Network+ Exam Guide

0-7897-2157-0

Written by Jonathan Feldman

Chapter Notes booklet is a supplement to the exam guide and may not be sold separately.

A Division of Macmillan USA
201 West 103rd Street
Indianapolis, Indiana 46290

Chapter 1

OSI Model

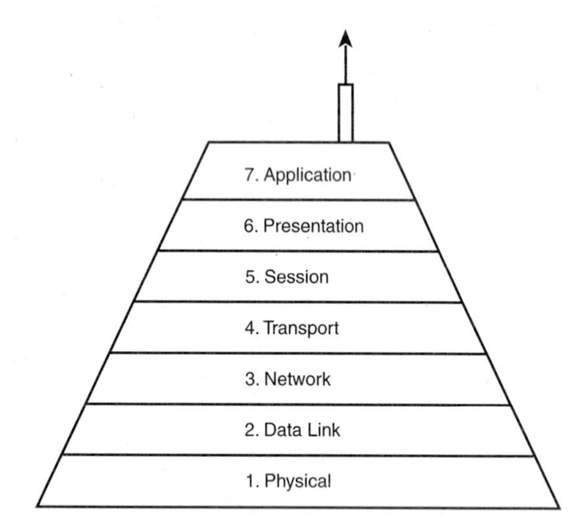

The OSI model.

- Layer 1 at the *bottom* of the cake.
- Each layer of the OSI model is supported by the layer beneath it.
- The physical layer supports all others.
- The application layer is supported by all others.

Mnemonic for OSI order:

All	(7. Application)
People	(6. Presentation)
Seem	(5. Session)
To	(4. Transport)
Need	(3. Network)
Data	(2. Data link)
Processing	(1. Physical)

Physical

Actual electrical impulses, radio waves, and so on, the electronics that power them, and the wires they travel on.

Data Link

How the network signal is encoded to represent information. Also includes any type of interdevice communication.

Network

The infrastructure that allows the information to get from point A to point C via point B. The network layer is the matrix that allows information to go from point to point.

Transport

How the data payload is structured; how the data gets there, and what kind of feedback can be expected by the sender. Defines connectionless transport versus connection-oriented transport.

- *Connectionless* = a note in class.
- *Connection-oriented* = telephone.

Session

The place where the traffic lights are located. Handles *flow control*, or the stopping and starting of data in a *session*. For example, Madge, in the trucker dispatch room, sets up the transfer of cargo and can delay a cargo if another is more important.

Presentation

Presents the data to the application. For example, a Web browser might be expecting encryption of the data. Or, an FTP program might need character conversion from one system to another. A classic example is from DOS to UNIX: The ASCII sequence CR-LF (carriage return-linefeed) must become a plain LF on its way from DOS to UNIX. Any kind of *data transformation services* are handled in this layer.

Application

The whole reason for networking is to be able to use a program that is network-enabled. A Web browser is an application, but it relies on the layers beneath it to work.

TIME to SWEAT and PRAY translates to:

- TIME Transport: Inner Message Express (How the message gets there).
- SWEAT Session: We Expect ASCII Traffic-lights (Flow control).
- PRAY Presentation: Rearranges Alphabet for You (Data modification).

Topologies

Paths that network data follow.

Physical topology = actual wire layout.

Logical topology = network signal path.

Point-to-Point

- Only *two* participants, such as in PPP dialup.
- Only two end points.

Bus

A broadcast technology:

- Shared by many devices (like the data bus on your PC). Example: Coaxial cable Ethernet.
- Problem: One station or one break in the wire can ruin it for everyone (Christmas lights).

Ring

An O-shaped ring:

- Can allow two-direction communication.
- More tolerant of faults than the bus topology (token ring, FDDI).

Star (or Spoke)

Many connections to its center:

- More fault tolerant than ring or bus, but requires more cable.
- Even many cable failures enable most users to keep on working.
- Requires hub equipment (10BASE-T).

Mesh

Many different paths to the same resource:

- Can be expensive, but they are the most fault-tolerant topology.
- ATM, X.25, Frame Relay.

Physical Wiring

Physical plant = wiring, power, and environmental conditions of your network.

Copper

Copper = most common data pipe.

Plenum

Cable intended to be run through air conditioning conduit in the ceiling.

- When it burns, it does not give off the toxic fumes that nonplenum cable does; thus, building codes mandate its use in a plenum.
- More expensive than nonplenum.

Nonplenum

Cable (usually cable with a PVC insulator jacket) can be used to run through ceilings without a plenum, or through an electrical conduit pipe.

- Toxic when it burns.
- Much cheaper than plenum cable.

Shielded

Cable has a metal conductive wrapping around it that helps to prevent electrical interference, such as RFI (Radio Frequency Interference) or EMI (Electro-Magnetic Interference) from affecting the integrity of the signal. Cable that is going to be run near motors or florescent lights should be shielded.

Unshielded

Cable has no conductive wrapping.

- More sensitive to the various types of interference.
- Much easier to work with than shielded cable.
- Far less expensive than shielded cable.

Twisted pair

Cable multiple pairs of twisted wires.

- Desirable electrically due to interference characteristics.
- Shielded twisted pair = STP.
- Unshielded twisted-pair cable = UTP. (UTP is the most common type of network cable.)

Stranded wire

Cable used in jumper wires. Many tiny fibers of copper make up each individual wire.

Solid wire

Cable most often used within conduits or walls.

- Each wire is a solid piece of copper.
- Solid wire cable is usually not appropriate for jumper cables.

Category V

Cat-5 cable.

- Can handle all but the very fastest of network data rates.
- UTP.
- Cannot be longer than 100 meters, including everything from the hub, to the wall plate, and including the patch cable from the wall plate to the PC.

Category III

Cat-3 cable predecessor to Cat-5.

- Both 10-Megabit Ethernet and 16-Megabit Token-Ring can use Cat-3 wire as a connector.
- A Cat-3 Ethernet run cannot be longer than 100 meters, including patch cables.

Coaxial, or Coax (Pronounced co-ax)

Cable that looks like television or cable box antenna wire. RG-58 cable most commonly used as Ethernet thinnet is 50 ohm.

IBM Type 1, or Type-1

Used by IBM in its token-ring networks. STP.

Copper Connectors

- RJ-45
- DB connectors
- IBM hermaphroditic
- BNC

RJ-45

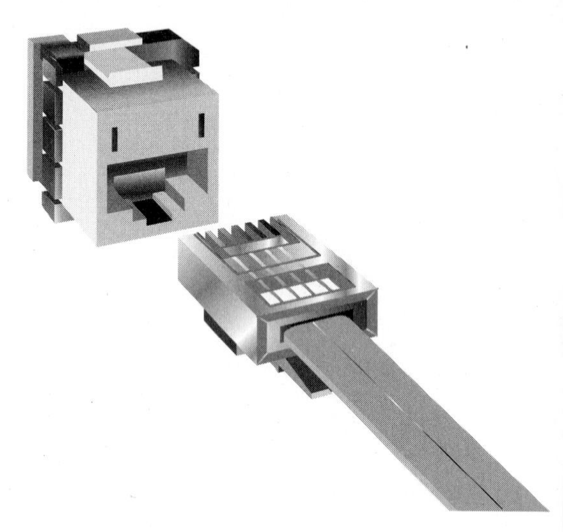

RJ-45 and socket.

RJ-45 premises wiring follows EIA/TIA-568A or EIA/TIA-568B standard.

RJ-45 connectors are used in

- 100BASE-T Ethernet.
- 16-Megabit token ring.
- Copper-based ATM.
- ISDN (Integrated Switched Digital Network) telephones and network devices.

DB and Hermaphrodite Connectors

IBM hermaphrodite (Left), DB-9 (Right).

DB-9: *token ring (STP).*

DB-15: *AUI (DIX) Ethernet (Shielded untwisted).*

BNC

BNC: 10BASE-2 Ethernet, coaxial cable.

Media converter = converts between types of media.

Transceiver = converter that also acts as a receiver and transmitter.

Fiber

Immune to electro-magnetic interference and power spikes, also the highest bandwidth cabling you can get.

Notoriously difficult:

- Connectors are labor-intensive to make.
- Everything from cables to connectors to testing gear is highly expensive.

Although the connectors are becoming easier and easier to work with, fiber is still a high-end commodity.

Wavelength: The distance between the beginning and the end of the wave is called the wavelength. Laser light has a predictable wavelength.

Attenuation: The amount of signal strength that light loses per unit of distance. Usually measured in decibels (dB) per kilometer (dB/km).

850 nanometer (850nm): found in low-speed networking equipment, such as Ethernet fiberoptic transceivers, and is only used for multimode fiber.

1300 nanometer (1300nm): found in high-end equipment, such as 100Mbps Ethernet, ATM, and FDDI gear. Can be used in single-mode or multimode fiber.

Multimode fiber

- Found within a building.
- Less expensive type of fiber.
- Core relatively large, at about 65 micrometers (65µm).
- Multimode signals bounce off of the sides of the core. There are short limits on distances that it can travel.

Single-Mode fiber

- Typically used for long distances—building a campus or metropolitan fiber ring.
- Small core: around 8 micrometers (8µm).

- Single-mode fiber signal does *not* bounce off of the sides of the fiber—signal can travel extremely large distances without losing strength.
- Expensive: higher cable and equipment cost.

Fiber Connectors

- SC
- ST
- MIC
- VF-45

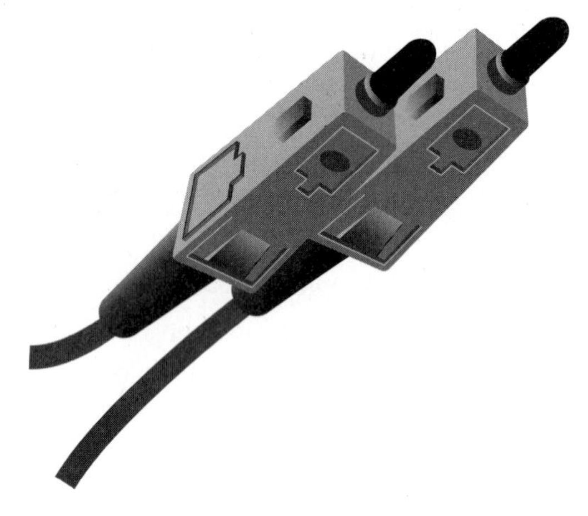

SC.

ST.

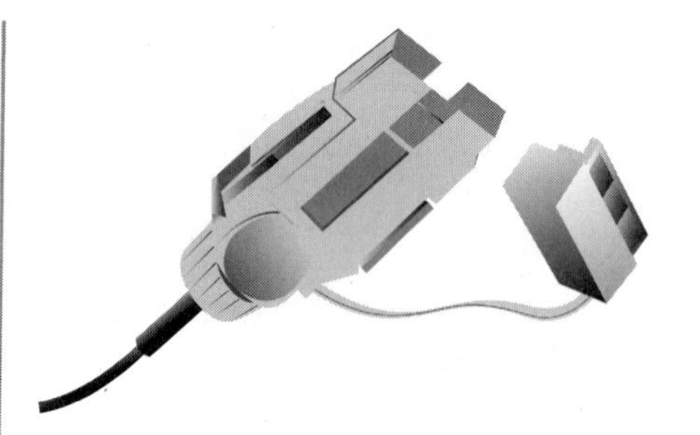

MIC.

Cleaving: Cutting a fiberoptic core by making a small nick on a side, followed by a quick pull.

Polishing: Needed so that the fiber end can adequately transmit light.

Jacket: Sheath around the cable.

Buffer: Padding within the sheath around the core (usually Kevlar).

Cladding: glass around the core.

Encoding

Digital

Either on or off. For example, using a flashlight to signal Morse code.

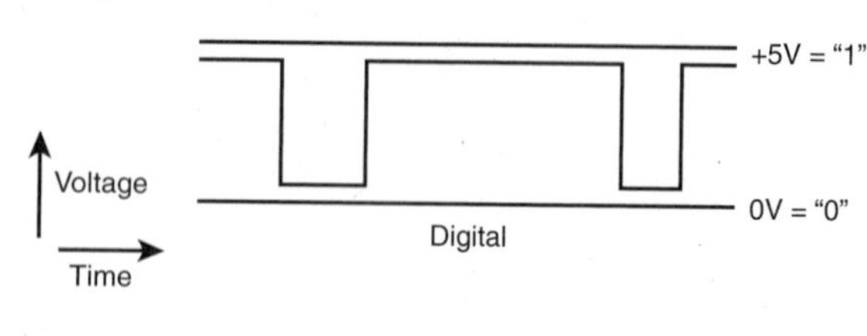

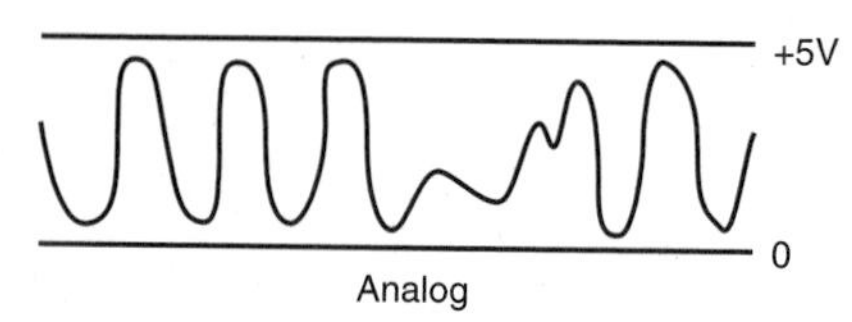

Analog

Many different levels of states. For example, American Sign Language or radio waves.

Broadband

Most common analog signaling method. Encodes multiple signals, or *bands* on the *medium* depending on the frequency. Like changing the station on the radio.

A given broadband signal comprises a *broad* range of *bands.*

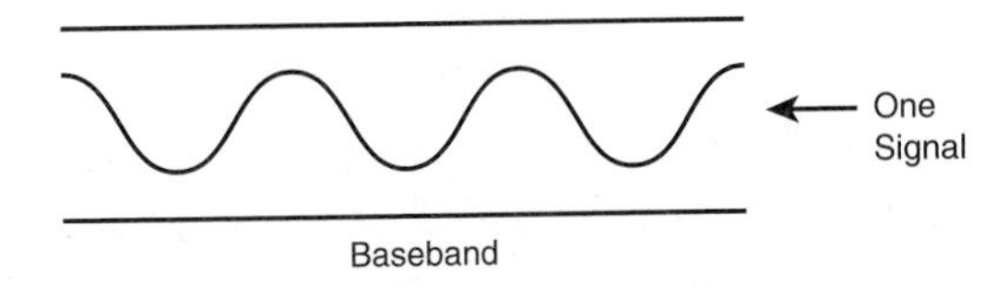

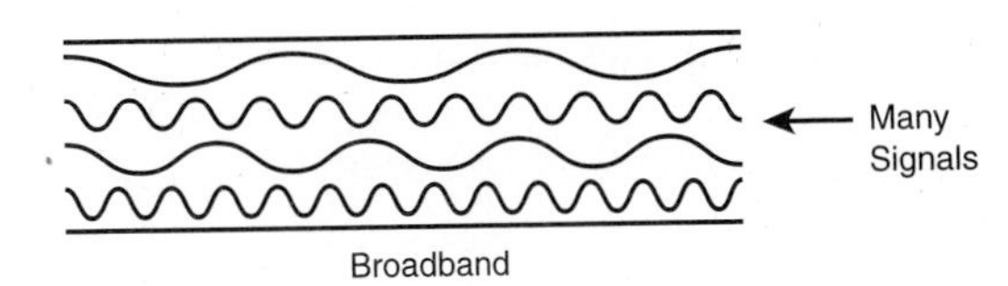

Baseband

When *one* signal occupies the entire wire, **the *base* of this signal is only one *band*.**

- Analog signals can be baseband or broadband.
- Digital signals are *always* baseband.

Duplex

Half duplex: communications between devices are turn taking.

- A transmit is done before a receive can take place, and vice versa.
- Traditionally how most local area networks (LAN) communication takes place.

Full duplex: simultaneous communications.

- Transmits can be done by one device while it simultaneously receives from another device.
- Circuitry more complex.
- Ethernet and token-ring devices now available that support are full duplex. Technologies like ATM have always been full duplex.

Data Link and Physical Signaling

Frame: One unit of device-to-device communication.

IEEE 802 standards: define physical signaling and datalink.

802.1, Internetworking

- Preamble to the rest of the 802 standards.
- Defines standards that are utilized by the rest of the standards.

802.2, Logical Link Control (LLC)

- Defines how a physical network type (the OSI physical layer) can talk to the upper layers of the OSI model.
- Defines Media Access Control (MAC).

802.3, Ethernet

Link layer using Carrier Sense with Multiple Access and Collision Detection (CSMA/CD).

- **C**omputer **S**ervice **M**en **A**ctively/(slash) **C**orporate **D**ifficulties.
- **C**omputer **S**ervice **M**en **A**pparently **C**an't **D**rive.

802.4

Obsolete standard for token bus.

802.5, Token Ring

Ring-topology broadcast network:

- Uses *token passing* as a method of arbitrating access to a shared medium.
- Rules are more complex, but they are *deterministic*; that is, they are not random, and events can be predicted.

802.6, Metropolitan Area Networks

Defines standards for Metropolitan Area Networks; that is, networks that span the geography of a city.

802.7, Broadband

802.8, Fiberoptic

802.9, Integrated Voice and Data

Provides a method to bring ISDN and Ethernet to a corporate desktop.

802.10, Interoperable LAN/MAN Security

Defines a mechanism to secure.

- LAN media via authentication (where each end identifies itself).
- Encryption (where data is not available to anyone but the sender and receiver).

802.11, Wireless Networks

Defines physical and media access control standards for wireless networking.

- Utilizes CSMA/CD media access control.
- Defines both infrared (DFIR, or Diffuse Infrared) and 2.4GHz (gigahertz) radio frequency choices.

802.12, 100BaseVG AnyLan

IEEE's Demand Priority Access LAN standard. First-come, first-served.

Network Protocols

TCP/IP

Transmission Control Protocol/Internet Protocol

- Most standard protocol.
- The protocol of the World Wide Web/Internet.

IPX/SPX

Internetwork Packet eXchange/Sequenced Packet eXchange

- Proprietary but widely used network protocol developed by Novell.
- Becoming obsolete.

NetBEUI

NetBIOS Extended User Interface:

- Incapable of leaving the physical segment that it originates from. That is, it is not *routable.*
- Seen in smaller Win95 networks.
- Method of transporting NetBIOS packets(Network Basic Input/Output System).

Traffic Control and Internetworking

Internetwork: Many network segments that are connected together.

Backbone: A high-speed central network that many lower-speed networks feed into.

Routers/Network Gateways

Network-layer devices that take data from one network and transfer it to another.

Routing Protocols

Allow routers to exchange information about available networks between themselves and client workstations.

Bridge

A data link-layer device that brings similar physical networks together.

- Errors, such as Ethernet collisions, do *not* get echoed.
- Bridges are limited to the LAN.
- They do not look at anything but data-link traffic.
- Bridges only connect similar types of physical networks together.

Brouters

A combination of a bridge and a router in one box.

Switches: Multiport Bridges

Application Gateways

Have nothing to do with the data link or network layers. Generally does some sort of data conversion; for example, Lotus mail to GroupWise mail.

Device	Data Link?	Network?	Wide Area?	App Layer?
Router	N	Y	Y	N
Bridge	Y	N	N	N
Switch	Y	N	N	N
Brouter	Y	Y	Y	N
App Gateway	N	N	Y	Y

Chapter 2

Network operating system (NOS): *Provides internal services to the computer and also external services to network clients.*

Host: *A workstation or server that provides TCP/IP services.*

Though a workstation can have a network service, a *server* is usually *dedicated* to providing network services.

Network Operating Systems

UNIX

First portable OS; many TCP/IP commands (ping, netstat, and so on) were originally UNIX commands.

Flavors of UNIX

- Linux (freely available UNIX): Red Hat, Slackware, Debian
- AIX: IBM's implementation of UNIX for their RS/6000 servers
- HP/UX: HP's implementation of UNIX
- SCO: Probably the most popular commercial Intel UNIX
- Sun Solaris

NetWare

Novell's file-and-print server, version 5.x has native TCP/IP support; older versions rely on proprietary IPX/SPX protocol.

- Requires DOS partition on system drive.
- Starts from SERVER.EXE.
- Latest release, Novell has added a GUI as well as part of its Native Java support.
- Good TCP/IP support and directory services support in the latest release.
- Excellent performance with file-and-print networking.

Windows NT/Windows 2000

The station wagon of the NOS world.

- Low entry price.
- Mid-range scalability.
- Combination of file-and-print and client/server services under one OS, meaning that fewer servers are necessary. (See following sections for definitions of file-and-print and client/server.)
- Good support for TCP/IP.

Directory Services

Large number of server-centric servers became unwieldy to administer. (Six servers that allow JJones required six user account creations.)

Allows one account to access many servers via network database. Directory databases are partitioned, usually by geographic distance/leased-line costs. Needs to be distributed for fault-tolerance.

Types

- Novell NDS: in wide use for many years
- Microsoft Active Directory: yet to ship
- UNIX NIS: not very secure or flexible

Replication: *Distributed DS database.*

Synchronization: *A database update.*

Replica: *A copy of a directory services database is called a replica.*

Replica ring: *The sum of all servers that have a replica on them.*

Organizational Unit (OU): *A unit of Directory Service hierarchy.*

Leaf object: *Detail record in the database; not limited to user or file permissions.*

Fault Tolerance and Data Integrity

Uninterruptable Power Supply (UPS) = protection from sags, spikes, brownouts, and temporary power failures.

Backup generator = protection against longer power loss.

Redundant server power supplies = power supply is single point of failure on typical PC.

Server power supply failure notification is via network, or audible.

Server Hard Drive Configurations: RAID

RAID: *Redundant Array of Inexpensive Disks.*

Disk volume: *The aggregate of several disks (several ways to combine disks to form a volume).*

Striping: *Data is spread over many physical drives. Plain striping offers speed, not reliability.*

Mirroring: *The same data is kept on more than one drive. This way, if one drive fails, the data is not lost.*

Duplexing: *The same data is kept on more than one drive, and a different interface card is used.*

If a mirrored volume loses a disk controller, even though the data might be intact, the data is still unavailable. If a duplexed volume loses a disk controller, the volume is still available.

Caching controllers have a certain amount of RAM on board.

- Can accept data from the server without the server having to wait for the physical I/O to complete.
- Provides a server a huge performance boost.
- Caching controller must have battery back up to be fault tolerant.

Type of RAID	Striped	Mirrored	Parity	Hot Spare Option
RAID 0	Y	N	N	N
RAID 1	N	Y	N	N
RAID 2	Y	N	Y	N
RAID 3	Y	N	Y	N
RAID 4	Y	N	Y	N
RAID 5	Y	N	Y	Y
RAID 10	Y	Y	Y	N

The practical use of RAID is usually limited to (in order of increasing expense) RAID 1, RAID 5, and RAID 10

Software RAID is available natively on Windows NT, NetWare, and with third-party software for UNIX. In practice, it's always better to have RAID on the controller because of CPU utilization issues.

Data Integrity and Recovery

RAID only protects data at the physical layer (garbage-in/garbage-out).

A malfunctioning application or hostile user can still destroy data!

Daily backups and a retention cycle are important for retaining data integrity.

Backup Methods

Full (or normal): Backs up all data on every volume to tape—method for highest data integrity.

Incremental: All data that has *changed* since the last backup is backed up.

Differential: All data that has *changed* since the last *full* backup is backed up.

OS Redundancy

Failover: *Two servers are dedicated to the same task; one is the hot standby, and one is the production server. Standby server waits until primary server dies and then jumps in and offers the same services.*

Clustering: *Multiple servers are used for the same task or groups of tasks. By participating in a clustering protocol, the servers as a group are more efficient than just one by itself could be.*

Workstations and Clients

Workstation: *Any user computer that participates in a network.* Needs

- Network Interface Card (NIC)
- Network Protocol Stack
- Client Software

Network protocol stack: *Interface between your network card driver and network applications. Called a stack in reference to the OSI model layers.*

Network client: *Software that enables you to take advantage of network services.*

A network protocol that is both able to and allowed to talk to a network client is said to be *bound* to that client. (Referred to in plural as bindings.)

Example of network clients:

- Web browser
- FTP client
- Email client
- Redirectors

Redirectors: *Redirect network resources to local references to make a networked resource appear to be local.*

File and print servers: *Specialize in providing shared file and printer access. They all require redirectors on the client workstations.*

UNC = Universal Naming Convention. All UNC resources are formatted as:

```
\\servername\resource
```

Types of Networking

Server based: *Workstations all rely on central server or group of servers for network services.*

Peer-to-peer: *All workstations are capable of providing some services to other workstations. They are both users and providers of resources.*

- Lack of central backup.
- Workstations are typically less fault tolerant than dedicated servers.

Client/Server: *Question/answer type of networking. More resource intensive on server, less so on client.*

File-and-print servers: *Provides entire file to client, not just the answer to a question. Less resource intensive on server, more so on client.*

Chapter 3

NIC

NIC = Network Interface Card.

Network card can't function without a functioning data bus:

- Legacy ISA
- Plug-and-Play (PnP) ISA
- PCI
- PCMCIA (PC Card)

Common problem: resource conflict. Plug-n-Play is supposed to eliminate conflict.

- Doesn't always play well with legacy ISA.
- Enabler—either BIOS or software driver—can be part of the problem.

Sources of Conflict

- IRQ: Interrupt ReQuest number. Typical legacy ISA bus only has IRQ 2, 5, 9, 10, 11, 12, and 14 available.
- DMA: Direct Memory Address channels.
- I/O ports: Hexadecimal memory addresses, direct mappings of hardware control functions.
- Memory mapped areas.

Hexadecimal Counting

Very important for finding overlapping I/O or memory areas.

- Count: 0 1 2 3 4 5 6 7 8 9 a b c d e f.
- The hard part is what to do after f—examples:

F + 1 = 10	FF + 1 = 100	3FF + 1 = 400
F + 2 = 11	FF + 2 = 101	3FF + 2 = 401

Sometimes BIOS needs upgrading (either PC or Network Card). Windows 9x System Control Panel applet lets you print a list of resources in use on system. (Look at this with the net card removed, and compare!)

Resolving Conflict

- BIOS can allow you to reallocate PnP IRQs so they do not conflict with legacy ISA.
- Jumpers on legacy ISA cards.
- Software settable ISA cards—will not be changeable if there is a current conflict!

Troubleshooting

For a workstation that won't connect to network

- Check link light.
- Swap out network cable.
- Reseat the network card.
- Run vendor diagnostics.
- Try loopback test. (Loopback is receive pins connected to transmit pins.) Loopback test usually accomplished by the use of a loopback plug. Some devices have a loopback switch—don't require loopback plug.

Network Attachment Devices

Ethernet

Ethernet's signaling is bus-based.

Modern Ethernet wired as a star:

- 10BASE-T (Cat-III wiring).
- 100BASE-TX (Cat-V Fast Ethernet).
- 100BASE-FX (Fiber-based Fast Ethernet).

Ethernet Physical bus (one coaxial wire):

- 10BASE-5 (thicknet—thick coaxial).
- 10BASE-2 (thinnet—thin coaxial).

Troubleshooting Ethernet

Try known good port of a hub or switch.

Try known good transceiver (if applicable).

Stacked hubs = one repeater device; cascaded hubs are each considered repeaters.

Each switch port is a point-to-point link; bus rules do *not* apply.

Switched hub has two shared buses; one for each speed of network.

Check for over-extended Ethernet bus.

5-4-3 Rule

- 5 subsegments in series (that is, in a row).
- 4 repeaters or concentrators.
- 3 populated subsegments (applies to coaxial only).

100BASE-T Rules

- Only two repeaters are allowed in any collision domain.
- The maximum inter-repeater cable length is 10m.

Ethernet Cable Budgets

Ethernet type	Distance limitations	Cable typically used
10-BASE-T	100 meters	UTP
100-BASE-T	100 meters	UTP
10-BASE-5 (AUI)	500 meters	Coaxial (thicknet)/ shielded
10-BASE-2 (BNC)	185 meters (Needs termination)	Coaxial (thinnet)

Token Ring

- 4 or 16 megabit speeds.
- RJ-45 or Hermaphrodite connectors.

Ring-in (RI): *Indicates where the data comes in. (Upstream).*

Ring-out (RO): *Where the data flows out of the MAU. (Downstream).*

NAUN: *Nearest Addressed Upstream Neighbor.*

Active Monitor: *Station in charge of ring.*

Standby Monitor: *All other stations, ready to take over if AM goes away.*

FDDI

Fiber Distributed Data Interface.

MIC (Media Interface Connector) connector keying:

A Multi-attach station's first port onto ring.

B Multi-attach station's second port onto ring.

M Concentrator Master port, used to connect S-type stations.

S Single-attach station.

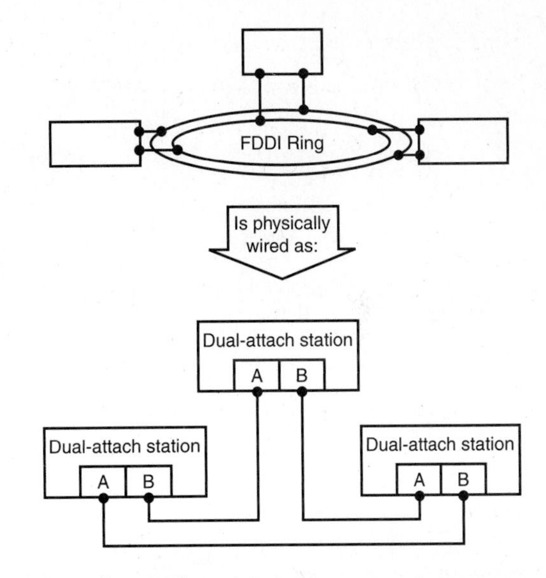

FDDI can be wired as a ring.

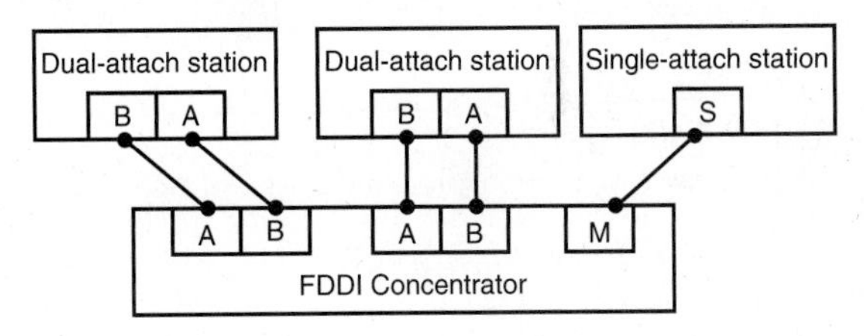

When a concentrator is in use, FDDI is wired as a star.

ATM

Asynchronous Transfer Mode: *No hubs; ATM is point-to-point, and uses switches.*

- Reasonably easy to create fault-tolerant mesh topologies.
- Ring topologies also possible.
- Fiber or copper.

Optical Carrier = OC unit (51.84Mbps).

- OC-3 = 155Mbps
- OC-12 = 622Mbps
- OC-24 = 1.2Gbps

Serial Synchronous/Leased

- Computer/Router (DTE) end: v.35 connector, shielded wire.
- Telephone company (network): RJ connector, needs CSU/DSU.

CSU/DSU = Channel Service Unit/Data Service Unit.

Common speeds: 1.53Mbps and 56Kbps.

Synchronize via a shared clocking signal.

Asynchronous (Asynch) Serial Links

No shared common clock signal.

Extra data bits to establish data synchronization, not as efficient as synch.

Common speeds:

- 9600
- 19,200
- 38,400
- 57,600
- 115,200

ISDN

ISDN = Integrated Services Digital Network; Baseband digital signal over standard telephone wire.

Most common type: BRI (Basic Rate Interface)

- Two 64K B channels and one D channel used for signaling.
- BRI, also known as 2B+1D.

Physical connection is UTP, typically with RJ-45 connector.

- Must end in premises NT device.
- NT device can be built into ISDN devices, such as ISDN network cards or Terminal Adapters (TA).

Need stand-alone NT1 for multiple ISDN devices.

- Simplest stand-alone NT device is NT1.
- NT1 has one U jack for out-of-premises, two S/T jacks for ISDN devices.

Wireless

802.11 standard specifies infrared, and two types of 2.1GHz radio signaling.

Like cell phones, radio networks have *access points* that act as wireless hubs for network.

Types of interference mitigation:

- FHSS—Frequency Hopping Spread Spectrum: Keep changing band every tenth of a second.
- DSSS—Direct Sequence/Spread Spectrum: Stretches the signal over a larger signal, making the signal more fault tolerant.

Chapter 4

Data link is the symbolic form of physical layer signals. Data link does not use *packets*; those are a network-layer concept.

Frame: *The smallest unit of a network conversation.*

Headers: *Various subunits to a frame, much like a database has fields.*

LLC/MA

- MAC = Media Access Control.
- LLC = Link Layer Control.
- LLC is higher than MAC (MAC is closer to physical).
- LMnoP = **L**LC, **M**AC, **P**hysical; MAC happens first, *then* LLC.

Access Control:

- CSMA/CD (implemented in Ethernet 802.3) is not deterministic; it is random and not predictable. (Ethernet contains the word three = .3 in 802.3 standard.)
- Token-passing (implemented in Token-Ring 802.5 and FDDI) is deterministic (*five* golden *rings*).
- Demand Priority (implemented in VG-AnyLAN 802.12)—deterministic.

MAC Addressing

MAC address or Burned In Number (BIA): *A unique number that with which each LAN card that gets manufactured must be encoded.*

MAC Address is six hex bytes (48 bits), as in 00-00-c9-52-88-11.

- These first three bytes of a MAC address are referred to as the OUI of the address.
- OUI stands for Organizationally Unique Identifier, and is assigned by the IEEE to the card manufacturer.

Using software-settable MAC addresses usually a bad idea; you run the risk of a duplicate MAC address causing a malfunction.

Stations normally listen to the wire, and process frames intended for them.

Promiscuous stations: *Listen to all frames.*

Link Layer Control

Responsible for error correction, and reliable, end-to-end transport of the data.

SAP (Service Access Point): *Indicator to network layer which type of data link/network protocol this frame is for.*

Control fields indicate command, response, connectionless or connection-oriented data.

SAP with SNAP = SAP with Sub Network Access Protocol.

SNAP includes additional five-byte header with another OUI and a protocol identifier.

Frames

Composed of MAC header, LLC header, payload and a MAC trailer.

Frame type: *The specific way that a frame is put together.*

Some frame types do not have the 802.2 LLC information in them.

Ethernet Datalink Preamble	Destination MAC Address	Source MAC Address	Length of rest of frame, w/o FCS	LLC SAP	Data Payload	Frame Check Sequence

A simple Ethernet frame.

Ethernet 802.3 -- Novell only; nonstandard & obsolete.

Ethernet Datalink Preamble	Destination MAC Address	Source MAC Address	Length of rest of frame, w/o FCS	Illegal SAP of "FFFF"	Data Payload	Frame Check Sequence

Ethernet 802.2 -- Frame with 802.2 LLC SAP

Ethernet Datalink Preamble	Destination MAC Address	Source MAC Address	Length of rest of frame, w/o FCS	LLC SAP	Data Payload	Frame Check Sequence

Ethernet _SNAP -- Frame with SAP LLC and SNAP

Ethernet Datalink Preamble	Destination MAC Address	Source MAC Address	Length of rest of frame, w/o FCS	LLC SAP	LLC SNAP	Data Payload	Frame Check Sequence

Ethernet _II -- Used with "Classic" TCP/IP, note presence of EtherType field

Ethernet Datalink Preamble	Destination MAC Address	Source MAC Address	EtherType	Data Payload	Frame Check Sequence

Token-Ring 802.2 -- Frame with SAP LLC

Token-Ring MAC fields	Destination MAC Address	Source MAC Address	LLC SAP	Data Payload	Frame Check Sequence	Token-Ring MAC fields

Token-Ring_ SNAP -- Frame with SAP LLC and SNAP

Token-Ring MAC fields	Destination MAC Address	Source MAC Address	LLC SAP	LLC SNAP	Data Check Sequence	Frame Check Sequence	Token-Ring MAC fields

A SAP is composed of two SAP bytes and up to two bytes of control information.

Wide Area Data Link

Typically not a shared broadcast medium; Point-to-Point instead = Don't need MAC.

Germane function of a wide area data link layer, then, is to perform

- Circuit setup (unlike LAN)
- Error detection
- Error correction
- Flow control

Hard-wired point-to-point = physical.

Going through a cloud like a telephone switch is virtual point-to-point.

Data-link, point-to-point protocols are

- PPP (Point-to-Point Protocol)
- SDLC (Synchronous Data Link Control)
- HDLC (High-level Data Link Control)

PPP

Most popular data-link protocol for the wide area.

PPP is not TCP/IP specific: like Ethernet or token ring, it can carry arbitrary protocols such as IPX/SPX or AppleTalk.

SDLC

IBM's Synchronous Data Link Control protocol.

Mainframe-oriented data-link protocol, usually used to carry the SNA network protocol.

HDLC

High Level Data Link Control.

Defined by the ISO; standards-based equivalent of SDLC.

HDLC ensures error detection and also does a certain amount of error correction. HDLC specifies several subprotocols:

- LAPB: Link Access Procedure, Balanced (X.25)
- LAPM: Link Access Procedure, Modems
- LAPD: Link Access Procedure, D-Channel (ISDN and Frame Relay)

Phone company can switch point-to-point data link with

- X.25
- Frame Relay

Packet switched data link can save equipment costs.

Bridges

Promiscuous mode devices.

Listens on one side of the bridge for transmissions, makes decision:

Is the destination known to the bridge?

- If not, drops the frame.
- If so, propagates the frame to the other side of the bridge.

The frame's source and destination fields do not change.

Spanning Tree

Bridges can be connected in a loop topology for redundancy's sake.

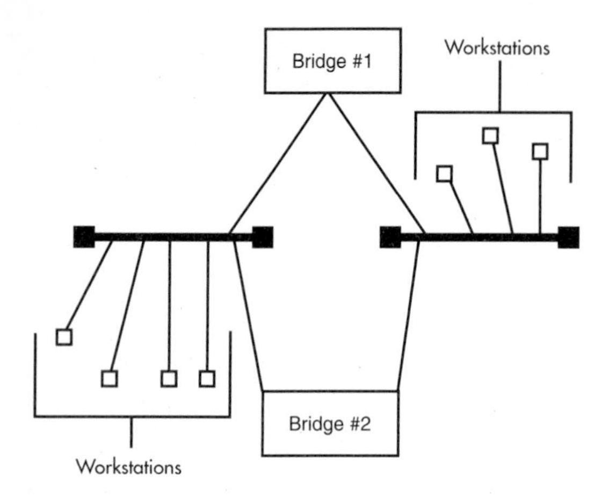

Creating a loop makes a set of bridged segments fault tolerant, but the bridges must have a way of dealing with the loop so that it doesn't become infinite.

Spanning Tree must be used to temporarily block one port so that an infinite loop isn't created.

BPDU = Bridge Protocol Data Units.

Root bridge get elected, distances calculated, port blockage selected.

802.1d is IEEE Spanning Tree.

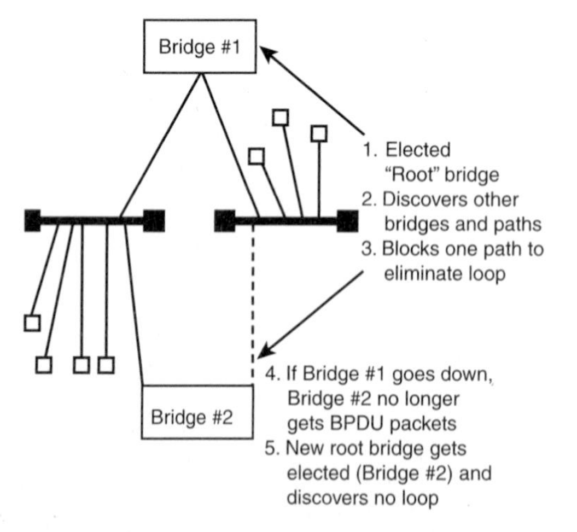

One bridge makes for a single point of failure; two bridges are fault-tolerant, but they create a loop topology that must be blocked by the Spanning-Tree algorithm.

Switches = Multiport Bridges

Store-and-forward waits until entire frame is received.

- Can discard frames that have errors in them.
- Storage and decision making creates delay (*latency*).

***Cut-through:** Starts to transmit the frame on its other ports before error detection is done.*

- Latency (delay) kept to a minimum.
- Bad frames are propagated to all ports; decreases reliability.

Switching/Bridging Pluses and Minuses:

Plus	Minus
Divides physical domain—more reliable network	Harder to use analysis tools
Workstations use common network numbers	Potential for broadcast storms
Error frames can be eliminated	Latency

Chapter 5

- Network layer is a way of organizing large amounts of communication in a partitioned way.
- If all nodes in a large business shared the same data link segment, congestion would prevent reliable communication.
- Segments are split into manageable data link domains—that is, into different network numbers—by the use of routers.
- Layer 3 of the OSI model.

Network Protocols:

- TCP/IP
- IPX/SPX
- NetBEUI

Packet Switching

Entire message gets chopped up into discrete elements called *packets.*

Packet switching: *A device switches between processing packets.*

Each subunit of a message could take *completely different paths* to the end-station. Example: Playing telephone in Mrs. Grinch's classroom.

Router: *A station that forwards packets between network nodes that are nonadjacent. Example: the students who pass the message.*

Node: *An autonomous unit on a packet-switched network. (Can be a router, or not a router).*

Network Numbering

Network number defines adjacency; you don't need a router to talk to someone on your same net number. Example: office workers dial 4 digits to call each other.

Protocol network numbers look different depending upon which protocol is in use.

Network Numbers

Type:	Full Address	Network	Node
IPX	205:0060201525f9	205	0060201525f9
Class A IP:	11.50.5.10	11	50.5.10
Class B IP:	167.195.168.10	167.195	168.10
Class C IP:	192.168.1.10	192.168.1	10-

See Chapter 7 for more about TCP/IP network numbers.

NetBEUI does *not* use network numbers: nonrouteable!

Routing Concepts

Nodes need help finding routers.

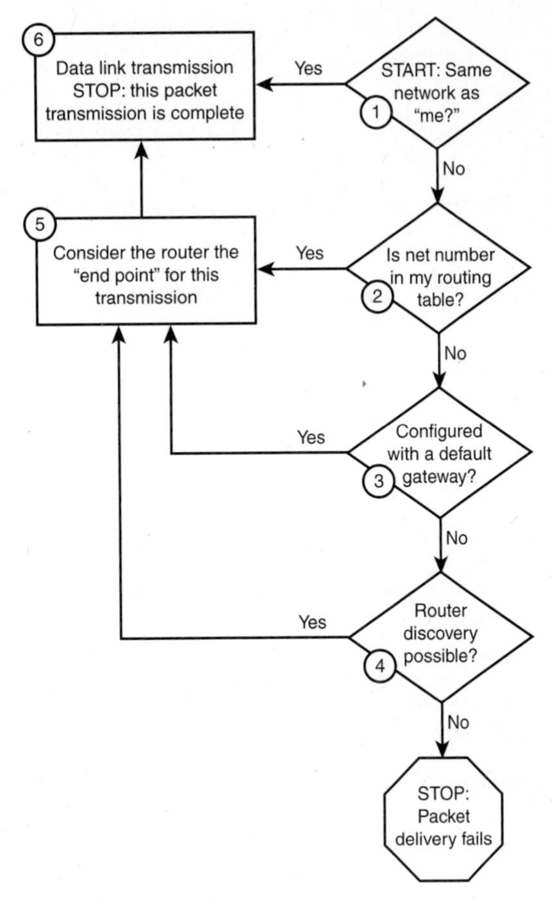

Node-to-router decision flowchart.

Router Tables

Basic router table shows each network number and corresponding routers that know about that network.

- All router entries in a routing table *must* refer to routers on the local network.
- Because routers are *multihomed hosts,* that is, they have more than one interface, they also have more than one protocol address.
- A router listed in a node's routing table must list a router's protocol address that is on the same network number as the node.

- Network entries may refer to arbitrary networks that the local station is not connected to.
- A node has as many *direct* entries in its routing table as it has active network cards.

Local or direct entry: *This is the attached network (packets don't need a router).*

Multi-homed host: *Any node with more than one network card.*

Default gateway routing table entry: *Gateway is a synonym for router, so default gateway means router to take when routing table doesn't specify where to go.*

- Often referred to as the 0 network.
- Usually set up by an installer.
- Most PCs have a *default gateway*, but routers can, as well.

Dynamic Versus Static Routes

Static routing = *routing table entries (route) are hand-entered.*

Dynamic routing = *routing table entries (routes) are received over the network via a routing protocol.*

- Dynamic routing protocols share their direct entries with other routers that learn about these networks.
- Each network protocol has *different* routing protocols.

Distance-vector routing protocol:

- Most concerned about the *direction* (vector) of the route, and *how far* the route is (distance, measured in number of routers crossed, or hops.)
- Distance-vector routing protocols know nothing about *how fast* a link might be, or whether it is a desirable link or not.

Link-state protocols chiefly concerned with the quality of the connection between routers.

- *Link-state* uses cost of a link in conjunction with how far the route is.
- Routers realize that using a faster link, even though it is more hops away, is more advantageous.
- Keeps track of current state of each router.
- Requires a bit more setup on the part of the network administrator, but they scale better for large networks.

Routing Protocol	Network Protocol	Type
RIP	IP	Distance-vector
RIP_II	IP	Distance-vector
OSPF	IP	Link-state
BGP	IP	Link-state
RIP	IPX	Distance-vector
NLSP	IPX	Link-state

Chapter 6

- Think of trucker transport reporting to session dispatch.
- How data gets from point A to point B.
- Name resolution.

Connection-Oriented Versus Connectionless

- Connection-oriented is *not* necessarily more secure than connectionless; connection-oriented messaging merely contributes towards security, but security requires cooperation of several layers.
- No guarantees that connection stream won't be hijacked by malicious user.

Connection-Oriented

Doesn't really have a physical pipe between points.

- *Does* have a virtual pipe.
- Accomplished via sequencing.
- Serial number that identifies the packet and gives it continuity with other packets in the exchange.
- Protocol stack uses sequence numbers to keep track of the connection's state.
- Upper layers do not need knowledge of sequence numbers; they actually treat it as a connected pipe.

Connectionless

Connectionless packets = datagrams.

- No good means of keeping track of conversation context.
- Upper layers must keep track of the state of the conversation.

Transport Type	Sequence #s?	Negatives
Connectionless	No	App must manage connection
Connection-oriented	Yes	Sequencing requires overhead

Naming

Naming service: *Translates symbolic names into numeric addresses.*

- This process is referred to a *name resolution.*
- Naming services enable you to specify `www.feldman.org` rather than 209.249.147.239.

You should always configure applications to point to symbolic names rather than numeric addresses.

If a user points to the address rather than a symbolic name, reconfiguration can cause the application to fail.

In real life, name services come from server software that provides name resolution to network clients.

Chapter 7

TCP/IP protocol suite

- Dominant network protocol on the planet.
- Not complicated for an application programmer to use.
- Reference implementations and source code available.
- Created by a diverse group of vendors, academics, and scientists; belongs to no one group.

RFC = *Request for Comment, used to extend and enhance the protocol suite.*

De facto standards can be RFCs.

Nonimplemented ideas can be RFCs, too.

STD = *Standard, when an RFC becomes accepted by everyone.*

Addressing

Any duplication of an address—node numbers or network numbers—on a TCP/IP network can lead to a serious malfunction.

Class:	Network Range	Default netmask
A	1 thru 126	255.0.0.0
B	128 thru 191	255.255.0.0
C	192 thru 223	255.255.255.0

Class determined by IP range.

Subnetting

Subnetting: *Changing the behavior of a class A, B, or C network so that it treats the network and node number differently.*

Subnet mask: *A value the administrator can indicate to routing equipment and servers that subnetting should be used.*

- Masks out the node number and keeps only the network number.
- Uses binary AND operations to do this.

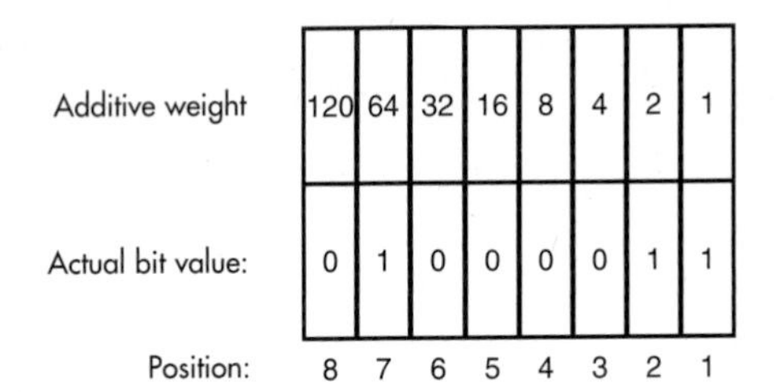

Adding the 1 columns, binary 0100 0011 = 67 decimal.

A logical AND of two numbers can only have the following results:

0 AND 0 = 0

0 AND 1 = 0

1 AND 0 = 0

1 AND 1 = 1

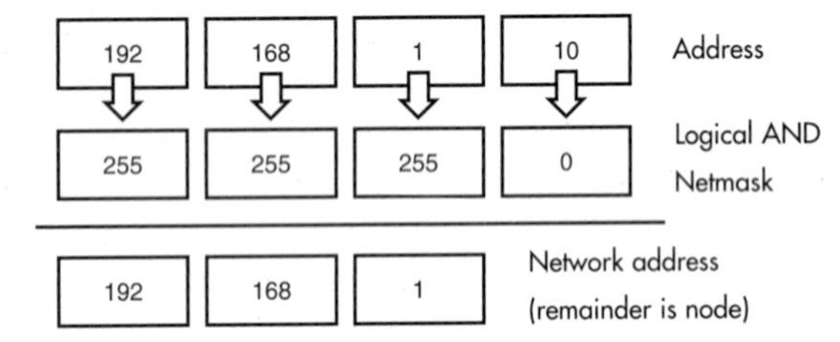

When you extend the subnet mask into an octet, you must calculate the last octet using the node number *plus the bits of the network number.*

A network mask works because, in binary, its 1s allow the network portion of the address to survive an AND operation. The 0s of a mask do NOT allow the node portion of the address to survive.

Broadcast

All 0s or all 1s not allowed as a node address, because these can be used as broadcast address.

Only all 0s *or* all 1s allowed as a broadcast address; using *both* is not allowed.

For a class C network with the default netmask (255.255.255.0)

- All ones broadcast address = 192.168.20.255
- All zeros broadcast address = 192.168.20.0

Special Addresses

Loopback

Useful for testing a workstation talking to itself—rules out network problems.

- 127.0.0.1

Private

An IP address for if you don't connect to the Internet, yet still have a network (such as a Windows network) that uses IP?

- 10.0.0.0 through 10.255.255.255 (class A style)
- 172.16.0.0 through 172.31.255.255 (class B style)
- 192.168.0.0 through 192.168.255.255 (class C style)

Protocol Suite

Internet Protocol (IP) = Package, address, and deliver.

Address Resolution Protocol (ARP) = Data link protocol: convert MAC to IP address.

Internet Control (ICMP) = Janitor Message Protocol interface; maintenance and problem reports.

User Datagram Protocol (UDP) = Application protocol—Connectionless.

Transmission Control Protocol = TCP Application protocol—Connection-oriented.

Ports

Service port number or ***socket number:*** *A unique application address required to run multiple network applications.*

Fully qualified address for a specific application on a specific server = servername:socket

Well Known Services:

Service Name	Function; Protocol(s); Socket
FTP	File Transfer Protocol; TCP; 21
Telnet	Terminal emulation; TCP; 23

SMTP	Simple Mail Transfer Protocol (Mail transmittal); TCP; 25
Domain	Domain Name Services (Translates net-names->address); TCP/UDP; 53
HTTP	Hyper Text Transfer Protocol (Web); TCP; 80
POP3	Post Office Protocol (mail pick-up); TCP; 110
NNTP	Network News Transfer Protocol (Usenet news); TCP; 119
IMAP	Interactive Mail Access Protocol (mail pickup); TCP; 143
Socks	Generic proxy; TCP; 1080
HTTP-proxy	Proxy for Web traffic; TCP; 8080

TCP/IP Name Resolution

- Is easier for the end user than remembering a string of numbers.
- Makes reconfiguration easier.

WINS, or ***Windows Internet Name System:*** *NetBIOS naming services for TCP/IP.*

- A workstation may have at most *two* WINS servers.
- WINS lives on UDP port 137, commonly known as NetBIOS-ns or nbname.

DNS, or ***Domain Naming System:*** *The venerable naming system used on the Internet.*

- Any more than three DNS servers specified in an IP stack's configuration are simply ignored.
- DNS lives at UDP port 53, as well as TCP port 53.
- Name server location must be specified by IP address.

Proxy

Proxy: *The middle man between you and somebody's Network Neighborhood.*

It is *not* a router; a router sets up a direct call, whereas a proxy intercepts and repackages the call.

Why people use proxies:

- Routing services are not desired or needed.
- Logging is important. (It's easier to do this with a server than with a network-layer device.)
- Bad IP addresses are being used (for example IP addresses that are not received from an ISP or that don't conform to RFC 1918). Thus, routing would be difficult without using special address translation software.

Two types of proxies:

- Application Proxies
- Generic Proxies

Most common application proxy is the HTTP proxy, which lives at TCP port number 8080.

- Only knows how to pass on HTTP requests; won't work for other services, such as FTP or Telnet.
- Understand the transactions, and can cache most recently used Web pages.

Most common generic proxy is the socks proxy, which lives at TCP port number 1080.

You should specify a workstation's proxy server as a symbolic name because it may change network location over time.

IP Workstation Configuration

Windows IP configuration (and examples)

Numeric:

IP address (167.195.160.6)

Netmask (255.255.255.0)

Default gateway (167.195.160.1)

DNS Server (167.195.162.12)

WINS (167.195.162.12)

Name:

Proxy (proxy.my.com)

Hostname (Jonathan)

Default DNS Domain (my.com)

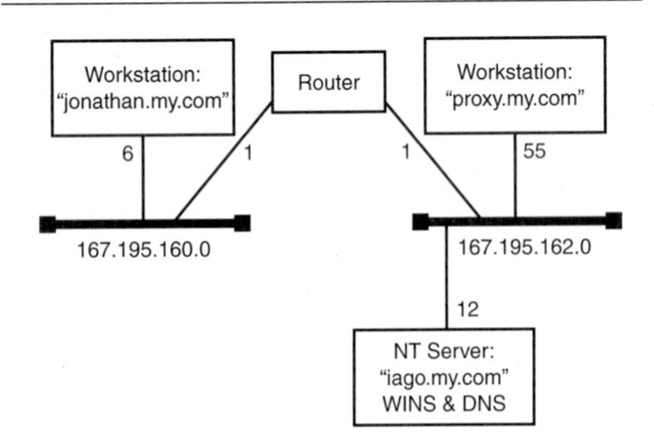

DHCP

DHCP: *Dynamic Host Configuration Protocol.*

- DHCP can be used for automatic workstation configuration.
- Workstation receives an address lease for a specific amount of time.
- Must renew with server after lease expires.
- Workstation not guaranteed to get the same address all of the time.

In addition to address and netmask, DHCP can also hand out

- Which WINS server to use
- Which DNS server to use
- Default DNS domain
- Default router

DHCP does not distribute proxy information.

Chapter 8

Workstation-Level TCP/IP Checklist

Configuration

Is the workstation configured appropriately for the segment? (The only thing that should be different between two workstations in the same workgroup is the *node numbers*. DNS configuration, WINS configuration, the netmask, and the default gateway should all be the same.)

Hardware

Is the hardware functioning? (NIC link light, good cable, connector, and so on.)

NIC/Stack Problems

Do your IP stack statistics give you any meaningful clues?

NIC/Stack Problems

Does your IP address respond?

Stack Problems

Does the loopback address respond?

Top-level TCP/IP Infrastructure Checklist

If an entire workgroup is having problems, you will naturally suspect an *infrastructure*, rather than a workstation, problem.

Name Services

Can you reach desired host using an IP address instead of a name?

Data Link to IP

Is any properly configured host on the local segment reachable by any other properly configured host?

Routing

Is the default router reachable? Is the remote host that you're trying to contact reachable by ICMP (different subnet)? If server is not ICMP reachable, at what point is the ball being dropped?

IP Application

If host is reachable, is anybody home on the application side?

Checking TCP/IP Information

Winipcfg/ipconfig/ifconfig: *Workstation configuration.*

Ping: *Node reachability via ICMP (no sockets involved).*

ARP: *Data link ARP cache.*

Netstat: *Routing table, protocol statistics, active sockets.*

Tracert/traceroute/iptrace: *Nodes traversed to get to end-station; the delays experienced between each.*

Telnet: *Whether TCP socket is listening.*

nbtstat: *NetBIOS name table.*

nslookup: *Various DNS information.*

IP Configuration Flags

winipcfg/all: *Shows all IP configuration of Win 95 or Win 98 workstation (graphical).*

ipconfig/all: *Shows all IP configuration of Win 98 or Win NT (text-based).*

Both `ipconfig` and `winipcfg` can use `/release_all` or `/renew_all` flags to release or renew a DHCP lease.

These tools are used to solve *local* problems. Global problems cannot be solved this way; for example, if DHCP is misconfigured at the server, or if static IP is configured on the same segment as DHCP.

Ping

Ping, like most TCP/IP applications

- Resolves a DNS alias into the real (or canonical) name
- Resolves the canonical name into an IP address
- Does not function on TCP or UDP level
- Functions on ICMP level
- No application sockets involved

Ping Times

- For a LAN, it usually should be in the <10ms (millisecond; 1000ms = 1 second) range.
- For a wide area connection, acceptable times tend to be under the 800ms range; anything above an eighth of a second is usually completely unacceptable.

If you are getting consistently unacceptable ping times, you'll probably want to do a tracert (see following) to narrow down which hop the delay is occurring on.

Reading Results

- Rule out stack problems by pinging loopback address, as in ping 127.0.0.1
- If you can ping by name, but cannot use a network application, the likelihood is that routing and name services are functioning, and that you have an application issue on the server.
- If you can't ping by name or by address, you might suspect some sort of routing problem.
- Try pinging default router; if you can't ping the router, you might suspect a data-link problem, and you'd want to ping the broadcast address to see if ARP is happening.

ARP

ARP = Address Resolution Protocol.

Ping broadcast address to make ARP cache record as many entries as it can. It takes a TCP/IP request to make ARP happen.

ARP cache: *shows ARP entries.*

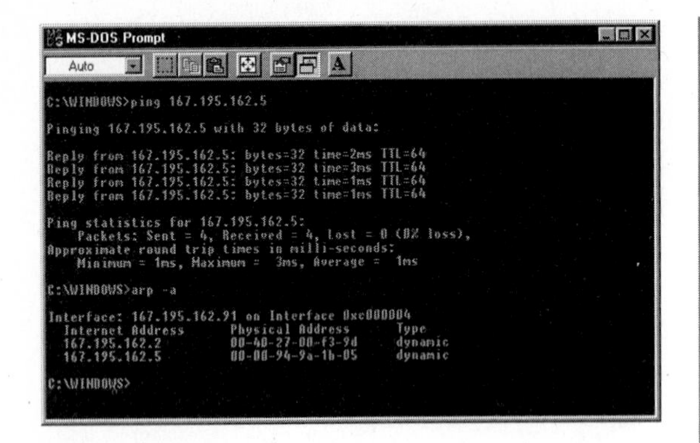

Netstat

Netstat can show

- Which sockets are in use
- Protocol stack and related data link statistics
- The local route table

The -n flag shows output numerically, not by name.

Netstat-a

- Shows all listening and active ports on the system.
- -a only shows socket state, not which app is using the socket.
- Any active service should show as listening.
- Sockets that are established show that a current conversation is occurring.

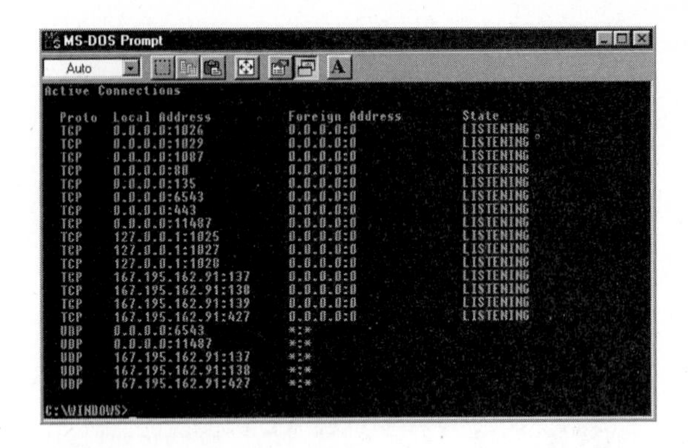

Ethernet Statistics

The TCP/IP stack's take on the interface statistics (not just Ethernet, but also token ring or whatever NIC you have).

Keep your eye on the errors and discards columns: Are they counting up?

Netstat –e Output

```
C:\WINDOWS>netstat -e
Interface Statistics
                                    Received          Sent
Bytes                                 192750         87334
Unicast packets                          596           461
Non-unicast packets                      227           237
Discards                                   0             0
Errors                                     0             0
Unknown protocols                          0
```

netstat -s -p tcp Output

```
TCP Statistics
  Active Opens                            = 23
  Passive Opens                           = 0
  Failed Connection Attempts              = 2
  Reset Connections                       = 0
  Current Connections                     = 4
  Segments Received                       = 552
  Segments Sent                           = 426
  Segments Retransmitted                  = 12
```

netstat -rn Output

```
Route Table
Active Routes:
  Network Address          Netmask  Gateway  Address        Interface  Metric
          0.0.0.0          0.0.0.0    167.195.161.10   167.195.161.61       1
        127.0.0.0        255.0.0.0         127.0.0.1        127.0.0.1       1
      167.195.0.0      255.255.0.0    167.195.161.61   167.195.161.61       1
   167.195.161.61  255.255.255.255         127.0.0.1        127.0.0.1       1
  167.195.255.255  255.255.255.255    167.195.161.61   167.195.161.61       1
        224.0.0.0        224.0.0.0    167.195.161.61   167.195.161.61       1
  255.255.255.255  255.255.255.255    167.195.161.61   167.195.161.61       1
```

This workstation showing the `netstat -rn` output is on the 167.195.161 network (see `netstat -rn` Output on previous page).

224 addresses are for *multicast.*

0.0.0.0 refers to the default route and points at the default gateway.

Traceroute

- `LOAD IPTRACE` on NetWare
- tracert on Windows
- traceroute on UNIX

Displays the point of entry of a packet into a router

See Sample traceroute output below.

If a packet stops trying to get to hop 2, it looks like this (see `timed out` below):

Traceroute itemizes each router that it goes through.

You can keep an eye on where a packet gets delayed or stopped:

- How long it takes between each hop
- Where the packet transmission stops

Telnet

TCP is a connection-oriented protocol. Any TCP socket can establish connection with another, regardless of app (Telnet to Web server socket Telnet server 80).

- You can type protocol commands if you know them (`Get /` for HTTP).
- If host is pingable, a failure to connect to a socket means that service is down.

You cannot telnet to a UDP port—UDP is connectionless—No sequencing relationship!

Nbtstat

`nbtstat -c` shows the most recently resolved name-to-number resolutions (see `nbtstat -c` below):

Most installations with NT server use WINS for IP.

Check WINS if name resolution is a problem.

Sample traceroute output

```
Tracing route to moshepc [192.168.3.55] over a maximum of 30 hops:
  1    164 ms    164 ms    162 ms   router1.feldman.org [192.168.1.5]
  2    170 ms    171 ms    166 ms   router2.feldman.org [192.168.2.2]
  3    235 ms    231 ms    234 ms   moshepc.feldman.org [192.168.3.55]
```

If a packet stops trying to get to hop 2, it looks like this:

```
        2      *         *         *      ➥Request timed out
```

nbtstat –c

```
C:\WINDOWS>nbtstat -c
Node IpAddress: [192.168.1.10] Scope Id: []
             NetBIOS Remote Cache Name Table

    Name               Type        Host Address     Life [sec]
--------------------------------------------------------------
DEGOBAH         <00>  UNIQUE      192.168.1.1          120
DEGOBAH         <20>  UNIQUE      192.168.1.1          360
```

Check workstation connections with `nbtstat -s` (see `nbtstat -s` below)

`nbtstat -A` *`ipaddress`* lists a machine's NetBIOS name table, and also tell you the machine's MAC address (see `nbtstat -A` *`ipaddress`* below):

Nslookup

Tells you two things:

- Whether a DNS server is responding
- Where the lookup is failing

The DNS is not a flat database; it queries other name servers all over the world when it doesn't know how to resolve a given name.

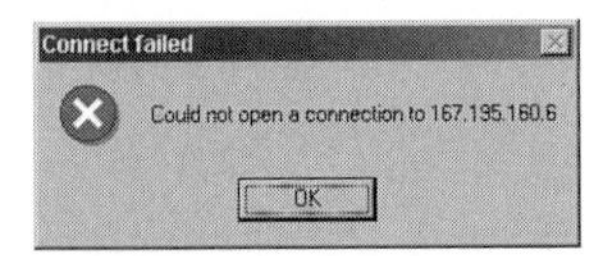

The most important thing about DNS for the exam is the order that a workstation looks up a name.

Someone at `company.com` looks up `www.stanford.edu`; DNS tries (in order):

1. `company.com`
2. `.com`
3. `.edu`
4. `stanford.edu`

Chapter 9

Remote node protocols include both dial-up and tunneling protocols

Dial up: *Connect a computer to a network using a local area code access number.*

- Topology is always point-to-point.
- Participants are workstation and dial-up server.

Tunneling: *Securely access a private network over a dial-up or LAN connection.*

nbtstat –s

```
C:\WINDOWS>nbtstat -s
                 NetBIOS Connection Table
Local Name             State    In/Out  Remote Host          Input    Output
------------------------------------------------------------------------------
DUKE          <00>  Connected  Out    DEGOBAH        <20>  687KB     31KB
DUKE          <03>  Listening
JFELDMAN      <03>  Listening
```

nbtstat –A *ipaddress*

```
C:\WINDOWS>nbtstat -a 192.168.1.1
       NetBIOS Remote Machine Name Table
   Name               Type         Status
---------------------------------------------
DEGOBAH       <20>  UNIQUE      Registered
DEGOBAH       <00>  UNIQUE      Registered
NABOO         <00>  GROUP       Registered
NABOO         <1C>  GROUP       Registered
NABOO         <1B>  UNIQUE      Registered
DEGOBAH       <03>  UNIQUE      Registered
NABOO         <1E>  GROUP       Registered
NABOO         <1D>  UNIQUE      Registered
..__MSBROWSE__.<01>  GROUP       Registered
MAC Address = 00-C0-F0-12-01-AE
```

PPP = Point-to-Point Protocol

Multiple network protocols can be transported.

Any type of point-to-point link: ISDN, modem or even T1 or X.25.

Set up dial-up networking in Windows setup.

Can negotiate for automatic configuration information.

Client and server configuration must agree.

Authentication:

- PAP = Password Authentication Protocol (cleartext passwords).
- CHAP = Challenge-Handshake Authentication Protocol (scrambled, hashed passwords).

SLIP = Serial Line IP

First invented for UNIX servers.

Windows dial-up lists SLIP as "SLIP: UNIX server," but other SLIP servers are available.

Mostly replaced by PPP.

Limitations:

- Each workstation must be manually configured; it will not autoconfigure the way PPP will.
- It only runs TCP/IP; other protocols such as NetBEUI or IPX/SPX are not supported.

PPTP = Point to Point Tunneling Protocol

Used for private data transfer over public networks.

Securing a point-to-point connection over the Internet accomplished by tunneling.

- A conversation between two end-points.
- Encapsulate either the same or another network protocol inside that first conversation.
- Tunnels don't have to be encrypted (first invented to transfer different network protocols over one-protocol link).
- Encrypted tunnels are called VPN (Virtual Private Network).

Found on Windows-based servers and workstations.

Not exclusively Windows-based.

Supports NetBEUI, IPX, and TCP/IP within the tunnel.

Windows version acts as "virtual NIC":

- You must have working connection to network before you use it.
- Specify IP address of PPTP server.
- PPTP server tunnels client request into internal network.

Modems

Relatively complex when compared with Ethernet.

Standard serial port settings for ISA bus:

Port	IRQ	I/O
COM1	4	3F8
COM2	3	2F8

Lower IRQ is for the higher COM port, and the even value IRQ value is for the odd COM port.

Simple loop back: just connect pin 2 to pin 3.

UART

UART: Universal Asynchronous Receiver and Transmitter: Brain of a serial port.

Nothing but a 16550 UART can handle transmissions much over 9600bps.

Internal modems have the serial port built in, thus the UART is also built in.

- Potential resource conflict with built-in COM1 or COM2.
- WinModems don't have UARTs—requiring the CPU to handle UART functions.
- Require higher performance PCs to operate correctly.

Speed

Typical serial line speeds:

300, 1200, 2400, 4800, 9600, 19200, 38400, 57600, and 115,200bps.

DTE speed = *Data Terminal Equipment speed. Speed between the modem and the computer.*

DCE speed = *Data Communication Equipment speed. Modem to modem speed.*

DTE speed can be different from DCE speed.

- Data compressing modem compresses the DTE stream into a smaller DCE stream.
- Hardware handshaking required.

ISDN Versus POTS?

Differences between POTS and ISDN

	BRI ISDN	POTS
Wiring	UTP	UTP
Signaling	Digital	Analog
Voice Channel	W/proper equip.	Yes
Telco stds	Many	One
Max Speed	2x64K=128K or 2x56K=115K	56K

Terminal Adapter = ISDN modem; attaches serially to PC, max 115,200bps.

ISDN bus card—can achieve full synchronous ISDN speeds.

ISDN achieves full line speed versus varying analog connection rates.

ISDN line more expensive than analog line.

ISDN SPID (Service Profile ID) varies according to ISDN switch type.

Remote Node Versus Remote Control

Remote node: *Your workstation becomes a host on the remote network (PPP, SLIP, PPTP, and so on).*

Access data using a file-and-print client or client-server programs.

Remote control: *You take control of a visual session on the remote network. Two categories: Workstation-based and Server-based.*

- Only mouse clicks and keyboard strokes are transmitted, rather than entire files or applications.
- Can be much faster than loading entire data files or applications over a slow network.
- Can be the best choice for tech support.
- Initiated over serial links or via remote node network.

Chapter 10

Authentication and Security

Authentication method*—How an individual access network resources.*

Credential called an *authentication token.*

Forms:

- Reusable password (password stays the same until administrator or user changes it).
- One time password (password changes every time).
- Certificates (digitally signed reusable tokens).
- Tickets (one-time digitally signed tokens).
- Biometric authentication (fingerprints, retina scans).

Security model: *Where the authentication takes place.*

Resource-based security:

- A car's combination lock.
- Windows share-level security.
- Doesn't identify person using the resource—no identity attached to the token.
- When security is compromised, token must be changed and redistributed.

User-level Security

User object requires a credential, the rest of network resources rely on user identity.

Security at a military base: Military ID identifies you/your face. If you are on access list, you can enter.

Directory services and most file-and-print servers have user-level security.

NT Domain model, Novell NDS, and UNIX PC/NFS:

- Auditing is easier than resource-level.
- Password changes only affect one person.
- Resources access lists can be changed without affecting others.
- Permissions have three levels with grouping:
    - Everyone
    - Function or department
    - Individual user

Share-Level Versus User-Level Authentication

- Resource level security is much better for large organizations with many users and many resources.
- Share level security can be better for smaller organizations with just a few resources.

Feature	Share-level	User-level
User auditing possible	No	Yes
Grouping possible	No	Yes
Easiest file and print sharing	Yes	No
One person leaves company; only one password at risk	No	Yes
n Resources require *n* passwords	Yes	No
n Users require *n* passwords	N/A	Yes

Password Policies

Password selection can be a big part of ensuring that your organization's data is secure.

Issues

- Password file availability
- Availability of Intruder Detection
- Mandatory password expiration
- Corporate culture
- User training
- Sensitivity of data

Password Disclosure Risks

- Password guessing obvious passwords (WarGames daemon dialing).
- Reading post-it or other user notes.
- Impersonating service personnel and asking for a password.
- Cracking readable password file(s). (Brute force encryption cracking, using widely available tools and cheap PCs hooked up to be massively parallel processors).

Defenses

- Intruder detection/lockout.
- Forced password changes.
- Good passwords.
- Using operating systems with publicly unavailable password files.
- Do not make it a practice to ask for a user's password, even while you're troubleshooting (use temporary passwords).

Bad Passwords

- Ego passwords or swear words (God, master, caesar, sex, ... darn, among others.)
- Words specific to cool cyberpunk, fantasy, or sci-fi novels/movies (snowcrash, neuromancer, lorien, moria, frodo, r2d2, deathstar, darth, and so on.)
- Organization or pop-culture acronyms (NASA, TMBG, BTO, and so on).
- Names (Joe, Mary, Bill, Eliza, and so on).
- Birthdays (082268, 8/22/68, 8-22-68, and so on).
- Dictionary words, English or otherwise (trattoria, cafe, doghouse, splendid).
- Cute numerical combinations (2hard2, work4love, 8pizza).

Good Passwords

- Unrelated combinations of words, numbers, and symbols (jinx$toy, pop24work, meow!dog, 10eat42).
- Acronyms (PDGMP = Please Don't Guess My Password; EIFTK = Elvis Is Forever The King, TW2HIB = The Way 2 Happiness Is Biking).
- Random alphanumeric combinations (5dj582, #2$58!, $zj3u20, and other horrible combinations).

Encryption

***Cipher**: Scrambles data in such a way that it is difficult/time consuming for intruders to read.*

***Key:** Used by the cipher to descramble (decrypt or decipher) or scramble (encrypt or encipher).*

***Key size:** How large, in bits, a given key is.*

Public and Private Keys

***Public key:** One-way encryption; the public key cannot decrypt the data: it can only encrypt the data for later decryption by the holder of a private key.*

***Private key:** A key that must be kept secret. Private keys can be used either to encrypt or decrypt data.*

Public key encryption—SSL (as with https://).

Private key encryption depends upon all keys being secret (Windows 2000).

Applications of Encryption

- Server-based: SSL, NetWare packet encryption, NT challenge-response, CHAP).
- Network layer: IPSEC (Network-layer TCP/IP), VPN.
- Data link layer: IEEE 802.10.
- Software applications: PGP (Pretty Good Privacy), WordPerfect, Microsoft Word, and so on.

Firewalls and Proxies

Lock on your front door.

Proxy server performs transactions on client's behalf.

Firewall = screening router, screens based on:

- Which interface a packet comes in on.
- Which network address the packet says it is from.
- Which network address the packet is going to.
- Which protocol/socket number the packet says it is coming from.

- Which protocol/socket number the packet is going to.
- Whether a packet is a response to a connection-oriented session.

Firewalls and proxies don't eliminate the need to secure other entries into your organization (dialup lines, and so on).

Chapter 11

SOP (Standard Operating Procedure): *A set of rules or standards that helps members of the organization do things in a consistent way.*

Examples:

- All users must pass a security background check before getting access to the network.
- All leased lines must be documented with the help desk prior to deployment.

Environment

Environment plays a significant role in server or other gear's longevity and reliability.

- Low-dust, low-humidity and temperature-controlled environment is best.
- Check manufacturer's specs to see what kind of air space a given piece of equipment needs.

Power Conditions

Room climate and positioning is only second to the room's power conditions.

Power conditions at any point on a network link can make or break that link.

Check the physical area:

- Are space heaters in use?
- Is a refrigerator or soft drink machine in the area?
- Is an air conditioner plugged into the area's circuit?
- Is an elevator on the same line as a given office?

Any A/C gear that pulls a large amount of voltage on a line can cause other devices connected to it to sag or brown out—not limited to previous list.

Keep power fluctuation in mind when you see power-related questions.

Equipment Readiness

If you have the exact same known good configuration on each workstation in a rollout, troubleshooting and deployment becomes easy.(IP address and workstation name will differ on each.)

Deploy factory-style assembly-line workstations:

- By using unattended setup options
- Using drive duplication

Written checklist for hardware items can be useful.

Servers

It's not a server until it has virus protection and a working backup!

Check the power draw on the UPS; that is, check how many amps it is currently supplying, add the amp draw of the new server, and see whether this is within the rating of the UPS line. (This is important: Typical software-oriented network administrators don't think of this.)

Check file and print and client-server services.

Label the server with

- Network name
- Protocol address
- Function (email server? Lotus Notes gateway?)

Infrastructure

Hubs, switches, and routers also need labels:

- Circuit ID (CSU/DSU)
- Protocol address (smart hubs, routers, and switches)
- ar-end connection, where appropriate

SCSI Cabling Issues

Jumper cables are part of any wire run's cable budget!

SCSI Cable Types & Maximum Cable Budget

SCSI Level:	Maximum cable run	Common connectors
SCSI 1	6m	DB-25, 50-pin
		Centronics, 50-pin mini-D
SCSI 2	6m	50-pin mini-D
Fast/Wide SCSI-2	3m	68-pin mini-D
SCSI 3 (Wide or narrow)	1.5m	68-pin mini-D

Be careful of getting tripped up by 36-pin Centronics—it's not SCSI; it's only used for parallel printers!

Before an Install

Before an install, plan for:

- Leased lines
- User names/passwords/appropriate login scripts
- Administrative accounts/supervisor privileges for your account
- IP address space/site configuration standards

Applications are ready when:

- Adequate disk space is available (best done *before* server goes into production)
- Printing resources are configured and available

Disk and print resources are best reconnected from a login script.

Print servers and printers should be labeled with server/queue names.

Chapter 12

Logistics of the Change Control System

Pilot Testing

For any new gear, procedures, or software, a pilot test system should have the same characteristics as the production system.

User Notification

- Get permission to perform user adds, deletes, or modifications.
- Get permission to move or delete old application data.
- Consult Standard Operating Procedures (SOP).
- Allow adequate time for users to plan their work week.

Baselining

Backing up systems before you change them:

- Consult documentation. Trust, but verify.
- Have good backups of all systems that you implement changes to.
- If systems aren't backup-enabled, document all settings.

Clone workstations don't need backing up if

- No user data is kept on hard drive
- Network profiles are in use

Workstation backup can be done by:

- Network agents
- File copy to network drive (replicated folder)

- Temporary image to network drive or local drive partition
- Removable storage

Implementation of the Change(s)

Change is 10 percent plan and 90 percent preparation.

Testing and Verifying the Changes

- Application testing is most important.
- Upper layers functional means that lower layers are functional, too.
- Manually reconnecting drives and printers:
  - Microsoft—`NET USE G: \\myserver\myshare; NET USE LPT1: \\myserver\myprinter.`
  - Novell—`MAP G:=\\myserver\myshare capture /Q=printer /L=1.`
  - Consider testing under load.

Rollback Plan

- Changing IP addresses or other configuration information back to previous values.
- Uninstalling software, or returning software to a previous version.
- Returning a server back to a previous patch level or OS version, sometimes requiring a restore from backup.
- Restoring workstation system DLLs to previous versions (restore from backup or previous workstation image).

Cleanup

After the changes, moves, or upgrades are done, remove the following:

- Test users
- Test data files
- Unzipped application install directories
- Old drivers

Chapter 13

Maintenance habits:

- **Daily**: backup.
- **Weekly**: Check for new virus patterns, check disk space.
- **Yearly**: Renew service contracts for critical equipment.
- **As needed**: apply necessary vendor patches, upgrades, and security fixes.

Backups

Good backups mean that you can recover from anything.

Developing a backup habit:

- What portion of data needs to be backed up every night?
- Will every server have a tape drive, or will you centralize your backups to back up over the network?
- What are the manufacturer recommended tape drive and tape cartridge specifications?
- Where is a secure place to store off-site copies of your data?
- What is the data retention cycle for the data that you are backing up?
- What verification scheme is in place to make sure that the backup data is reliable?

Backup window: *Amount of daily server idle time where you can back data up.*

Full backups: *The easiest and most reliable backup if you have the tape space and a large enough backup window.*

Incremental: *Back up all data since last full or incremental backup.*

- Only one copy of each file version
- Least amount of data per backup

Differential: *Back up all data since last full backup.*

- Writes more data per backup session than an incremental backup, but less than a full backup.
- More than one copy of each version of a file.

NOS keep track of backup status in two ways:

- Archive attribute
- Modification time

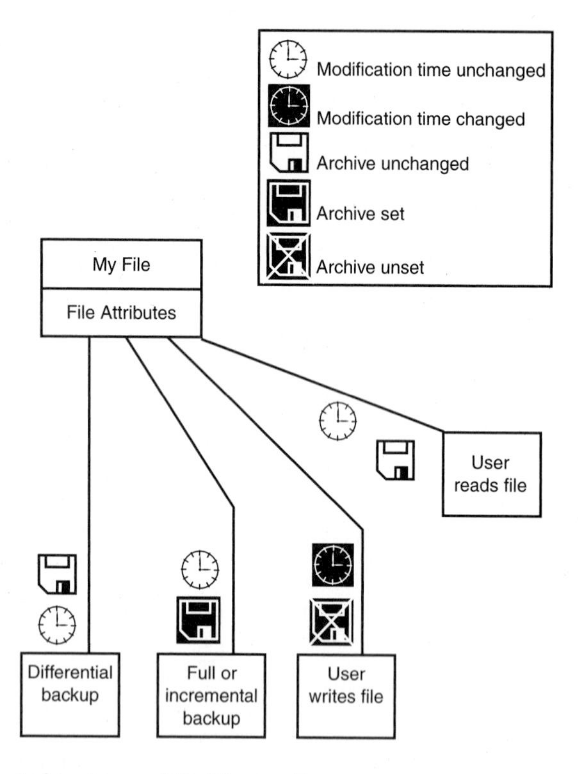

Archive Bits and Modification Times

Comparison of Backup Methods

Backup Method	File on More Than One Tape	Amount of Tape/ Time Required for Backup
Full	Most	Unset
Differential	Medium	Unchanged
Incremental	Least	Unset

Prevent Tape Damage

To prevent tape damage, you will want to follow manufacturer's specifications about the following:

- What type of climate to keep tapes in (typically air-conditioned, low-humidity environments).
- How to store tapes (typically with the spools perpendicular to the floor, *not* flat).
- How often to clean tape drives (typically weekly).
- How many times a tape can be used (varies according to tape type).

Backup Verification

Necessary to ensure good data reliability.

Tape Rotation

- Required if you want to keep data past a certain point.
- Multiple sets that represent a different period of time are called multigenerational backups.
- Part of tape rotation is off-site storage, which can help your business recover in the event of a fire, hurricane, or other disaster.

Virus Protection

Necessary against

- Mail-attachment viruses
- Executable viruses
- Boot sector viruses
- Macro viruses

Stand-alone virus protection for workstations is not sufficient.

Virus Protection Suite

- Workstation protection.
- Virus pattern update via login scripts or other server-based mechanism.
- Mail gateway protection.
- Server protection for different Network Operating Systems.

Virus Signature File

Also called a ***pattern file:*** Proprietary file that allows virus protection software to detect and remove viruses.

Your virus protection vendor is the only source of signature files because there is no standard format for a signature file.

Patches

Periodic application of software patches and other fixes to the network is a necessary evil.

Avoid being the guinea pig: Patch servers and software after the patch has been available for several months

Hotfixes: *Small, discrete fixes released by the manufacturer to solve specific problems, usually for specific customers using specific configurations.*

Patches: *Larger fixes intended for the general user community that have usually been more thoroughly tested than hotfixes.*

Service Pack: *The accumulation of many patches into one distribution file.*

If you have publicly accessible servers, such as Web servers or FTP servers, it's in your best interest to patch these servers with security fixes as soon as humanly possible.

Chapter 14

Prioritizing

Picking priorities enables you to handle multiple problems in an appropriate order.

Problem determination and response mnemonic, SSS:

- Scope
- Seriousness
- Service

Seriousness

What kind of impact the problem has on the business

Item	Seriousness
Can't browse the Web	Low
Workstation malfunction	Low
Can't log in	Medium
Can't print	Medium
Deleted data (depending on scope)	Medium
User issues	Medium
Customer issues	High
Server down	High
Security problem	High

Scope

How widespread a problem is

Group affected	Scope
Single user	Narrow
Multi user	Medium
Single workgroup	Medium
Multiple workgroups	Broad
Enterprise	Broad

Priority Pick Chart

1 is the highest priority, and 4 is the lowest:

	Serious	Not Serious
Wide scope	1	3
Narrow scope	2	4

Scope is usually second fiddle to seriousness.

Can determine where you start looking for the problem.

Problem Response: Service

Subjective data is less reliable than objective data (Problem might be reported incorrectly!)

- Question a less trained observer thoroughly.
- Trust what a trained observer says.
- Gather empirical evidence yourself.

A user might need the following types of service:

- Handholding—Talking a user through normal operations.
- Information Transfer—Teaching a user about a new procedure.
- Technical service:
  - Quick fix
  - Workaround
  - Embarking upon troubleshooting

Chapter 15

- Think about the problem using a limited set of OSI-like layers.
- Get objective problem determination data.
- Perform local troubleshooting procedures.
- Call on vendor services.

For high-level troubleshooting purposes, considering four key OSI layers is appropriate:

- Physical
- Data link
- Network
- Application

Order of Operations

Mnemonic:

- *Babies* IDENTIFY with their parents.
- *Teens* are more interested in RECREATion than anything else.
- When *college students* are ISOLATEd from their parents, FORMULATing new alcoholic beverages is the order of the day.
- *Young adults* can IMPLEMENT the marriage ritual.
- *Young couples* tend to have babies, which TESTs their sanity.
- *Their first baby* is the most photographed and DOCUMENTed baby.
- The *new parents* get more FEEDBACK on their child-rearing skills than they want.

CompTIA troubleshooting order of operations:

1. Identify

Identify the exact issue—find out what is going on (problem determination).

2. Re-Create

Re-create the problem—make sure the same thing happens to you when you try the problem operation.

3. Isolate

Isolate the cause—simplify the situation. That is, if a person can't get from point A to point D, see if you can get to point B or C.

4. Formulate

Formulate a correction—after you find the cause, plan what you are going to do. (If a user's network client isn't coming up because of disk errors, run ScanDisk and install the client.)

5. Implement

Implement the correction—address the cause that you have isolated; put your plan into action.

6. Test

Test—make sure that the problem is corrected by your solution. It's always a good idea to completely restart a machine, so that you can be sure that the solution is permanent.

7. Document

Document the problem and the solution—always let the help desk and your peers know about how you solved the issue; obviously, handholding doesn't need to be documented, but a report of a complex troubleshooting session can help the next person address the same issue more quickly.

8. Feedback

Give feedback—mke sure that your supervisor and the user know about any issues that prevented you from solving the problem more quickly.

Probing the Problem

Most important thing you can do is to change the conditions of the scenario.

- See how it changes, or if it goes away, as you change the conditions.
- Problem's reaction to the changed condition provides you with knowledge about its nature.

Try with a different

- User
- Workstation
- Server
- NOS

A controlled experiment, consisting of changing one element of the problem at a time, is a good way to gather empirical data about a problem. Ensure consistent problem behavior by trying the change more than once.

Physical Problems

Power Problems

- Check power light, fans
- Try with line conditioner or UPS

Cable Problems

- Cable scope
- Swap known good

Can't find the other end to test?

- Fox-and-hound (inductive tone generator and detector)
- Generator goes at known end.
- Detector used at unknown end.

Electronic Malfunction

- Swap known good.

Resource Problem

Rule out PC resource problems by checking

- ScanDisk
- System monitor
- Resource meter

Things that tend to kill network devices, or make networked programs malfunction are the following:

- A lack of memory
- A lack of CPU time
- Too much disk I/O
- Damaged disk surfaces

Data Link

- You can infer a diagnosis of a data-link segment by using workstation statistics and ARP.
- For a definitive diagnosis, use a data scope.

Network

Establish

- Reachability
- Good statistics, few errors

Tools that can establish top-level reachability and statistic gathering include the following:

- `Ping` (TCP/IP ICMP reachability)
- `Nslookup` (TCP/IP name services: DNS)
- `Nbtstat` (Microsoft TCP/IP name services: WINS)
- `Tracert` (TCP/IP router reachability)
- `Netstat-s` (TCP/IP statistics)

- `LOAD IPXCON` (Novell IPX, IPX statistics)
- `LOAD IPXPING` (Novell IPX, IPX reachability)

Application

- Don't forget to try to use the network resources yourself to rule out server-based problems.
- If you (or anyone else) can use a resource and another user cannot, check permissions.
- If permissions are okay, check the system and application logs.

Workstation Configuration

- Verify the configuration, either manually, or by re-loading or cloning the workstation image.
- Check for virus protection and up-to-date pattern file.

Vendor Resources

Vendor Web sites typically include the following:

- Minimum patch lists
- Knowledge base search engines
- Compatibility matrix
- Frequently Asked Questions

Tech support includes the following:

- Email
- Telephone

Both are more effective when you document what you've already done.

Both require follow up.

Follow-up leads to *escalation* if a first-level technician can't help.

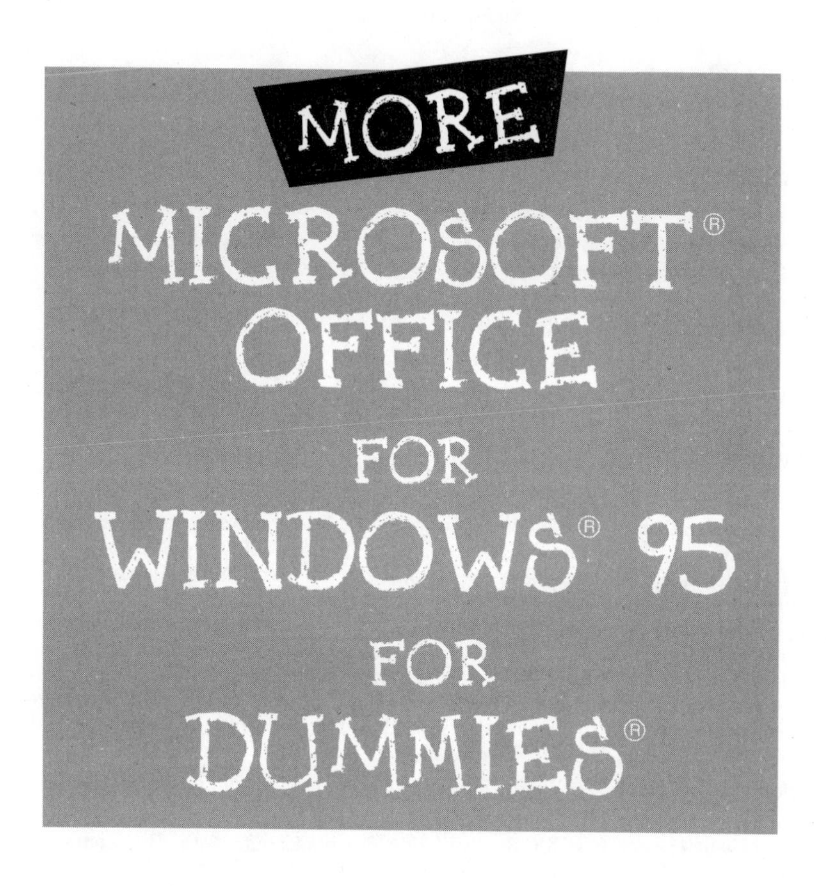

by Wallace Wang

IDG Books Worldwide, Inc.
An International Data Group Company

Foster City, CA ♦ Chicago, IL ♦ Indianapolis, IN ♦ Southlake, TX

MORE Microsoft® Office For Windows® 95 For Dummies®

Published by
IDG Books Worldwide, Inc.
An International Data Group Company
919 E. Hillsdale Blvd.
Suite 400
Foster City, CA 94404

www.idgbooks.com

Library of Congress Catalog Card No.: 96-076359

ISBN: 0-7645-0009-0

Printed in the United States of America

10 9 8 7 6 5 4 3 2 1

1A/QV/QW/ZW/IN

Distributed in the United States by IDG Books Worldwide, Inc.

Distributed by Macmillan Canada for Canada; by Contemporanea de Ediciones for Venezuela; by Distribuidora Cuspide for Argentina; by CITEC for Brazil; by Ediciones ZETA S.C.R. Ltda. for Peru; by Editorial Limusa SA for Mexico; by Transworld Publishers Limited in the United Kingdom and Europe; by Academic Bookshop for Egypt; by Levant Distributors S.A.R.L. for Lebanon; by Al Jassim for Saudi Arabia; by Simron Pty. Ltd. for South Africa; by Pustak Mahal for India; by The Computer Bookshop for India; by Toppan Company Ltd. for Japan; by Addison Wesley Publishing Company for Korea; by Longman Singapore Publishers Ltd. for Singapore, Malaysia, Thailand, and Indonesia; by Unalis Corporation for Taiwan; by WS Computer Publishing Company, Inc. for the Philippines; by WoodsLane Pty. Ltd. for Australia; by WoodsLane Enterprises Ltd. for New Zealand. Authorized Sales Agent: Anthony Rudkin Associates for the Middle East and North Africa.

For general information on IDG Books Worldwide's books in the U.S., including information on discounts and premiums, contact IDG Books Worldwide at 800-434-3422 or 415-655-3000.

For information on where to purchase IDG Books Worldwide's books outside the U.S., contact IDG Books Worldwide's International Sales department at 415-655-3078 or fax 415-655-3281.

For information on foreign language translations, contact IDG Books Worldwide's Foreign & Subsidiary Rights department at 415-655-3018 or fax 415-655-3281.

For sales inquiries and special prices for bulk quantities, contact IDG Books Worldwide's Sales department at 415-655-3200 or write to the address above.

For information on using IDG Books Worldwide's books in the classroom or for ordering examination copies, contact IDG Books Worldwide's Educational Sales department at 800-434-2086 or fax 817-251-8174.

About the Author

Wallace Wang

Before buying a book, many people like to know who the author is so that they can determine whether the author's credentials may somehow make the book more pertinent or valuable in some obscure way. So to help you make a snap decision on whether to buy this book or not, here's a quick look at my resume.

Name: Wallace Wang

E-mail address: 70334.3672@compuserve.com

Objective: To convince people that they're not stupid; it's the poorly designed computers and software that are.

Work and Education Experience

1979	Graduated from high school with absolutely no marketable skills or direction whatsoever. Support your local school system.
1983	Graduated from Michigan State University with an (appropriately abbreviated) Bachelor of Science degree in Materials Science, the only engineering major I could find that offered the most non-technical electives. Also pursued a dual degree in English that I never completed because I felt I already knew how to get a minimum-wage job all by myself.
1983–1985	Worked as a technical writer for General Dynamics, home of the nuclear-tipped cruise missile. Got in trouble once for referring to General Dynamics as a "bomb factory," so from that point on I bought chocolate-covered doughnuts for my boss, hoping to clog his arteries with cholesterol and induce a fatal heart attack.
1985–1987	Worked as a computer programmer for the Cubic Corporation doing absolutely nothing at all. Spent many days sitting at a desk, staring out the window, and pretending I was the vice president of the United States.
1987–1991	Worked as a writer/editor for a San Diego computer magazine called *ComputerEdge,* where I met Dan Gookin (*DOS For Dummies*), Tina Rathbone (*Modems For Dummies*), and Andy Rathbone (*Windows For Dummies*). At one time, Dan Gookin and I got in trouble with the FBI for printing a fake FBI poster of myself, proclaiming that I was a criminal for buying a Macintosh computer.

1990–Present	Decided to pursue stand-up comedy and began performing at The Comedy Store in La Jolla and Hollywood, California.
1993–Present	Got married and soon became the owner of three cats named Bo, Scraps, and Tasha.
1994	Appeared on "A&E's Evening at the Improv."
1995	Became a columnist for *Boardwatch Magazine*.
1996	Wrote this book.
1997	Helped bring peace to the Middle East.
1998	Invented a perpetual motion machine.
1999	Developed a cure for cancer.
2000	Discovered the missing number that would solve Albert Einstein's Grand Unified Field Theory. That number is 4.
2001	Wrote to Arthur C. Clarke and told him his book was wrong.

ABOUT IDG BOOKS WORLDWIDE

Welcome to the world of IDG Books Worldwide.

IDG Books Worldwide, Inc., is a subsidiary of International Data Group, the world's largest publisher of computer-related information and the leading global provider of information services on information technology. IDG was founded more than 25 years ago and now employs more than 7,700 people worldwide. IDG publishes more than 250 computer publications in 67 countries (see listing below). More than 70 million people read one or more IDG publications each month.

Launched in 1990, IDG Books Worldwide is today the #1 publisher of best-selling computer books in the United States. We are proud to have received 8 awards from the Computer Press Association in recognition of editorial excellence and three from Computer Currents' First Annual Readers' Choice Awards, and our best-selling *...For Dummies®* series has more than 19 million copies in print with translations in 28 languages. IDG Books Worldwide, through a joint venture with IDG's Hi-Tech Beijing, became the first U.S. publisher to publish a computer book in the People's Republic of China. In record time, IDG Books Worldwide has become the first choice for millions of readers around the world who want to learn how to better manage their businesses.

Our mission is simple: Every one of our books is designed to bring extra value and skill-building instructions to the reader. Our books are written by experts who understand and care about our readers. The knowledge base of our editorial staff comes from years of experience in publishing, education, and journalism — experience which we use to produce books for the '90s. In short, we care about books, so we attract the best people. We devote special attention to details such as audience, interior design, use of icons, and illustrations. And because we use an efficient process of authoring, editing, and desktop publishing our books electronically, we can spend more time ensuring superior content and spend less time on the technicalities of making books.

You can count on our commitment to deliver high-quality books at competitive prices on topics you want to read about. At IDG Books Worldwide, we continue in the IDG tradition of delivering quality for more than 25 years. You'll find no better book on a subject than one from IDG Books Worldwide.

John Kilcullen
President and CEO
IDG Books Worldwide, Inc.

IDG Books Worldwide, Inc., is a subsidiary of International Data Group, the world's largest publisher of computer-related information and the leading global provider of information services on information technology. International Data Group publishes over 250 computer publications in 67 countries. Seventy million people read one or more International Data Group publications each month. International Data Group's publications include: **ARGENTINA:** Computerworld Argentina, GamePro, Infoworld, PC World Argentina; **AUSTRALIA:** Australian Macworld, Client/Server Journal, Computer Living, Computerworld, Digital News, Network World, PC World, Publishing Essentials, Reseller; **AUSTRIA:** Computerwelt, PC TEST; **BELARUS:** PC World Belarus; **BELGIUM:** Data News; **BRAZIL:** Annuário de Informática, Computerworld Brazil, Connections, Super Game Power, Macworld, PC World Brazil, Publish Brazil, SUPERGAME; **BULGARIA:** Computerworld Bulgaria, Networkworld/Bulgaria, PC & MacWorld Bulgaria; **CANADA:** CIO Canada, ComputerWorld Canada, InfoCanada, Network World Canada, Reseller World; **CHILE:** Computerworld Chile, GamePro, PC World Chile; **COLUMBIA:** Computerworld Colombia, GamePro, PC World Colombia; **COSTA RICA:** PC World Costa Rica/Nicaragua; **THE CZECH AND SLOVAK REPUBLICS:** Computerworld Czechoslovakia, Elektronika Czechoslovakia, PC World Czechoslovakia; **DENMARK:** Communications World, Computerworld Danmark, Macworld Danmark, PC World Danmark, PC World Danmark Supplements, TECH World; **DOMINICAN REPUBLIC:** PC World Republica Dominicana; **ECUADOR:** PC World Ecuador, GamePro; **EGYPT:** Computerworld Middle East, PC World Middle East; **EL SALVADOR:** PC World Centro America; **FINLAND:** MikroPC, Tietoverkko, Tietoviikko; **FRANCE:** Distributique, Golden, Info PC, Le Guide du Monde Informatique, Le Monde Informatique, Reseaux & Telecoms; **GERMANY:** Computer Business, Computerwoche, Computerwoche Extra, Computerwoche Focus, Electronic Entertainment, GamePro, I/M Information Management, Macwelt, PC Welt; **GREECE:** GamePro, Macworld & Publish; **GUATEMALA:** PC World Centro America; **HONDURAS:** PC World Centro America; **HONG KONG:** Computerworld Hong Kong, PCWorld Hong Kong, Publish in Asia; **HUNGARY:** ABCD CD-ROM, Computerworld Szamitastechnika, PC & Mac World Hungary, PC-X Magazine; **INDIA:** Computerworld India, PC World India, Publish in Asia; **INDONESIA:** InfoKomputer PC World, Komputek Computerworld, Publish in Asia; **IRELAND:** ComputerScope, PC Live!; **ISRAEL:** PC World 32 BIT, People & Computers; **ITALY:** Computerworld Italia, Computerworld Italia Special Editions, Lotus Italia, Macworld Italia, Networking Italia, PC Shopping, PC World Italia, PC World/Walt Disney; **JAPAN:** Macworld Japan, Nikkei Personal Computing, SunWorld Japan, Windows World Japan; **KENYA:** East African Computer News; **KOREA:** Hi-Tech Information/Computerworld, Macworld Korea, PC World Korea; **MACEDONIA:** PC World Macedonia; **MALAYSIA:** Computerworld Malaysia, PC World Malaysia, Publish in Asia; **MEXICO:** Computerworld Mexico, GamePro, Macworld, PC World Mexico; **MYANMAR:** PC World Myanmar; **NETHERLANDS:** Computable, Computer! Totaal, LAN Magazine, Macworld, Net Magazine; **NEW ZEALAND:** Computer Buyer, Computerworld New Zealand, MTB, Network World, PC World New Zealand; **NICARAGUA:** PC World Costa Rica/Nicaragua; **NIGERIA:** PC World Africa; **NORWAY:** Computerworld Norge, Computerworld Privat, CW Rapport Klient/Tjener, CW Rapport Nettverk & Telecom, CW Rapport Offentlig Sektor, IDG's KURSGUIDE, Macworld Norge, Multimedia World, PC World Ekspress, PC World Nettverk, PC World Norge, PC World's Produktguide, Windows Spesial; **PAKISTAN:** Computerworld Pakistan, PC World Pakistan; **PANAMA:** GamePro, PC World Panama; **PARAGUAY:** PC World Paraguay; **P. R. OF CHINA:** China Computerworld, China Infoworld, Computer & Communication, Electronic Product World, Electronics Today, Game Camp, PC World China, Popular Computer Week, Software World, Telecom Product World; **PERU:** Computerworld Peru, GamePro, PC World Profesional Peru, PC World Peru; **POLAND:** Computerworld Poland, Computerworld Special Report, Macworld, Networld, PC World Komputer; **PHILIPPINES:** Computerworld Philippines, PC Digest, Publish in Asia; **PORTUGAL:** Cerebro/PC World, Correio Informático/Computerworld, Mac•In/PC•In Portugal; **PUERTO RICO:** PC World Puerto Rico; **ROMANIA:** Computerworld Romania, PC World Romania, Telecom Romania; **RUSSIA:** Computerworld Rossiya, Network World Russia, PC World Russia; **SINGAPORE:** Computerworld Singapore, PC World Singapore, Publish in Asia; **SLOVENIA:** MONITOR; **SOUTH AFRICA:** Computing S.A., Network World S.A., Software World; **SPAIN:** Computerworld España, COMUNICACIONES WORLD, Dealer World, Macworld España, PC World España; **SWEDEN:** CAP&Design, Computer Sweden, Corporate Computing, MacWorld, Maxi Data, MikroDatorn, Nätverk & Kommunikation, PC/Aktiv, PC World, Windows World; **SWITZERLAND:** Computerworld Schweiz, Macworld Schweiz, PCtip; **TAIWAN:** Computerworld Taiwan, Macworld Taiwan, PC World Taiwan, Publish Taiwan, Windows World; **THAILAND:** Thai Computerworld, Publish in Asia; **TURKEY:** Computerworld Monitör, MACWORLD Turkiye, PC WORLD Turkiye; **UKRAINE:** Computerworld Kiev, Computers & Software Magazine, PC World Ukraine; **UNITED KINGDOM:** Acorn User, Amiga Action, Amiga Computing, Amiga, Appletalk, CD Powerplay, CD-ROM Now, Computing, Connexion, GamePro, Lotus Magazine, Macaction, Macworld, Open Computing, Parents and Computers, PC Home, PC Works, The WEB; **UNITED STATES:** Cable in the Classroom, CD Review, CIO Magazine, Computerworld, Computerworld Client/Server Journal, Digital Video Magazine, DOS World, Electronic, InfoWorld, I-Way, Macworld, Maximize, MULTIMEDIA WORLD, Network World, PC World, PUBLISH, SWATPro Magazine, Video Event, WebMaster; **URUGUAY:** PC World Uruguay; **VENEZUELA:** Computerworld Venezuela, GamePro, PC World Venezuela; and **VIETNAM:** PC World Vietnam

10/17/95a

Dedication

This book is dedicated to my parents, Herbert and Ruth Wang, my wife, Cassandra, and Bo and Scraps, my cats.

Publisher's Acknowledgments

We're proud of this book; please send us your comments about it by using the Reader Response Card at the back of the book or by e-mailing us at `feedback/dummies@idgbooks.com`. Some of the people who helped bring this book to market include the following:

Acquisitions, Development, & Editorial

Project Editor: Colleen Rainsberger

Assistant Acquisitions Editor: Tammy Goldfeld

Copy Editors: Tamara S. Castleman, Joe Jansen, Rebecca A. Whitney

Technical Reviewer: Jim McCarter

Editorial Manager: Mary C. Corder

Editorial Assistant: Chris H. Collins

Production

Project Coordinator: Sherry Gomoll

Layout and Graphics: Cameron Booker, Cheryl Danski, Maridee Ennis, Todd Klemme, Jane Martin, Drew R. Moore, Elizabeth Cardenas-Nelson, Mark Owens, Brent Savage, Gina Scott

Proofreaders: Christine Meloy Beck, Michael Bolinger, Nancy Price, Robert Springer, Carrie Voorhis, Karen York

Indexer: David Heiret

General & Administrative

IDG Books Worldwide, Inc.: John Kilcullen, President & CEO; Steven Berkowitz, COO & Publisher

Dummies, Inc.: Milissa Koloski, Executive Vice President & Publisher

Dummies Technology Press & Dummies Editorial: Diane Graves Steele, Associate Publisher; Judith A. Taylor, Brand Manager; Myra Immell, Editorial Director

Dummies Trade Press: Kathleen A. Welton, Vice President & Publisher; Stacy S. Collins, Brand Manager

IDG Books Production for Dummies Press: Beth Jenkins, Production Director; Cindy L. Phipps, Supervisor of Project Coordination; Kathie S. Schnorr, Supervisor of Page Layout; Shelley Lea, Supervisor of Graphics and Design

Dummies Packaging & Book Design: Erin McDermit, Packaging Coordinator; Kavish+Kavish, Cover Design

♦

The publisher would like to give special thanks to Patrick J. McGovern, without whom this book would not have been possible.

♦

Author's Acknowledgments

Thanks go to Bill Gladstone and Matt Wagner of Waterside Productions. I always have to acknowledge my book agents because I want to make sure that I get my royalty checks on time.

Another big round of heart-felt warmth and thanks goes to Fred Burns, Ron Clark, Terry Mayfield, Frank Manzano, Pete Balistreri, Dante, and Leo Fontaine of The Comedy Store in La Jolla, California. These guys didn't help with this book one bit, so I really don't know why I'm thanking them at all.

More thanks go out to the following comedians whose humor has inspired, enlightened, and entertained me during the writing of this book: Bill Hicks, George Wallace, Dennis Miller, Paula Poundstone, George Carlin, Jay Leno, David Letterman, Will Durst, Emo Phillips, and Robert Klein. These people didn't help me write this book either, but at least they made me laugh a lot while I was doing all the hard work.

Final thanks go to Cassandra the Wife, Bo the Cat, Scraps the Cat, Tasha the Cat, and the person who first invented the tradition of the Acknowledgements page for pure ego-gratification on the part of the author. Without the invention of the Acknowledgements page, these paragraphs could never have been written and you would look rather silly right now just staring at a blank piece of paper.

Contents at a Glance

Cartoons at a Glance

By Rich Tennant • Fax: 508-546-7747 • E-mail: the5wave@tiac.net

"ALRIGHT, STEADY EVERYONE. MARGO, GO OVER TO TOM'S PC AND PRESS 'ESCAPE',...VERY CAREFULLY."

page 359

The 5th Wave By Rich Tennant

"A STORY ABOUT A SOFTWARE COMPANY THAT SHIPS BUG-FREE PROGRAMS ON TIME, WITH TOLL-FREE SUPPORT, AND FREE UPGRADES? NAAAH – TOO WEIRD."

page 7

AFTER SPENDING 9 DAYS WITH 12 DIFFERENT VENDORS AND READING 26 BROCHURES, DAVE HAD AN ACUTE ATTACK OF TOXIC OPTION SYNDROME.

page 303

"I HEARD THEY WANTED TO FILL OUT THE SHOW A LITTLE THIS YEAR."

page 149

"ALL THIS STUFF? IT'S PART OF A SUITE OF INTEGRATED SOFTWARE PACKAGES DESIGNED TO HELP UNCLUTTER YOUR LIFE."

page 273

"For further thoughts on that subject, I'm going to download Leviticus and go through the menu to Job, chapter 2, verse 6, file 'J.' It reads..."

page 229

Table of Contents

Introduction

Look at most program manuals (or even most computer books), and you'll notice a striking difference between this book and all the rest. Almost every computer manual or book organizes their explanations according to the way the program works, not how you work.

Focusing on menu commands forces you to learn how the program works, which is like learning to drive by focusing on how your transmission works. Most people don't care how their transmission works, just as long as it works. Likewise, most people don't care about the particular order of menu commands as long as they know how to use them to get something done.

So rather than display endless dialog boxes or pull-down menu commands and exhaustively explain what each command does, this book takes a different approach. This book describes how to accomplish certain tasks and then explains how to use various menu commands to get the job done. After you get familiar with using various commands, you'll have the confidence you need to start experimenting with Microsoft Office for Windows 95 on your own.

This book won't make you a Microsoft Office expert overnight, but it will show you how to take full advantage of each program that makes up Microsoft Office for Windows 95. Just pick through the tips and tricks you need, and you'll gradually learn more about the programs and features you need the most. Within a short time, you'll soon know enough about Microsoft Office to work faster, more efficiently, and more productively than ever before (unless, of course, you don't want to).

Who Should Buy This Book

If you plan to buy Microsoft Office for Windows 95 or already have a copy installed on your computer, you can use this book to guide you through the mental landmines of frustration that accompany the task of learning any new computer program.

If you're not already familiar with the basics of Microsoft Office, grab a copy of *Microsoft Office For Windows 95 For Dummies* first. (Make sure that you get that particular book, easily spotted by its bright yellow and black cover. Accept no substitutes or cheap imitations!)

When you're familiar with starting Microsoft Office and saving data, you can make maximum use of this book, which shows you the more advanced techniques buried inside Microsoft Office for Windows 95. You'll soon discover how to harness the power of Microsoft Office to get your work done faster and easier than ever before, regardless of your previous experience with computers.

How This Book Is Organized

Rather than throw the pages of this book together in random order, I divided it into several parts. Each part covers a specific program of Microsoft Office. Whenever you need help (or just want to look like you're doing something at work while you're really flipping through the cartoons), browse through this book, find the part that covers the topic you're looking for, toss this book aside, and get back to work before your boss catches you goofing off.

Part I: Power Writing with Microsoft Word

Whether you write letters, memos, newsletters, novels, or ransom notes, you'll find that Microsoft Word provides a feature to make your task easier. This part of the book reveals various time-saving shortcuts so that you can spend your time being creative instead of wrestling with the program's limitations (known in the advertising brochures as "features").

Part II: Crunching Numbers with Microsoft Excel

Besides letting you type numbers in a spreadsheet and calculating a result, Excel enables you to design and print reports that don't look like spreadsheets, create spreadsheets with multiple pages, automate your spreadsheets with macros, and even help you check your formulas to make sure that the answers you're getting actually make sense.

Part III: The Microsoft PowerPoint Dog-and-Pony Show

Although everyone nods their head in appreciation when they hear the phrase, "Looks aren't everything," nobody really believes it. After all, if they had to rely on their talent rather than their looks, most of the cast for the TV show *Baywatch* would be sweeping floors in a fast-food restaurant somewhere in Los Angeles.

Because looks really are everything, PowerPoint helps you create pretty presentations to dazzle the competition and pacify your supervisors when you should really be working and doing something productive.

Part IV: Staying Organized with Microsoft Schedule+

Everyone would love to be more organized so that they can accomplish the tasks that really mean something to them. Unfortunately, most of us have to work, which gobbles up most of our precious time. So to help you plan your time more effectively, use Microsoft Schedule+ to turn your $2,000 computer into a $49.95 electronic organizer.

By using Microsoft Schedule+ daily, you can plan dreams for the future, set goals for turning your dreams into reality, schedule tasks for reaching your goals, and eventually live the type of life you really want to live instead of settling for endless days of mediocrity that provide the main source of revenue for psychiatrists all over the world.

Part V: Storing Information in Microsoft Access

For those of you using the Professional edition of Microsoft Office for Windows 95, you get to play around with a bonus program called Microsoft Access, which is a special database program that lets you store names, addresses, phone numbers, part numbers, invoices, or any other type of information that you think you might need at a future date. (Storing the names of valuable business contacts is wise. Storing your report cards from third grade probably is not.)

By letting you decide how you want to store, organize, and display information, Access gives you the power to create your own custom programs to track inventory, print reports, or store customer names and addresses.

Part VI: The Part of Tens

This part of the book lists some of the more common commands you need to know to use Microsoft Office. In addition, this part describes various online resources where you can get the latest program updates, bug reports, and news about Microsoft Office, the most powerful software suite in the universe.

How to Use This Book

You can use this book as a reference, as a tutorial, or as a shield (it's thick enough). Don't feel the need to read every page of this book. Instead, just browse through the parts that interest you and ignore the rest.

Although it's unlikely that you'll always use every program in Microsoft Office, take some time to browse through the parts of the book that describe the programs you don't use very often.

Fooling around with spreadsheets might seem dull if you're not an accountant or engineer, but by playing around with it, you just might find a way to make it useful in your own personal life or business. You paid for Microsoft Office, so you might as well try all of its programs. At the very least, you can just erase the programs you don't use off your hard disk and never bother with them again.

How much do you need to know?

As long as you know how to turn on a computer and use a mouse, you should be able to follow the instructions in this book with no major, trauma-inducing problems. If you find Windows 95 to be somewhat of a strange beast to master, however, you may want to get a copy of *Windows 95 For Dummies* by Andy Rathbone (published by IDG Books Worldwide, Inc.).

Conventions

To avoid confusion later on (since computers do such a good job of sowing confusion without anyone's help), it's important to understand the following terms:

- When you look at the screen, you may see two items: a blinking *cursor* (which appears as a vertical, blinking line) and an *I-beam pointer* (which sometimes appears as a white arrow if it appears over certain parts of the screen).
- The blinking *cursor* moves whenever you use the keyboard, such as typing a letter or number, or pressing one of the four (up, down, left, right) arrow keys. The *I-beam pointer* moves whenever you move the mouse.
- *Clicking* means pressing the left mouse button once and letting go. Clicking is how you activate buttons in the toolbar, for example.
- *Double-clicking* means pressing the left mouse button twice in rapid succession. Double-clicking typically activates a command.

- *Dragging* selects items you want to move, delete, or format. To drag, place the I-beam pointer to the left of the item that you want to select, hold down the left mouse button, and move the mouse in the desired direction. When you release the mouse button, Windows 95 selects that item. You can tell when an item is selected because it appears in white against a black background.
- *Right-clicking* means clicking the mouse button to the right. (Some mice have three buttons, so ignore the middle button for now.) Right-clicking usually displays a shortcut menu on the screen.

Icons used in this book

This icon highlights information that can be helpful (as long as you don't forget it, of course).

This icon marks certain steps or procedures that can save you time when you use Microsoft Office.

Watch out! This icon warns you of potential trouble you might run into while using Microsoft Office.

This icon highlights detailed information that's nice to know but not essential for using Microsoft Office.

Choosing commands in Microsoft Office 95

Microsoft Office gives you two ways to choose commands:

- Clicking the mouse on a button or menu command
- Pressing a keystroke combination such as Ctrl+S (which means hold down the Ctrl key, press the S key, and then release both keys at the same time)

Most keyboard shortcuts involve holding down the Ctrl or Alt key (typically located to the left and right of the spacebar on your keyboard) in combination with one of the function keys (the keys labeled F1, F2, F3, and so on) or a letter key (A, B, C, and so on).

Use the method that you like best. Some people use the mouse, some use the keyboard, some use both, and some just hire another person to do all their hard work for them instead.

Your first tip

Don't be afraid to experiment, fool around, or play with any of the multitude of commands available in Microsoft Office. Any time you choose a command by mistake, you can tell Microsoft Office to take back your last command by pressing Ctrl+Z (hold down the Ctrl key, press the Z key, and let go of both keys simultaneously).

Now that you know how to undo commands, feel free to pick a command at random, just to see what happens. Then press Ctrl+Z to return your data to normal. By freely experimenting with Microsoft Office and keeping the handy Ctrl+Z keystroke ready at all times, you can practically teach yourself how to use many features of Microsoft Office all by yourself through the same way that most people learn best anyway: trial and error.

Getting Started

Now that you have a copy of Microsoft Office on your computer (you did pay for it, didn't you?), you're all set to start using all of its advanced features that Microsoft buried in the most obscure places. But don't worry. As you pick up various tips and tricks from this book, you'll soon see that Microsoft Office really can make you more productive with your computer in ways you may never have dreamed about until now. So what are you waiting for? Stop reading this paragraph and turn the page.

Part I

Power Writing with Microsoft Word

"A STORY ABOUT A SOFTWARE COMPANY THAT SHIPS BUG-FREE PROGRAMS ON TIME, WITH TOLL-FREE SUPPORT, AND FREE UPGRADES? NAAAH – TOO WEIRD."

In this part . . .

Aside from playing games, most people use a computer to write with a word processor (provided that they can get their computer to work in the first place). Microsoft Word provides plenty of time-saving shortcuts, such as macros (which can automate your writing), templates (so that you don't have to waste time formatting your documents yourself), and automatic index- and table-of-contents–generating features.

As usual, Microsoft tried (emphasis on *tried*) to make these advanced features of Word accessible to everyone, but you're likely to get confused trying to find out about them from Word's sparse documentation and help screens. Dig through this part of the book to master the secrets yourself.

Chapter 1

Customizing Microsoft Word

In This Chapter

- Customizing the way Word saves documents
- Modifying print settings
- Using WordPerfect settings
- Creating and changing toolbars and menus
- Customizing keystroke combinations

Microsoft has poured tons of money into the development of Word for Windows to ensure that their word processor is the easiest to use and the most powerful on the market, but they can't please everybody. Some people may not like the way Word looks, the particular menu commands or keystrokes needed to accomplish a task, or where the program stores documents when you save them. Fortunately, whenever you don't like something about Word, you have the power to change it. (If only voting could be as effective.)

Rather than suffer silently, take some time to customize Word so that it looks and works like the type of program you want it to be.

Fiddling with the Way Word Works

Word can overwhelm you with the number of ways it offers to change its behavior. Rather than exhaustively list all these options and then leave you to figure out what to do next, the following sections describe some of the default features you may find most useful to change.

Saving your files

What happens if you write a 29-page report and forget to save it when the power goes out? Right! Not only do you lose all 29 pages, but you also feel like kicking yourself, smashing your computer — and cursing out the entire computer industry.

To prevent this type of violent behavior, which is normally associated with disgruntled postal workers, Word offers several helpful options for saving files:

- Backup copies
- AutoSave
- Fast saves

Creating backup copies

Normally when you save a file, Word wipes out the old version of the file and replaces it with the new one. So if you write a letter, save it, revise it, save the revision, and then decide that you liked your first draft better, guess what? You've just lost your first version the moment you saved the revised version of the file.

To prevent this type of catastrophe from occurring, Word provides a feature that creates a backup copy of each saved file. If you use the Always Create Backup Copy option, each time you save a file, Word stores the original file under a new filename (called "Backup of" followed by the original filename). Then it saves the revised file under the original filename.

Suppose that you have the Always Create Backup Copy option turned on when you write a nasty letter to your boss, which you save in a file called Hate Letter to Joe. After a moment's reflection, you decide that Joe doesn't deserve a hate letter, so you revise that file and save it. Word saves this revision under the Hate Letter to Joe filename and the original file under the Backup of Hate Letter to Joe.

Even better, what happens if someone or something destroys your Hate Letter to Joe file? You normally have to resort to screaming or crying. If you have been using the Always Create Backup Copy option, however, you can open the Backup of Hate Letter to Joe and retrieve most of your original document.

The more often you save a file, the more current the Backup file. Many people like to save their files every 5, 10, or 15 minutes, although the time interval you choose depends on how much data you're willing to lose. If you're willing to lose 10 minutes' worth of data, save your file every 10 minutes.

So if you want to send Joe the first, nasty version of the letter, send him the Backup of Hate Letter to Joe. If you experience a sudden change of heart, send Joe the nicer, second version of the letter, which is the Hate Letter to Joe file.

You can use the Always Create Backup Copy option only if you're using Word as a separate program. If you're using Word within a binder (a unique file format specially designed to hold multiple Word, Excel, or PowerPoint data in a single file), the Always Create Backup Copy option does not work. For more information on working with binders, see *Microsoft Office For Windows 95 For Dummies,* by Wallace Wang (published by IDG Books Worldwide, Inc.).

Be aware that saving a backup copy of a file essentially doubles the amount of disk space your files occupy. If disk space is scarce, you may not want to use this option.

To turn on the Always Create Backup Copy option, follow these steps:

1. **Choose Tools⇨Options.**

   The Options dialog box appears.

2. **Click the Save tab, shown in Figure 1-1.**
3. **Click the Always Create Backup Copy check box so that a check mark appears.**
4. **Click OK.**

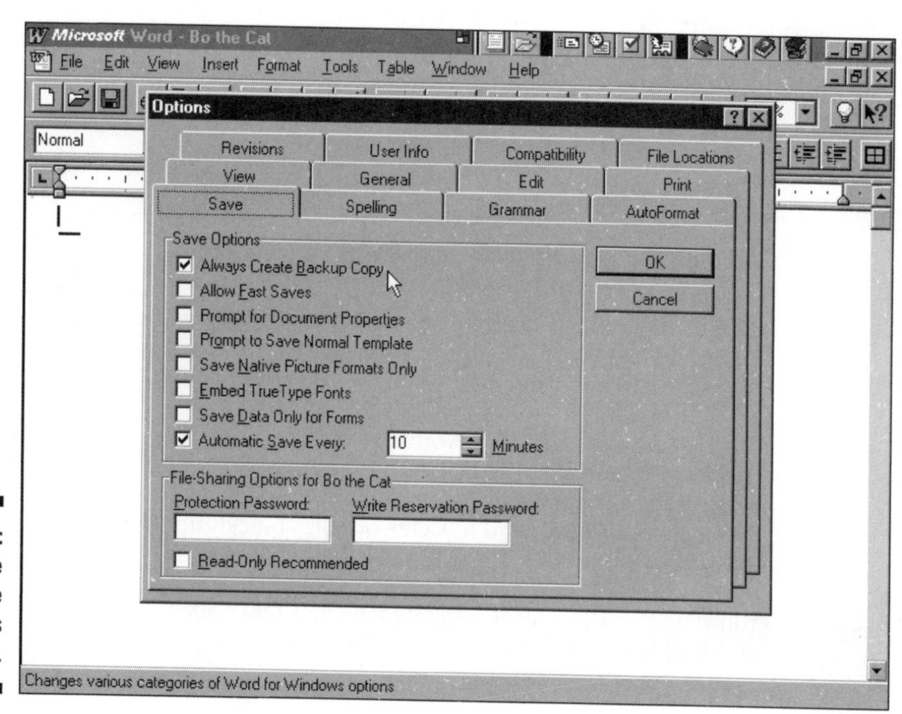

Figure 1-1: The Save tab in the Options dialog box.

Saving files automatically with AutoSave

Saving your Word documents periodically as you work is a good idea, but most people forget to do it. Fortunately, Word provides a feature that saves your documents automatically. Just tell Word how often you want to save your document, such as every 8, 10, or 29 minutes.

Suppose that you told Word to save your document every seven minutes. As you write, Word patiently waits until seven minutes are up. Then it springs into action and saves your document, interrupting your writing like a well-meaning, but irritating, elementary school teacher.

Because Word has to interrupt your writing to save your document, you might want to experiment and choose an AutoSave setting that isn't so intrusive, such as every 10, 15, or 20 minutes. Just remember that the longer the setting, the less likely Word can help you if the power goes out right before the AutoSave feature runs. Saving your files automatically every ten minutes should be adequate.

To turn on or modify the AutoSave option, follow these steps:

1. **Choose Tools⇨Options.**

   The Options dialog box appears.

2. **Click the Save tab (refer to Figure 1-1).**
3. **Click the Automatic Save Every check box so that a check mark appears.**
4. **Type a number in the Minutes box.**
5. **Click OK.**

Saving files quickly with Fast Saves

If you get nothing else from this chapter, memorize the mantra, "Save your work periodically, or else you may be really sorry." Unfortunately, saving a large document can take a long time. To make the process of saving a file faster and therefore less annoying, use the Allow Fast Saves option.

The Fast Saves option tells Word, "See this huge file I just modified? Save only the changes I made since the last time I saved the file, and don't bother saving the whole thing all over again." By saving just the changes you make to a file, the Fast Saves option allows Word to save your files quickly so that you can get back to work.

You cannot use the Always Create Backup Copy option and the Fast Saves option at the same time.

To turn on the Fast Saves option, follow these steps:

1. **Choose Tools⇨Options.**

   The Options dialog box appears.

2. **Click the Save tab (refer to Figure 1-1).**
3. **Click the Allow Fast Saves check box so that a check mark appears.**
4. **Click OK.**

"Where did I save that document?"

Unless you specify otherwise, Word cheerfully stores your files in a default directory, such as C:\My Documents. If you want to store your Word documents in a different directory, you have two choices:

- Specify a directory each time you save a new file (which can be a nuisance)
- Change the default directory

You can change the default directory only if you're using Word as a separate program. If you're using Word within a binder, you won't be able to change the default directory.

To change the default directory where Word will store your files (unless you specify otherwise), follow these steps:

1. **Choose Tools⇨Options.**

   The Options dialog box appears.

2. **Click the File Locations tab, shown in Figure 1-2.**
3. **Click** `Documents` **under the File Types column heading.**
4. **Click Modify.**

   A Modify Location dialog box appears, as shown in Figure 1-3.

5. **Choose the drive and directory you want for your new default directory and then click OK.**
6. **Click Close.**

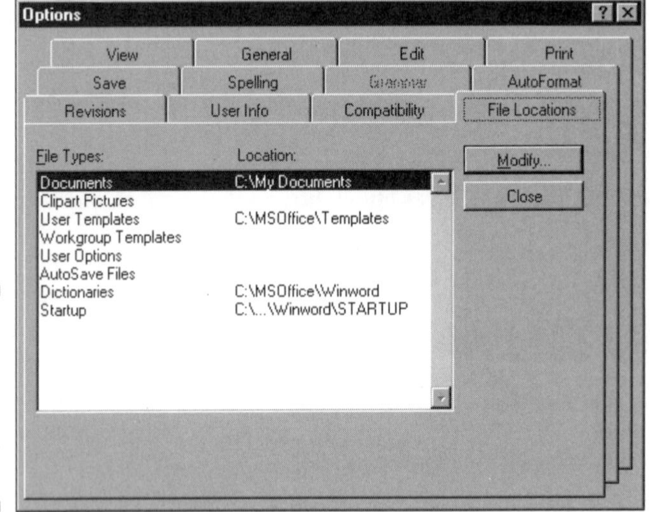

Figure 1-2: The File Locations tab in the Options dialog box.

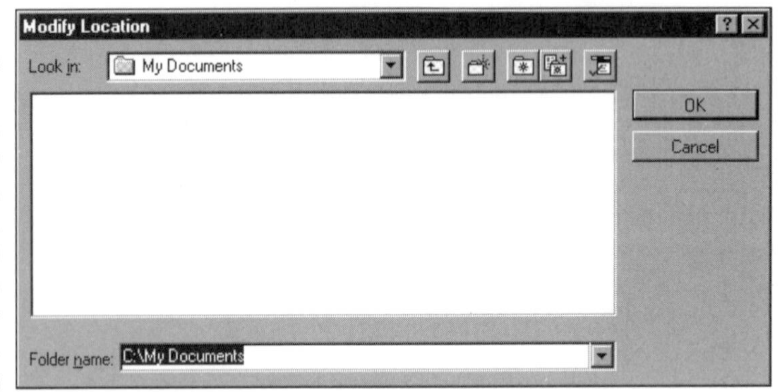

Figure 1-3: In the Modify Location dialog box, you tell Word where to store your files.

Printing stuff

The way your document appears in print depends partly on your printer. You can modify certain print options to make printing faster or more convenient, however.

Draft printing

If you have an old, dot-matrix printer that takes forever to print and chatters noisily when it's working, you may want to choose draft printing. (Draft printing works with laser and inkjet printers, too.) Draft printing simply means that Word takes less time to print your document.

As the name implies, a draft printing of a document looks horrible but is acceptable enough for proofreading. Besides printing your text at a much lower resolution, draft printing may also omit any graphics you have embedded in your document.

To choose draft printing, follow these steps:

1. **Choose Tools⇨Options.**

   The Options dialog box appears.

2. **Click the Print tab, shown in Figure 1-4.**
3. **Click the Draft Output check box so that a check mark appears.**
4. **Click OK.**

Reversing the print order

If you have one of those odd laser printers that stacks documents with the last page on top and the first page on the bottom, you probably want to reverse the print order. Reversing the print order means just that: The last page prints first, and the first page prints last.

To reverse the print order, follow these steps:

1. **Choose Tools⇨Options.**

   The Options dialog box appears.

2. **Click the Print tab (refer to Figure 1-4).**

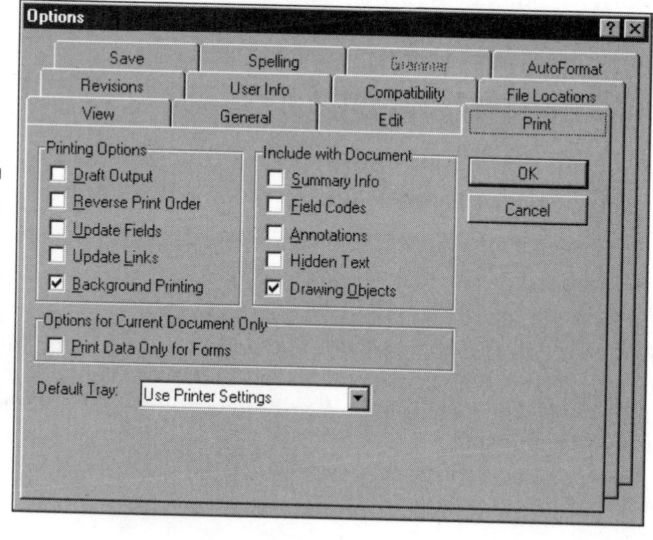

Figure 1-4: You can specify what happens to your printed documents by using the Print tab in the Options dialog box.

3. Click the Reverse Print Order check box so that a check mark appears.

4. Click OK.

Making Word act like WordPerfect 5.1 for DOS

Years ago, during the ancient days of personal computers, the most popular word processor in the world was WordPerfect 5.1. Because companies adopted WordPerfect all over the planet, thousands of innocent people forced themselves to memorize bizarre WordPerfect 5.1 keystroke commands. (Anyone still remember what Shift+F7 does in WordPerfect 5.1?)

When Microsoft Windows took over the personal computer market, it helped to sink the popularity of WordPerfect 5.1. Many people still remember WordPerfect commands, however, to the extent that the use of another word processor, such as Word, is difficult.

To help those poor souls who can't get WordPerfect commands out of their minds, Word can mimic the appearance of and keystroke commands in WordPerfect 5.1. You can then use your WordPerfect knowledge to get work done while you use Word.

Although making Word mimic WordPerfect can help you adjust to using Word, you may be better off just to forget your WordPerfect commands and spend a day or two fumbling around using Word's commands instead. Then, if you ever have to use Word on somebody else's computer, you won't be completely confused when the other copy of Word isn't customized to act like WordPerfect.

Four options are available to help you switch from WordPerfect to Word:

- Help for WordPerfect users
- Navigation keys for WordPerfect users
- Blue background, white text
- Full screen (which displays nothing on-screen except the text you type)

Displaying help for WordPerfect users

If you want to make the gradual switch from WordPerfect to Word, Microsoft is more than happy to accommodate you. To this end, Word contains a special help file that shows you your familiar WordPerfect commands and then their equivalent Word commands.

By gradually weaning you away from WordPerfect, this special help file ensures that your transition to Word is as painless as possible. After all, you don't really want to stick with WordPerfect 5.1 and the ugliness of MS-DOS, do you?

To use help for WordPerfect users, follow these steps:

1. **If you are using Word in a binder, choose Section⇨View Outside.**

   Skip this step if you're using Word as a separate program.

2. **Choose Help⇨WordPerfect Help.**

   The Help for WordPerfect Users dialog box appears, as shown in Figure 1-5.

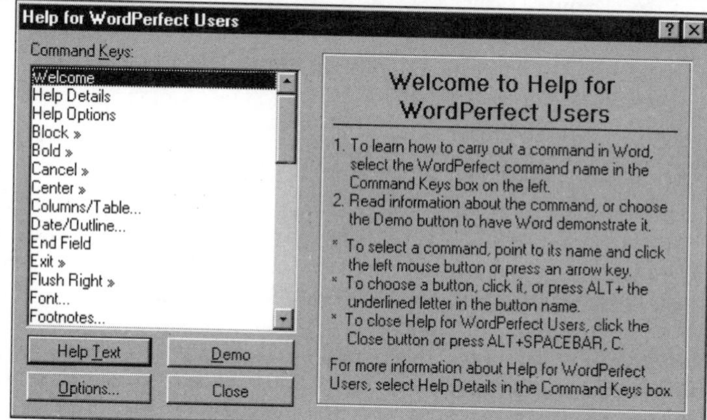

Figure 1-5: WordPerfect Users can use this dialog box to get help with Word.

3. **Click a topic under the Command Keys heading.**

   A brief explanation of your chosen topic appears on the right side of the Help for WordPerfect Users dialog box.

4. **Click Close.**

Using WordPerfect navigation keys

Despite the perfectly standard way you can move the cursor around in any Microsoft Windows program, old habits are tough to break. Many diehard WordPerfect users may still try to press Home+Home+Up arrow to move the cursor to the top of the document and press Home+Home+Down arrow to move the cursor to the bottom of the document.

If you don't want to give up the WordPerfect navigation keys, you don't have to. Just tell Word to use the WordPerfect navigation keys by following these steps:

1. **If you are using Word in a binder, choose Section⇨View Outside.**

   Skip this step if you're using Word as a separate program.

2. **Choose Tools⇨Options.**

   The Options dialog box appears.

3. **Click the General tab, shown in Figure 1-6.**

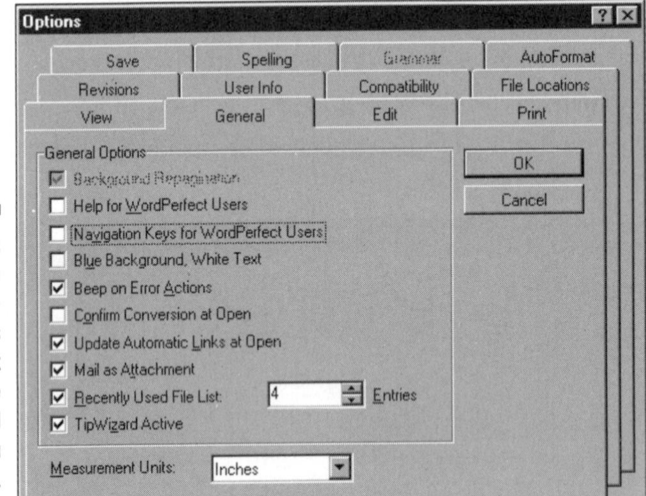

Figure 1-6: The General tab in the Options dialog box has some Word options you can change.

4. **Click the Navigation Keys for WordPerfect Users check box so that a check mark appears.**
5. **Click OK.**

Mimicking WordPerfect screen colors

Microsoft Word displays text in black against a white background, but the old WordPerfect 5.1 displayed text in white against a blue background. Important? Hardly, although it may be easier on your eyes to see text this way. But if you're going to customize Word to act like WordPerfect 5.1, you may as well go all the way and have Word display text just like WordPerfect 5.1 does.

To make Word use WordPerfect screen colors, follow these steps:

1. **Choose Tools⇨Options.**

   The Options dialog box appears.

2. **Click the General tab (refer to Figure 1-6).**
3. **Click the Blue Background, White Text check box so that a check mark appears.**
4. **Click OK.**

   Microsoft Word immediately changes your screen colors to look like WordPerfect 5.1.

Mimicking WordPerfect Full Screen mode

To WordPerfect 5.1 purists, nothing is more inviting to writing than staring at a blank screen. If you don't like the distraction of the Word pull-down menus, toolbars loaded with cryptic-looking buttons, or status bars that clutter the screen with information about lines, columns, and sections, you can make them all go away.

To display a screen without pull-down menus, toolbars, status bars, or rulers, choose View⇨Full Screen.

While in Full Screen mode, you can display pull-down menus by using the keystroke commands shown in Table 1-1.

Table 1-1 Keystroke Commands to Use in Full-Screen Mode

Keystroke Command	*Displays This Pull-Down Menu*
Alt+F	File menu
Alt+E	Edit menu
Alt+V	View menu
Alt+I	Insert menu
Alt+O	Format menu
Alt+T	Tools menu
Alt+A	Table menu
Alt+W	Window menu
Alt+H	Help menu

Making Word 7.0 mimic Word 2.0

To no one's surprise, each version of Word looks and acts slightly different from the preceding version. Getting used to the new version can be disorienting at best and downright confusing at worst.

The most prominent difference between Word 7.0 and Word 2.0 is the appearance of the toolbar. If you hate the Word 7.0 toolbar, you can have Word display the Word 2.0 toolbar instead. Just display the Toolbars dialog box and click in the Word for Windows 2.0 check box.

After you choose the Full Screen command from the View menu, Word immediately removes everything from your screen except for any text you may have typed. Of course, then you can't use your mouse to choose menu or toolbar commands either, but if you want to relive the good old days of WordPerfect 5.1, this hindrance won't seem like much of a handicap.

In case you get tired of looking at a screen with nothing but text on it and want to return to Word's normal appearance, follow these steps:

1. **Press Alt+V.**

   The View menu appears, floating in thin air like a disembodied spirit, as shown in Figure 1-7.

2. **Press U, or click Full Screen with the mouse.**

Messing Around with Toolbars

Rather than force you to memorize obscure keystroke commands or dig through pull-down menus, Word lets you choose commands by clicking buttons organized in a toolbar. As long as you know which command a particular button represents, you can choose that command by clicking its button.

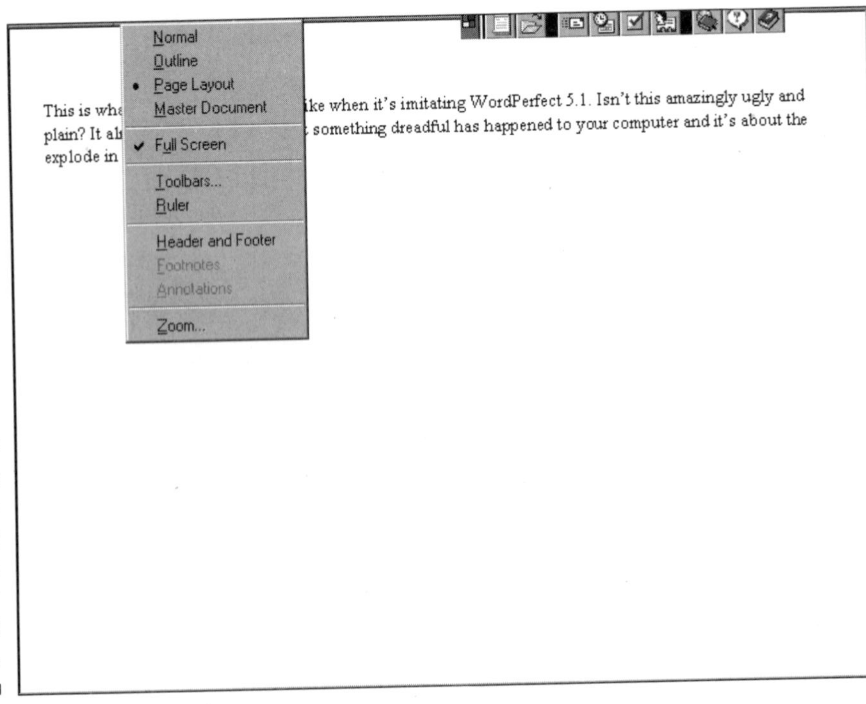

Figure 1-7: The View menu floating in thin air over a blank screen.

Microsoft Word provides ten toolbars, all of which display buttons for formatting your document or adding information from a database. Figure 1-8 shows what happens if you get carried away and display all ten toolbars at once.

Of course, if you display all ten toolbars, you barely have enough room left to write anything, which is the whole purpose of having Word in the first place. You'll probably never need all ten toolbars at the same time, so you can simply make one or more of the Word toolbars appear or disappear, depending on what you need at the time.

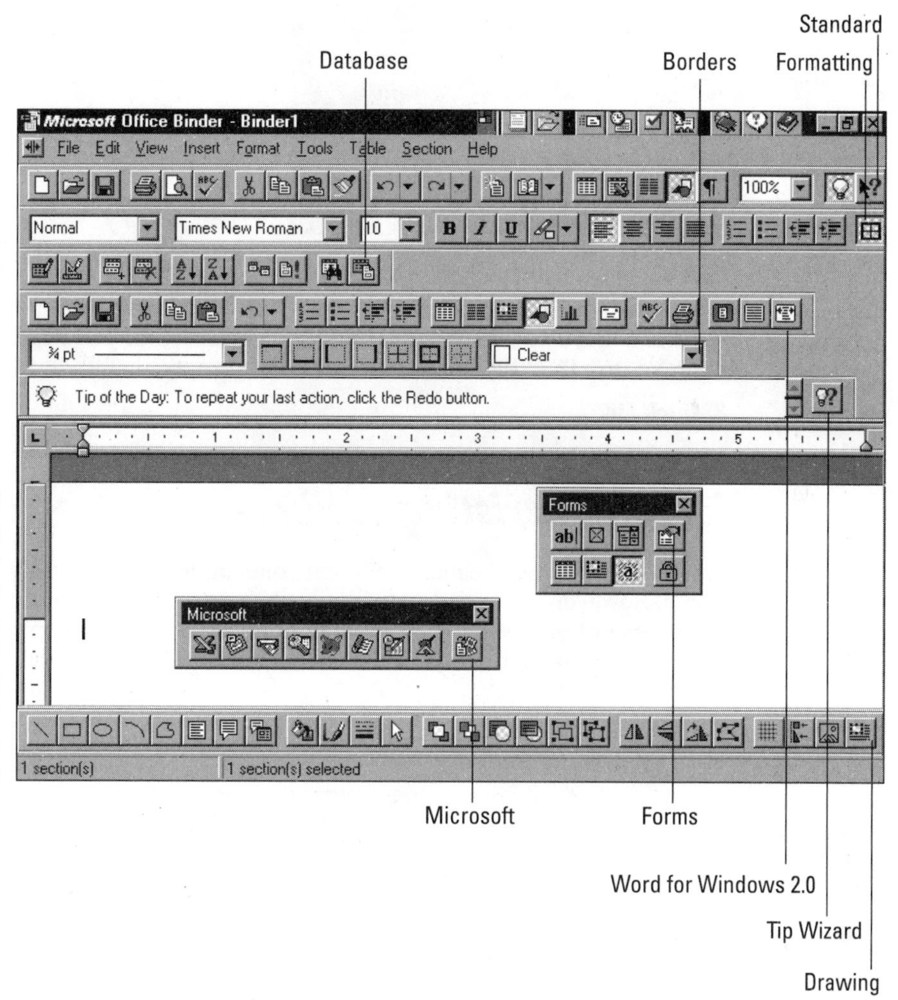

Figure 1-8: Toolbar heaven! Word with every possible toolbar displayed.

To make a toolbar appear or disappear, follow these steps:

1. **Choose View⇨Toolbars.**

   The Toolbars dialog box appears, as shown in Figure 1-9.

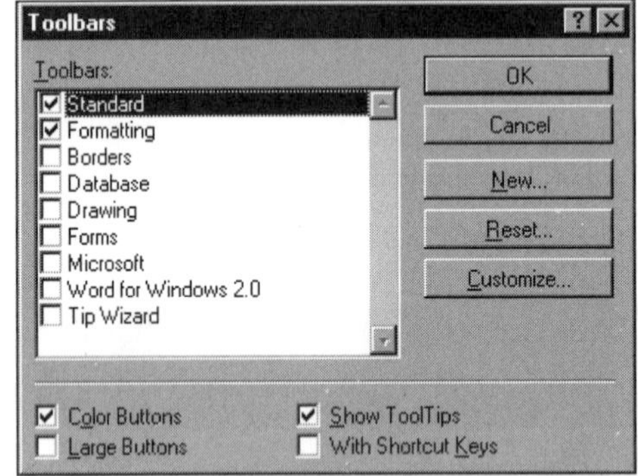

Figure 1-9: Choosing the toolbars you want Word to display on your screen.

2. **For each toolbar you want displayed, click in the corresponding check box so that a check mark appears. For each toolbar you want hidden, make sure that the toolbar's check box is empty.**

3. **Click OK.**

Modifying existing toolbars

Microsoft Word buries the most common commands in its multitude of built-in toolbars. However, you may find that you rarely use certain commands on the toolbars or that you really need other commands that don't appear on them. Rather than fume and suffer, take charge of your life and modify the toolbars to your liking.

Removing buttons from a toolbar

Because Word's toolbars are already crowded with buttons, the first step toward modifying a toolbar is to remove the buttons you don't want.

To remove a button from a toolbar, follow these steps:

1. **If you're using Word in a binder, choose Section⇨View Outside.**

   Skip this step if you're using Word as a separate program.

2. **Choose View⇨Toolbars.**

   The Toolbars dialog box appears (refer to Figure 1-9).

3. **Highlight the toolbar you want to modify, and click in its check box so that a check mark appears.**
4. **Click Customize.**

   Word displays the Customize dialog box with the toolbar you chose highlighted, as shown in Figure 1-10.

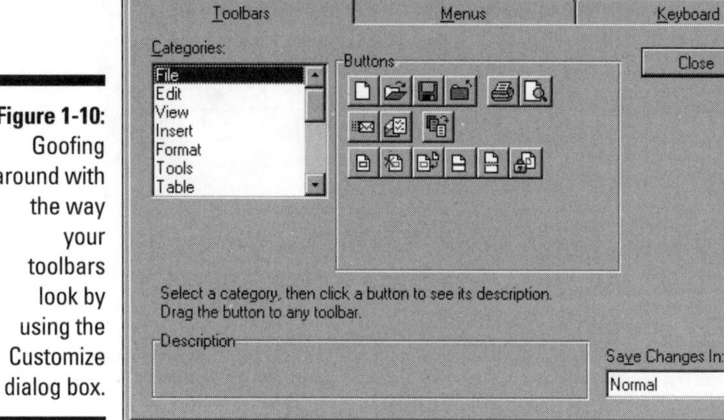

Figure 1-10: Goofing around with the way your toolbars look by using the Customize dialog box.

5. **Point to the button on the toolbar you want to remove, hold down the left mouse button, and drag the button anywhere off the toolbar, as shown in Figure 1-11.**
6. **Release the left mouse button.**

   Microsoft Word immediately removes the button from the toolbar.
7. **Click Close.**

Adding buttons to a toolbar

You can add buttons to a toolbar at any time. It's usually a good idea, however, to first remove any buttons you don't want. Then you can make room for your new buttons.

To add a button to a toolbar, follow these steps:

1. **If you're using Word in a binder, choose Section⇨View Outside.**

   Skip this step if you're using Word as a separate program.
2. **Choose View⇨Toolbars.**

   The Toolbars dialog box appears (refer to Figure 1-9).

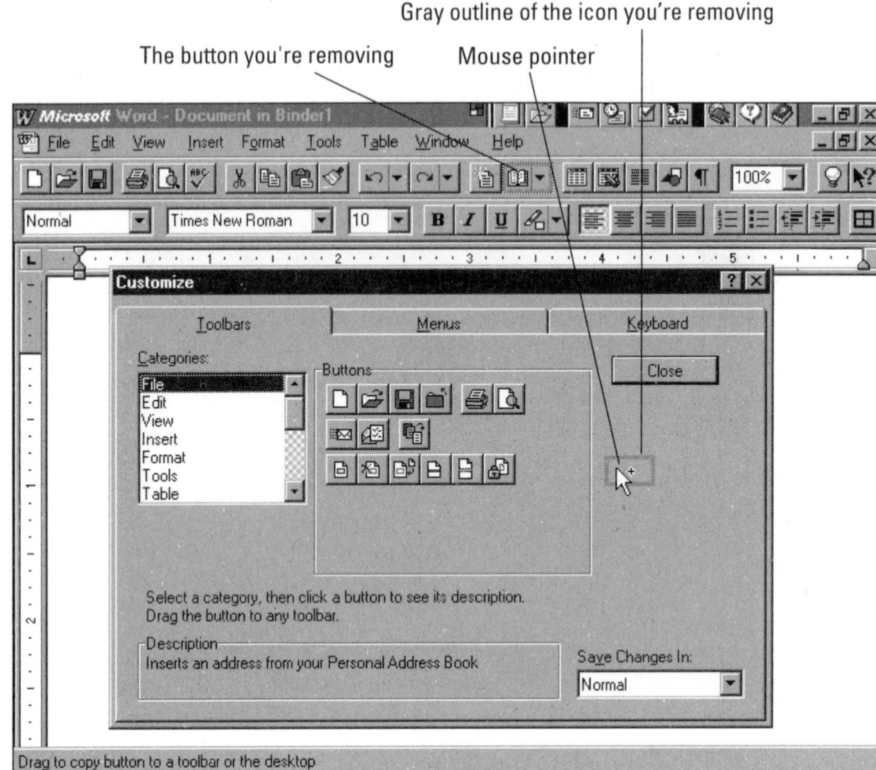

Figure 1-11: Removing a button from a toolbar.

3. **Highlight the toolbar you want to modify, and click in its check box so that a check mark appears.**
4. **Click Customize.**

   Word displays the Customize dialog box with the toolbar you chose, as shown in Figure 1-10.
5. **Click a category displayed in the Categories list box.**

   To add a formatting command to a toolbar, for example, click Format in the Categories list box. Word displays some buttons in the Buttons group.
6. **Point to the button you want to add, hold down the left mouse button, and drag the button to the location on the toolbar where you want it to appear, as shown in Figure 1-12.**
7. **Release the mouse button and click Close.**

Gray outline of the button you're adding

Mouse pointer

The button you're adding

Figure 1-12: Adding a button to a toolbar.

Resetting your toolbars to their original condition

If you mess up your toolbars totally beyond recognition, you can restore them to their original state. Feel free to experiment with your toolbars as wildly as possible!

To reset a toolbar, follow these steps:

1. **If you're using Word in a binder, choose Section⇨View Outside.**

   Skip this step if you're using Word as a separate program.

2. **Choose View⇨Toolbars.**

   The Toolbars dialog box appears (refer to Figure 1-9).

3. **Highlight the toolbar you want to reset.**

4. **Click Reset.**

   A Reset Toolbar dialog box appears, as shown in Figure 1-13.

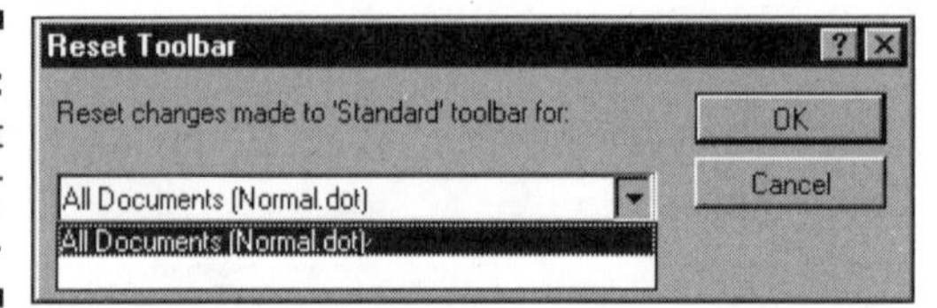

Figure 1-13: The Reset Toolbar dialog box.

5. **Click OK.**

   Microsoft Word resets your toolbar to its original state.

6. **Click OK in the Toolbars dialog box.**

Making your own toolbars

Creating custom toolbars can be much more fun than messing around with existing toolbars. You can combine your favorite commands to create a custom toolbar perfectly matched to your needs.

To make your own toolbar, follow these steps:

1. **If you're using Word in a binder, choose Section⇨View Outside.**

   Skip this step if you're using Word as a separate program.

2. **Choose View⇨Toolbars.**

   The Toolbars dialog box appears (refer to Figure 1-9).

3. **Click New.**

   A New Toolbar dialog box appears, as shown in Figure 1-14.

New Toolbar
Toolbar Name:
Make Toolbar Available To:
All Documents (Normal.dot)
OK
Cancel

Figure 1-14: Naming your new toolbar.

4. **Type a name for your toolbar in the Toolbar Name box, and then click OK.**

   The Customize dialog box appears next to your toolbar, as shown in Figure 1-15.

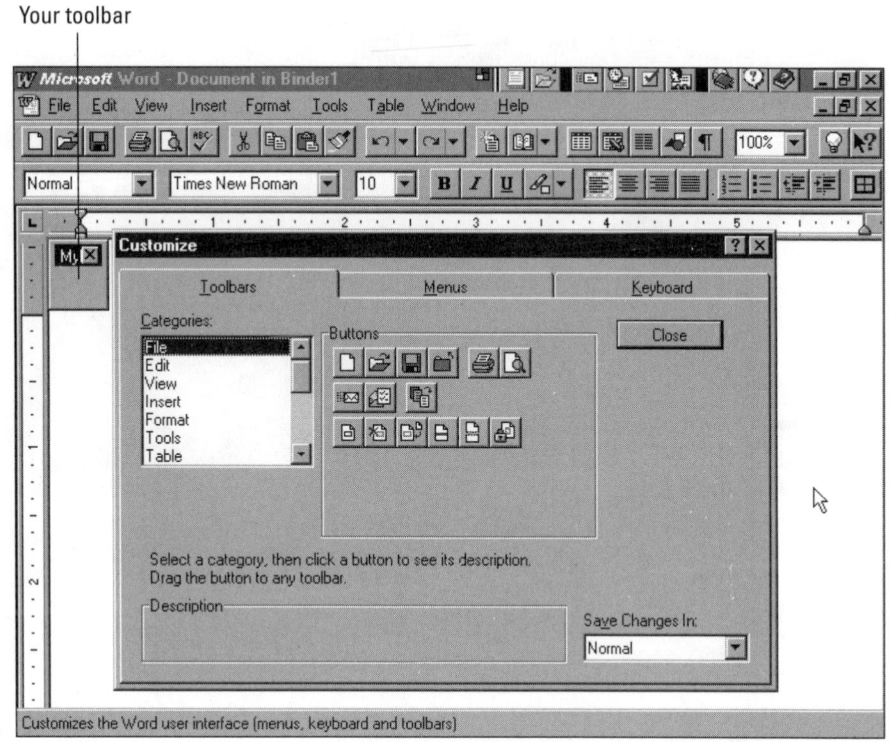

Figure 1-15: Your newly created toolbar.

5. **Click a category displayed in the Categories list box.**

   For example, to add an editing command to a toolbar, click Edit in the Categories list box. Word displays some buttons in the Buttons group.

6. **Point to the button you want to add, hold down the left mouse button, drag the button to the location on the toolbar where you want it to appear, and release the mouse button.**

   Figure 1-16 shows your newly created toolbar with some buttons on it.

7. **Click Close when you're done filling your toolbar with buttons.**

   Your newly created toolbar appears on-screen, ready to use.

To move your floating toolbar, point to the blue title bar of the toolbar, hold down the left mouse button, drag the mouse to where you want the toolbar to appear, and release the mouse button.

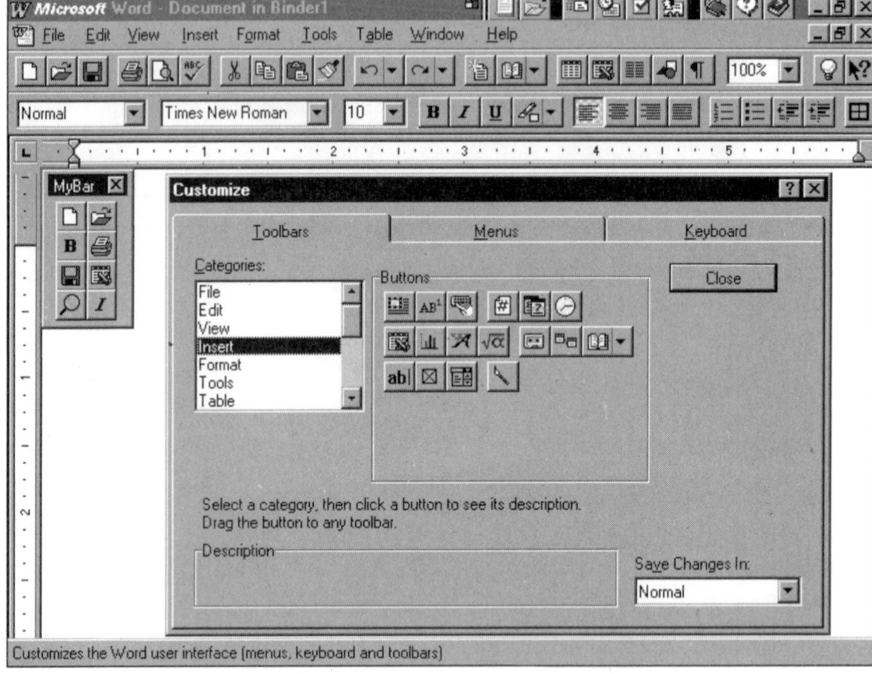

Figure 1-16: Your newly created toolbar with some buttons on it.

Changing the shape of your toolbar

If you don't like the ugly shape of your toolbar (when it appears as a floating toolbar), you can change its shape to resemble a flattened sausage, a squat little box, or a rectangle, as shown in Figure 1-17.

Figure 1-17: Three different shapes for your toolbar.

To change the shape of your toolbar, follow these steps:

1. **Move the mouse pointer to the left, right, top, or bottom edge of the toolbar.**

The mouse pointer turns into a double-pointing arrow that points left and right or up and down.

2. **Hold down the left mouse button and drag the mouse until the gray outline of the toolbar turns into the shape you want, as shown in Figure 1-18.**
3. **Release the mouse button.**

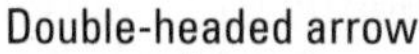

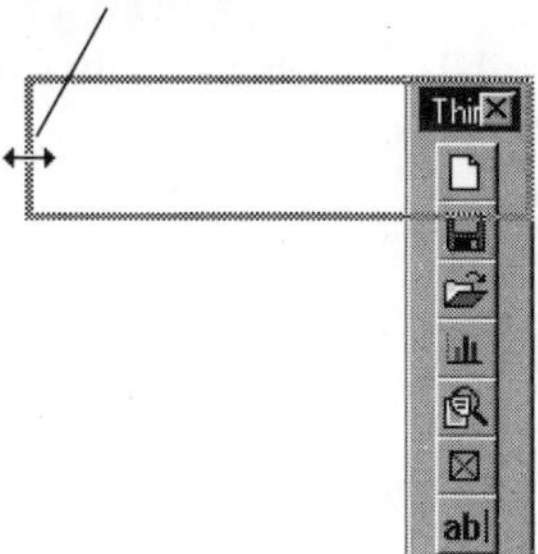

Figure 1-18: Changing the shape of a toolbar.

Deleting your toolbar

You can delete any of your own toolbar creations from the face of the earth, but you cannot delete any of the Word toolbars.

To delete one of your toolbars, follow these steps:

1. **If you're using Word in a binder, choose Section⇨View Outside.**

   Skip this step if you're using Word as a separate program.

2. **Choose View⇨Toolbars.**

   The Toolbars dialog box appears (refer to Figure 1-9).

3. **Highlight the toolbar you want to delete.**
4. **Click Delete.**

   A dialog box appears, asking whether you really want to delete your toolbar.

5. **Click Yes.**
6. **Click OK in the Toolbars dialog box.**

Make sure that you really want to delete one of your toolbars. After you delete a toolbar, you cannot undelete it if you change your mind later.

Displaying toolbars in different ways

Word can display a toolbar two ways:

- At the top of the screen as a long, skinny, horizontal strip
- As a floating toolbar

To change the way a toolbar appears, just double-click any gray portion of the toolbar. (Make sure that you don't double-click a button by mistake.) The moment you double-click a toolbar, it changes its shape from a horizontal strip to a floating toolbar and vice versa. Figure 1-19 shows you what the Standard and Formatting toolbars look like as floating toolbars.

Making Menus Your Way

After you become accustomed to the fact that you can modify the Word toolbar buttons, take a deep breath and get ready for a surprise: You can modify the Word pull-down menus as well.

This feature not only provides incredible flexibility so that you can customize Word to your liking, but also gives you a great way to mess up somebody else's copy of Word for a hilarious April Fool's joke.

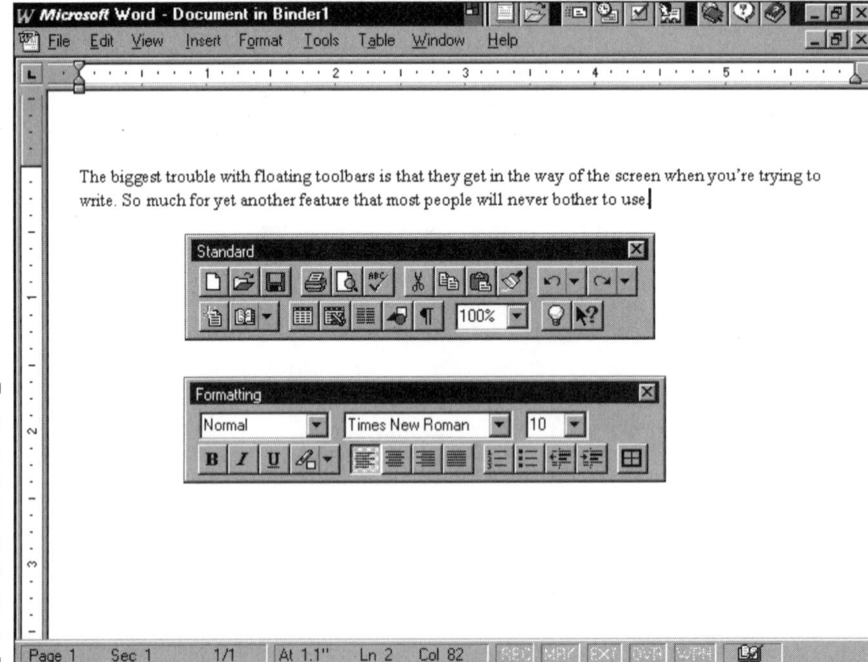

Figure 1-19: The Standard and Formatting toolbars as floating toolbars.

Modifying an existing menu

Word provides plenty of pull-down menus in the vain hope that you'll be able to find a specific command easily. After you wade through the Word pull-down menus, however, you may realize that you never use certain commands or that you use other commands not easily found on the menus. So rather than force yourself to adapt to Word, modify its menus to suit your needs.

Renaming menu titles

Some of the Word pull-down menu titles may be too terse for you, so Word lets you create more descriptive menu titles. If the Insert menu title doesn't make any sense to you, for example, just rename it to something more memorable, such as Stick In (see Figure 1-20).

Because you can't change menu titles in Excel, Schedule+, Access, or PowerPoint, your Word menu titles will be different from your other Office applications.

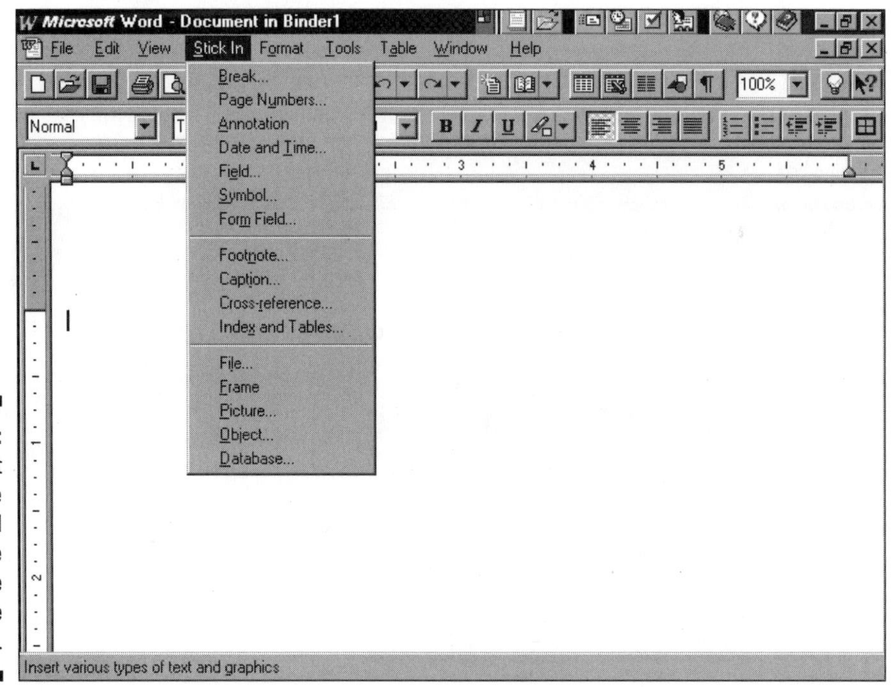

Figure 1-20: The Insert menu title replaced with the more descriptive Stick In title.

To rename a pull-down menu title, follow these steps:

1. **If you're using Word in a binder, choose Section⇨View Outside.**

   Skip this step if you're using Word as a separate program.

2. **Choose Tools⇨Customize.**

   The Customize dialog box appears.

3. **Click the Menus tab, shown in Figure 1-21.**

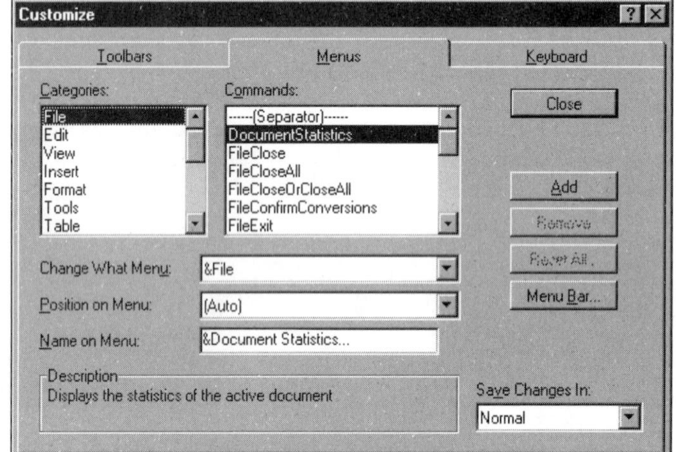

Figure 1-21: The Menus tab in the Customize dialog box.

4. **Click Menu Bar.**

   A Menu Bar dialog box appears, as shown in Figure 1-22.

Figure 1-22. Renaming a menu title.

5. **In the Position on Menu Bar list box, click the menu title you want to change, such as &Edit or &View.**

6. **Type the new menu title in the Name on Menu Bar box.**

   Note: To underline a letter in a menu title, put an ampersand character (&) in front of the letter. To display Stick In on the menu title, for example, you type **&Stick In**.

7. **Click Rename and then click Close.**
8. **Click Close in the Customize dialog box.**

   Word displays your new pull-down menu title.

Removing pull-down menus from sight

Word uses pull-down menus to group related commands. If you rarely use commands on the Table or View pull-down menus, however, you may as well hide that particular pull-down menu. That way, you don't have to look at it anymore.

To remove a pull-down menu from sight, follow these steps:

1. **If you're using Word in a binder, choose Section➪View Outside.**

   Skip this step if you're using Word as a separate program.

2. **Choose Tools➪Customize.**

   The Customize dialog box appears.

3. **Click the Menus tab (refer to Figure 1-21).**
4. **Click Menu Bar.**

   A Menu Bar dialog box appears (refer to Figure 1-22).

5. **Click the pull-down menu title you want to hide from view.**
6. **Click Remove.**

   A dialog box appears, asking whether you're sure that you want to delete this menu.

7. **Click Yes and then click Close.**
8. **Click Close in the Customize dialog box.**

   Microsoft Word hides your chosen pull-down menu title from view.

Removing commands from pull-down menus

You may want to remove commands that are buried in a pull-down menu. By weeding out seldom-used commands, you can make your menus shorter and easier to use.

To remove a command from a menu, follow these steps:

1. **If you're using Word in a binder, choose Section⇨View Outside.**

   Skip this step if you're using Word as a separate program.

2. **Choose Tools⇨Customize.**

   The Customize dialog box appears.

3. **Click the Menus tab (refer to Figure 1-21).**
4. **Click in the Change What Menu list box, and choose the pull-down menu (such as &File, &Insert, or T&able) that contains the command you want to remove.**
5. **Click in the Position on Menu list box, and then click the command you want to remove.**
6. **Click Remove and then click Close.**

Adding new commands to menus

To further customize your pull-down menus, you can not only delete seldom-used commands, but you can also add your own frequently used commands. In this way, you can make sure that your pull-down menus display only the commands you want.

To add a command to a menu, follow these steps:

1. **Choose Section⇨View Outside.**

   Skip this step if you're using Word as a separate program.

2. **Choose Tools⇨Customize.**

   The Customize dialog box appears.

3. **Click the Menus tab (refer to Figure 1-21).**
4. **Click in the Categories list box and choose a pull-down menu title.**

   If you want to add a command to the Edit menu, for example, choose Edit in the Categories list box.

5. **Click in the Commands list box, and then choose the command you want to add.**
6. **Click in the Position on Menu list box and choose one of the following:**
   - **(Auto):** Lets Word put your command wherever it wants
   - **(At Top):** Puts your command at the top of the menu
   - **(At Bottom):** Puts your command at the bottom of the menu
   - **Click a menu command:** Puts your command directly underneath the menu command you chose

7. **Click Add.**

   If you clicked a menu command in step 5, click Add Below.

8. **Click Close.**

   Word displays your newly added command in the pull-down menu you chose.

Making your own pull-down menus

If you modify the existing pull-down menus and menu commands but Word still seems too restrictive, go ahead and make your own pull-down menus. Load them up with your favorite commands.

To make your own pull-down menu, follow these steps:

1. **If you're using Word in a binder, choose Section⇨View Outside.**

   Skip this step if you're using Word as a separate program.

2. **Choose Tools⇨Customize.**

   The Customize dialog box appears.

3. **Click the Menus tab (refer to Figure 1-21).**
4. **Click Menu Bar.**

   A Menu Bar dialog box appears (refer to Figure 1-22).

5. **Type a title for your pull-down menu in the Name on Menu Bar box.**

   Remember to type an ampersand (&) in front of the letter you want underlined. If you type *Do &Nothing,* for example, Word displays it as `Do Nothing`.

6. **Choose one of the following:**
   - **(First):** Puts your pull-down menu on the far left side of the menu bar
   - **(Last):** Puts your pull-down menu on the far right side of the menu bar
   - **Click a menu title:** Puts your pull-down menu immediately after the menu title you chose

7. **Click Add.**

   If you clicked a menu title in step 5, click Add After.

8. **Click Close.**
9. **Click in the Categories list box, and choose a category.**
10. **Click in the Commands list box, and choose the command you want to add.**

11. **Click in the Position on Menu list box, and choose one of the following:**
    - **(Auto):** Lets Word put your command wherever it wants
    - **(At Top):** Puts your command at the top
    - **(At Bottom):** Puts your command at the bottom
    - **Click a menu command:** Puts your command directly underneath the menu command you chose
12. **Click Add.**

    If you clicked a menu command in step 5, click Add Below.
13. **Repeat steps 9 – 12 for each command you want to add to your pull-down menu.**
14. **Click Close.**

    Word displays your newly added command in your chosen pull-down menu.

Resetting your pull-down menus

If you hid, renamed, deleted, or added pull-down menu titles or commands and want to get rid of all your changes, simply restore the menus to their default settings by using the Reset All command in the Customize dialog box.

To reset your pull-down menus, follow these steps:

1. **If you're using Word in a binder, choose Section⇨View Outside.**

   Skip this step if you're using Word as a separate program.
2. **Choose Tools⇨Customize.**

   The Customize dialog box appears.
3. **Click the Menus tab (refer to Figure 1-21).**
4. **Click Reset All.**

   A dialog box appears, asking whether you want to remove all your menu changes.
5. **Click Yes and click Close.**

   Word displays your pull-down menu titles in their original, pristine state.

You can always tell when you (or somebody else) has changed your menu titles because the Reset All button appears. If no one has changed your menu titles, the Reset All button appears dimmed. Rather than reset your menu titles, you can instead remove individual menu titles by clicking the Remove button.

Removing menu titles from your pull-down menus

Rather than wipe out any changes you've made to your menu titles, you can selectively remove the titles. Then, if someone adds a menu title you don't want to use, you can remove it without removing any other menu titles you may have added.

To remove a single menu title from your pull-down menus, follow these steps:

1. **If you're using Word in a binder, choose Section⇨View Outside.**

   Skip this step if you're using Word as a separate program.

2. **Choose Tools⇨Customize.**

   The Customize dialog box is displayed.

3. **Click the Menus tab, as shown in Figure 1-21.**
4. **Click the Change What Menu list box, and click the menu (the File menu, for example) that contains the menu title you want to remove.**
5. **Click the Position on Menu list box, and highlight the menu title you want to remove.**
6. **Click Remove.**
7. **Click Close.**

   Word removes your chosen menu title from the pull-down menu.

Customizing the Keyboard

Pull-down menus can be handy, but when you're in the middle of some furious typing, the last thing you want to do is take your hands off the keyboard, grab the mouse, point to a pull-down menu or toolbar, and click a command.

As a shortcut, Word lets you choose certain commands by pressing keystroke combinations. For example, you can press Ctrl+S to choose the Save command, Ctrl+P to choose the Print command, and Shift+F7 to choose the Thesaurus command.

Unfortunately, you can't use all commands by pressing keystrokes. Not all keystroke commands are intuitive, either. (Pressing Ctrl+S to choose the Save command makes sense, but who came up with Shift+F7 to choose the Thesaurus command?)

Assigning your own keystroke combinations

To mold Word to the way you work, you can assign custom keystrokes to represent your favorite commands. Then you can just press a button (or two) rather than use the pull-down menus.

To assign a keystroke to a command, follow these steps:

1. **If you're using Word in a binder, Choose Section⇨View Outside.**

   Skip this step if you're using Word as a separate program.

2. **Choose Tools⇨Customize.**

   The Customize dialog box appears.

3. **Click the Keyboard tab, shown in Figure 1-23.**

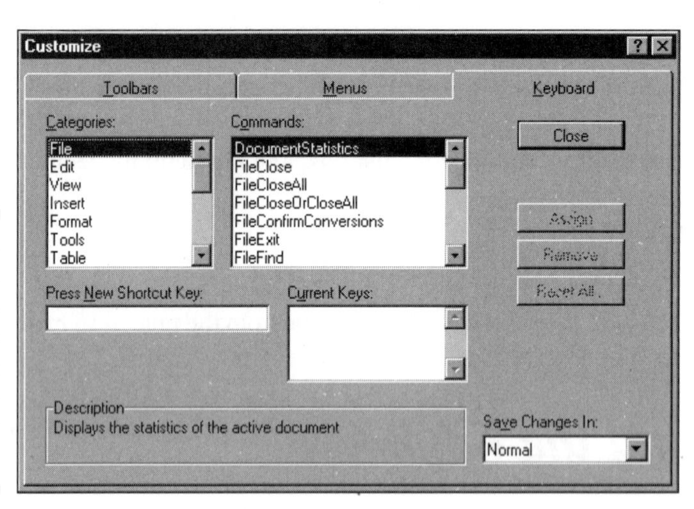

Figure 1-23: Discombobulate your fingers by changing the keystrokes Word uses.

4. **Click in the Categories list box and choose a category.**
5. **Click in the Commands list box and choose a command.**
6. **Click in the Press New Shortcut Key box, and press the keystroke combination you want to represent the command you chose in step 4.**

   For example, press Ctrl+F9 or Alt+L.

7. **Click Assign.**

   Microsoft Word displays all the keystroke combinations in the Current Keys list box.

8. Click Close.

Microsoft Word is now ready to use your newly assigned keystroke combination.

Removing all your keystroke combinations

If you don't want to keep your keystroke combinations, you can get rid of them.

To remove all your keystroke combinations, follow these steps:

1. **If you're using Word in a binder, choose Section⇨View Outside.**

   Skip this step if you're using Word as a separate program.

2. **Choose Tools⇨Customize.**

   The Customize dialog box appears.

3. **Click the Keyboard tab (refer to Figure 1-23).**
4. **Click Reset All.**

   A dialog box appears, asking whether you want to remove all your keystroke assignments.

5. **Click Yes and then click Close.**

You can always tell when you (or somebody else) has assigned new keystroke combinations to your copy of Word, because the Reset All button appears in the Customize dialog box. If no one has changed your keystroke combinations, the Reset All button appears dimmed.

Removing your keystroke combinations individually

Rather than ruthlessly wipe out every single keystroke combination you may have created, you can remove just the ones you don't want to use anymore.

To remove a single keystroke combination, follow these steps:

1. **If you're using Word in a binder, choose Section⇨View Outside.**

   Skip this step if you're using Word as a separate program.

2. **Choose Tools⇨Customize.**

   The Customize dialog box is displayed.

3. Click the Keyboard tab, as shown in Figure 1-23.
4. Click the Categories list box, and highlight the menu (the Edit menu, for example) that contains the command with the keystroke combination you want to remove.
5. Click the Commands list box, and highlight the command with the keystroke combination you want to remove.
6. Click the keystroke combination in the Current Keys box.
7. Click Remove.
8. Click Close.

Chapter 2

More about Macros

In This Chapter

- Recording macros as toolbar buttons, menu items, and keystroke combinations
- Fine-tuning your macros
- Deleting macros
- Using macros in different documents

To help you work faster, Word lets you create *macros,* which act like shortcuts. A macro is simply a file that contains one or more instructions. When you want to repeat those instructions, rather than type them or click menu commands to make Word follow them, you just tell Word to follow the instructions stored in your macro.

Suppose that you have to type a long-winded phrase, such as *Acme's Super Acne Medication Cream,* or choose multiple commands to create a three-column document over and over again. You can type all those words or choose various commands multiple times and risk making a mistake, or you can use a macro.

If you use a macro, you have to type the words or choose the commands only once. You use Word's macro feature to "capture" them (like a bug in amber) and then "replay" them at the touch of a button. In this way, a macro lets you perform complicated tasks without thinking, which is the way most people act when they're working for somebody else anyway.

Recording Your Own Macros

When you record a macro, you can store it in one of three ways:

- **As a toolbar button:** If you store a macro on a toolbar, you choose it by simply clicking its button.
- **As a menu command:** If you store a macro on a menu, you choose it by pulling down the menu and then clicking the macro's name.

- **As a unique keystroke combination (such as Ctrl+W):** If you store a macro as a keystroke combination, you can quickly choose the macro by pressing the proper keystrokes. (The only hard part is remembering the macro's particular keystroke combination.)

Which method should you use? It depends on how you like to use Word. If you want simple point-and-click access to your macros, store your macros as toolbar buttons. If you don't want macros cluttering your screen, store them as menu commands. If you want to access your macros faster than you can by clicking either toolbar buttons or menu commands, store the macros as keystroke combinations.

Macros as toolbar buttons

When you record a macro as a toolbar button, you need to choose two things:

- A button to represent the macro
- A toolbar (such as the Standard or Formatting toolbar) on which to store the macro

To record a macro and store it as a toolbar button, follow these steps:

1. **If you're using Word in a binder, choose Section⇨View Outside.**

   Skip this step if you're using Word as a separate program.

2. **Choose Tools⇨Macro.**

   A Macro dialog box appears, as shown in Figure 2-1.

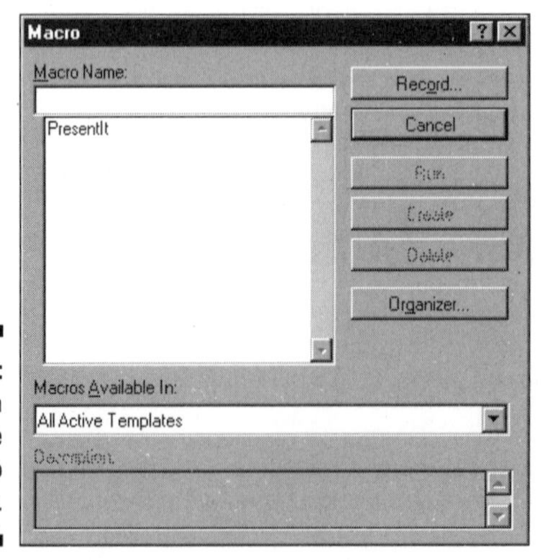

Figure 2-1: Naming a macro in the Macro dialog box.

3. Type a descriptive name for your macro (one word only, no spaces are allowed) in the Macro Name box.

4. Click Record.

The Record Macro dialog box appears, as shown in Figure 2-2.

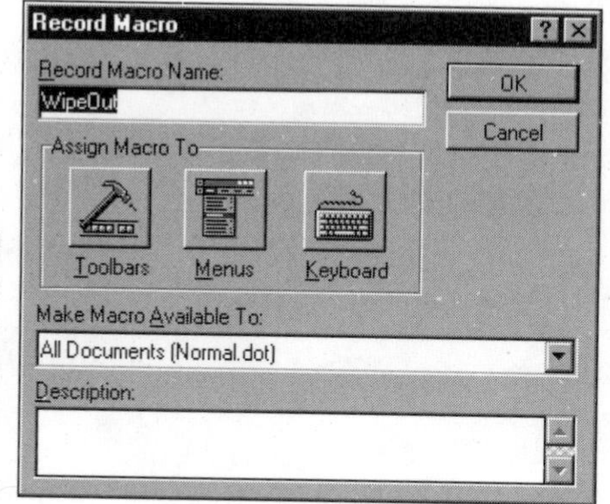

Figure 2-2: Get ready to record those keystrokes!

5. Click the Toolbars button in the Assign Macro To group.

The Customize dialog box appears with the Toolbars tab displayed, as shown in Figure 2-3.

6. Point to the macro name displayed in the list box, hold down the left mouse button, and drag the mouse to the toolbar on which you want to store your macro.

Your macro button appears as a gray outline, as shown in Figure 2-4.

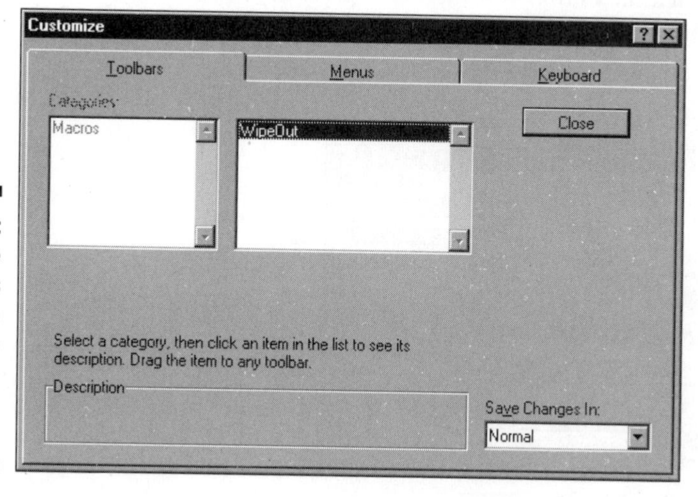

Figure 2-3: On the Toolbars tab, you choose where a macro will live.

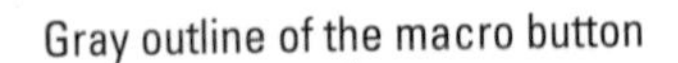

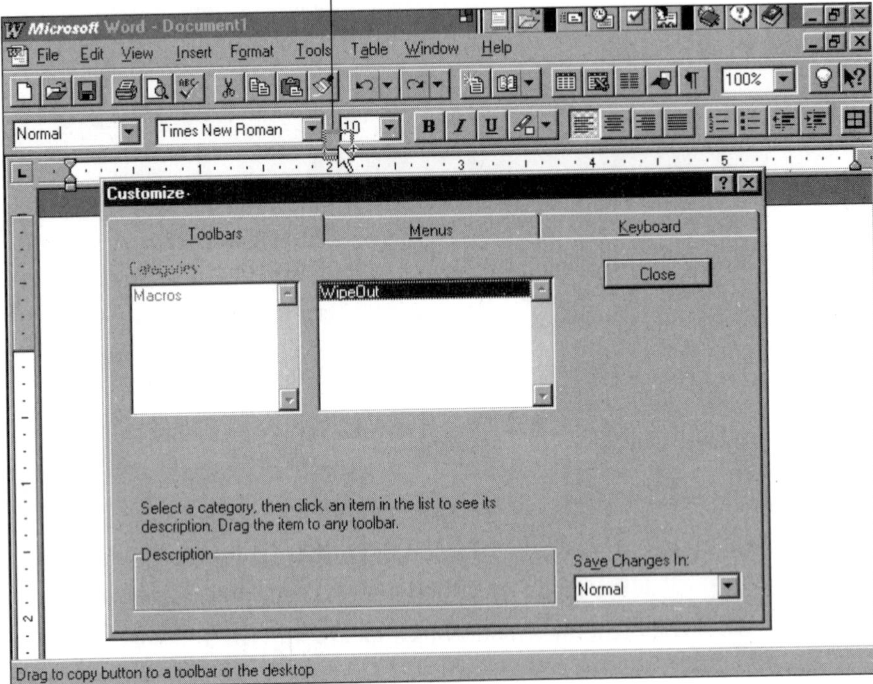

Figure 2-4: Dragging a macro button to a toolbar.

7. **After you place the button on a toolbar, release the mouse button.**

   The Custom Button dialog box appears, as shown in Figure 2-5.

8. **Click the button you want to represent your macro and then click Assign.**

   The Customize dialog box appears again.

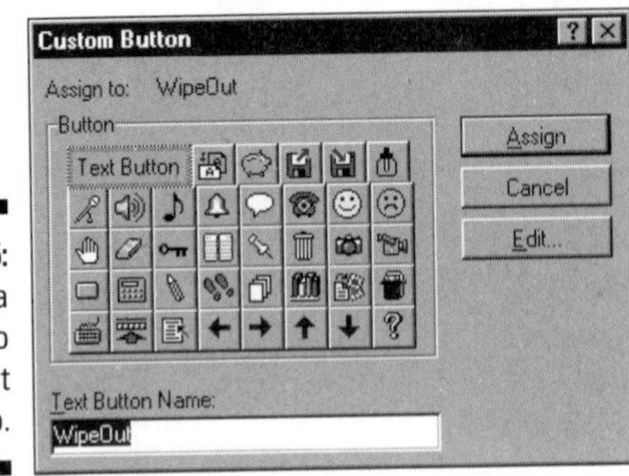

Figure 2-5: Picking a critter to represent your macro.

9. **Click Close.**

   The Macro Recording toolbar appears, floating in the middle of the screen (see Figure 2-6). Notice that the mouse pointer displays a cassette tape icon to let you know that Word is recording your macro.

10. **Press any keys or choose any command you want to store in your macro.**

   When you're recording a macro but don't want to record certain keystrokes or commands, you can temporarily "turn off" the macro recorder by clicking the Pause button (refer to Figure 2-6). To turn the macro recorder back "on," just click the Pause button again.

11. **Click the Stop button on the Macro Recording toolbar.**

Congratulations! You've just recorded a macro. To use this macro at any time, just click its toolbar button.

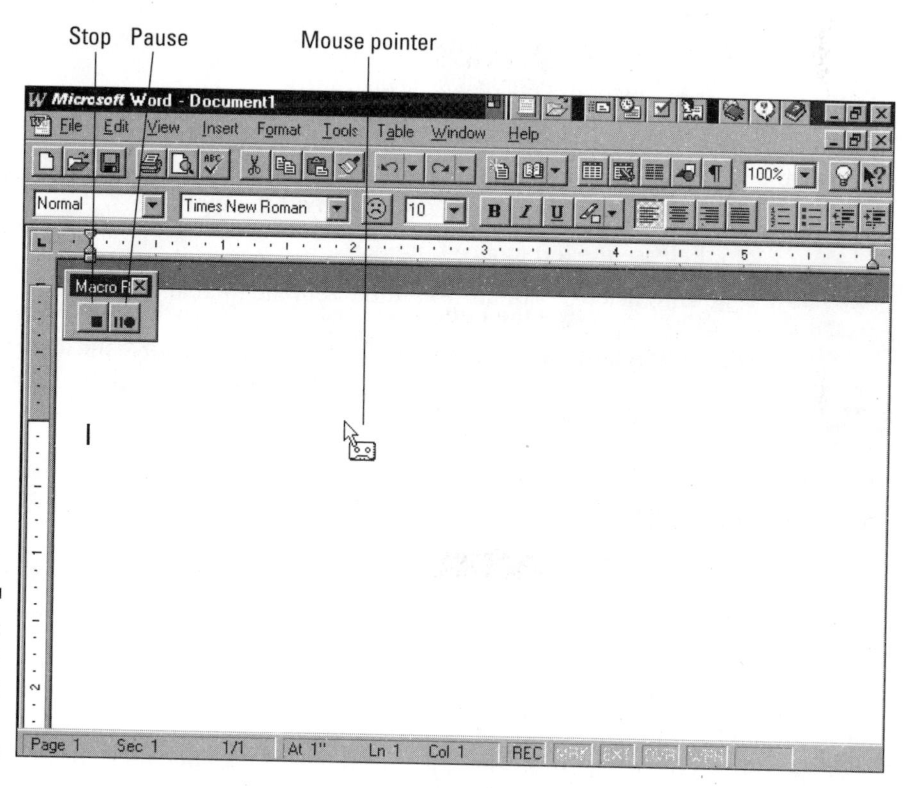

Figure 2-6: The Macro Recording toolbar.

To remove the macro button from your toolbar, follow these steps:

1. **Choose View⇨Toolbars.**

   The Toolbars dialog box appears.

2. **Highlight the toolbar that contains the macro icon you want to remove.**

3. **Click Reset.**

These steps remove *all* changes, including any other macro icons you may have added or any modifications you may have made to the toolbar itself.

If you want to remove just one macro button from your toolbar without completely resetting your toolbar, follow these steps:

1. **If you're using Word in a binder, choose Section⇨View Outside.**

   Skip this step if you're using Word as a separate program.

2. **Choose Tools⇨Customize.**

   The Customize dialog box is displayed.

3. **Click the Toolbars tab.**

4. **Click the macro button you want to remove, hold down the left mouse button, and drag the macro button off the toolbar.**

5. **Release the left mouse button.**

   Word deletes your macro button from the toolbar.

When you remove a macro from a toolbar, you just remove the icon; the macro still exists on your hard disk. To delete macros, see the section "Deleting a macro from the face of the earth," later in this chapter.

Macros as menu commands

When you record a macro as a menu command, you need to choose two things:

- A descriptive name for the macro
- A pull-down menu (such as the Tools or View menu) in which to store the macro

To record a macro and store it as a command on a pull-down menu, follow these steps:

1. **If you're using Word in a binder, choose Section⇨View Outside.**

   Skip this step if you're using Word as a separate program.

2. **Choose Tools➪Macro.**

   The Macro dialog box appears (refer to Figure 2-1).

3. **Type a descriptive name for the macro (one word only, no spaces are allowed) in the Macro Name box.**

4. **Click Record.**

   A Record Macro dialog box appears (refer to Figure 2-2).

5. **Click the Menus button in the Assign Macro To group.**

   The Customize dialog box appears with the Menus tab displayed, as shown in Figure 2-7.

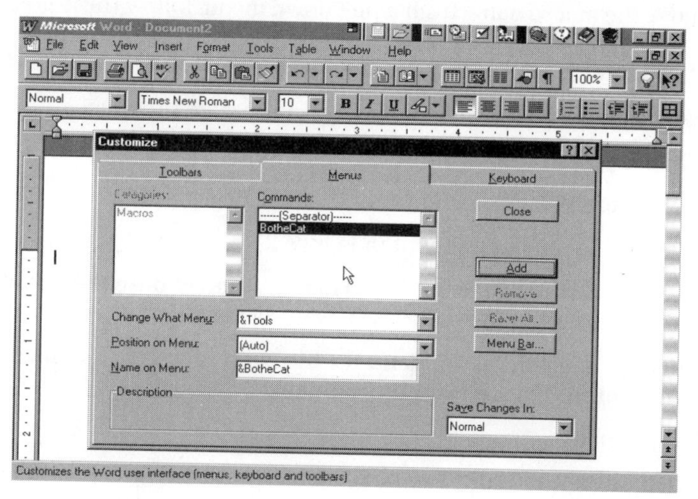

Figure 2-7: Putting a macro on a menu.

6. **Click in the Change What Menu list box, and choose the pull-down menu on which you want your macro name to appear.**

7. **Click in the Position on Menu list box and choose one of the following:**

   - **(Auto):** Lets Word put your command wherever it wants
   - **(At Top):** Puts your command at the top
   - **(At Bottom):** Puts your command at the bottom
   - **Click a menu command:** Puts your macro directly below the menu command you chose

8. **Click Add.**

   If you clicked a menu command in step 7, click Add Below.

9. **Click Close.**

   The Macro Recording toolbar appears, floating in the middle of the screen (refer to Figure 2-6). Notice that the mouse pointer displays a cassette tape icon to let you know that Word is recording your macro.

10. **Press any keys or choose any command you want to store in your macro.**

11. **Click the Stop button on the Macro Recording toolbar.**

    To use this macro at any time, just display the pull-down menu on which you stored the macro name (in step 6) and click the macro name displayed on the menu.

To remove the macro name from a pull-down menu, follow these steps:

1. **If you're using Word in a binder, choose Section⇨View Outside.**

   Skip this step if you're using Word as a separate program.

2. **Choose Tools⇨Customize.**

   A Customize dialog box appears.

3. **Click the Menus tab, shown in Figure 2-8.**

4. **Click in the Change What Menu list box, and choose the pull-down menu containing the macro you want to remove.**

5. **Click in the Position on Menu list box, and highlight the macro name you want to remove from the menu.**

6. **Click Remove.**

7. **Click Close.**

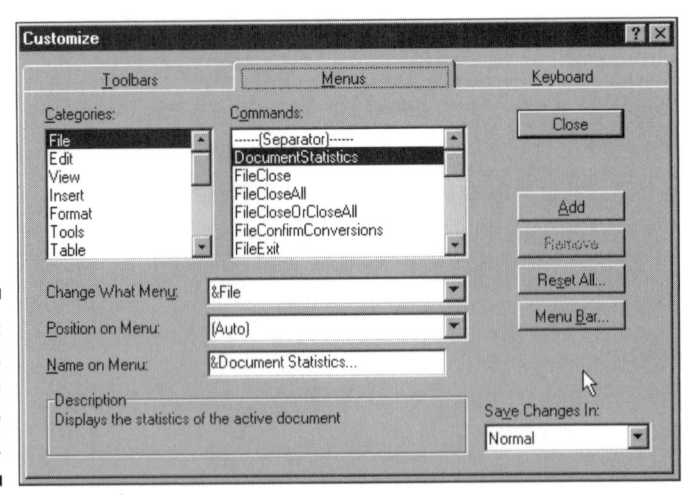

Figure 2-8: The Menus tab in the Customize dialog box.

When you remove a macro from a pull-down menu, that macro still exists on your hard disk — it's just hiding. To delete macros, see the section "Deleting a macro from the face of the earth," later in this chapter.

Macros as keystroke combinations

When you record a macro as a keystroke combination, you need to choose two things:

- A descriptive name for your macro
- A unique two- or three-keystroke combination to represent your macro

To record a macro and store it as a keystroke combination, follow these steps:

1. **If you're using Word in a binder, choose Section⇨View Outside.**

   Skip this step if you're using Word as a separate program.

2. **Choose Tools⇨Macro.**

   The Macro dialog box appears (refer to Figure 2-1).

3. **Type a descriptive name for the macro (one word only, no spaces are allowed) in the Macro Name box.**

4. **Click Record.**

   The Record Macro dialog box appears (refer to Figure 2-2).

5. **Click the Keyboard button in the Assign Macro To group.**

   The Customize dialog box appears with the Keyboard tab displayed, as shown in Figure 2-9.

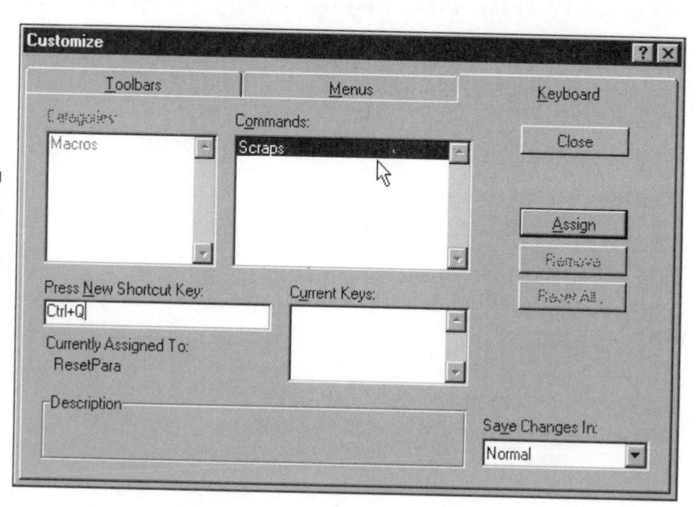

Figure 2-9: Type a couple of cheater shortcut keys you can press to execute a macro.

6. **Click in the Press New Shortcut Key box, and press the keystroke combination you want to represent your macro.**

   Make sure that you choose a unique keystroke combination. Don't choose Ctrl+S, for example, because Word has already assigned Ctrl+S to represent the Save command.

7. **Click Assign.**

   Your keystroke combination appears in the Current Keys list.

8. **Click Close.**

   The Macro Recording toolbar appears, floating in the middle of the screen (refer to Figure 2-6). Notice that the mouse pointer displays a cassette tape icon to let you know that Word is recording your macro.

9. **Press any keys or choose any command you want to store in your macro.**

10. **Click the Stop button on the Macro Recording toolbar.**

    To use this macro at any time, press the keystroke combination you assigned in step 6.

Editing Your Macros to Perfection

You may want to edit a macro for two reasons:

- The macro doesn't work 100 percent correctly.
- The macro contains keystrokes or commands you don't need anymore.

Understanding the ugly way macros look

Before you start blindly editing your macros (and risk messing them up so that they don't work at all), you have to understand the parts of a macro.

A typical macro begins and ends with the following lines:

```
Sub MAIN
End Sub
```

Never erase or modify the Sub MAIN or End Sub lines. If you do, your macro won't work anymore.

Between the Sub MAIN line and the End Sub line are the keystrokes or commands you stored in your macro. For example, the following macro types the phrase *Acme's Super Acne Medication Cream* on-screen and then "presses" Enter to move the cursor to the next line:

```
Sub MAIN
Insert "Acme's Super Acne Medication Cream"
InsertPara
End Sub
```

The `Insert` command types whatever appears between quotation marks. Macros that type numbers or letters on-screen always use the Insert command. The `InsertPara` command appears whenever you press Enter while recording a macro.

If you move the cursor around by pressing the arrow keys, your macro may contain one or more of the commands shown in Table 2-1.

Table 2-1 Cursor-Movement Macro Commands

Macro Command	*What It Does*
CharLeft	Moves the cursor left a specific number of spaces. CharLeft 4, for example, moves the cursor to the left four spaces.
CharRight	Moves the cursor right a specific number of spaces. CharRight 5, for example, moves the cursor to the right five spaces.
WordLeft	Moves the cursor left a specific number of words. WordLeft 2, for example, moves the cursor to the left two words.
WordRight	Moves the cursor right a specific number of words. WordRight 3, for example, moves the cursor to the right three words.
StartOfLine	Moves the cursor to the beginning of a line.
EndOfLine	Moves the cursor to the end of a line.
LineUp	Moves the cursor up a specific number of lines. LineUp 1, for example, moves the cursor up one line.
LineDown	Moves the cursor down a specific number of lines. LineDown 8, for example, moves the cursor down eight lines.
PageDown	Moves the cursor down a specific number of pages. PageDown 7, for example, moves the cursor down seven pages.
PageUp	Moves the cursor up a specific number of pages. PageUp 6, for example, moves the cursor up six pages.

Learning more about Word's macro language

Although the macro commands listed here may give you an idea of what to expect when you edit a macro, you may want to know where you can find a complete listing of all the available macro commands. Guess what? You won't find such a listing in any of your Word or Microsoft Office for Windows 95 manuals.

Because macros are a fairly advanced feature, Microsoft decided not to slaughter a tree just to give you a manual that lists all the Word macro commands. Microsoft must believe that saving a tree is more important than wasting paper printing macro command listings in a manual that 99 percent of the population will never use or care about.

So if you want a listing of all macro commands available in Word, you have to order The Word Developer's Kit by calling 1-800-MS-PRESS or 615-793-5090. Have a credit card ready— yours, preferably.

By getting creative with all the available macro commands, you can completely customize your own word-processing program within Word. If you want that type of excitement in your life, by all means learn about all the macro commands. But for most people, just recording simple macros is more than enough to meet their needs.

If you record menu commands in a macro, the macro contains the name of the pull-down menu title plus the command, as shown in Table 2-2.

Table 2-2 Some Typical Macro Commands

Command within Macro	*Menu Equivalent*
ToolsWordCount	Tools⇨WordCount
EditClear	Edit⇨Clear
ViewPage	View⇨Page Layout

Editing your macros

If your macro needs adjusting to make it work properly, feel free to edit it. Simply follow these steps:

1. **If you're using Word in a binder, choose Section⇨View Outside.**

   Skip this step if you're using Word as a separate program.

2. **Choose Tools⇨Macro.**

   The Macro dialog box appears (refer to Figure 2-1).

3. **Click the macro name you want to edit and click Edit.**

   Microsoft Word displays your macro on-screen, as shown in Figure 2-10.

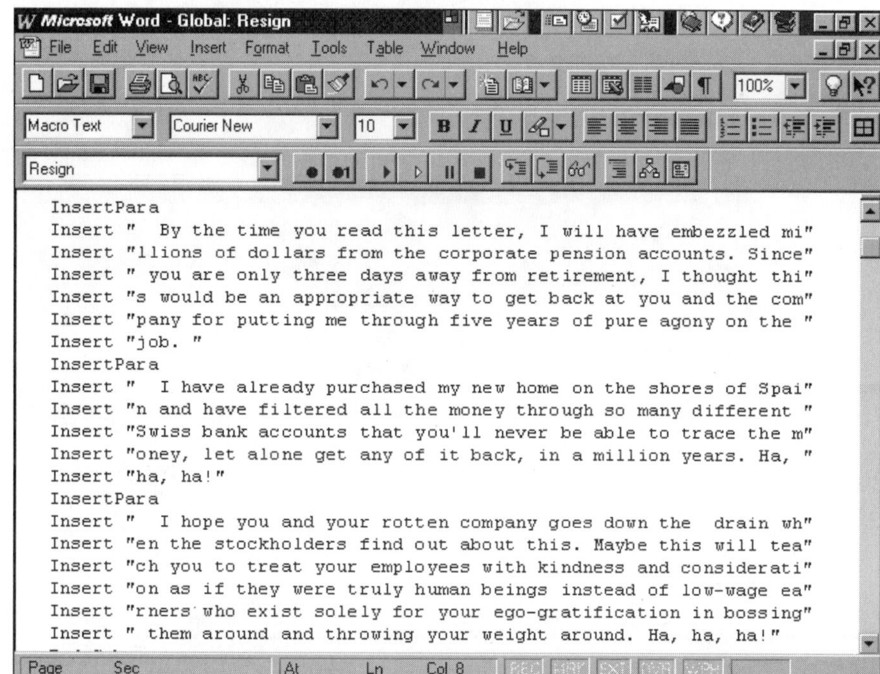

Microsoft Word - Global: Resign
File Edit View Insert Format Tools Table Window Help
Macro Text
Courier New
10
Resign
InsertPara
Insert " By the time you read this letter, I will have embezzled mi"
Insert "llions of dollars from the corporate pension accounts. Since"
Insert " you are only three days away from retirement, I thought thi"
Insert "s would be an appropriate way to get back at you and the com"
Insert "pany for putting me through five years of pure agony on the "
Insert "job. "
InsertPara
Insert " I have already purchased my new home on the shores of Spai"
Insert "n and have filtered all the money through so many different "
Insert "Swiss bank accounts that you'll never be able to trace the m"
Insert "oney, let alone get any of it back, in a million years. Ha, "
Insert "ha, ha!"
InsertPara
Insert " I hope you and your rotten company goes down the drain wh"
Insert "en the stockholders find out about this. Maybe this will tea"
Insert "ch you to treat your employees with kindness and considerati"
Insert "on as if they were truly human beings instead of low-wage ea"
Insert "rners who exist solely for your ego-gratification in bossing"
Insert " them around and throwing your weight around. Ha, ha, ha!"
Page Sec At Ln Col 8

Figure 2-10: The contents of a typical macro.

4. **Make changes to your macro as though you're editing a normal document.**
5. **Choose File⇨Close.**

   A dialog box appears, asking whether you want to save your changes.
6. **Click Yes.**

Before you edit a macro, save a copy of it — just in case you wreck the original when you edit it. To make a copy of a macro, choose File⇨Save Copy As right after you open the macro in step 3.

Renaming your macros

After you create a macro, you may suddenly get a better idea for a more descriptive name for your macro.

To rename an existing macro, follow these steps:

1. **Choose Tools⇨Macro.**

   The Macro dialog box appears (refer to Figure 2-1).

2. **Click Organizer.**

   The Organizer dialog box appears, as shown in Figure 2-11.

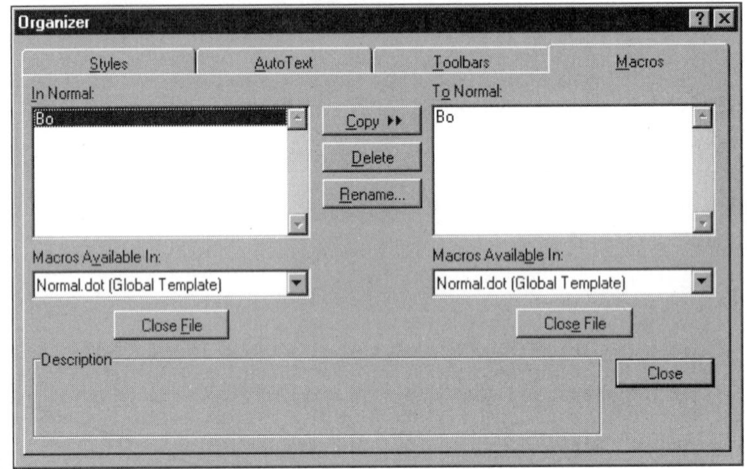

Figure 2-11: What a handy-dandy place to store all your macros!

3. **Click the macro that you want to rename.**

4. **Click Rename.**

   A Rename dialog box appears, as shown in Figure 2-12.

Figure 2-12: Pick a cool name for your macro.

5. **Type a new name for your macro in the New Name box and click OK.**

6. **Click Close.**

Wiping Out Macros

At some point, you may want to delete one or more of the macros you create. You can erase a macro in two ways:

- Record a new macro by using the name of a macro you previously created
- Delete the macro

Recording over an existing macro

When you record over an existing macro, you wipe out the existing macro and replace it with a new macro that has the same name as the deleted macro. This method is similar to taking your brother's tape cassette recording of the Rolling Stones and recording children's nursery rhymes over it. The tape cassette may still be titled "The Rolling Stones," but the cassette contains something completely different.

To record over an existing macro, follow these steps:

1. **If you're using Word in a binder, choose Section⇨View Outside.**

   Skip this step if you're using Word as a separate program.

2. **Choose Tools⇨Macro.**

   A Macro dialog box appears (refer to Figure 2-1).

3. **Click the macro name you want to record over and click Record.**

   The Record Macro dialog box appears (refer to Figure 2-2).

4. **Click OK.**

   A dialog box appears, asking whether you want to replace the existing macro.

5. **Click Yes.**
6. **Type the characters or choose the commands you want to store in your macro.**
7. **Click the Stop button on the Macro Recording toolbar.**

When you record over an existing macro, Word wipes out any toolbar buttons, menu commands, or keystroke combinations previously assigned to that macro name. To assign a new toolbar button, menu command, or keystroke combination to your macro, see the respective sections "Macros as toolbar buttons," "Macros as menu commands," and "Macros as keystroke combinations," earlier in this chapter.

Deleting a macro from the face of the earth

If you decide that you'll never need a certain macro again, you can just delete it for good. To delete a macro, follow these steps:

1. **Choose Tools⇨Macro.**

   The Macro dialog box appears (refer to Figure 2-1).

2. **Click the macro name you want to delete and click Delete.**

   A dialog box appears, asking whether you really want to delete your macro.

3. **Click Yes.**

   Your macro is gone for good!

4. **Click Close.**

Sharing Macros between Documents

When you create a macro, Word stores it in the template used to create the document. For example, every time you create a new document, Word uses the NORMAL.DOT template unless you specify a different template to use. (For more information about templates, see Chapter 3.)

After you create several useful macros, you may want to copy them to other templates. That way, you can use your macro no matter which template you use to create another document.

For example, you may store all macros related to faxes in a FAX.DOT template, all macros related to form letters in a FORM.DOT template, and all macros related to business reports in a DULL.DOT template.

To copy your macros to a different template, follow these steps:

1. **Choose Tools⇨Macro.**

   The Macro dialog box appears (refer to Figure 2-1).

2. **Click Organizer.**

   The Organizer dialog box appears (refer to Figure 2-11).

3. **In the list box on the left, click the macro you want to copy.**

4. **Click the Close File button that appears to the right of the Organizer dialog box.**

   Microsoft Word renames the Close File button as the Open File button.

Beware of macro viruses

Because Word's macro language is basically a miniature programming language, people have been able to use it to create computer viruses. These macro viruses infect your document files and spread to your template files. Every time you create a new document based on an infected template file, your new document files become infected. And if you share an infected document file with someone else, the macro virus infects that person's template files, too.

To protect yourself from macro viruses, get an antivirus program, such as Norton Antivirus or McAfee's VirusScan that checks Word documents for macro viruses. That way, you can safely share your macros with others without worrying about infecting their computer with a macro virus.

5. **Click the Open File button.**

   The Open dialog box appears, as shown in Figure 2-13.

6. **Click the template in which you want to store your macro and click Open.**
7. **Click Copy>>.**
8. **Click Close.**

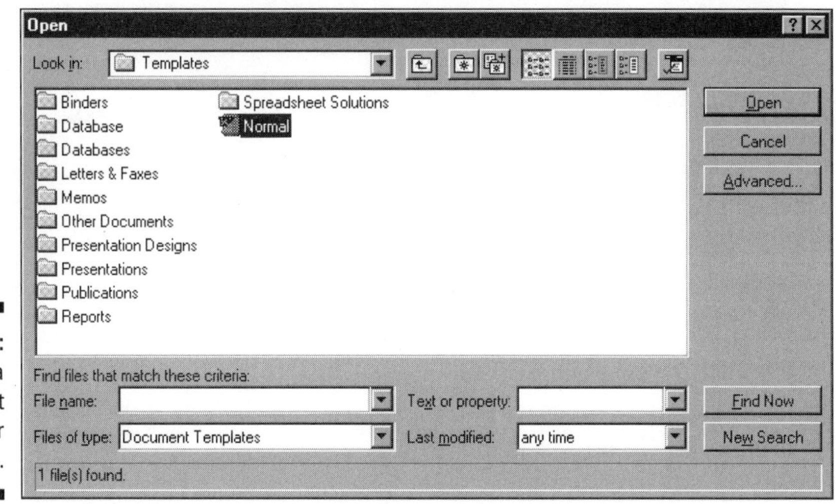

Figure 2-13: Choosing a storage spot for your macro.

Chapter 3

Formatting Text with Styles and Templates

In This Chapter

- Using styles to format your text
- Creating templates to make document formatting easier
- Storing your templates somewhere else

Two of Word's most useful features are styles and templates. A *style* lets you define a specific way to format text. A *template* lets you store multiple styles so that you can use them over and over again.

If you do a great deal of writing that requires unusual formatting (such as writing screenplays, typing financial reports, or pasting together ransom notes), styles and templates can help you work faster than usual.

Formatting Text with Styles

To help make your writing look good, Word gives you the option of creating and storing predefined styles. A *style* is simply a specific way to format text, such as the font, font size, alignment, color, boldface, italicization, and underlining.

By creating a predefined style, you don't have to keep highlighting text and changing all these formatting options by yourself every time you need a particular style. Instead, just click the text you want to format and choose a style, and Word formats your text for you automatically.

Styles are not the same as macros. A *style* defines the formatting of text but not the text itself. A *macro* can type text for you automatically but does nothing to define the formatting of that text. For more information about macros, see Chapter 2.

Creating a style

Whenever you need to format text in a specific way over and over again, you should create a style. When you create one, you have to define the following items:

- The style name
- Whether the style is based on an existing style
- Whether the style affects an entire paragraph or just a single word
- The style to use for the paragraph that follows the one you're formatting

The style name lets you identify the specific style you want to use. Although you can name your styles anything you want (including four-letter words), using memorable style names (such as Hanging Indent, Dialogue, or Headline) is a good idea.

To save time when you create new styles, you can use an existing style as a starting point. That way, you don't have to waste time creating styles from scratch when all you have to do is slightly modify an existing style. This technique is similar to copying someone else's term paper and then rewriting it a little instead of writing your own term paper from scratch.

When you create a style, you have to decide whether you want to create a character style or a paragraph style. A *character style* changes the formatting for one or more characters. A *paragraph style* changes the format for an entire paragraph. Most of the time, styles affect the format for an entire paragraph because changing the format of a single character (or group of characters) by yourself is usually easy to do without creating a style.

After you create a style, you can define the style for the paragraph that appears after the one you're formatting. That way, if two styles normally appear one after the other, Word can choose the second style for you automatically.

For example, you may create a style, called Character, that centers character names in a screenplay. After using the Character style, Word can immediately choose a style called Dialogue, which formats dialogue on the page. In this way, you can continue typing without having to stop to choose the Dialogue style. Figure 3-1 shows four possible styles within a document.

To create your own style, follow these steps:

1. **Choose Format⇨Style.**

   The Style dialog box appears, as shown in Figure 3-2.

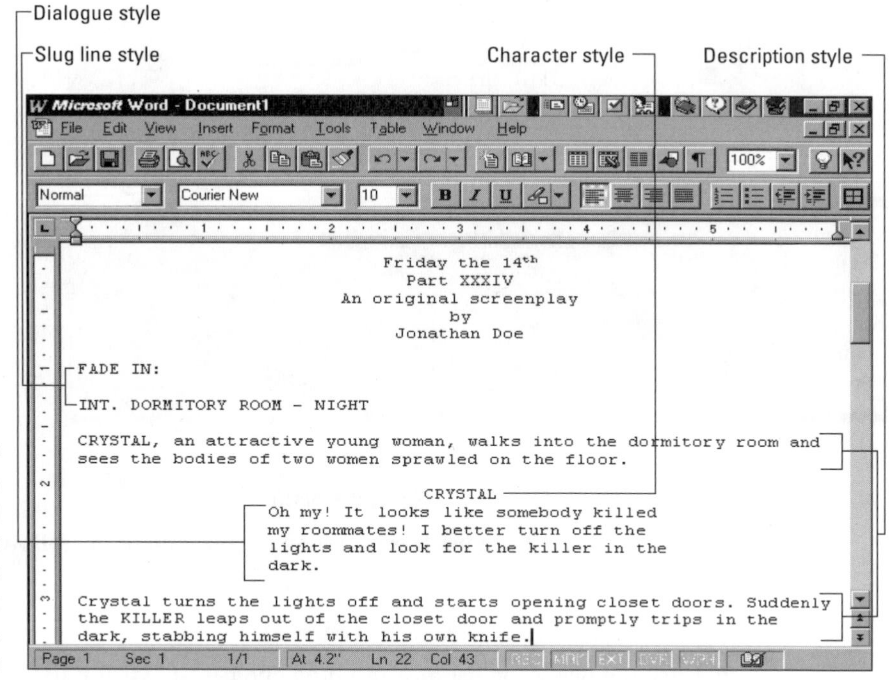

Figure 3-1: A typical document uses different styles.

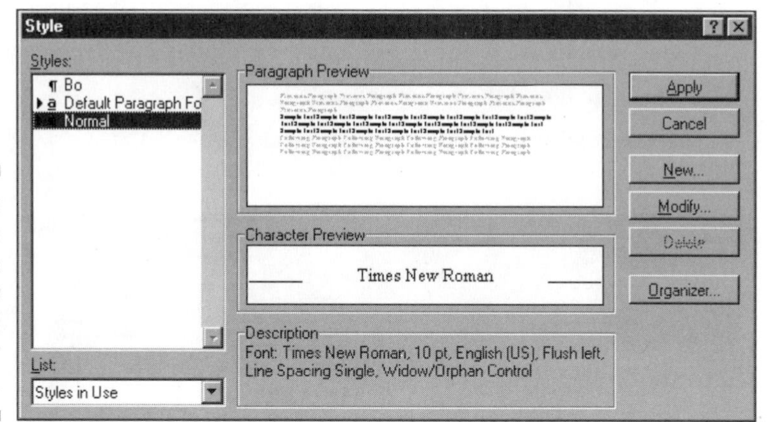

Figure 3-2: The Style dialog box shows how text will look in your chosen style.

2. Click New.

The New Style dialog box appears, as shown in Figure 3-3.

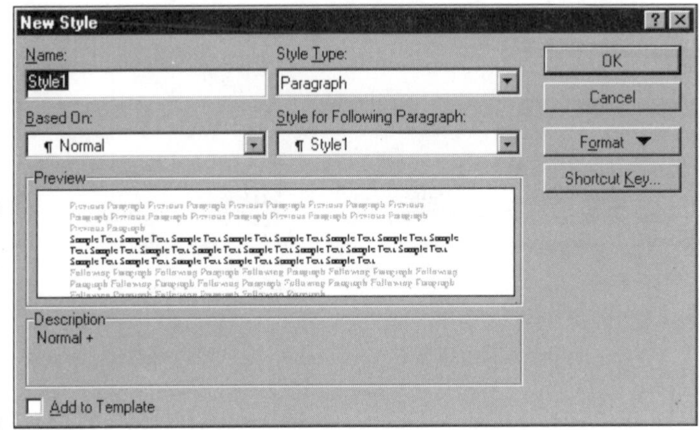

Figure 3-3: In the New Style dialog box, you can define your own styles.

3. **Type a name for your style in the Name box.**
4. **Click the Style Type list box and then choose one of the following:**
   - Paragraph (format an entire paragraph)
   - Character (format a single word)
5. **Click the Based On list box and then choose an existing style you want to use to help create your new style.**
6. **Click the Style for Following Paragraph list box and choose a style you want Word to use in the paragraph immediately after your new style.**
7. **Click Format and then choose Font.**

   The Font dialog box appears, as shown in Figure 3-4.

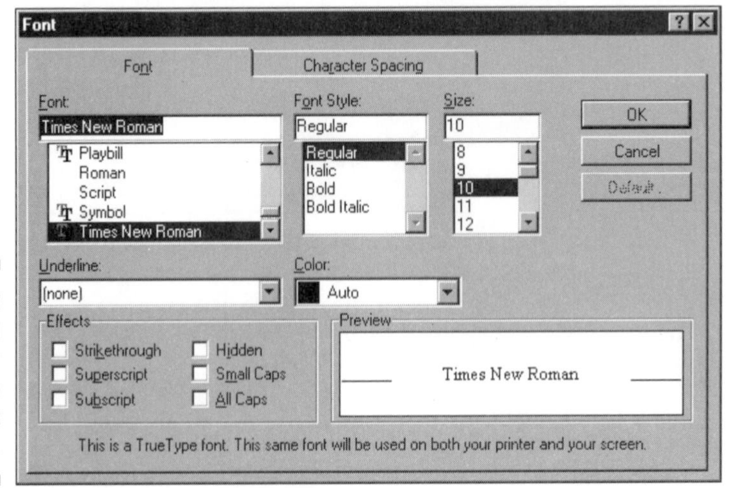

Figure 3-4: Choosing a font for your style in the Font dialog box.

8. **Chose the font, font style, and size you want to use and then click OK.**
9. **Click Format and then choose Paragraph.**

   The Paragraph dialog box appears, as shown in Figure 3-5.

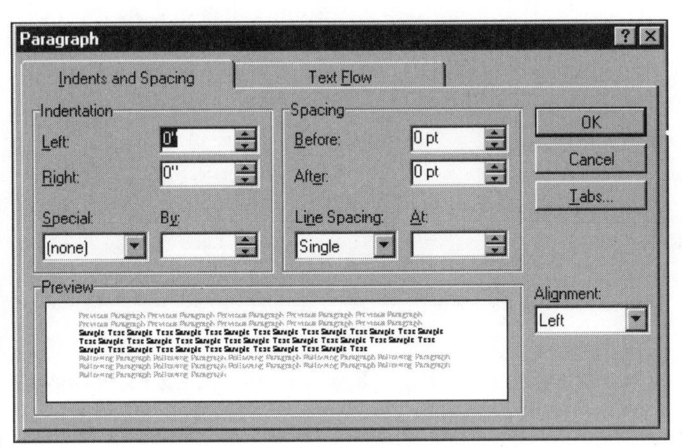

Figure 3-5: In the Paragraph dialog box, you can stretch out a paragraph in one long line or clump a bunch of paragraphs together.

10. **Choose the left or right indentation and the line spacing and then click OK.**
11. **Click Format and choose Tabs.**

    The Tabs dialog box appears, as shown in Figure 3-6.

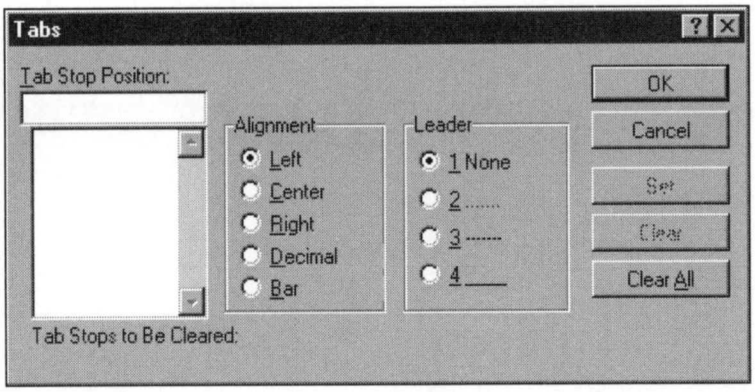

Figure 3-6: Set "rest stops" for your text in the Tabs dialog box.

12. **Choose the tab stop position, alignment, and leader and then click OK.**
13. **Click Format; choose Border, Language, Frame, or Numbering; and then define any options you want to save in your style.**
14. **Click Shortcut Key.**

    The Customize dialog box appears, as shown in Figure 3-7.

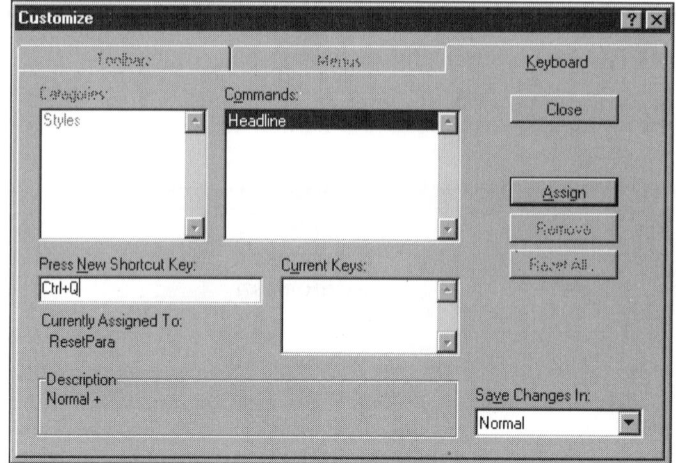

Figure 3-7: Giving your style a keystroke assignment.

15. **Click the Press New Shortcut Key box and press the keystroke combination you want to assign to your style.**
16. **Click Assign and then click Close.**
17. **Click the Add to Template check box if you want to save your style for use in other documents.**
18. **Click OK.**

    The Style dialog box appears again.

19. **Click Close.**

    Your style is now ready to use.

If you click the Add to Template check box in step 17, Word saves your style to your document template. Your style is then available for you to use every time you create a new document based on that template.

Using a style

After you create a style, you can celebrate if you want. However, you'll probably want to use your style instead. You can use a style in two ways:

- Choose the style name from the Style list box displayed on the Formatting toolbar.
- Press the keystroke combination assigned to the style you want to use (assuming that you assigned a keystroke combination to your style when you created it).

If you have hidden the Formatting toolbar, you won't be able to see the Style list box. To display a hidden Formatting toolbar, choose View➪Toolbars and click the formatting check box.

To use a style that affects an entire paragraph, follow these steps:

1. **Move the cursor (or click the mouse) anywhere in the paragraph you want to format.**
2. **Click the Style list box and then choose the style name you want to use. (Or press the keystroke combination assigned to the style you want to use.)**

   Microsoft Word magically formats the entire paragraph according to the style.

To use a style that affects a single word, follow these steps:

1. **Highlight the word or words you want to format.**
2. **Click the Style list box and then choose the style name you want to use. (Or press the keystroke combination assigned to the style you want to use.)**

   Microsoft Word magically formats the entire paragraph according to the style.

Editing a style

After you create a style, you may decide that it doesn't work quite the way you want. In this case, you can always modify a style.

Be careful when you modify a style. If you've used a specific style to format text and then later change that style, guess what? Word automatically reformats all your text according to the newly modified style. Modify a style only if you're absolutely sure that you want all the text formatted with that style to change as well. Otherwise, create a new style instead.

Character styles versus paragraph styles

A character style can format a single character, word, or group of words; a paragraph style can format an entire paragraph. What happens, however, if you use a character style to format words and then later use a paragraph style to format the entire paragraph?

Fortunately, Word isn't as dumb as you may expect. Any characters formatted by using a character style retain their formatting. The paragraph style simply formats all text within a paragraph except for text formatted by character styles. Isn't that comforting?

To edit an existing style, follow these steps:

1. **Choose Section⇨View Outside.**

   Skip this step if you're using Word as a separate program.

2. **Choose Format⇨Style.**

   The Style dialog box appears (refer to Figure 3-2).

3. **In the Styles list box, highlight the style you want to edit.**

4. **Click Modify.**

   The Modify Style dialog box appears, as shown in Figure 3-8.

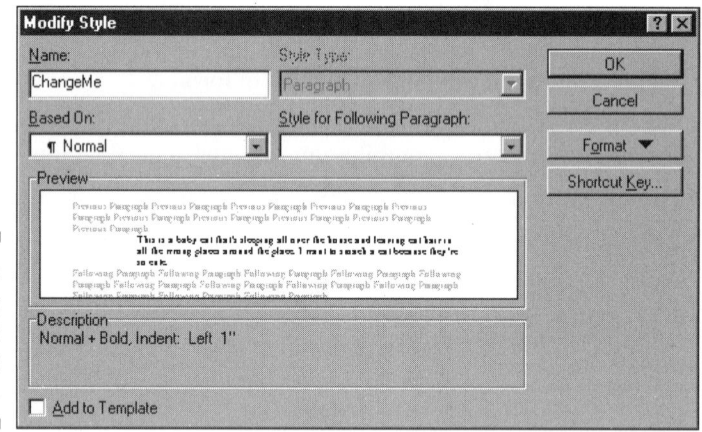

Figure 3-8: Changing the way an existing style looks.

5. **Click Format and choose one of these options to modify your style:**

   - Font
   - Paragraph
   - Tabs
   - Border
   - Language
   - Frame
   - Numbering

6. **Click Shortcut Key if you want to assign a keystroke combination to the style.**

   The Customize dialog box appears (refer to Figure 3-7).

7. **Click the Press New Shortcut Key box and press the keystroke combination you want to assign to your style.**
8. **Click Assign and then click Close.**
9. **Click the Add to Template check box if you want to save your style for use in other documents.**
10. **Click OK.**

    The Style dialog box appears again.
11. **Click Close.**

    Your newly modified style is now ready to use.

To edit a style quickly, follow these steps:

1. **Highlight any text formatted by the style you want to change.**
2. **Make any changes you want to the style.**
3. **Click the Style list box and choose the name of the style you just modified.**

    The Reapply Style dialog box appears, as shown in Figure 3-9.
4. **Click OK.**

    Microsoft Word reformats all text previously formatted with your newly modified style.

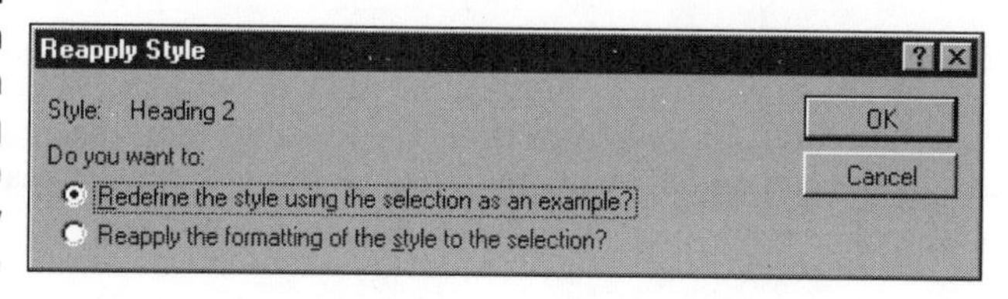

Figure 3-9: You can redefine an existing style in the Reapply Style dialog box.

Wiping out a style

You may occasionally create a style and then later decide that you don't need it after all. To wipe out a style from the face of the earth, follow these steps:

1. **Choose Format⇨Style.**

    The Style dialog box appears (refer to Figure 3-2).

2. **Highlight in the Styles list box the style you want to delete, destroy, obliterate, or otherwise eliminate.**
3. **Click Delete.**

   A dialog box appears and asks whether you're sure that you want to delete your chosen style.
4. **Click Yes.**

   Kiss your style good-bye forevermore.
5. **Click Close.**

   The moment you delete a style, any text formatted in that style reverts to the Normal style.

If you delete a style, you can never undo, retrieve, undelete, or recover it, so make sure that you really want to delete a style before you make a mistake and regret your decision afterward.

Creating Document Templates

If you create documents that require bizarre formatting, tab settings, or paragraph indentations, you may want to create styles or macros to modify those settings at the touch of a button (or the click of a mouse). If you regularly create these types of documents, creating your own, unique document templates instead is much easier.

A document template acts like a cookie cutter for text. Just modify a document once and save all the formatting in the document as a template. Then, the next time you want to create a document with all the fancy formatting, spacing, and indentations already created for you, just create a new document based on your template.

Suppose that you use Word to create a newsletter that has a boldface headline in large print and two columns that divide the page in half. Setting up the column spacing, width, and headline formatting every time you want to create another newsletter is a tiresome task, which makes this the perfect job to give to someone who makes less money per hour than you do.

To save time, create your newsletter only once and save it as a template. The next time you create a newsletter, create a new document based on your newsletter template. Then you can just focus on typing the text, because the template will have already set up all the headline formatting and columns for you.

Document templates can contain the following items:

- Text, such as your company name, that must appear in every document based on your template
- Graphics, such as a company logo, that must appear in every document based on your template
- Any formatting or ruler settings you may have changed
- Any styles you may create
- Any macros you may create

Using a template

To show you the power of templates, Word contains several templates that some poor Microsoft employee got paid to create for you. To give you as many different ways as possible to accomplish the same task and to provide maximum possibility for confusion, Microsoft provides two ways to view and use a Word template:

- From within a new document
- From the Windows 95 desktop

If you don't choose a template, Word shrugs its shoulders and assumes that you just want to use a blank template called Normal.

Choosing a template from within a document

If you've already created and opened a document, you can tell Word, "Hey, I want my document to use a different template instead."

To choose a template for your Word document, follow these steps:

1. **Choose Format⇨Style Gallery.**

   The Style Gallery dialog box appears, as shown in Figure 3-10.

2. **Click a template you want to view, such as Elegant Fax or Professional Report.**

3. **Click the Example or Style Samples radio button in the Preview group.**

   Click the Example radio button to see how attractive your document can look if you know what you're doing (see Figure 3-11). Click the Style Samples radio button to see the type of formatting the template can create (see Figure 3-12). Either way, Word shows you how the template displays text.

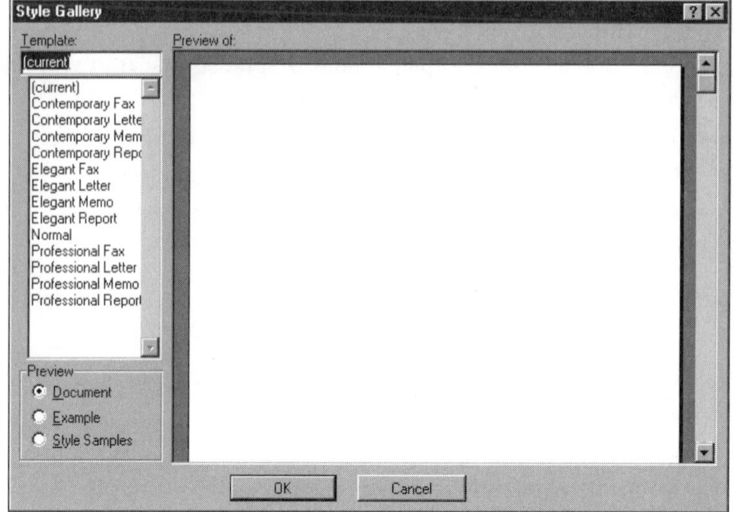

Figure 3-10: The Style Gallery dialog box displays all the available templates you can use.

4. **Click OK when you find a template you want to use.**

   Your chosen template is ready to use. Just choose a style from the Style list box on the Formatting toolbar.

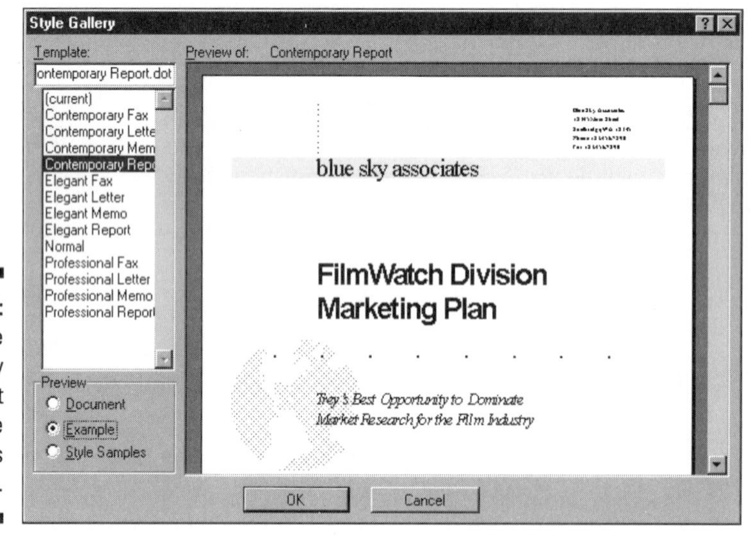

Figure 3-11: The Contemporary Report template displayed as an example.

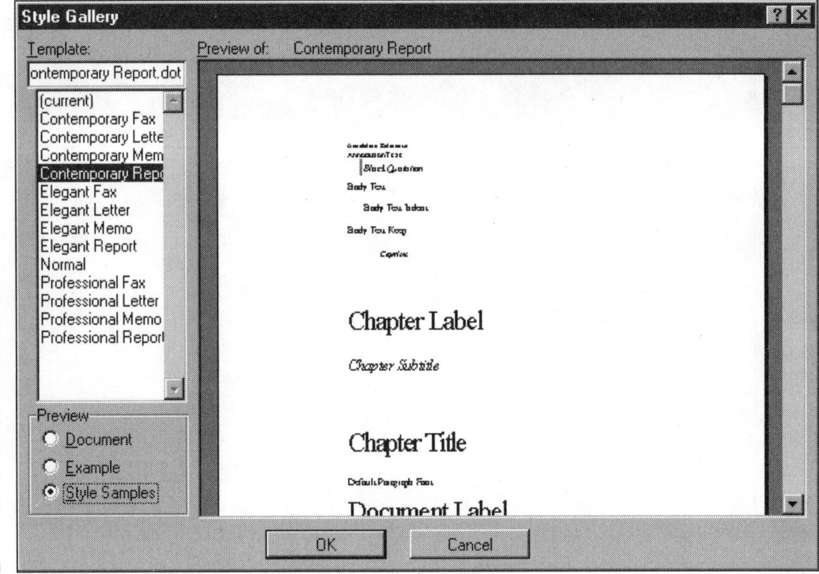

Figure 3-12: The Contemporary Report template displayed as a style sample.

Choosing a template from the Windows 95 desktop

If you know that you want to use a template to create a new Word document, choosing a template directly from the Windows 95 desktop is easier than opening a blank document and then changing the template.

When you choose a template from the Windows 95 desktop, Word runs as a separate program.

To view and choose a template from the Windows 95 desktop, follow these steps:

1. **Choose one of the following:**
   - **Click the Start button on the Windows 95 taskbar, and then click New Office Document.**
   - **Click the Start a New Document button on the Microsoft Office Shortcut Bar.**
2. **Click one of the following tabs:**
   - **Letters & Faxes**
   - **Memos**
   - **Reports**

   The New dialog box appears, as shown in Figure 3-13.

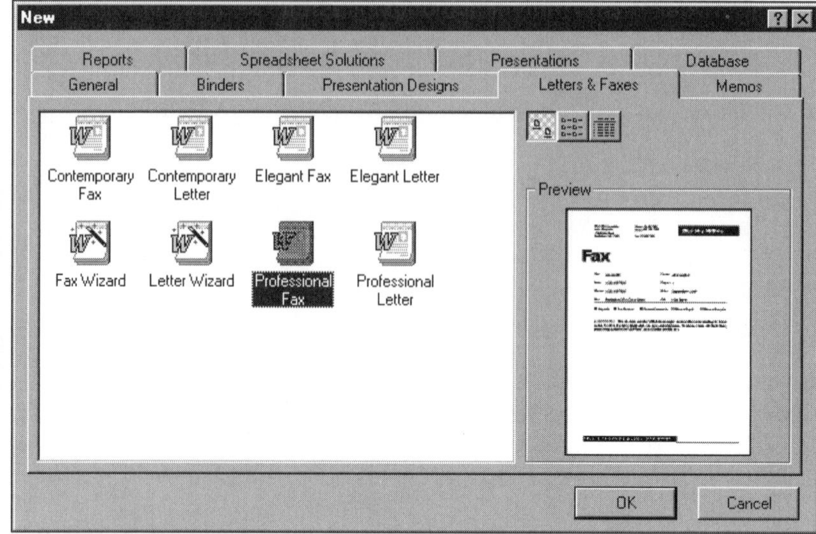

Figure 3-13: Choosing the Letters & Faxes tab in the New dialog box.

3. **Click the template icon you want to use and then click OK.**

   Microsoft Word displays a new document based on your chosen template.

Creating a template by modifying an existing one

As though using a personal computer or Microsoft Office isn't traumatizing enough, you can subject yourself to additional psychological distress by creating your own document templates from scratch.

If someone creates a template for you or if you don't really like the templates that come with Word, change them. Modifying an existing template is much easier than creating a new template, just as copying someone else's work is easier than doing the work yourself.

To modify an existing template, follow these steps:

1. **Choose Section⇨View Outside.**

   Skip this step if you're using Word as a separate program.

2. **Choose File⇨Open.**

   The Open dialog box appears, as shown in Figure 3-14.

3. **Click the Files of type list box and choose Document Templates.**

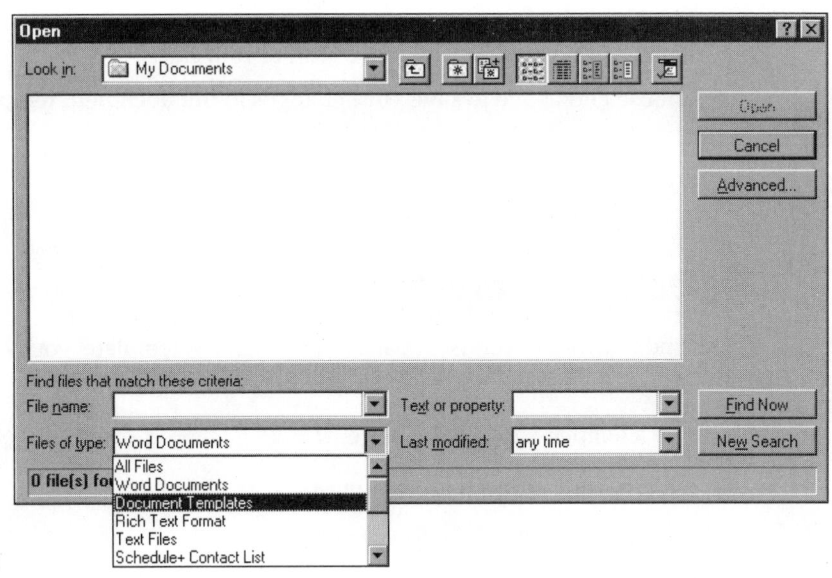

Figure 3-14: The Open dialog box.

4. **Click the template you want to modify and then Open.**

   You may have to search for the templates, which are usually stored in the C:\MSOffice\Templates directory. Word displays your chosen document template, as shown in Figure 3-15.

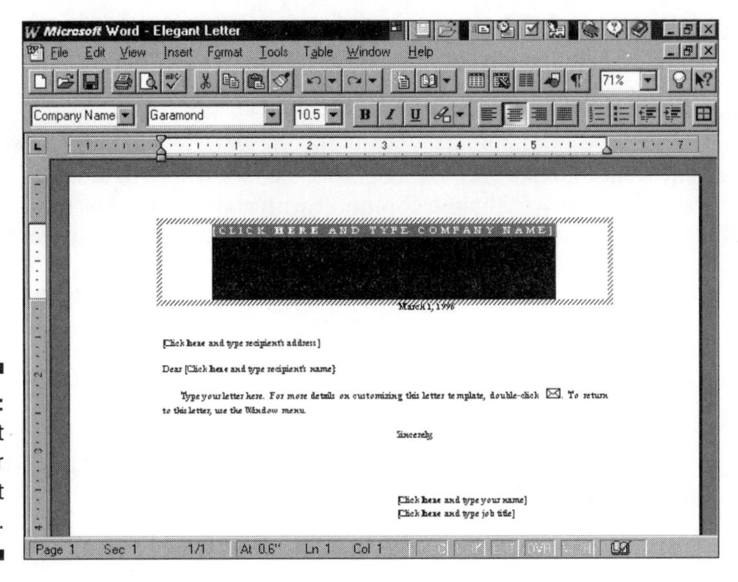

Figure 3-15: The Elegant Letter document template.

5. **Click the style you want to modify and change any settings you want, such as paragraph indentation, font, or font size.**
6. **Choose File⇨Save to save your changes in the document template.**

If you choose File⇨Save As in step 6, you can create a new template, based on the original one, without changing the original template.

Deleting a template

If you find that you never use a particular document template, you can wipe it out and save a minuscule amount of hard disk space in the process.

To delete a template, follow these steps:

1. **Click the Start button on the Windows 95 taskbar.**
2. **Choose Programs⇨Windows Explorer.**
3. **Click the document templates you want to delete and press Delete.**

   You may have to dig through various directories, such as C:\MSOffice\Templates\Memos, to find the template. A Confirm File Delete dialog box appears after you press Delete.
4. **Click Yes.**

Changing the location of your templates

Microsoft Office normally stores your document templates in a default directory, such as C:\MSOffice\Templates. If this method lives up to your idea of freedom of choice, then dictatorships are probably for you. For the rest of you, though, who may want to make your own decisions about where to store document templates (in case you share a computer with someone and want to keep your templates separate), you can choose any drive or directory you want.

To change the directory in which Microsoft Office stores your templates, follow these steps:

1. **Choose Tools⇨Options.**

   The Options dialog box appears.
2. **Click the File Locations tab and highlight User Templates, as shown in Figure 3-16.**

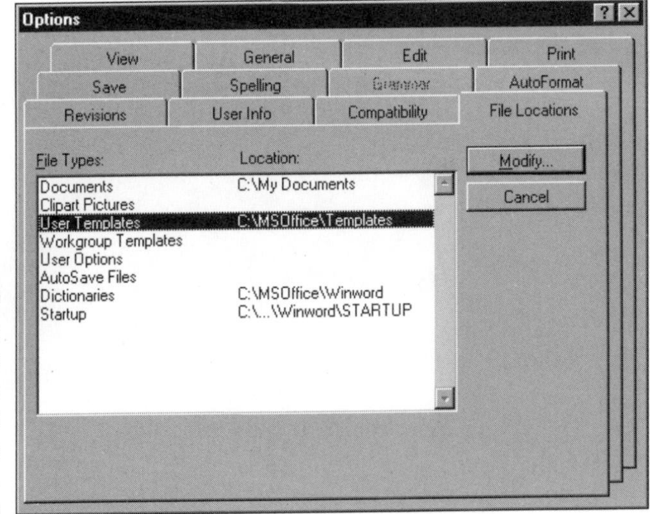

Figure 3-16: The File Locations tab in the Options dialog box.

3. Click Modify.

The Modify Location dialog box appears, as shown in Figure 3-17.

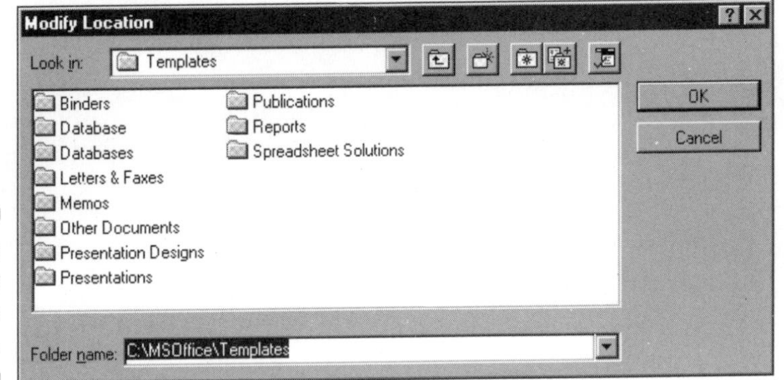

Figure 3-17: The Modify Location dialog box.

4. Click the new directory in which you want to store your document templates and click OK.

5. Click Close.

If you change the directory in which you store your Word document templates, you also change the directory in which Microsoft Office looks for Excel, PowerPoint, and Office templates and binders.

Chapter 4

Making Your Own Forms

In This Chapter

- Filling in the blanks with a form template
- Making your forms more visually pleasing
- Giving users the opportunity to fill out forms online
- Distributing your online forms to others

In addition to letting you create letters, memos, business reports, and other boring documents, Word lets you create forms. Rather than create a form on your computer, print it, and force someone to use the archaic method of using a pen or pencil to fill it out, Word lets you create a form so that someone can complete it electronically on a computer screen. That way, you don't have to kill a tree in order to print your form on paper (a form that someone will probably just throw out anyway).

Creating a Form Template

Everyone has seen a tax form or an employment application form. A *form* simply provides blank spaces on which you fill in information, such as your name, the date, your telephone number, or whom to contact in case you have a terrible accident at work.

You can create two types of forms:

- Printed forms
- Online forms

Printed forms involve nothing fancier than creating a form in Word and then printing it for someone else to fill out. If all you want to do is create paper forms, you can stop reading this chapter and just use a typewriter and a photocopying machine to make all your forms instead.

Online forms represent a futuristic fantasy in which we have a truly paperless office (either because society wants to conserve natural resources or because society has already plowed over all the rain forests and no paper is left anyway). With an online form, people sit at a computer and fill out your form by using a keyboard and a mouse.

Because an online form is a special Word document, you may have to create a form template before you can create a form document. After you create a form template, you can create your online forms for people to fill out.

Every time you want someone to fill out your online form, you have to create a new document based on your form template. (That's why you need a form template: If you just created a form and had someone fill it out online, you would have to create a new blank form all over again for someone else to fill out.)

A *document* is a file that contains your text. A *template* is a file that defines the format for any text that appears in your document. To find out more about the wonders of templates, see Chapter 3.

To create a form template, follow these steps:

1. **Choose Section⇨View Outside.**

   Skip this step if you're using Word as a separate program.

2. **Choose File⇨New.**

   The New dialog box appears, as shown in Figure 4-1.

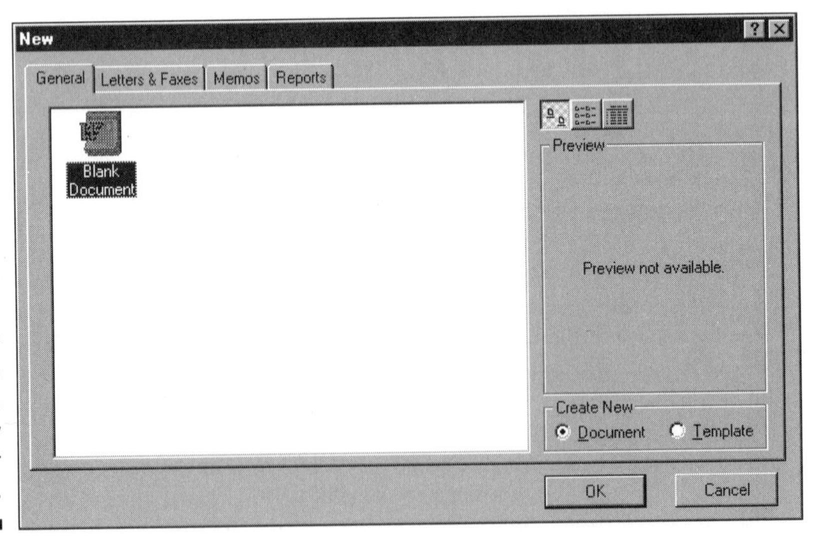

Figure 4-1: The New dialog box, waiting for you to create a new document or template.

3. **Click the Template radio button in the Create New group and then click OK.**

4. **Choose File⇨Save or press Ctrl+S.**

   The Save As dialog box appears.

5. **Type a name for your form template (such as Tax Form, Invoice, or Job Application) and then click Save.**

   At this point, your form template doesn't do anything until you design the text and graphics you want to display.

Designing Pretty Forms

After you create a form template, you have to design the form that people will see and admire for generations to come. Most forms contain one or more of the following elements:

- **Text:** "Name" or "Ship to," for example
- **Lines:** Show someone where to write or just make your form look nice
- **Graphics:** A company logo, for example
- **Fields:** Enables someone to fill out your form online

The Forms toolbar contains funny-looking buttons that let you easily design a form. To display the Forms toolbar, follow these steps:

1. **Choose View⇨Toolbars.**

   The Toolbars dialog box appears, as shown in Figure 4-2.

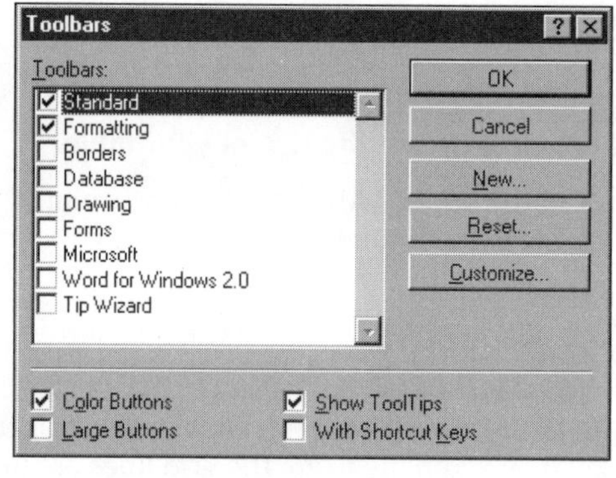

Figure 4-2: In the Toolbars dialog box, you can choose to hide or display your toolbars.

2. **Click the Forms check box so that a check mark appears and then click OK.**

   The Forms toolbar appears, as shown in Figure 4-3.

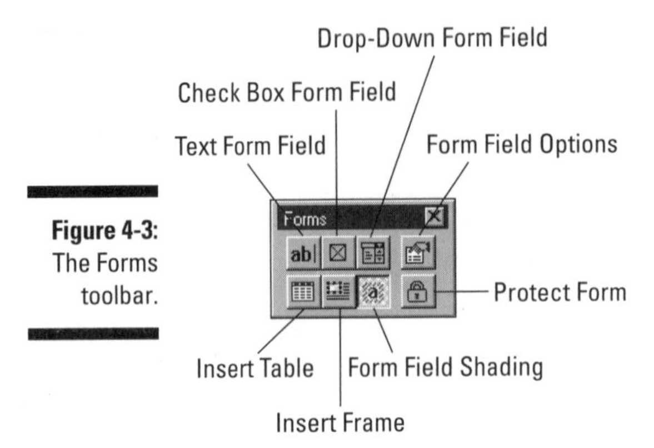

Figure 4-3: The Forms toolbar.

Before you create a form in Word, draw the form on paper. That way, you can quickly design your form by using paper and pencil. (You'll have to wing it because *Paper-and-Pencil Drawings For Dummies* has yet to be published.) After you know which type of information you want on your form, you can begin struggling with the process of designing your form in Word.

Drawing tables on a form

The basic element for designing a form is the table, which lets you organize text, graphics, and form fields in convenient rows and columns. After you create one or more tables on your form, you can begin inserting text, graphics, and form fields (as shown in Figure 4-4).

To draw a table on your form, follow these steps:

1. **Click the Insert Table button on the Forms toolbar.**

   A grid appears, as shown in Figure 4-5.

2. **Click one of the grid boxes to define the size of your table.**

   If you click the grid box in the second row and the third column, for example, you create a table two columns wide and three columns long.

3. **Release the mouse button.**

   Word draws your table on the form.

The grid lines in a table appear only when you're creating or editing a form. If you print the form or display it as an online form, the grid lines are invisible.

Stretching or shrinking your table

Word has no sense of aesthetics, which means that, after you create a table, it probably won't be the exact size you want. You then have to stretch or shrink its width and height to your liking.

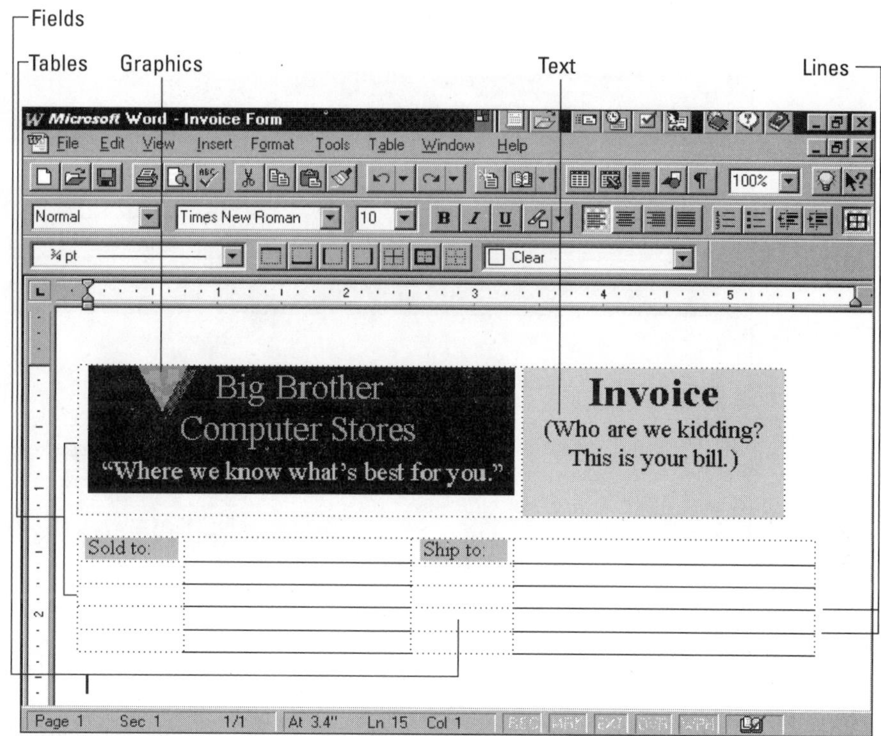

Figure 4-4: A typical form divided into tables.

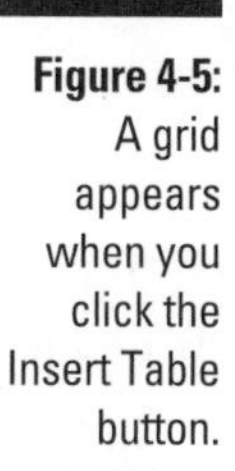

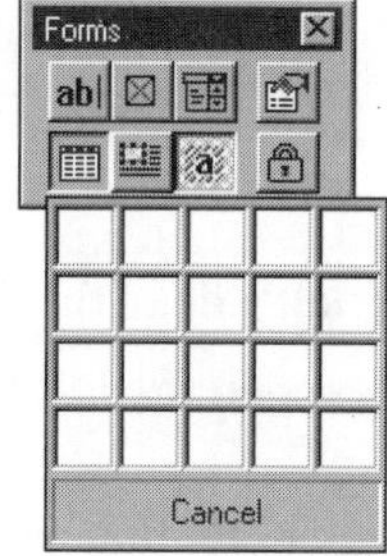

Figure 4-5: A grid appears when you click the Insert Table button.

To change the width of your table columns, follow these steps:

1. **Move the mouse pointer directly over any vertical grid line until the mouse pointer turns into two parallel lines with left- and right-pointing arrows, as shown in Figure 4-6.**
2. **Hold down the left mouse button and drag the mouse right or left.**
3. **Let go of the mouse button when you're happy with the width of the table column.**

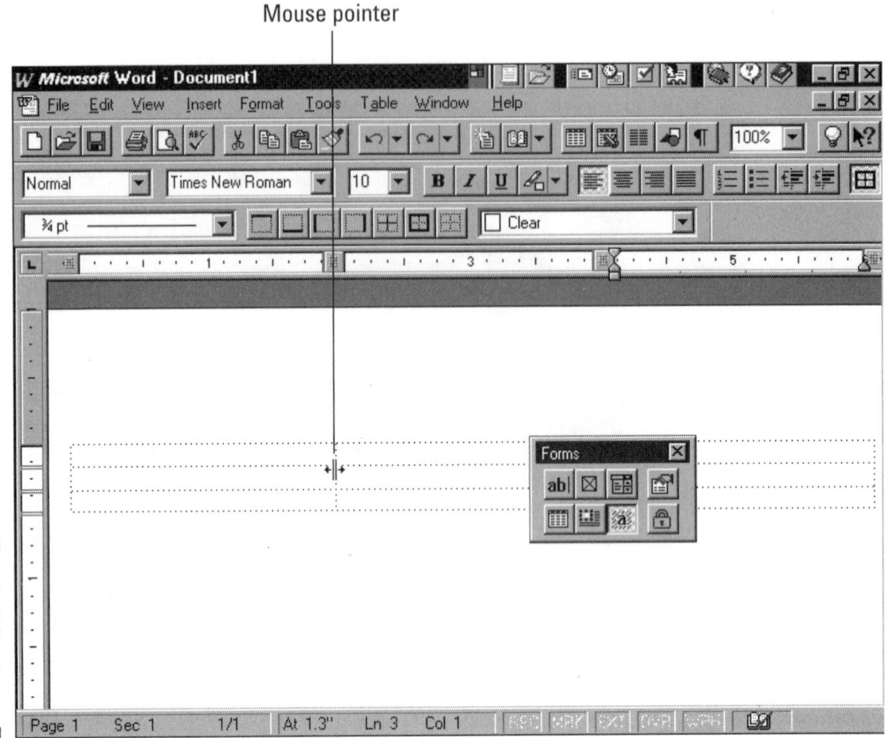

Figure 4-6: Changing the width of a table column.

If you want to change the height of individual rows in your table, follow these steps:

1. **Click in the row you want to adjust.**

   Double parallel lines appear on the ruler on the left side of the screen.

2. **Move the mouse pointer to the ruler that appears on the left side of your screen.**

3. **Move the mouse pointer over the double parallel line that represents the row you want to make taller or shorter.**

   The mouse pointer turns into an up- and down-pointing arrow.

4. **Hold down the left mouse button and drag the mouse up or down.**

5. **Release the mouse button when the row is the height you want.**

Deleting rows, columns, and entire tables

Like everything else in life, you may make a mistake and have to delete a row or column in your grid. Fortunately, Word lets you selectively delete rows and columns. Or you can take out your aggressive tendencies and wipe out an entire table.

If you delete a row, column, or table, you also delete any text or graphics within that row, column, or table. If you accidentally delete a row, column, or table, you can undelete it by immediately pressing Ctrl+Z.

To delete a column, follow these steps:

1. **Click the column you want to delete.**
2. **Choose Table⇨Select Column.**

   Word highlights your chosen column.
3. **Press the right mouse button.**

   A pop-up menu appears, as shown in Figure 4-7.
4. **Choose Delete Columns.**

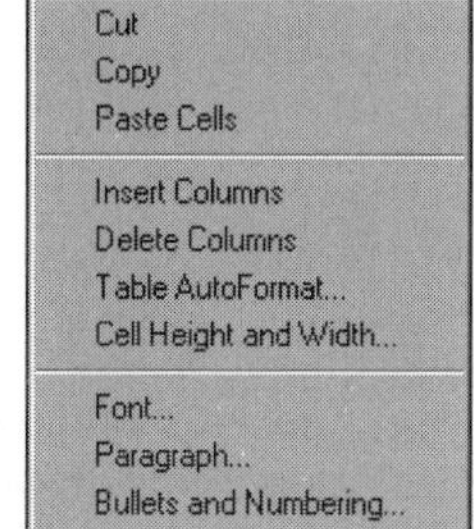

Figure 4-7: A pop-up menu.

To delete a row, follow these steps:

1. **Click the row you want to delete.**
2. **Choose Table⇨Select Row.**

   Word highlights your chosen row.
3. **Press the right mouse button.**

   A pop-up menu appears (refer to Figure 4-7).
4. **Choose Delete Rows.**

To delete an entire table, follow these steps:

1. **Click anywhere inside the table you want to delete.**
2. **Choose Table⇨Select Table.**

   Word highlights your entire table.
3. **Choose Edit⇨Cut or press Ctrl+X.**

   Word obliterates your entire table, right before your eyes.

Putting text on a form

This section describes some typical uses for text:

- As a label to identify a field, such as "Name," "Marital Status," or "How many years did you repeat the third grade?"
- For nonfunctional purposes, such as displaying "We are an equal opportunity employer" at the bottom of your form

To add text to a form, follow these simple steps (which any moron — even your boss — can understand): Click the grid box in which you want the text to appear, and then type your text.

Text can appear on a form by itself or inside a grid box in a table. Which method should you use? If you want to align text, it's easier to put your text in a table (grid box). If you don't need to align your text in any particular way, it's easier just to put it on a form without first creating a table to hold it.

Placing pretty graphics on a form

Graphics usually serve no functional purpose other than to make a form look good. Common uses for graphics include displaying a company logo or decorative picture that makes your form look less like the intimidating corporate piece of paper it really is.

To add graphics created by another program to a form, follow these steps:

1. **Click the form at the place where you want the picture to appear (inside a grid box in a table, for example).**
2. **Choose Insert⇨Picture.**

   The Insert Picture dialog box is displayed. Using this box, you can choose a picture stored anywhere on your computer.
3. **Click the picture you want to add and click OK.**

If you feel artistic, you can draw an image from within Word. To draw an image, follow these steps:

1. **Choose View⇨Toolbars.**

   The Toolbars dialog box appears (refer to Figure 4-2).
2. **Click the Drawing check box so that a check mark appears and then click OK.**

   The Drawing toolbar (see Figure 4-8) appears at the bottom of your screen.

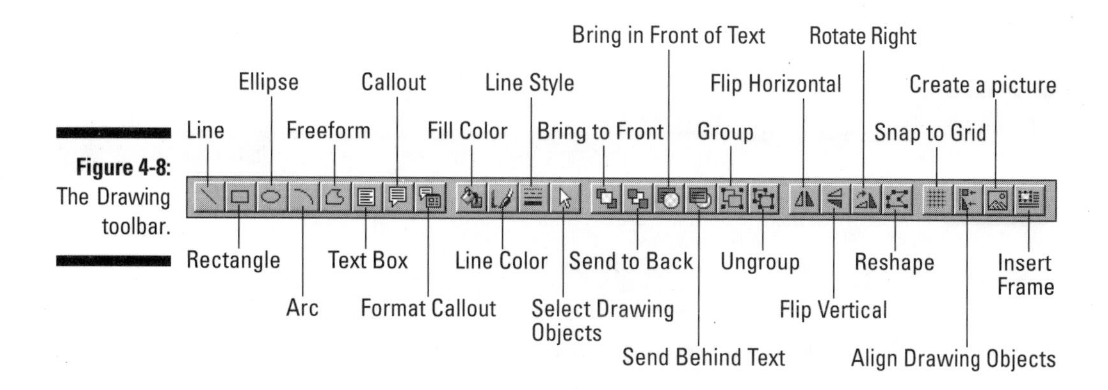

Figure 4-8: The Drawing toolbar.

3. **On the Drawing toolbar, click the tool you want to use.**
4. **Click the grid box in which you want to draw your image, and then draw away (good luck!).**

Adding borders and shading to your grid

When you create a grid (a table), its outline appears as a dotted line. This dotted line never appears when you print your form; it exists solely to help you design your form.

To make parts of your grid visible, you can draw borders (to create a blank line for someone to fill out, such as Name: __________) or add shading to make certain parts of your form easier to read.

You can create a "fill-in-the-blank" line in two ways:

- Choose a bottom border for a grid box.
- Type the underscore (_) key in a grid box. (It's the key between the 0 and the = keys on your keyboard.)

Choose a bottom border if you want a line to extend the width of the grid column. Type a line if you don't want a line to extend the entire width of the grid column.

To draw borders on your grid, follow these steps:

1. **Choose View⇨Toolbars.**

   The Toolbars dialog box appears (refer to Figure 4-2).

2. **Click the Borders check box so that a check mark appears and then click OK.**

   The Borders toolbar (see Figure 4-9) appears in the top part of your screen.

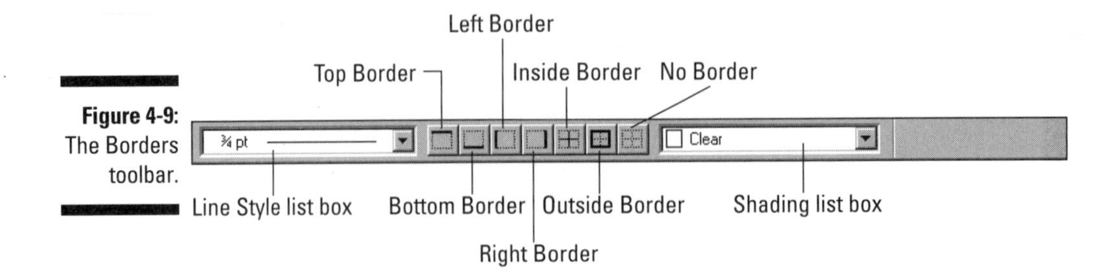

Figure 4-9: The Borders toolbar.

3. **Click the grid box to which you want to add a border.**
4. **Click one of the following buttons on the Borders toolbar:**
   - **Top Border**
   - **Bottom Border**
   - **Left Border**
   - **Right Border**
   - **Inside Border**
   - **Outside Border**

   Word then cheerfully draws your chosen border.

If you've drawn a grid and want to draw lines on all the grid lines, simply select the entire grid and then click the Outside Border and Inside Border buttons on the Borders toolbar.

Creating Online Forms with Form Fields

When you create an online form that someone can fill out by using a computer (as opposed to writing answers on a printed form), you have to use form fields. A *form field* simply displays on-screen a "fill-in-the-blank" space in which someone can type an answer or choose from a list of answers (such as Male or Female in response to a blank asking for "Gender"). Form fields provide the only area in which someone can type anything on your online form.

You can add three types of form fields to your form:

- Text
- Check box
- Drop-down

No matter which type of form field you add, you probably have to type some descriptive text next to it, just so that people know which type of information the form field expects, such as "Whom to contact in case of an emergency."

Making a text form field

Text form fields can hold text, such as names; numbers, such as ages; dates, such as 05/06/96; or times, such as 12:34. After you know which type of information you want your text form field to display, you can also define these items:

- The maximum length of text to display
- Any default text you want to display automatically
- The format of your text

To put a text form field on a form, follow these steps:

1. **Click the spot where you want the text form field to appear (inside a grid box, for example).**
2. **Click the Text Form Field button on the Forms toolbar.**

   Word immediately draws your text form field as a gray rectangle, as shown in Figure 4-10.
3. **Click the Form Field Options button on the Forms toolbar.**

   The Text Form Field Options dialog box appears, as shown in Figure 4-11.
4. **Click the Type list box and choose the type of text you want to display:**
   - Regular text
   - Number
   - Date
   - Current date
   - Current time
   - Calculation
5. **Click the Maximum Length box and then choose a length.**
6. **Click the Default list box and then type the text you want to appear automatically in the text form field.**
7. **Click the Format list box and choose a format in which to display your text.**
8. **Click OK.**

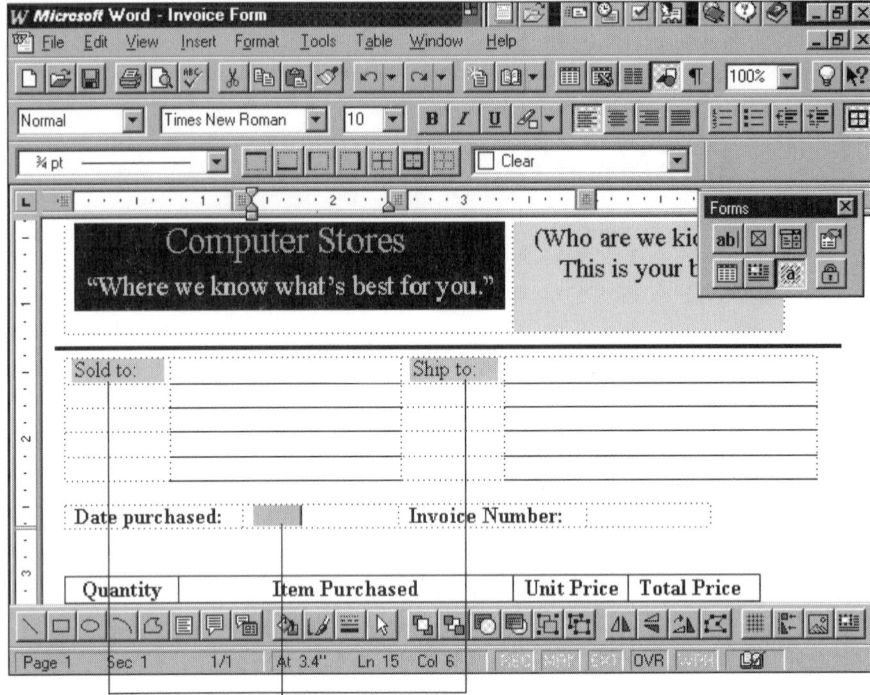

Figure 4-10: Placing a text form field.

Text Form Field Options

Type: Regular Text
Default Text:
Maximum Length: Unlimited
Text Format:
Run Macro On
Entry:
Exit:
Field Settings
Bookmark: Text2
Fill-in Enabled
OK
Cancel
Add Help Text...

Figure 4-11: Choosing the type of text you want to display.

Using a check box form field

Check box form fields are used for Yes or No responses, such as "Are you available for travel?" or "Do you object to drug testing?" To add a check box form field to your form, complete the following steps:

1. **Click the spot where you want the check box form field to appear (inside a grid box, for example).**

2. **Click the Check Box Form Field button on the Forms toolbar.**

   Word immediately draws your check box form field as a small box, as shown in Figure 4-12.

3. **Type any descriptive next to the check box form field.**
4. **Click the check box and then the Form Field Options button on the Forms toolbar.**

   The Check Box Form Field Options dialog box appears, as shown in Figure 4-13.

5. **Click one of the following radio buttons:**
   - **Exactly:** Lets you choose a point size if you want to change the size of your check box
   - **Auto:** Lets Word choose the size of your check box
6. **Click one of the following radio buttons:**
   - Not Checked
   - Checked
7. **Click OK.**

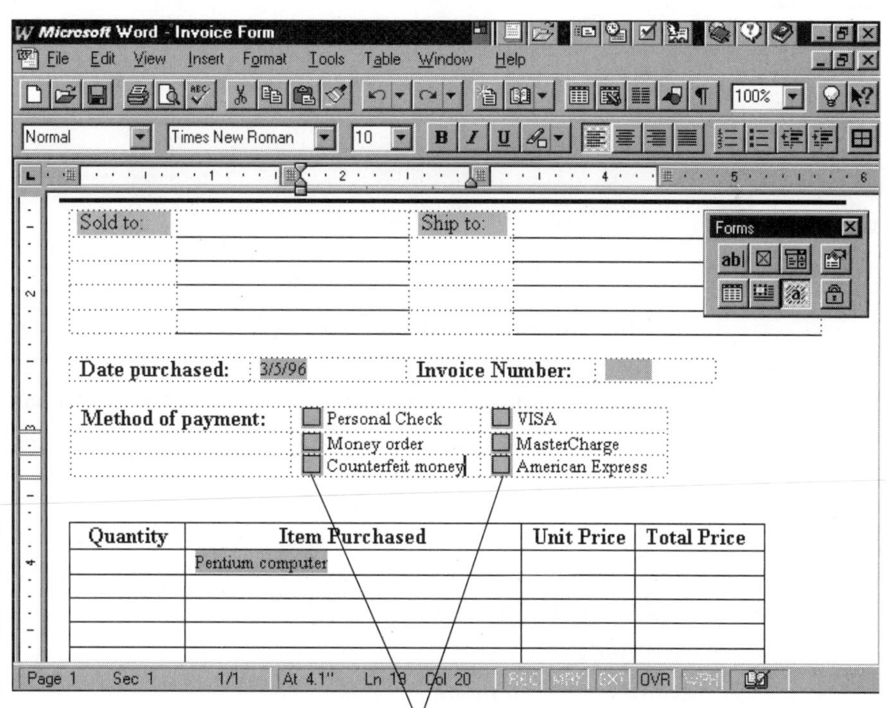

Figure 4-12: Placing a check box form field.

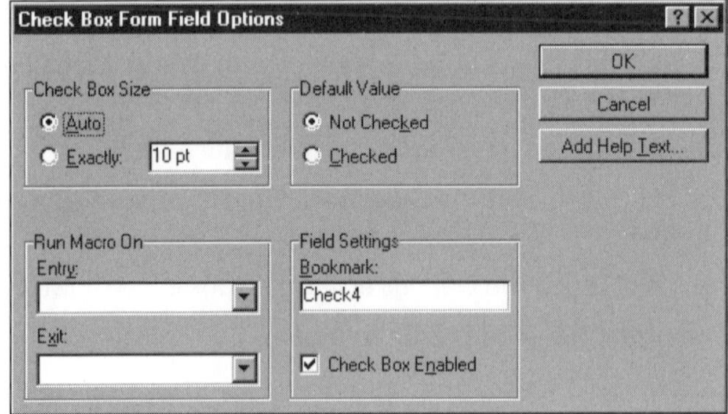

Figure 4-13: Changing the options for your check box form fields.

Creating a drop-down form field

Drop-down form fields let users choose from a list of acceptable answers. For example, you may have a question that asks for marital status and a drop-down form field that offers four choices, as shown in Figure 4-14.

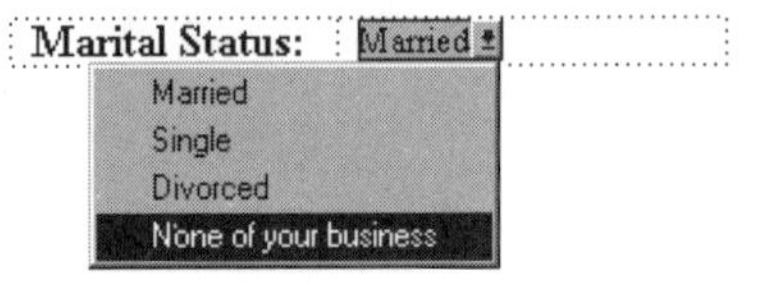

Figure 4-14: What a drop-down form field looks like.

To create a drop-down form field, follow these steps:

1. **Click the spot where you want the check box form field to appear (inside a grid box, for example).**
2. **Click the drop-down Form Field button on the Forms toolbar.**

   Word immediately draws your drop-down form field as a gray rectangle.
3. **Click the Form Field Options button on the Forms toolbar.**

   The Drop-Down Form Field Options dialog box appears, as shown in Figure 4-15.
4. **In the Drop-Down Item box, type an item you want to appear in the drop-down form field.**
5. **Click Add.**

   Word displays your item in the Items in Drop-Down List box.

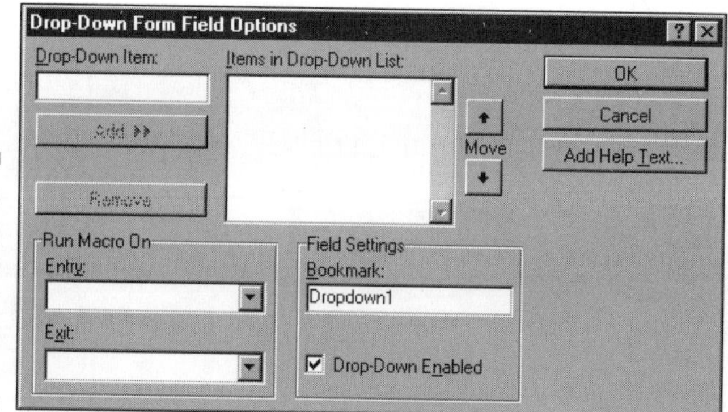

Figure 4-15: Changing the options for your drop-down form fields.

6. **Repeat steps 4 and 5 until you've typed all the items you want to appear in your drop-down form field.**

   In case you add an item you later want to remove, click that item and click Remove.

7. **Click OK.**

Adding Online Help

After carefully designing your form and placing your text, check box, or drop-down form fields in the most aesthetically pleasing positions possible, you're almost ready to use your form template to create online forms.

After you design your form, however, you may want to add some help prompts to assist any clueless users. If a user has no idea which type of information a particular text form field should contain, for example, he or she can press F1 to make your online form display an explanation on the status bar at the bottom of the screen or in a dialog box, as shown in Figure 4-16.

To create online help for your form fields, follow these steps:

1. **Click the form field to which you want to add online help.**
2. **Click the Form Field Options button on the Forms toolbar.**

   The Form Field Options dialog box appears.

3. **Click Add Help Text.**

   The Form Field Help Text dialog box appears, as shown in Figure 4-17.

4. **Click the Status Bar tab and then the Type Your Own radio button.**
5. **Type any helpful suggestions you want to appear on the status bar.**

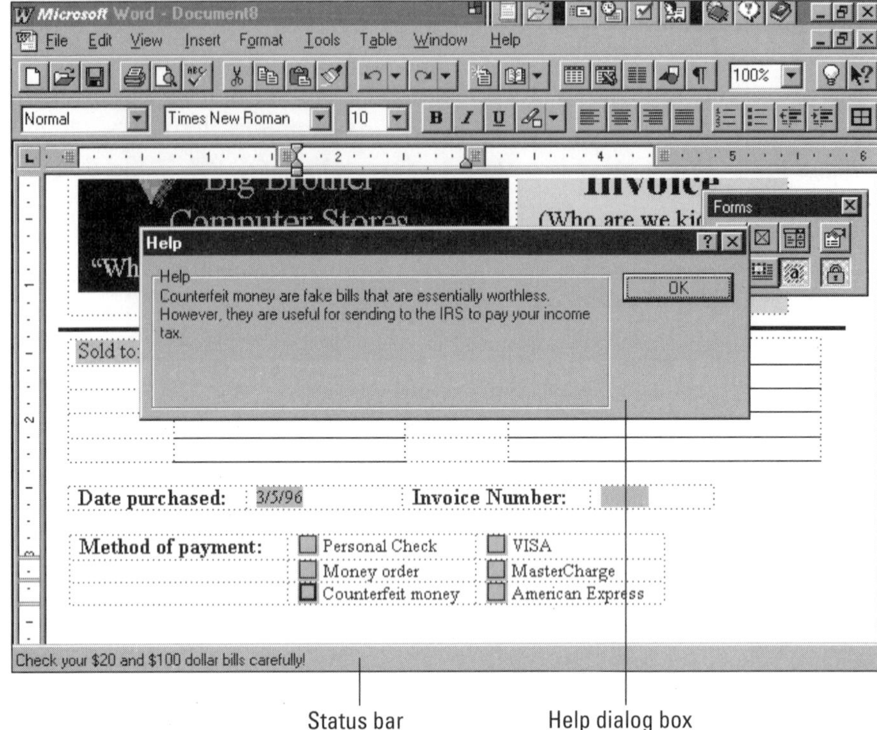

Figure 4-16: Displaying help by using the status bar and a pop-up dialog box.

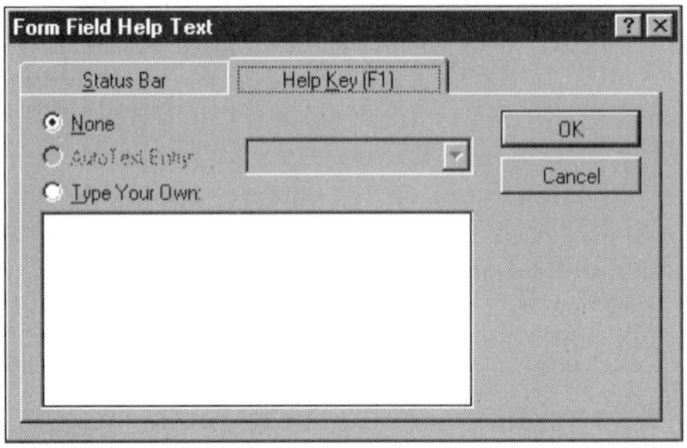

Form Field Help Text

Status Bar | Help Key (F1)

None

AutoText Entry:

Type Your Own:

OK

Cancel

Figure 4-17: Type some fancy explanations for using your forms.

6. **Click the Help Key (F1) tab and then the Type Your Own radio button.**
7. **Type any helpful suggestions you want to appear in the help dialog box if the user presses F1.**
8. **Click OK twice.**

Sharing Your Online Forms

After you've spent countless hours designing your form to perfection, you'll eventually want to distribute it to others so that they can use it too. When you're absolutely sure that your form template is finished, it's time to save and protect your form template.

Protecting your form template means that, when you create a document (online form) based on your form template, the document lets users type information only in form fields and nowhere else.

Saving and protecting your precious form templates

To save and protect a form template, follow these steps:

1. **Click the Protect Form button on the Forms toolbar.**
2. **Choose File⇨Save, or press Ctrl+S.**
3. **Choose File⇨Close.**

Creating an online form from a form template

After you save and protect a form template, you can create your online forms based on your form template.

Every time you create an online form based on a form template, you're creating a brand-new Word document. The form template never changes, no matter how many online forms you may create from it. To find out more about templates, see Chapter 3.

To create an online form based on a form template, follow these steps:

1. **Choose Section⇨View Outside.**

   Skip this step if you're using Word as a separate program.
2. **Choose File⇨New.**

   The New dialog box appears.
3. **Click the form template you want to use and then click OK.**

   Word displays your form.

Filling out an online form

An online form looks exactly like a form template. The main difference is that you can't move the cursor anywhere except in different form fields. Although you can use a mouse to fill out an online form, you eventually have to use the keyboard to type certain information, such as a name, address, or naughty word that will get you trouble if you send it over the Internet.

In case you don't like using your mouse, Table 4-1 lists the keystroke commands you can use to navigate around an online form.

Table 4-1 Keystroke Commands for Navigating around an Online Form

Keystroke Command	*What It Does*
Down arrow or Tab	Moves the cursor to the next form field
Up arrow or Shift+Tab	Moves the cursor to the preceding form field
Spacebar or X	Selects (or deselects) a check box form field
F4 or Alt+down arrow	Displays items in a drop-down form field
F1	Displays a Help dialog box (if you created text for it)

For users to be able to view and fill out an online form, they must use Word to load the online form. If they don't have Word, they can't view or fill out your online form — so there!

Chapter 5

Creating an Index and Table of Contents

In This Chapter

- Organizing your ideas in an index
- Helping readers find topics by creating a table of contents
- Organizing multiple documents with a master document

Because writing is a pain in the neck for most people, anything that can make the job easier is welcome. Short of doing all the writing for you, Microsoft Word does the next best thing — it provides special features to help you create an index and a table of contents (almost) automatically.

After all, which would you rather do: Write a 300-page document and go back — page by page — to create a table of contents and index yourself or have Word create the table of contents and index for you as you write?

If you prefer to let Word do the difficult work for you, continue reading. If you prefer to do everything yourself, why did you bother getting a computer?

Making Your Very Own Index

An *index* simply organizes your document's main ideas by page number. That way, people can find quickly what they're looking for without having to read your entire document. Because most people don't like reading anyway, indexes can be a great way to encourage people to at least browse through your text (and maybe even increase our national literacy rate in the process).

To create an index, you must decide which words or topics you want to include in your index, the page numbers on which each word or topic appears, and in which visually pleasing format to organize your index.

Indexing a book or document is an art in itself. Although Word can help make the task of indexing easier, it can't help you decide which words, topics, or synonyms you want to index.

Selecting words and individual page numbers

Most indexes list topics and individual page numbers, as shown here:

> Stinger hand-held missile, 49

In this example, "Stinger hand-held missile" is the index entry, and "49" is the page number on which it appears.

To mark words for an index, follow these steps:

1. **Highlight the word or words you want to appear in your index.**
2. **Press Alt+Shift+X.**

   A Mark Index Entry dialog box appears, as shown in Figure 5-1. Your highlighted word or words appear in the Main Entry box.
3. **Edit the word or words in the Main Entry box so that they look the way you want in your index.**
4. **In the Subentry box, type any index subentries you want to include.**
5. **Click one of these radio buttons:**
   - **Cross-reference:** Directs readers to a related index entry
   - **Current Page:** Lists the current page for your index entry
6. **Click Mark.**

   Word marks your selected word or words by inserting an index entry next to them, as shown in Figure 5-2.

Figure 5-1: Highlighting words to appear in your index.

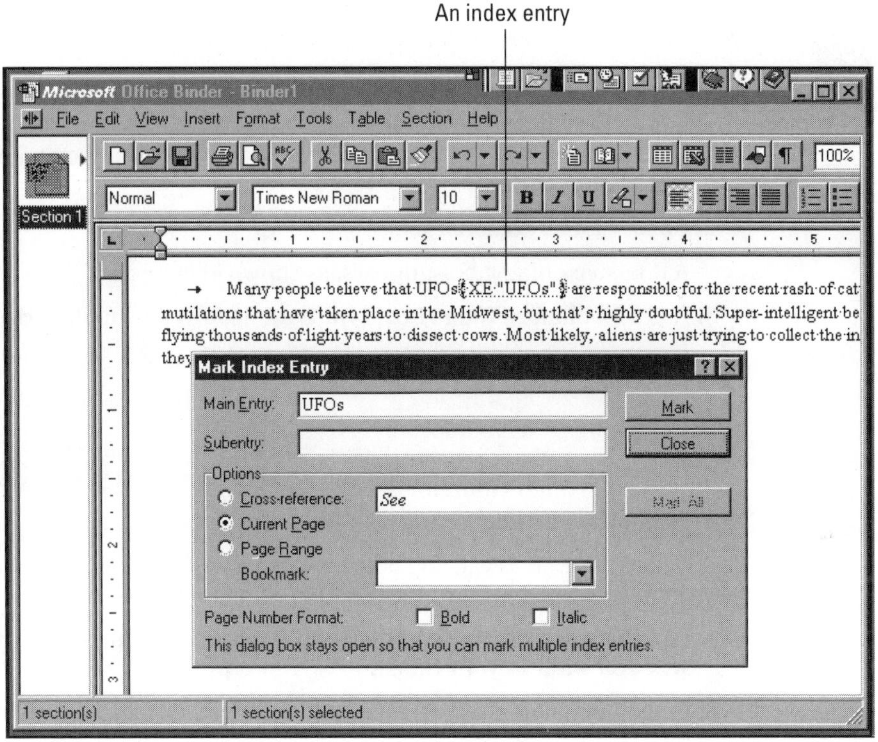

An index entry

Figure 5-2: Word inserts an index entry next to your chosen index word or words.

7. **Repeat steps 1 through 6 until you've marked all the words you want to appear in your index.**
8. **Click Close.**

Marking words and page ranges for your index

Most of the time, the words you select for your index appear on a single page. Sometimes, however, an index topic may span two or more pages, Some index entries may occasionally span a range of pages, as shown in this example:

CIA, selling Stinger missiles illegally, 58-63

In this example, "CIA, selling Stinger missiles illegally" is the index entry, and "58-63" represents the page range in which users can find the index entry.

When you index a page range, you follow slightly different steps to include in your index your chosen index topic and its page range.

To mark words and page ranges for an index, follow these steps:

1. **Highlight the text (spanning one or more pages) that you want to include in your index.**
2. **Choose Edit⇨Bookmark.**

   A Bookmark dialog box appears, as shown in Figure 5-3.
3. **In the Bookmark Name box, type a name for your bookmark.**

   Your bookmark name must be a single word, so be creative and make it descriptive, too.
4. **Click Add.**
5. **Highlight the word or words you want to appear in your index.**
6. **Press Alt+Shift+X.**

   A Mark Index Entry dialog box appears (refer to Figure 5-1). Your highlighted word or words appear in the Main Entry box.
7. **Edit the word or words in the Main Entry box so that they appear the way you want in your index.**
8. **In the Subentry box, type any index subentries you want to include.**
9. **Click the Page Range option button.**
10. **Click the Bookmark list box, and choose the bookmark name you created in step 3.**
11. **Click Mark.**

    Word marks your selected word or words by inserting an index entry next to them.

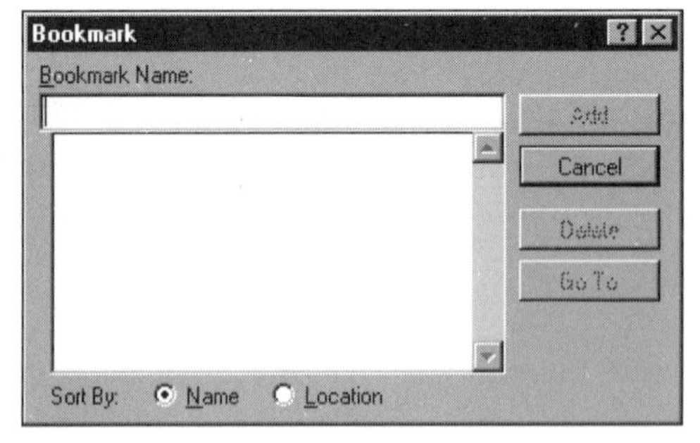

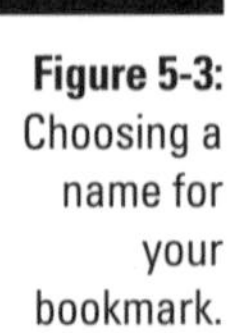

Figure 5-3: Choosing a name for your bookmark.

12. **Repeat steps 1 through 11 until you've marked all the words you want to appear in your index.**
13. **Click Close.**

Displaying your index in print

Every time you mark a word or words to appear in your index, Word stores the words in its tiny, electronic brain. When you finally choose all your index entries, you're ready to display the index in print so that you can take a look at it.

Word wouldn't seem like a real program, of course, if it didn't offer you a billion different options that most people never use. When you create an index, Word bombards you with multiple ways to guarantee that your index looks nice.

Before you can create an index, you have to mark at least one word you want to include in your index.

This list shows some of the available options that affect the look of your index:

- Index format
- Alignment of page numbers
- Number of columns used

The index format simply lets you choose the overall look of your index, such as the fonts used for the letter headings.

The alignment of page numbers means that Word can display page numbers next to an index entry (such as "Dog food, 4"), or it can align all page numbers on the right side of the page.

The number of columns is practically self-explanatory. Choosing two columns displays your index on a single page in two columns, and choosing three columns displays your index in three columns.

To choose the appearance of an index, follow these steps:

1. **Move the cursor to the spot where you want your index to appear.**
2. **Choose Insert⇨Index and Tables.**

   An Index and Tables dialog box appears, as shown in Figure 5-4.
3. **Click the Index tab.**

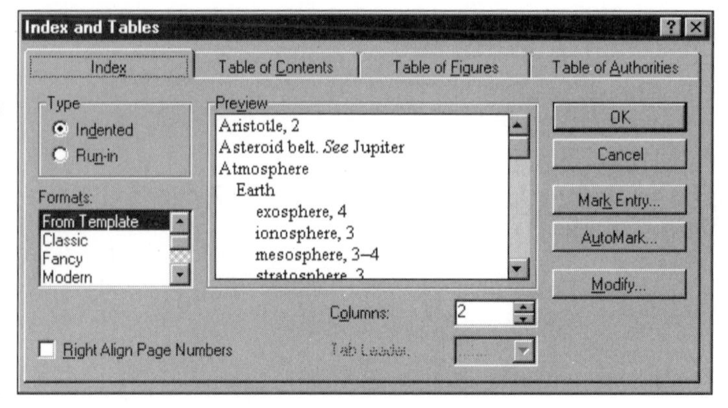

Figure 5-4: Using the Index and Tables dialog box to choose the appearance of an index.

4. **In the Formats list box, click the format you want (Modern or Bulleted, for example).**

   In the Preview box, Word shows you what your index will look like.

5. **Click either the Indented or Run-in radio button in the Type group.**
6. **If you want to right-align your index page numbers, click the Right Align Page Numbers check box.**
7. **Click the Columns list box, and choose the number of columns you want.**
8. **Click the Tab Leader box, and choose a tab leader.**

   Note: If you don't choose to right-align your page numbers, the Tab Leader box appears dimmed.

9. **Click OK.**

You can create an index only in the same document that contains the word or words you select to appear in your index. After Word creates your index and you're absolutely sure that none of the index entries will change, you can cut the index and paste it into a new document.

Creating an index (almost) automatically

Because computers are supposed to make our lives easier, you may be happy to know that Word can create an index almost automatically, with just a little help from you. Before Word can perform its automatic indexing magic for you, you must first create a separate file that contains two lists of words.

One list of words must contain the entries you want to appear in your index. The second list of words must contain the words stored in your Word document that you want to mark as an index entry.

You might have these two lists, for example:

CIA	Central Intelligence Agency
DIA	Defense Intelligence Agency
EIEIO	Farmer's Intelligence Agency
polling people	Gathering information
psoriasis	Skin irritation

Because the words you type in both lists are case sensitive, if Word finds the string "Polling people," it doesn't store it in the index. Word stores that string in your index only if it finds it typed exactly as "polling people" (in lowercase letters).

Using the preceding list as a guideline, Word searches through your document for all occurrences of the words that appear in the list on the left. Whenever Word finds the phrase "polling people," for example, it looks in the list on the right to determine how to store this entry in your index.

Assuming that "CIA" appears on pages 59–65, "DIA" appears on page 90, "EIEIO" appears on page 493, "polling people" appears on pages 78 and 90, and "psoriasis" appears on page 746, Word creates the following index for you:

Central Intelligence Agency, 59–65

Defense Intelligence Agency, 90

Farmer's Intelligence Agency, 493

Gathering information, 78, 90

Skin irritation, 746

To create a list of words so that Word knows what to look for in your document and how to store those words in your index, follow these steps:

1. **Choose File⇨New.**

   (If you're using Word within a binder, choose Section⇨Add, choose Word document, click OK, and then choose Section⇨View Outside.)

   Word displays your new blank document.

2. **Choose Table⇨Insert Table.**

   An Insert Table dialog box appears. Make sure that the dialog box displays the settings for creating a table composed of two columns and two rows.

3. **Click OK.**

   Word creates a table that consists of two rows and two columns.

4. **In the left column, type the word or words** (CIA, **for example) you want Word to search for in your document.**

5. **In the right column in the same row, type the way you want this word or words to appear in your index** (Central Intelligence Agency, **for example).**

6. **Repeat steps 4 and 5 until you create a list that contains all the words you want Word to search for and store in your index.**

   You may have to add rows as necessary by choosing Table⇨Insert Rows.

7. **Choose File⇨Save. (If you're viewing Word outside of a binder, choose File⇨Save Copy As.)**

   A Save As dialog box appears.

8. **Type a name for your document in the File name box, and then click Save.**

9. **Switch to the document that contains the words you want to index.**

10. **Choose Insert⇨Index and Tables.**

    An Index and Tables dialog box appears (refer to Figure 5-4).

11. **Click the Index tab.**

12. **Click AutoMark.**

    An Open Index AutoMark File dialog box appears, as shown in Figure 5-5.

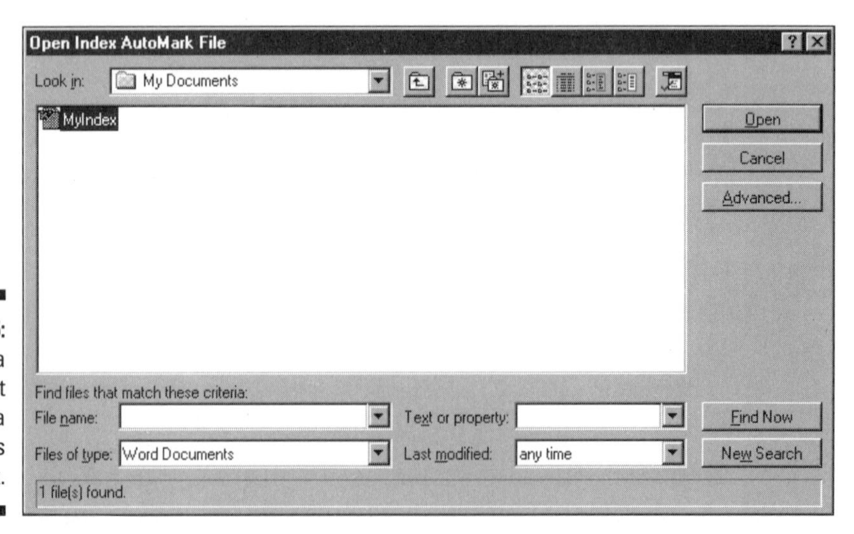

Figure 5-5: Opening a file that contains a list of words to index.

13. **Click the Word document that contains your two lists of words, and then click Open.**

    Word silently marks all your selected words.

14. **Move the cursor to the spot where you want the index to appear.**
15. **Choose Insert⇨Index and Tables.**

    The Index and Tables dialog box appears (refer to Figure 5-4).

16. **Make any changes to the format of your index, and click OK when you're done.**

    Word magically displays your automatically created index.

Updating your index

Ideally, you should create your index last, after you already know that you won't be changing your text. Because human beings don't always like being told what they can do and when they can do it, Word can accommodate those people who insist on changing their text after they've already created an index. Whenever you create an index, you can always update it if you decide later that you want to add a word to your index.

To update an index, follow these steps:

1. **Highlight the word or words you want to add to your index.**
2. **Press Alt+Shift+X.**

   A Mark Index Entry dialog box appears (refer to Figure 5-1).

3. **Click Mark.**
4. **Repeat steps 1 through 3 for every word you want to add to your index.**
5. **Click Close.**
6. **Choose Insert⇨Index and Tables.**

   The Index and Tables dialog box appears (refer to Figure 5-4).

7. **Click the Index tab.**
8. **Click OK.**

   A dialog box appears and asks whether you want to replace your selected index.

9. **Click Yes.**

   Word updates your indexes. Aren't computers wonderful?

Word can create an index based on words stored in only one document. If you want to create an index based on words stored in separate documents, you have to create a master document, discussed later in this chapter, in the section "Working with Master Documents."

Creating a Table of Contents

An index lets readers quickly find separate topics that may be scattered throughout a large document, such as a book or magazine. A *table of contents,* however, lets your readers see which topics your book or document discusses. Like an index, a table of contents also lists page numbers so that readers can find quickly what they're looking for without having to read the entire manuscript.

Before you can create a table of contents, you must first create headings within your document (such as the heading for this section, "Creating a Table of Contents") and format them by using Word's style feature.

Using Word's built-in styles to format headings

To quickly format headings to create a table of contents, use the built-in styles Heading 1, Heading 2, and Heading 3, as shown in Figure 5-6.

To create a table of contents, follow these steps:

1. **Format all the document headings you want to include in your table of contents by using Heading 1, Heading 2, or Heading 3.**
2. **Place the cursor in the document where you want the table of contents to appear, such as at the beginning of your document.**
3. **Choose Insert⇨Index and Tables.**
4. **Click the Table of Contents tab to display the tab, as shown in Figure 5-7.**
5. **In the Formats list box, click the format you want, such as Modern or Fancy.**

   Word shows you in the Preview box what your table of contents will look like.

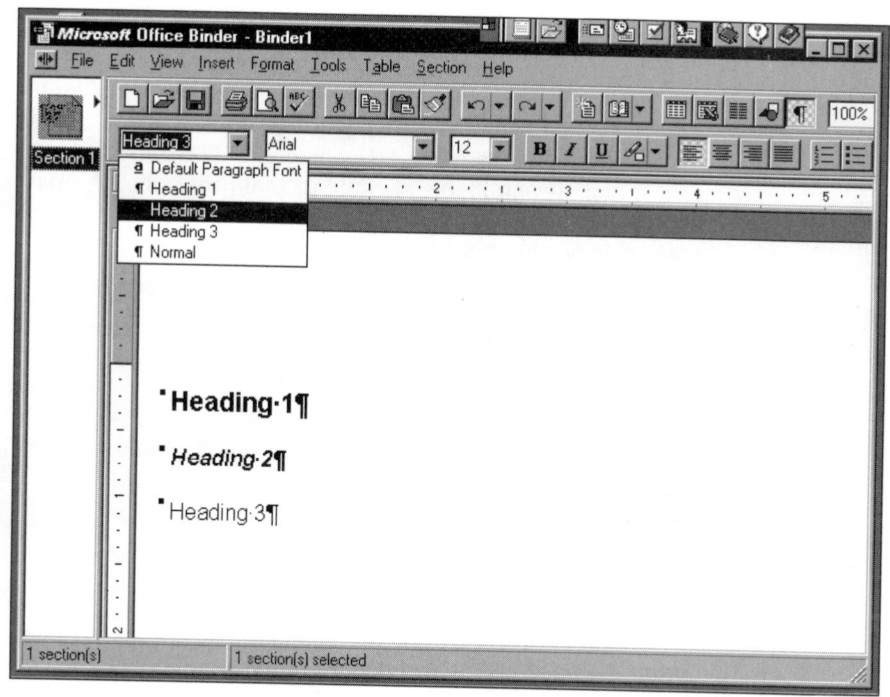

Figure 5-6: Heading styles are stored in the Style list box.

6. **If you want to show page numbers, click the Show Page Numbers check box.**

   Because you're working with the table of contents, this option really shouldn't be available, but Word wants to give you a choice anyway. After all, what good is a table of contents without page numbers?

7. **Click the Right Align Page Numbers check box if you want your index page numbers to be right-aligned on the page.**

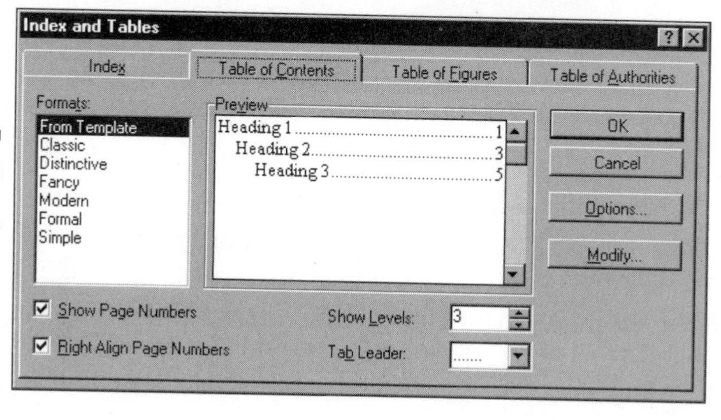

Figure 5-7: Defining a Table of Contents in the Index and Tables dialog box.

8. **Click the Show Levels list box, and choose how many levels you want to display.**

   Word gives you the option of creating a detailed table of contents or a more general one. For example, you may want to create a detailed table of contents using the Heading 1, Heading 2, and Heading 3 styles. Or you may want a more general table of contents that uses only Heading 1 styles. If you want to include only Heading 1, Heading 2, and Heading 3 styles in your table of contents, choose 3.

9. **Click the Tab Leader box, and then choose a tab leader.**

   A tab leader consists of text or symbols that appear between a table of contents entry and its page number, as in this example:

   Euphemisms for Confusing the Public...............................23

   In this case, the tab leaders are the periods (dots) between the phrase "Euphemisms for Confusing the Public" and the page number 23.

   Note: If you don't choose to right-align page numbers, the Tab Leader box appears dimmed.

10. **Click OK.**

    In the blink of an eye (or longer, depending on the speed of your computer), Word creates your table of contents for you, as shown in Figure 5-8.

Using your own styles to format headings

For stubborn nonconformists (if you're a nonconformist, you probably shouldn't even be using Microsoft programs), you can also create a table of contents based on your own styles rather than use the Heading 1, Heading 2, and Heading 3 styles all the time. (To learn how to create your own styles, see Chapter 3.)

To create a table of contents based on your own styles, follow these steps:

1. **Format all the document headings by using your own particular styles.**
2. **Place the cursor in the document on the spot where you want the table of contents to be inserted (such as at the beginning of your document).**
3. **Choose Insert⇨Index and Tables.**
4. **Click the Table of Contents tab to display the tab (refer to Figure 5-7).**
5. **In the Formats list box, click the format you want, such as Modern or Fancy.**

   Word shows you in the Preview box what your table of contents will look like.

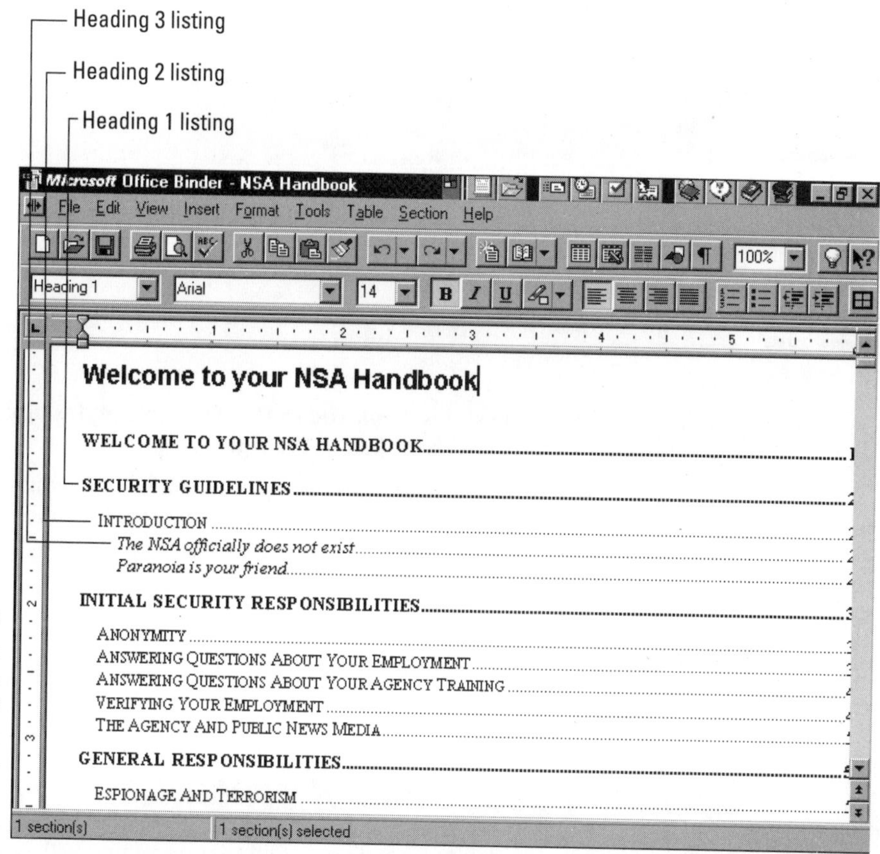

Figure 5-8: A sample table of contents created by Word.

6. **If you want to show page numbers, click the Show Page Numbers check box.**
7. **Click the Right Align Page Numbers check box if you want to right-align the page numbers in your table of contents.**
8. **Click the Show Levels list box, and choose how many levels you want to display.**
9. **Click the Tab Leader box, and choose a tab leader.**

   If you don't choose to right-align page numbers, the Tab Leader box appears dimmed.

10. **Click Options.**

   A Table of Contents Options dialog box appears, as shown in Figure 5-9.

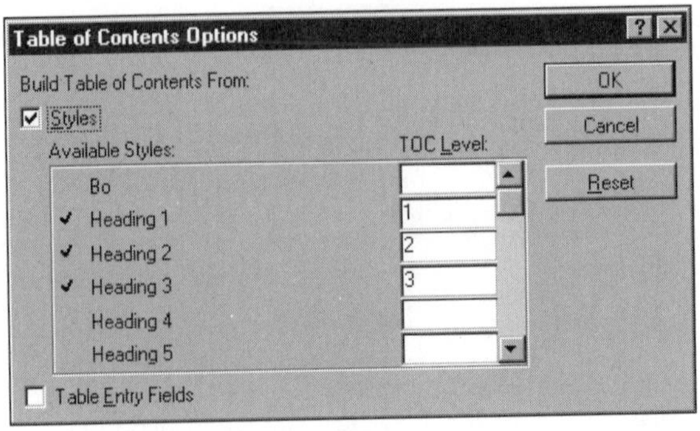

Figure 5-9: Choosing the heading levels you want to use.

11. **Scroll through the styles displayed in the Available Styles box, and type a number in the TOC Level box to the right.**

    For example, type **1** to make the style appear as a main heading in your table of contents, or type **2** to make the style appear as a subheading.

12. **Click OK.**

    The Index and Tables dialog box appears again.

13. **Click OK.**

    Word creates your table of contents for you.

Updating your table of contents

Whenever you add or delete a heading or text that may change the page numbering, you have to update your table of contents all over again. To update a table of contents, follow these steps:

1. **Make any changes to your document or headings.**
2. **Move the cursor to anywhere inside the table of contents you want to update.**

   Word displays your table of contents in a shade of gray.

3. **Press F9.**

   An Update Table of Contents dialog box appears, as shown in Figure 5-10.

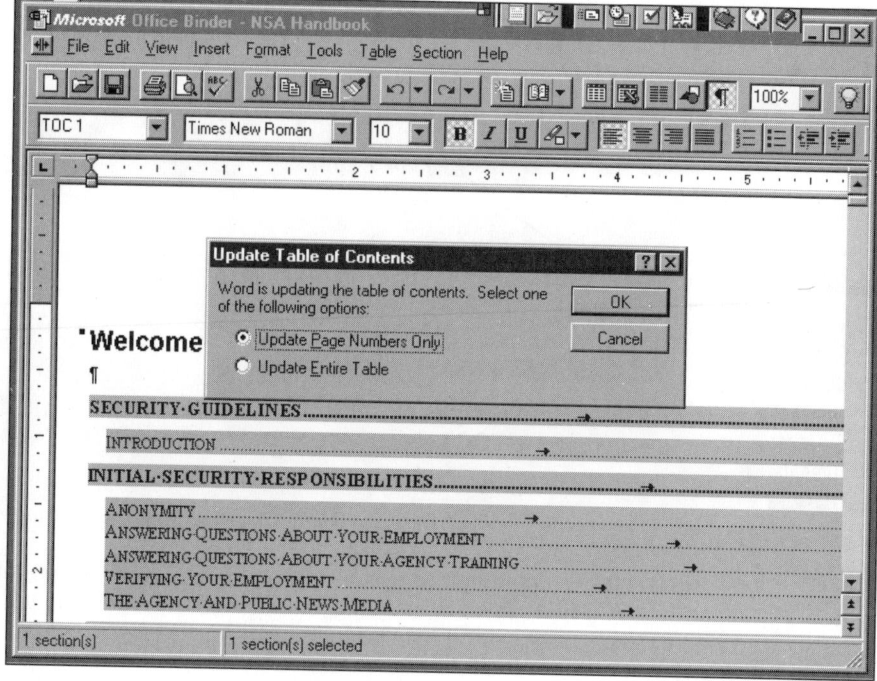

Figure 5-10: Placing the cursor inside a table of contents and clicking turns it gray.

4. **Click one of the following radio buttons:**
   - **Update Page Numbers Only**
   - **Update Entire Table**
5. **Click OK.**

   Word updates your entire table of contents.

Working with Master Documents

Most people write with Word in one of three ways:

- Cram everything into a single document.
- Store chapters or logical sections in separate documents.
- Store chapters or logical sections in separate documents with all documents saved in a single binder.

If you cram everything into a single document, it can be difficult to edit the document easily. If you store chapters in separate documents, you can't easily create an index or table of contents. To help deal with this apparent paradox, Word offers the mysterious master document.

A *master document* is an outline stored in a separate file. Every heading in an outline acts as a link to another file, called a *subdocument,* as shown in Figure 5-11.

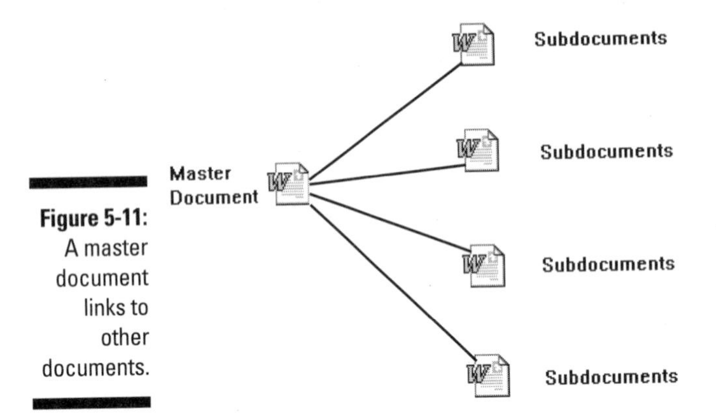

Figure 5-11: A master document links to other documents.

By using a master document, you can view and edit individual subdocuments separately or display them in one long, continuous document, which enables you to create an index or table of contents.

Any changes you make to a master document appear automatically in the appropriate linked subdocument. Likewise, any changes you make to a linked subdocument appear automatically in the master document.

By using a master document, you can create an accurate index and table of contents while keeping text stored in separate files for easy editing and viewing.

Creating a master document from scratch

The best time to create a master document is when you want to write a large document (a novel, a business report, or a legal paper suing someone for no apparent reason other than money, for example) and you want to store parts of it in separate files.

By first creating a master document, you can outline your ideas before you waste time writing aimlessly. After you organize your ideas, you can begin writing.

To create a master document, follow these steps:

1. **Choose Section⇨View Outside.**

   Skip this step if you're using Word outside of a binder.

2. **Choose View⇨Master Document.**

   Word displays the Outlining and Master Document toolbar, as shown in Figure 5-12.

3. **Type one or more headings using the Heading 1 style (refer to Figure 5-12), where each heading can represent a chapter title.**

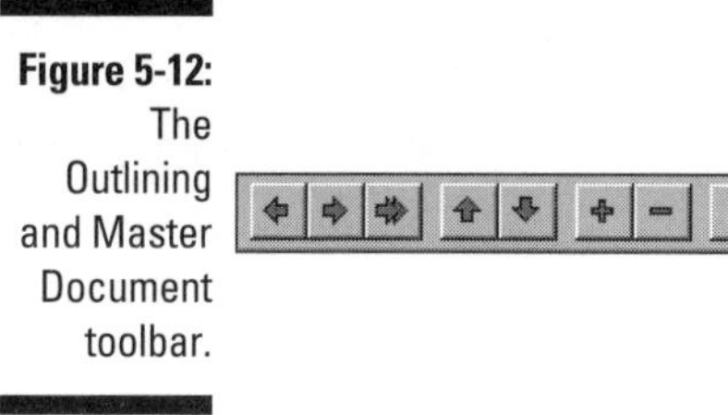

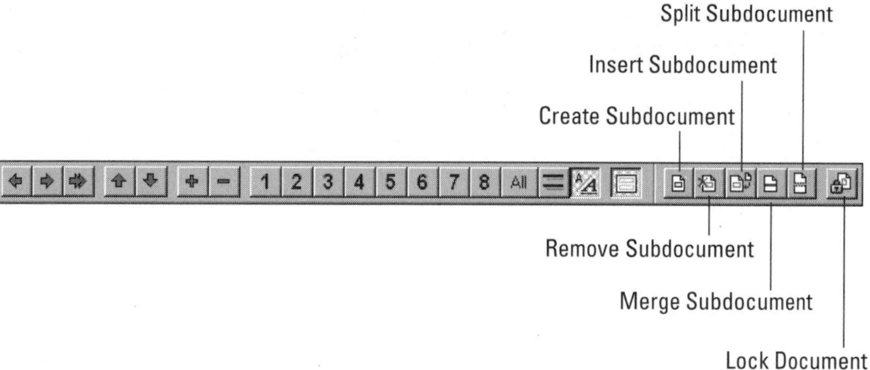

Figure 5-12: The Outlining and Master Document toolbar.

4. **Place the cursor in a heading you want to use to create a subdocument.**

5. **Click the Create Subdocument button.**

   Word draws a gray box around your heading and displays a subdocument icon, as shown in Figure 5-13.

6. **Double-click the subdocument icon.**

   Word displays your subdocument all by itself, as shown in Figure 5-14.

7. **Type the text you want to store in your subdocument.**

8. **Choose File⇨Close when you finish typing your text.**

   Word displays a dialog box, asking you whether you want to save your document.

9. **Click Yes.**

   A Save As dialog box appears.

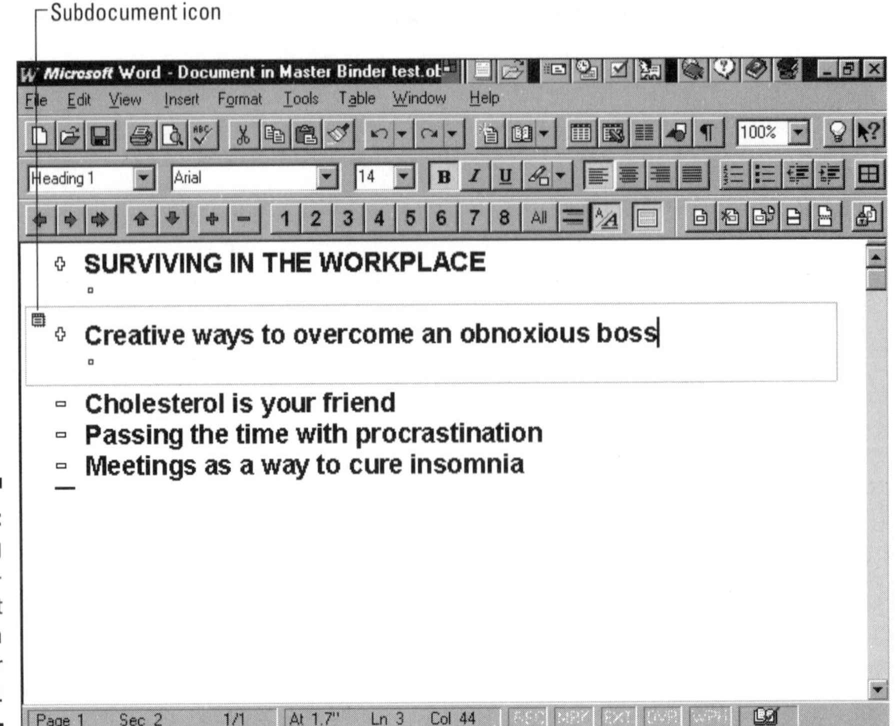

Figure 5-13: Creating a sub-document within a master document.

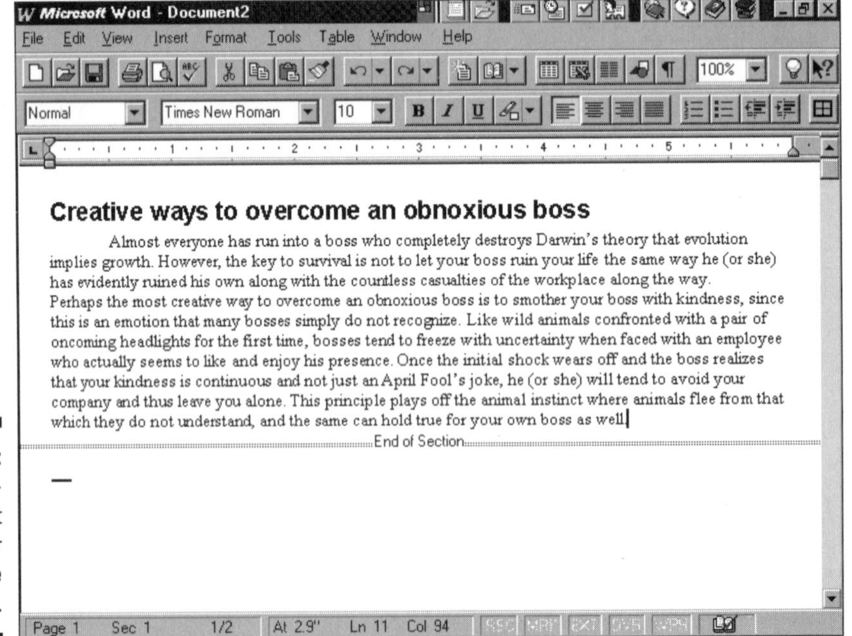

Figure 5-14: A sub-document waits for you to type something.

10. **Type a name for your subdocument in the File name box, and then click Save.**

    Word displays your subdocument's text in the master document, as shown in Figure 5-15.

11. **Repeat steps 4 through 10 for every heading you want to convert into a subdocument.**

If you create a master document within a binder, you must store your subdocuments as separate files outside your binder. You cannot store a subdocument in a binder because Microsoft Office cannot update subdocuments stored inside a binder.

Creating a master document from an existing document

Rather than create a master document from scratch, you can also convert an existing document into a master document. This trick can be handy if you've already created a huge document and suddenly decide that it's getting too bulky to edit and read easily.

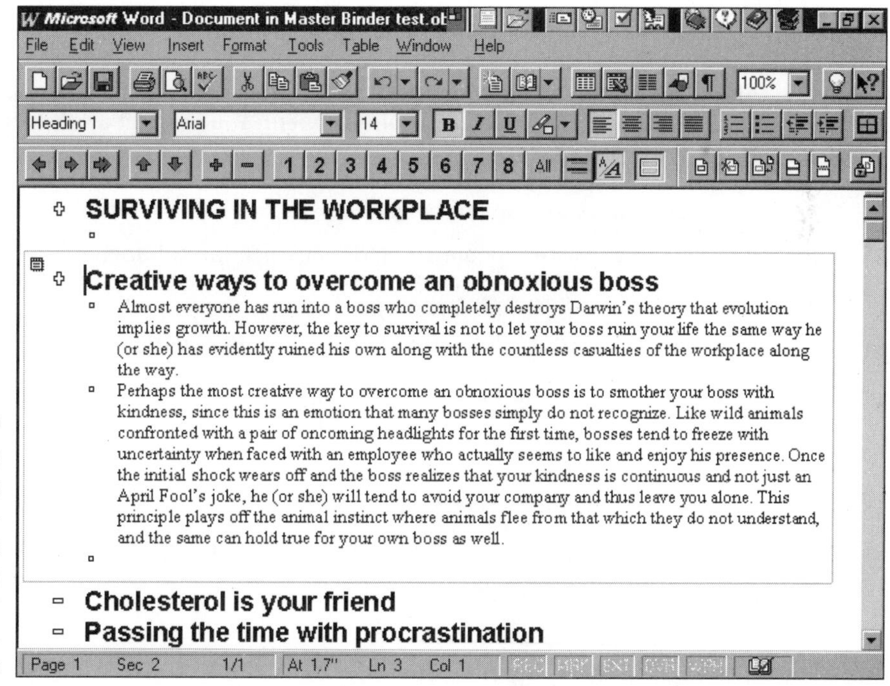

Figure 5-15: The text from a subdocument appears in a master document.

To convert a document into a master document, follow these steps:

1. **Open the document you want to convert into a master document.**
2. **Click a heading in your document and format it by using the Heading 1, Heading 2, Heading 3, or Heading 4 style.**
3. **Choose View⇨Master Document.**
4. **Highlight the heading and the text you want to convert into a subdocument.**
5. **Click the Create Subdocument button.**
6. **Repeat steps 4 and 5 for every heading and text you want to convert into a subdocument.**
7. **Choose File⇨Save As.**

   A Save As dialog box appears.
8. **Type a name for your master document in the File name box, and then click Save.**

   Word automatically saves your subdocuments as separate files; it uses the heading as the filename for the subdocument.

Editing a subdocument

After you create a master document and one or more subdocuments, you might want to edit the text stored in a subdocument. You can edit a subdocument in two ways:

- Open the subdocument by itself.
- Open the master document, and then open the subdocument.

No matter which method you choose, any changes you make to the subdocument appear automatically in the master document.

To edit a subdocument by itself, follow these steps:

1. **Choose File⇨Open.**

   An Open dialog box appears.
2. **Click the subdocument you want to edit, and then click Open.**
3. **Edit your subdocument.**
4. **Choose File⇨Save.**
5. **Choose File⇨Close.**

To edit a subdocument from within a master document, follow these steps:

1. **Choose Section⇨View Outside.**

   Skip this step if you're using Word outside of a binder.

2. **Choose File⇨Open.**

   An Open dialog box appears.

3. **Click the master document that contains the subdocument you want to edit, and then click Open.**
4. **Edit the subdocument text you want to change.**
5. **Choose File⇨Save.**

Collapsing and expanding subdocuments

Cramming multiple subdocuments into a master document lets you view your entire text, which can be as long as several hundred pages. Because scrolling through a long document is about as convenient as reading a copy of *War and Peace* written on a roll of toilet paper, you may be happy to know that Word can temporarily hide and display subdocuments.

By hiding one or more subdocuments, you can selectively view your subdocuments without being overwhelmed by the entire text in every subdocument. When you want to want to see the text stored in a hidden subdocument, just display it again.

To hide (or "collapse") a subdocument, follow these steps:

1. **Open your master document.**
2. **Move the cursor to the subdocument heading you want to collapse.**
3. **Click the Collapse button, as shown in Figure 5-16.**

   Word hides your subdocument's text.

To display (or "expand") a subdocument, follow these steps:

1. **Open your master document.**
2. **Move the cursor to the subdocument heading you want to expand.**
3. **Click the Expand button (refer to Figure 5-16).**

   Word displays your subdocument's text again.

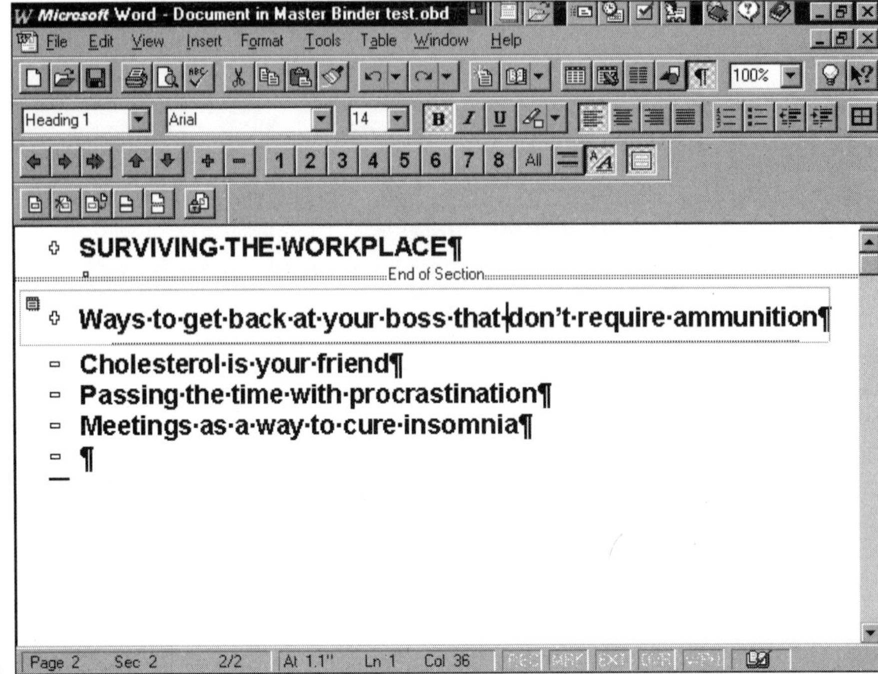

Figure 5-16: Collapsing a subdocument within a master document.

Rearranging linked subdocuments

After you create a master document and one or more subdocuments, you can quickly rearrange the position of your subdocuments just by moving the subdocument heading around. Without this fancy feature, you would have to go through the cumbersome process of highlighting huge chunks of text, cutting them, and then pasting them where you want.

To rearrange a subdocument, follow these steps:

1. **Open your master document.**
2. **Move the cursor to the subdocument heading you want to move.**
3. **Click the Move Up or Move Down button (refer to Figure 5-16).**

   Word magically moves your subdocument's heading and text. Isn't that easy?

Adding, splitting, merging, and removing subdocuments

After you create a master document, you can add new documents at any time; split large subdocuments into smaller, more manageable chunks; or remove subdocuments for good. By using a master document to organize multiple files, you can edit your entire text easily without losing your mind.

Adding a subdocument

Most of the time, you create subdocuments within a master document. Suppose that someone creates a document for you, however, and that you want to include it in your master document. Fortunately, Word is happy to let you add an existing document to your master document at any time.

To add an existing document to a master document, follow these steps:

1. **Choose Section➪View Outside.**

   Skip this step if you're using Word outside of a binder.

2. **Choose View➪Master Document.**
3. **Place the cursor where you want to insert your subdocument.**
4. **Click the Insert Subdocument button (refer to Figure 5-16).**

   An Insert Subdocument dialog box appears, as shown in Figure 5-17.

5. **Click the Word document you want to add to your master document, and then click Open.**

   Word shoves your chosen file inside your master document.

Splitting and merging subdocuments

Sometimes a subdocument may become so large that it's too clumsy to use. In that case, you can split a subdocument into smaller subdocuments to keep them to a more manageable size.

To split a subdocument, follow these steps:

1. **Choose Section➪View Outside.**

   Skip this step if you're using Word outside of a binder.

2. **Choose View➪Master Document.**
3. **Place the cursor at the beginning of a paragraph in which you want to split a subdocument.**

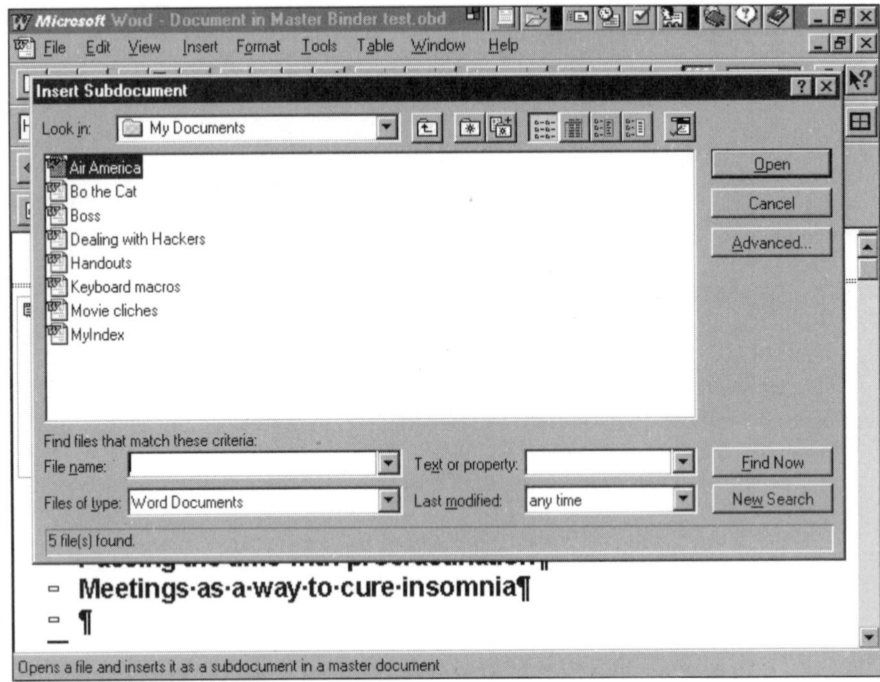

Figure 5-17: The Insert Subdocument dialog box.

4. **Click the Split Subdocument button (refer to Figure 5-17).**

   Word splits your subdocument at the cursor's location.

Just as you may have to split apart large subdocuments, you may also have to combine smaller subdocuments.

To merge one or more subdocuments, follow these steps:

1. **Choose Section⇨View Outside.**

   Skip this step if you're using Word outside of a binder.

2. **Click the subdocument icon that represents the first subdocument you want to merge.**

   Word highlights the subdocument heading and text.

3. **Hold down the Shift key and click the next subdocument icon that represents the next subdocument you want to merge.**

   Word highlights the subdocument heading and text.

4. **Repeat step 3 for every subdocument you want to combine.**

5. **Click the Merge Subdocument button (refer to Figure 5-17).**

   Word merges your subdocuments into a single subdocument.

Removing a subdocument

You may have a subdocument you no longer need. When this situation occurs, just remove the subdocument from the master document.

When removing a subdocument from a master document, the subdocument still exists on your hard disk as a separate Word file. Removing a subdocument does not delete the file from the face of the earth. To delete the document from your hard disk, load the Windows Explorer, click the document you want to delete, and then press Delete.

To remove a subdocument, follow these steps:

1. **Choose Section⇨View Outside.**

   Skip this step if you're using Word outside of a binder.

2. **Choose View⇨Master Document.**
3. **Click the subdocument icon that represents the subdocument you want to remove.**

   Word highlights the subdocument heading and text.

4. **Press Delete or Backspace.**

Chapter 6

Sharing Word Documents

In This Chapter

- Converting files so that you can use them with other word-processing programs
- Using annotations to hide your comments
- Viewing both original and revised text with revision marks
- Using Word to create e-mail
- Creating Web pages with the Internet Assistant

Not everyone has joined the lemminglike march toward Microsoft software dominance. Although many people use Microsoft Word, others are perfectly happy using rival programs such as WordPerfect, Ami Pro (now called WordPro, as if that isn't a silly name), Works, or even older versions of Word.

If you want to share documents with people who absolutely refuse to use Word, take heart: You can always convert your Word documents to a file format that another word processor can understand. If you're fortunate enough to share files with other Word users, you can use many fancy features to mark up and edit text without having to print a copy on paper or use your red pen to mark up the text by hand.

By sharing Word files on disk, on a network, or over a modem, you can view, edit, and comment on text without wasting paper printing it all. When your document looks perfect, you can print it for the world to see.

Converting Files for Use with Other Word Processors

Because Word (along with WordPerfect) dominates the word-processing market, you may wonder about the wisdom of converting your Word documents into other word-processing formats. After all, if people don't have the good sense (unlike you) to use Word, it's obvious that they should rush out and switch to Word right away (which is what Microsoft wants).

Using the Word Viewer to share Word documents

If everyone used Microsoft Word, you could just hand people your files so that they could read them with their own copy of Word. But because not everyone uses Word, you can use a special program called Word Viewer.

Word Viewer is essentially a crippled version of Microsoft Word. The primary difference is that the Word Viewer lets people only read and print documents — you can never edit them using the Word Viewer, no matter how hard you may try.

The other big difference is that the Word Viewer program is free to copy or give away; if you try to copy or give away Microsoft Word, however, you can go to jail for it.

By giving everyone you know a copy of the Word Viewer, you can share your documents without having to convert your Word files to a strange file format, such as WordPerfect. You can download a free copy of the Word Viewer from CompuServe, America Online, or directly from the Microsoft Web site at `http://www.microsoft.com`.

Despite Microsoft's best marketing efforts, there are still two good reasons you may have to convert a Word file:

- You create a file using Word but you want to give that file to someone who uses a different word-processing program.
- Someone gives you a file created by another word-processing program and you want to edit and view it in Word.

Converting a Word file into another file format is called exporting a file. When you *export* a file, you make a copy of your original Word document and save this second copy in a different file format, such as a WordPerfect file.

When someone gives you a file created by a different word-processing program and you want to edit the file in Word, you import the file. When you *import* a file, you load the file in Word and save a copy of it as a Word document.

Exporting a Word file to another file format

Word knows how to export files into various versions of WordPerfect (Word's archenemy). But what if you want to export a Word document for a different word-processing program, such as Ami Pro, WordPro, WordStar, NisusWriter, WriteNow, or any of the other obscure programs that never hit it big in either the IBM or Macintosh market?

In these cases, you can export a Word file to one of the following formats:

- **Text Only:** Exporting a Word document to a text file enables any word-processing program to use that file, even obscure programs for MS-DOS or programs that run on different computers, such as the Macintosh or the Amiga.
- **Text Only with Line Breaks:** This file format is the same as the Text Only format except that it saves line breaks between paragraphs. If you save a file by using the Text Only format and it smashes your paragraphs together in one huge blob of text, you have to save your file by using the Text Only with Line Breaks format instead.
- **MS-DOS Text:** Exporting a Word document to this format creates a text file that can be used by any word-processing program that runs under MS-DOS or Windows.
- **MS-DOS Text with Line Breaks:** This file format is the same as the MS-DOS Text format except that it saves line breaks between paragraphs. If you save a file by using the MS-DOS Text format and it crams your paragraphs into one huge lump of text, you have to save your file by using the MS-DOS Text with Line Breaks format instead.
- **Rich Text Format:** Exporting a Word document into this special format creates a file that every Microsoft program — even Macintosh programs — can use, such as Works for MS-DOS. Whenever you want to save a file for use in another Microsoft program, save the file as a Rich Text Format file. Because Microsoft dominates the software industry so completely, many other programs also know how to use Rich Text Format.

When you export a Word file, first try saving your file in Rich Text Format — this format saves both your text and all your formatting, such as italics, fonts, and type sizes. If the Rich Text Format fails, try exporting your Word file as a WordPerfect file because 99 percent of the word-processing programs in the world can recognize WordPerfect files. If that still fails, you have to resort to using either the MS-DOS Text or the Text Only format. Good luck.

To export a Word file and save it in a different word-processing file format, follow these steps:

1. **Choose Section⇨View Outside from the menu bar.**

   Skip this step if you're using Word outside of a binder.

2. **Choose File⇨Save As.**

   If you're using Word within a binder, choose File⇨Save Copy As. The Save As dialog box appears.

3. **Click the Save as type list box and then choose a file format.**

4. **Type a name for your file in the File name box.**

   It's a good idea to save your exported file under a name that's different from your original Word document to avoid any confusion between the two.

5. **Click Save.**

Making Word export files flawlessly

Sometimes, despite its best efforts, Word can't always export a document flawlessly into another file format. When this happens, you may have to modify the way Word saves files.

To modify the way Word saves files, follow these steps:

1. **Choose Tools⇨Options.**

   The Options dialog box appears.

2. **Click the Compatibility tab, shown in Figure 6-1.**
3. **Click the Recommended Options For list box and choose a file format.**

   A couple of format options are Word for MS-DOS and Custom.

4. **Click one or more of the check boxes listed in the Options list box.**
5. **Click OK.**

Making Word export your files flawlessly may require endless amounts of trial and error and experimentation with different options.

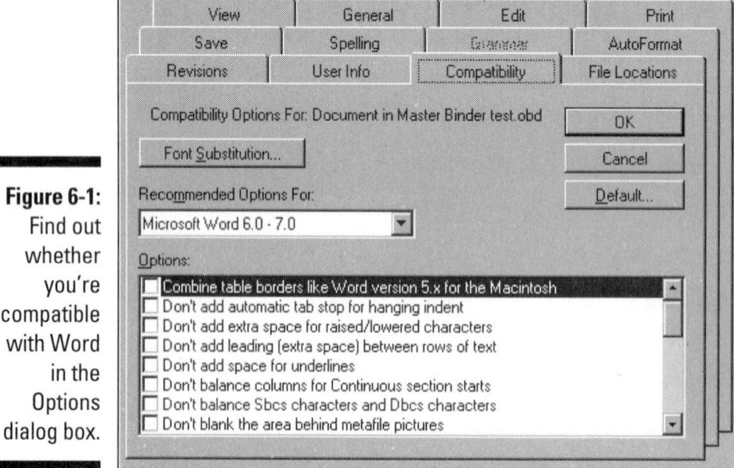

Figure 6-1: Find out whether you're compatible with Word in the Options dialog box.

Importing a file into Word

Word can import files created by a variety of programs, including WordPerfect, Excel, Schedule+, and older versions of Word.

How to import a file into Word

To import a file into Word, follow these steps:

1. **Load Word as a separate program (not within a Microsoft Office binder).**
2. **Choose File⇨Open.**

   The Open dialog box appears.
3. **Click the Files of type list box and choose the file format you want to import.**

   Some possible import options are WordPerfect 5.*x*, Rich Text Format, and Text Files.
4. **Click the file you want to import and then click Open.**

   If all goes well, Word displays the text exactly as it appears in its original file format. Most likely, though, you have to read through your newly imported file and slightly edit the text.

How to import a file into a Microsoft Office binder

If you have a foreign file format you want to add to a Microsoft Office binder, you first have to convert (import) the foreign file into a Word document and then add it to your Microsoft Office binder.

To import a file into a Microsoft Office binder, follow these steps:

1. **Load Word as a separate program (not within a Microsoft Office binder).**
2. **Choose File⇨Open.**

   The Open dialog box appears.
3. **Click the Files of type list box and choose the file format you want to import.**

   Some possible import options are WordPerfect 5.*x*, Rich Text Format, and Text Files.
4. **Click the file you want to import and then click Open.**

   If all goes well, Word displays the text exactly as it appears in its original file format. Most likely, though, you have to read through your newly imported file and slightly edit the text.

5. **Choose File⇨Save to save your newly imported file as a genuine, 100 percent authentic Word document.**
6. **Open the Microsoft Office binder to which you want to add your newly converted file.**
7. **Choose Section⇨Add from File.**

   The Add from File dialog box appears.
8. **Click the Word document you saved in step 5 and then click Add.**

Hiding Comments with Annotations

When you print a letter or report, you can pass it around to others and let them mark it up with comments about how to improve or alter your text. When you share Word documents on a floppy disk or online over a modem or network, however, you don't have the convenience of scribbling comments in the side margins of a page.

At the simplest level, you could just shove your comments right into the middle of the text — something like "Hey, this last sentence doesn't make any sense!" Interrupting the flow of text is not only intrusive, but you also have to go through the trouble of deleting all those comments, one by one. Only then can you print a clean copy of your text.

As a simpler solution, Word offers annotations. An *annotation* is a comment that you type directly into a Word document but that doesn't appear when you print the document unless you specifically tell Word to print it.

If you convert (export) a Word document to another file format (WordPerfect, for example), you may lose all your annotations.

Creating an annotation

An annotation lets you bury a comment directly in a Word document. Rather than display your annotation intrusively right in the middle of existing text, Word puts an annotation mark in your text so that other people can see it. Word displays your actual annotation in a separate annotation window at the bottom of your screen, as shown in Figure 6-2.

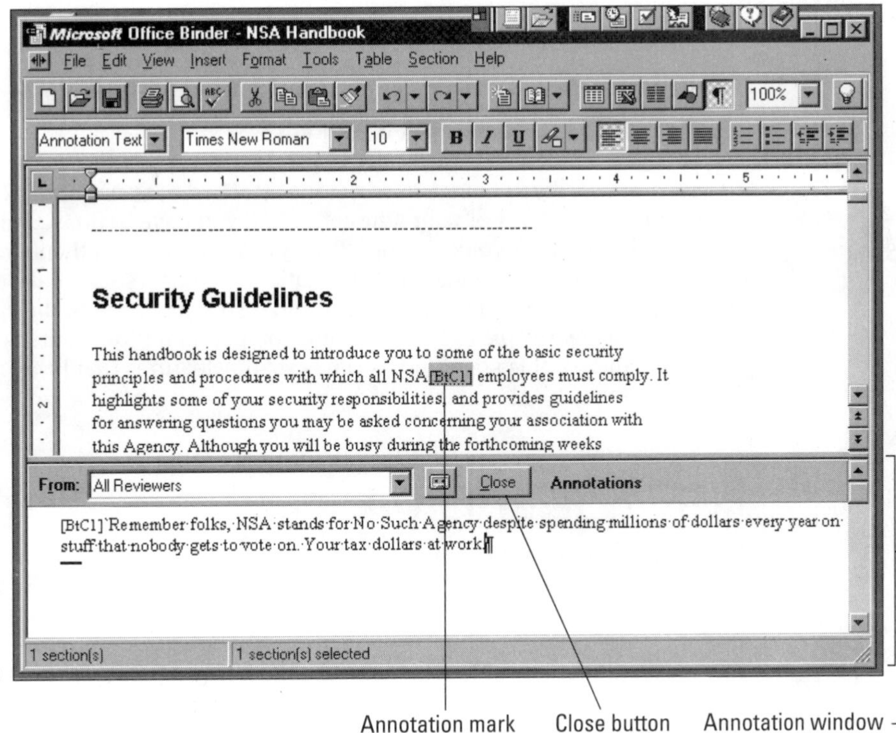

Figure 6-2: A typical annotation in a document.

Each annotation mark contains the following parts:

- **The initials of the person who created the annotation.** Word creates the annotation abbreviation from the name you gave it when you installed Microsoft Office on your computer. If you entered your name in Microsoft Office as Bo the Cat, your initials are BtC. To change your initials, choose Tools⇨Options, click the User Info tab, and type your new initials in the Initials box.
- **The sequential number of the annotation.** If you entered your name as Bo the Cat in Microsoft Office, your first annotation mark would appear as [BtC1], your second annotation mark would appear as [BtC2], and so on.

To create an annotation, follow these steps:

1. **Move the cursor to the location in the text where you want to add an annotation.**
2. **Choose Insert⇨Annotation.**

   At the cursor location in your text, Word places an annotation mark and displays the annotation window at the bottom of your screen (refer to Figure 6-2).

3. **Type your comments in the annotation window.**
4. **Repeat steps 1–3 for each annotation you want to add.**
5. **Click the Close button when you finish.**

Believe it or not, if you have a microphone attached to your computer, you can add a sound file as part of your annotation. All you have to do is create a sound file (for example, your voice saying, "Bob, you're fired!") and then store it as an annotation. If someone reads your annotation and has a sound card on his or her computer, that person can hear your voice blaring through the speakers. Of course, not many people are likely to add sound annotations, but it's nice to know that Microsoft is spending its time creating features that bring us closer to science fiction.

Viewing annotations

After your fellow cowriters insert their annotations throughout your Word document and return the file to you, you can read their annotations. You can follow their advice or (more likely) ignore their comments.

To view annotations within a document, follow these steps:

1. **Choose View⇨Annotations.**

   Word displays the annotation marks in the document and opens the annotation window at the bottom of the screen.

2. **Click the annotation mark for the comment you want to view.**

   Word politely displays the comment in the annotation window. If you want to view annotations from only a certain reviewer, click in the From list box in the annotation window and choose that reviewer's initials.

3. **Click the Close button when you finish viewing the annotations.**

If a document has no annotations, the Annotations command in the View menu appears dimmed.

Deleting an annotation

Annotations are meant to be temporary. After all, you don't have to store a comment in a document after you respond to the comment.

To delete an annotation, follow these steps:

1. **Choose View⇨Annotations.**

   Word displays annotation marks in the document and opens the annotation window at the bottom of the screen.

2. **Highlight the annotation mark that contains the annotation you want to delete.**

3. **Press Delete or Backspace.**

   This action deletes the annotation mark and the comments in the annotation window.

4. **Click Close.**

Printing a document with annotations

You may occasionally want to print your document with annotations so that you can see all annotations at one time. To print all the annotations in a document, follow these steps:

1. **Choose Tools⇨Options.**

   The Options dialog box appears.

2. **Click the Print tab.**

3. **Click the Annotations check box in the Include with Document group.**

4. **Click OK.**

   The next time you print your document, Word also prints your annotations along with it.

Marking up Text with Revision Marks

Annotations are great for making comments, but what if you want to get right into the text and modify it yourself? With paper copies of text, you can *mark up* the text (make revision marks) with a red pen, indicating where to delete, add, or rearrange words. With Word, you also can indicate where you delete, add, or rearrange words in your text file.

On a paper copy of your marked-up text, you can easily see your revision marks. Word, however, normally doesn't let you see the original text that you cross out and modify. If you want to modify text and still be able to view the original text *and* your revisions, use a special feature called revision marks.

The *revision marks* feature lets you edit a text file without deleting the original text. If you later decide to keep the original version, you can recall the original text without having to retype it. If you decide to include your revisions, you can wipe out the original version and retain the revised text.

If you convert (export) a Word document to another file format (WordPerfect, for example), you may lose all your revision marks.

Turning revision marks on or off

When you turn on the revision marks feature, Word distinguishes between your original text and your revised text. This feature enables you to customize the color and appearance of your original text, your revised text, and the revision lines that appear in the margins of your edited text.

To turn revision marks on or off, follow these steps:

1. **Choose Tools⇨Revisions.**

   The Revisions dialog box appears, as shown in Figure 6-3.

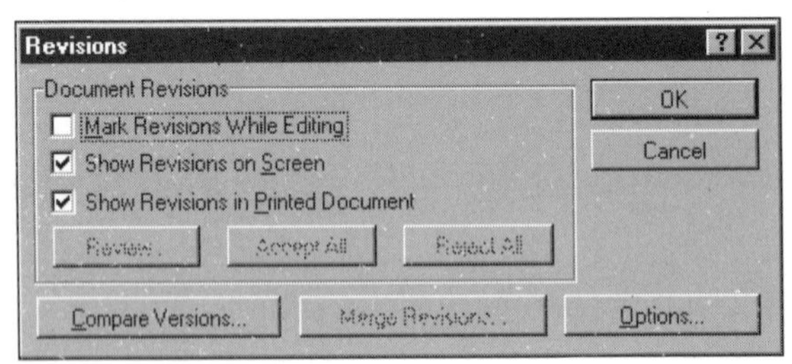

Figure 6-3: Letting Word know where you want revisions to show up.

2. **Click the Mark Revisions While Editing check box so that a check mark appears.**

   If the check box is empty, Word doesn't retain any of your revision marks as you make changes in the text.

3. **Click Options.**

   The Options dialog box appears, as shown in Figure 6-4, with these options available for customizing the appearance of your revised text:

   - **Inserted Text:** Choose the color and appearance of any new text you add.
   - **Deleted Text:** Choose the color and appearance of any text you delete.
   - **Revised Lines:** Choose the color and appearance of the revision marks that appear in the margins of your document. Revision lines help you easily locate revised text.

4. **Customize the way Word displays the color and appearance of inserted text, deleted text, and revised lines.**

   For example, you can make inserted text appear red with an underline or make deleted text appear yellow with strikethrough.

5. **Click OK twice.**

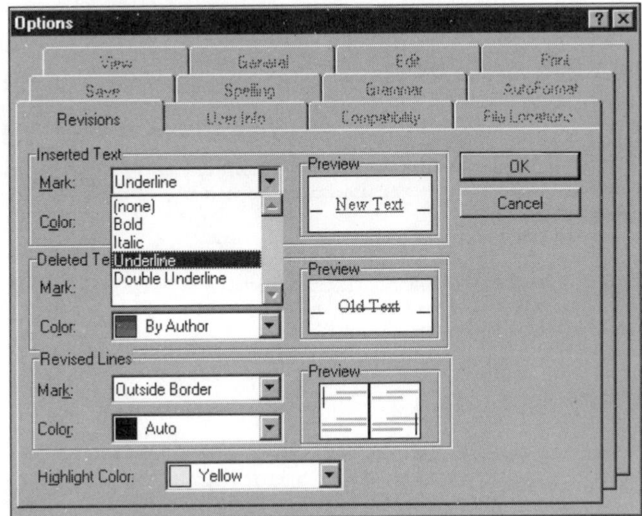

Figure 6-4: Telling Word how to display your revision marks.

From now on, every time you add, delete, copy, or move text, Word displays the original text and the new text in the colors and appearance you chose in step 4. Figure 6-5 shows what a document with multiple revision marks looks like.

Reviewing revision marks one by one

After an editor, co-worker, or critic has littered your document with revision marks, you have to go through them and selectively accept or reject each one. To review your revision marks one by one, follow these steps:

1. **Press Ctrl+Home to move the cursor to the top of your document.**

2. **Choose Tools➪Revisions.**

   The Revisions dialog box appears (refer to Figure 6-4).

3. **Click Review.**

   The Review Revisions dialog box appears, as shown in Figure 6-6.

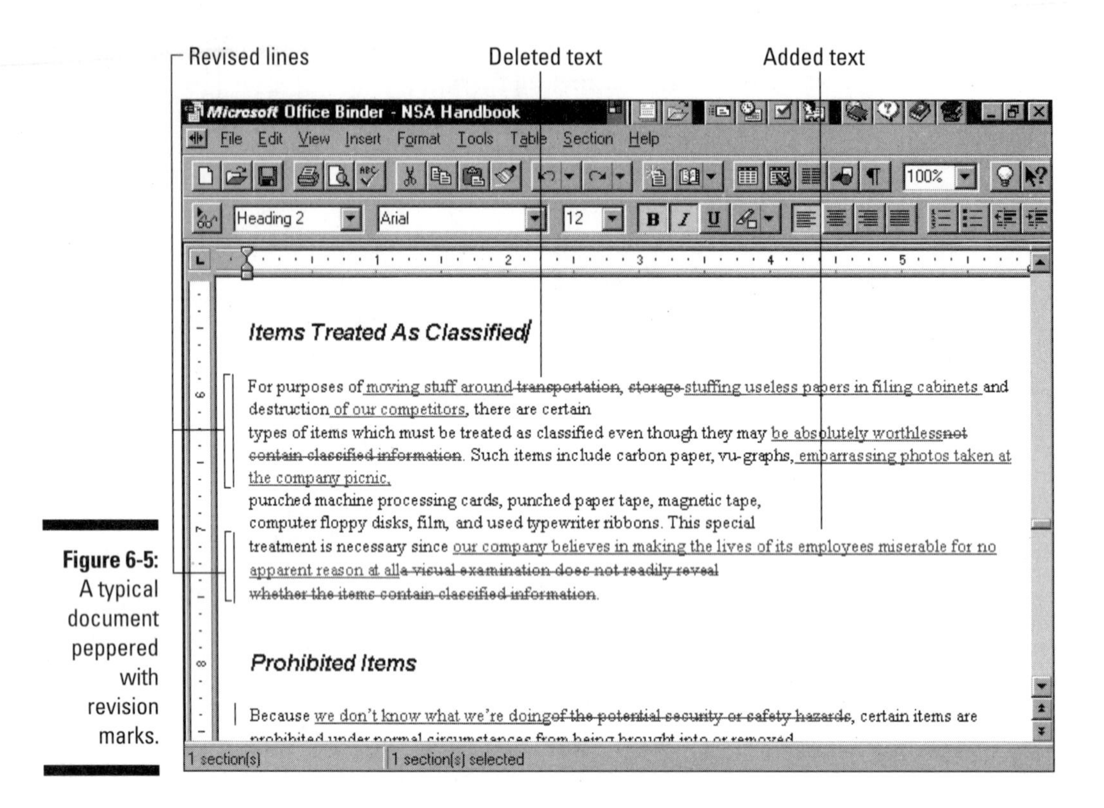

Figure 6-5: A typical document peppered with revision marks.

4. **Click the Find button (that's the *right* Find button).**

   Word highlights the first revision mark it finds.

5. **Click Hide Marks to see what your text will look like if you accept the revision.**

6. **Click Show Marks to see the original text in addition to your revised text.**

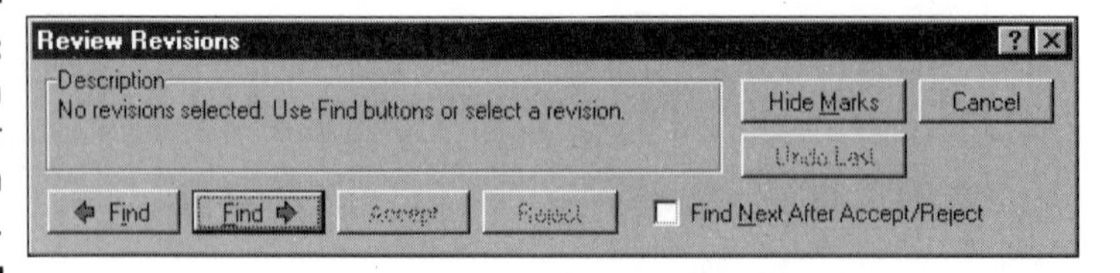

Figure 6-6: Looking high and low for revision marks.

7. **Click Accept or Reject.**

   If you click Accept, Word removes the revision mark and displays any added text as part of your document. If you click Reject, the revision mark disappears.

8. **Repeat steps 4–7 for each revision mark you want to review.**
9. **Click Close.**

Reviewing revision marks all at one time

In case you're feeling lazy or you have complete confidence (or no confidence) in the person who created all those revision marks in your document, you can accept (or reject) all the revision marks at one time.

To accept or reject all revision marks in a document without first reviewing them, follow these steps:

1. **Choose Tools⇨Revisions.**

   The Revisions dialog box appears (refer to Figure 6-3).

2. **Click Accept All or Reject All.**

   A dialog box appears, asking whether you're sure that you know what you're doing.

3. **Click Yes.**
4. **Click OK.**

If you accept or reject all your revision marks and suddenly change your mind, press Ctrl+Z immediately to undo your last action.

Using Word to Send E-mail

In another attempt to make it painless for the entire world to adopt Microsoft programs, the company makes it easy for you to use Word to create all your e-mail, in case you have an Internet account or subscribe to an online service (such as Microsoft Network or CompuServe) that also lets you use the Microsoft Exchange Program. By using Word as your e-mail editor, you don't have to learn to use a new program just to write e-mail messages.

If you plan to send huge e-mail messages over the Internet or an online service, you can spend less time using the phone lines if you save your e-mail as a file and then use a compression program such as PKZIP or WinZIP to squash the file. When you send a "zipped" file to someone else, the recipient must use a similar compression program to "unzip" your file before reading it.

Installing Word as an e-mail editor

In case you haven't installed Word as an e-mail editor (or if you don't know whether you have), follow these steps:

1. **Run the Microsoft Office for Windows 95 setup program again so that the Setup dialog box appears.**
2. **Click Add/Remove.**

   The Microsoft Office for Windows 95 Maintenance dialog box appears, as shown in Figure 6-7.
3. **Click Microsoft Word to highlight it and then click Change Option. (Make sure not to click in the check box next to Microsoft Word, or else you'll deselect Word.)**

   The Microsoft Word dialog box appears, as shown in Figure 6-8.
4. **Click the WordMail check box so that a check mark appears, and then click OK.**

   If a check mark is already displayed, WordMail is already installed. You can click Cancel and stop right here.
5. **Click Continue.**

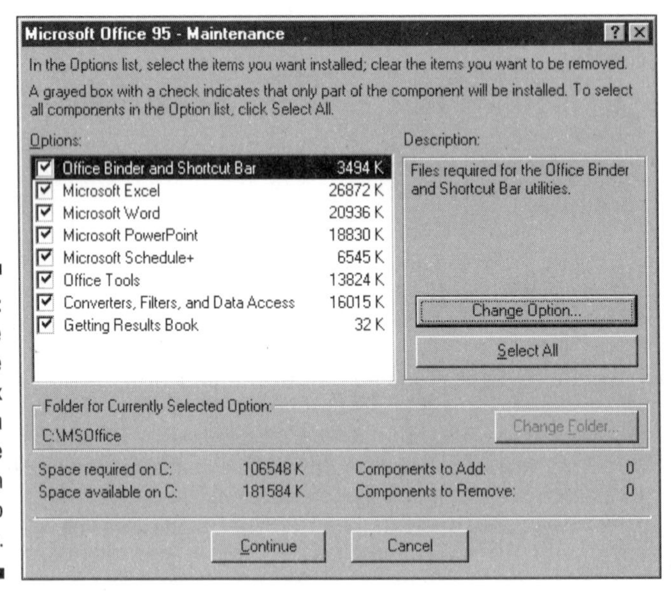

Figure 6-7: The Maintenance dialog box lets you choose which options to modify.

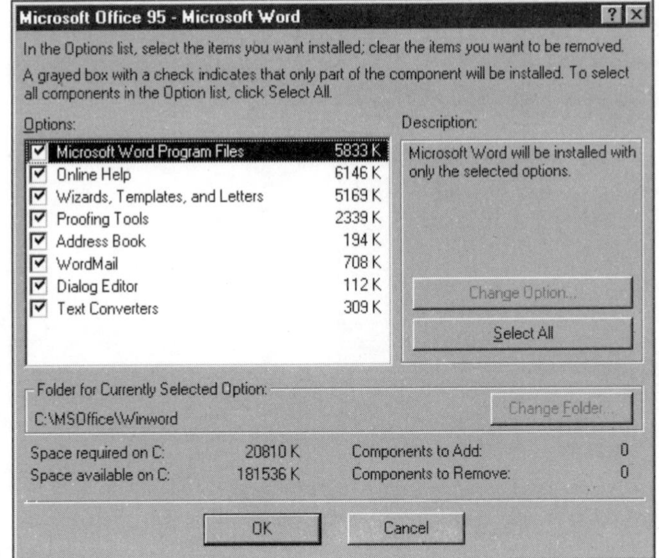

Figure 6-8: Choosing which Word options to modify.

Using WordMail to write e-mail

After you install the WordMail feature, you can use Word to write your e-mail if you also use the Microsoft Exchange program that comes with Windows 95.

To install Word as your e-mail editor within Microsoft Exchange, follow these steps:

1. **Load Microsoft Exchange.**
2. **Choose Compose⇨WordMail Options.**

   The WordMail Options dialog box appears, as shown in Figure 6-9.
3. **Click the Enable Word as Email Editor check box so that a check mark appears.**
4. **Click Close.**

   From now on, whenever you write an e-mail message within Microsoft Exchange, Word pops up as your e-mail editor, as shown in Figure 6-10.

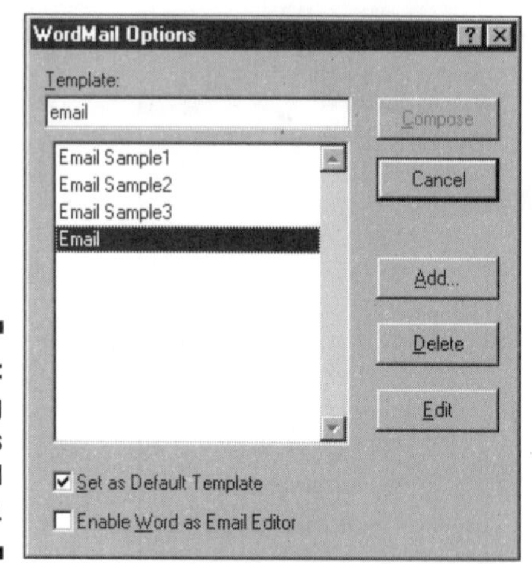

Figure 6-9: Installing Word as your e-mail editor.

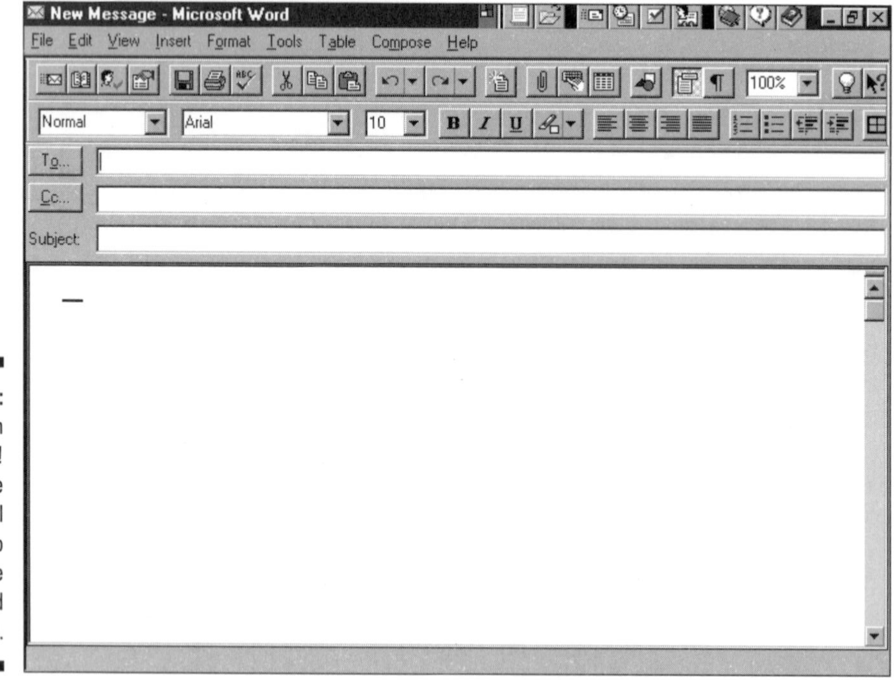

Figure 6-10: A clean slate! Use the WordMail screen to compose and send your e-mail.

Making Your Own Web Pages with Word and the Internet Assistant

After the surging popularity of the Internet apparently made Microsoft suddenly realize that it risked being run over on the mythical information superhighway, the company has been releasing tons of free Internet software to gain market share quickly and continue its dominance in the computer industry. To help accomplish this feat, Microsoft has released a free program named the Internet Assistant. (You can download it for free from CompuServe, America Online, The Microsoft Network, or Microsoft's Web site at `http://www.microsoft.com`.)

When you install the Internet Assistant on your computer, Word adds a Switch to Web Browse/Edit View button to the Formatting toolbar, as shown in Figure 6-

The Switch to Web Browse/Edit View button

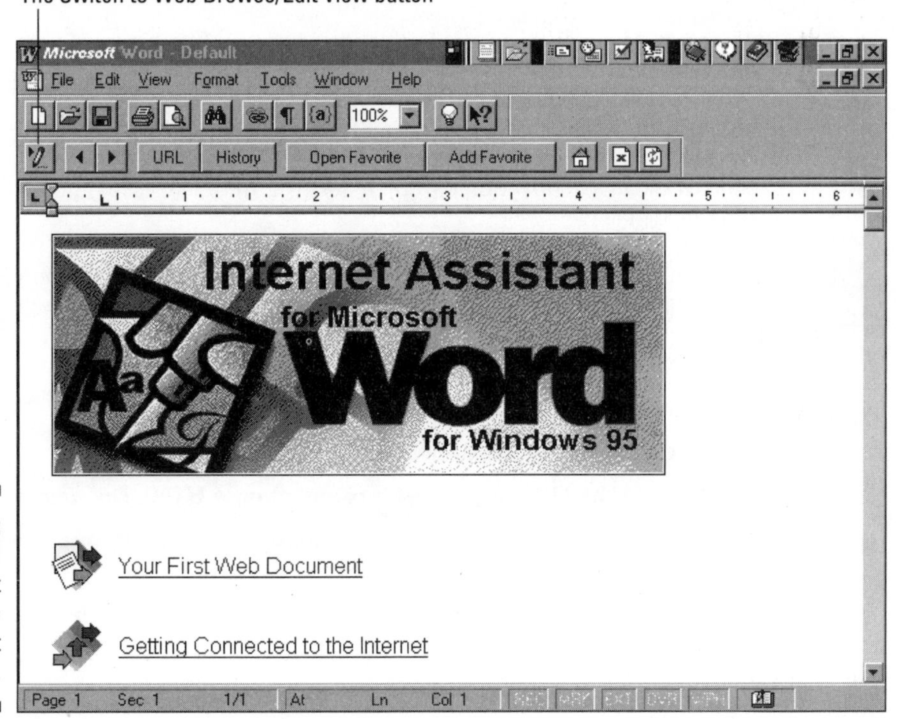

Figure 6-11: Let Word help you get to the Internet Assistant.

The Internet Assistant lets you create and edit Web pages from within Word. That way, you can turn all your Word documents into Web pages and share them over the Internet with people from all over the world. Because all Web pages follow a cryptic standard known as HTML (HyperText Markup Language), you can convert your Word documents into Web pages and enable anyone (even folks who use a Macintosh, Amiga, or Sun workstation) to view your Word documents.

Dissecting a Web page in Word

If you spend much time browsing through the World Wide Web, you may find some fascinating Web pages that use all sorts of special effects, such as scrolling text, frames, and blinking messages. To learn how other people create those fancy Web pages, use your Web browser to save your Web page as an HTML document. (If you're using the Microsoft Internet Explorer, choose File⇨Save As. Just remember that not all browsers let you save a Web page.)

When you save a Web page by using your browser, the browser saves the Web page text but may not save any graphics that appear on the Web page.

After you've saved a Web page as an HTML file on your hard disk, you can load that Web page into Word and examine the HTML source code. By studying this code, you can see how other Webmasters (or Webmistresses) perform their Web page magic.

To examine the HTML source code for a Web page you've saved on your hard disk, follow these steps:

1. **Load Microsoft Word as a separate program outside of a binder.**
2. **Choose File⇨Open.**

   The Open dialog box appears.
3. **Click in the Files of type list box and choose HTML Document.**
4. **Click in the Look in list box and choose the directory or drive in which you have stored your HTML files (Web pages).**
5. **Click the HTML file (Web page) you want to view and click Open.**

   Word displays the text of your saved Web page, as shown in Figure 6-12.
6. **Choose View⇨HTML.**

   Word displays the HTML toolbar and your Web page HTML source code, as shown in Figure 6-13.

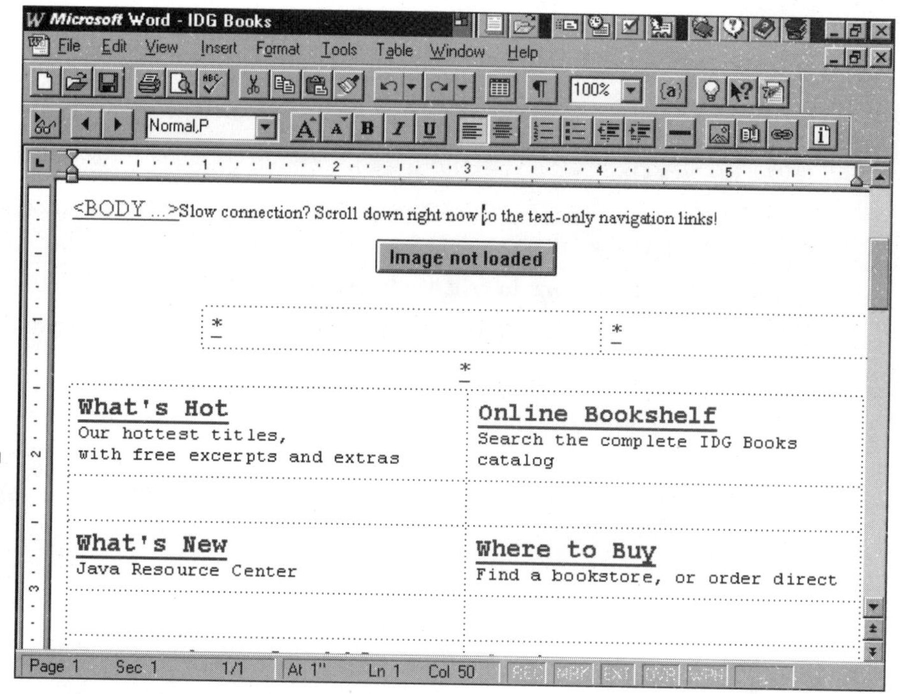

Figure 6-12: Displaying a Web page without fancy graphics.

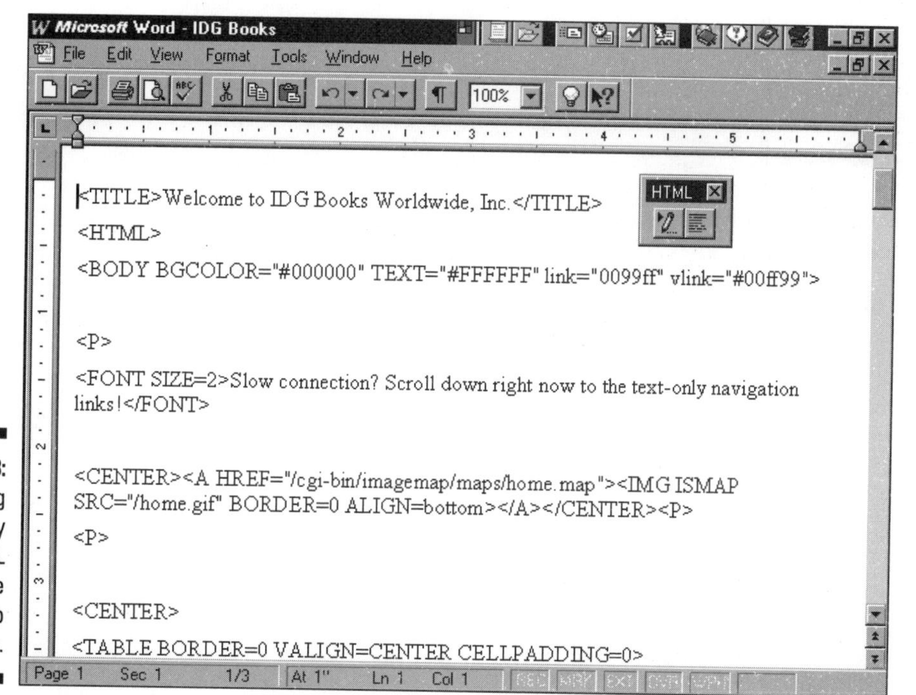

Figure 6-13: Revealing the ugly HTML source code for a Web page.

7. **To make your HTML source code look a little more attractive, click the Auto Format HTML icon on the HTML toolbar, as shown in Figure 6-14.**

   A dialog box appears and lets you know that Word successfully formatted the HTML source code.

8. **Click OK.**

   Now you can browse through the HTML source code to study how another Web page works.

9. **Click the Return to Edit Mode button.**

   The dialog box appears and asks whether you want to save your changes.

10. **Click Yes.**

    Word displays the Web page again (refer to Figure 6-12).

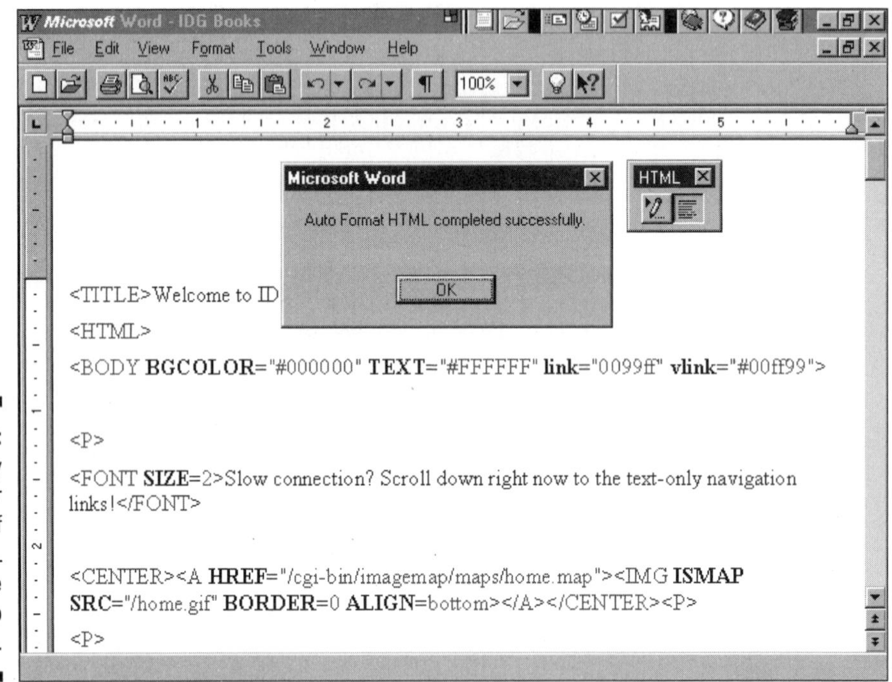

Figure 6-14: A slightly cleaner version of the HTML source code for a Web page.

Making a Web page by using Word

Although it's helpful to use Word to examine existing Web pages, you may want to use the program to create your own Web pages from scratch. Just type, format, and rearrange your text as though you were writing an ordinary business report, résumé, or letter of resignation.

After you've created a Word document (or loaded an existing Word document), follow these steps to turn it into a Web page (an HTML file):

1. **Choose File⇨Save As.**

   The Save As dialog box appears.

2. **Click in the Save as type list box and choose HTML Document.**
3. **Type a new name for your file in the File name box and click Save.**

   Word takes a few seconds (or more if you have a slow computer) to convert your Word document into a genuine HTML file (Web page).

4. **Choose View⇨HTML Source.**

   Word shows you the HTML code it created from your Word document.

5. **Click the Return to Edit Mode icon on the toolbar.**

   Word displays your Web page again. Now you can either stop and be happy with the Web page that Word has helped you create or (more likely) modify your Web page by adding hypertext links and graphics.

Making your Web page look prettier

After creating and saving a Word document as an HTML file, you may want to add a horizontal line (for some reason, Internet Assistant calls it a "horizontal rule"). This line separates paragraphs (to help people more easily read your Web page) or turns text into a marquee so that it scrolls or slides across the screen.

To add a horizontal rule, follow these steps:

1. **Click in your Web page at the spot where you want to add the horizontal rule.**
2. **Choose Insert⇨Horizontal Rule.**

   Word draws a horizontal rule, as shown in Figure 6-15.

Horizontal Rule

Microsoft Word - Movie cliches (web page)

ALCOHOL

Only men are alcoholics. Any hopeless alcoholic can quit drinking when faced with an important challenge. The instant the alcoholic stops drinking, all his faculties return and he faces no annoying withdrawals.

ALIENS

If there is more than one or two of an alien race, they are always roughly the same size as humans. Aliens usually speak English and have same colloquialisms. planet.

All members of alien species wear the same outfits, including clothing, hairstyles, and jewelry. This makes them readily identifiable. Aliens who do not dress like aliens are hiding something.

This may, in fact, be a consequence of the fact that aliens all have single, monolithic cultures: one language, one religion, one outfit, per planet.

Figure 6-15: A horizontal rule in a Web page on movie cliches.

To add a scrolling marquee for text, follow these steps:

1. **Highlight the text you want to turn into a scrolling marquee.**
2. **Choose Insert⇨Marquee.**

   The Marquee dialog box is displayed, as shown in Figure 6-16, with these options:

   - **Right radio button and Left radio button:** Choose whether the text scrolls from the right or the left.
   - **Delay box:** Specify the number of milliseconds to pause when scrolling. The smaller the number, the faster the marquee scrolls.
   - **Amount box:** Indicate the number of pixels to move the marquee. The smaller the number, the smoother the marquee scrolls.
   - **Scroll radio button:** Make the text continually scroll across the screen.
   - **Slide radio button:** Make the text slide across the screen and then stop when it reaches its destination.
   - **Alternate radio button:** Make the text scroll across the screen and continually bounce from one side to the other.

- **Height box:** Specify the height of your marquee text.
- **Width box:** Specify (what else?) the width of your marquee text.
- **Align with Text group of radio buttons (Top, Middle, and Bottom):** Indicate the placement of text next to the marquee text.
- **Background Color list box:** Choose the background color of your marquee to make it look nice as it scrolls across the screen.

3. **Choose the options you want for your marquee text and click OK when you're finished.**

You cannot see how your scrolling marquee looks unless you view it with a Web browser that can display marquee text, such as Microsoft's own Internet Explorer (what a coincidence). Not all Web browsers can display marquee text; if a browser can't display marquee text, it just displays the text on-screen without the fancy marquee special effects — effectively ignoring all the hard work you put into creating the marquee in the first place.

Adding and removing hyperlinks

What's a Web page without links to other parts of the same Web page or to other computers across the world? Because links form the heart of the World Wide Web, it's only natural that the Internet Assistant lets you create links within your Web pages.

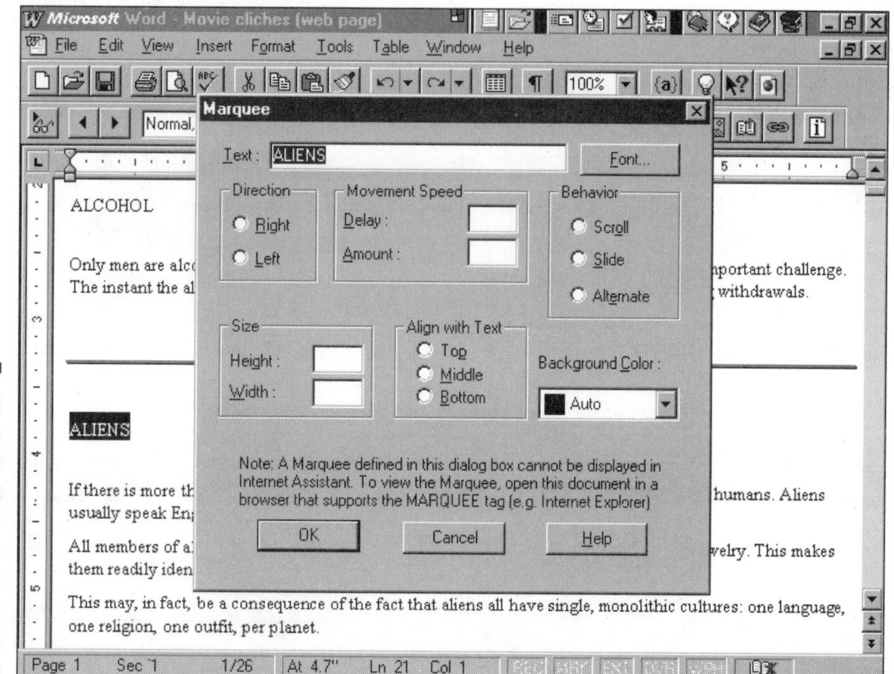

Figure 6-16: The Marquee dialog box helps you get ready to turn text into a scrolling marquee.

You can create two types of links: internal and external. An *internal link* simply jumps to another part of your Web page, such as from the top of the Web page to a paragraph at the bottom of the Web page. An *external link* points to a Web page located on a different computer, such as one located in another city, country, or continent. (If space travel ever becomes a reality, you will eventually be able to link to other planets.)

Creating an internal link within a Web page

To create an internal link, follow these steps:

1. **Highlight the destination text.**

   If you want a link to jump to the bottom of your Web page, for example, highlight the text at the bottom of your Web page.

2. **Choose Edit⇨Bookmark.**

   The Bookmark dialog box appears, as shown in Figure 6-17.

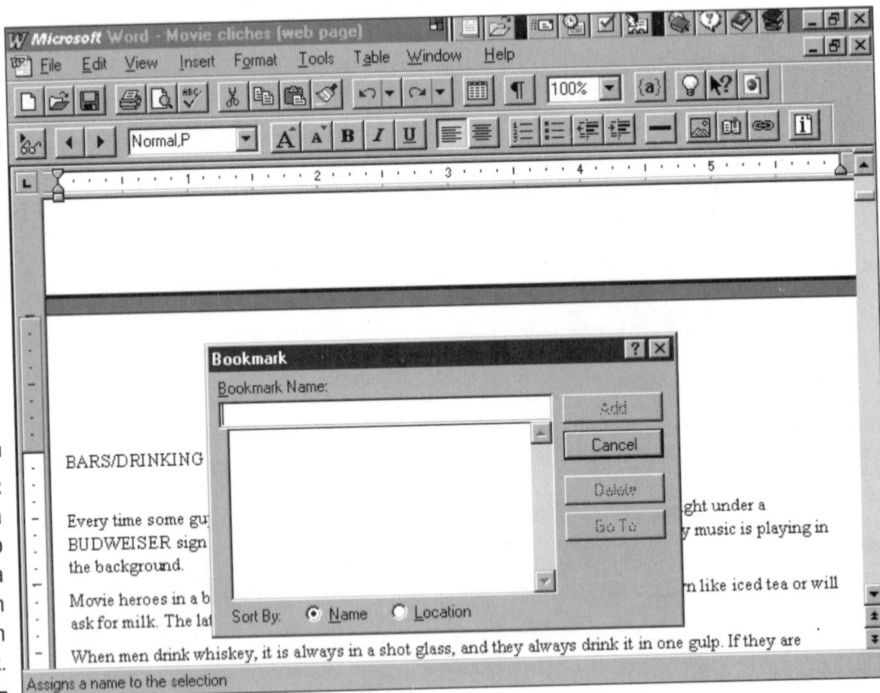

Figure 6-17: Using a bookmark to create a destination for an internal link.

3. **Type a name for your bookmark and click Add.**
4. **Highlight the text you want to turn into an internal hyperlink.**
5. **Choose Insert⇨HyperLink.**

   The Hyperlink dialog box appears, as shown in Figure 6-18.
6. **Click in the Bookmark Location in File list box and highlight the bookmark name you specified in step 3.**
7. **Click OK.**

External links are out of your control. If your Web page points to a Web page on another computer, that computer could crash or shut down, leaving your external link pointing to a suddenly non-existent Web page. Whenever you use external links, check often to make sure that the link still points to a valid Web page.

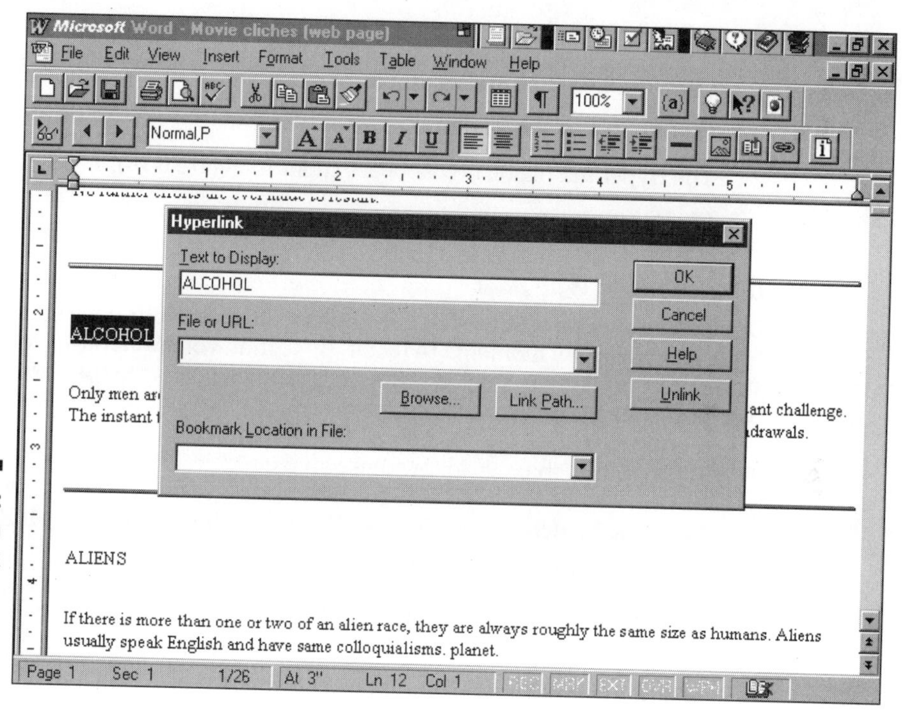

Figure 6-18: Creating an internal link with the Hyperlink dialog box.

To create an external link, follow these steps:

1. **Highlight the text you want to turn into an external hyperlink.**
2. **Choose Insert⇨HyperLink.**

   The Hyperlink dialog box appears (refer to Figure 6-18).
3. **Type the URL address of the Web site to which you want to link.**

   If you want to link your Web page to the IDG Books Web page, for example, you type `http://www.idgbooks.com` in the File or URL box.
4. **Click OK.**

After creating an internal or external link, you may later decide to remove the link.

To remove a link, follow these steps:

1. **Click the text designated as a hyperlink.**
2. **Choose Insert⇨HyperLink.**

   The Hyperlink dialog box appears (refer to Figure 6-18).
3. **Click Unlink.**

Browsing your Web page

Designing a Web page is the fun part. Before you post your page on a Web site, however, take a few moments to test it. By testing your Web page, you can make sure that everything is spelled correctly, graphics appear in the correct location, and your hyperlinks actually work.

To browse your Web page, follow these steps:

1. **Click the Switch to Web Browse View. (Or choose View⇨Web Browse.)**

   Word displays the Formatting toolbar, shown in Figure 6-19.
2. **Click your hyperlinks to make sure that they work.**

   If you click an external hyperlink, Word tries to connect to the Internet. If you don't have a modem or Internet account, you just have to trust that your external links work.
3. **Choose File⇨Save when you're finished.**

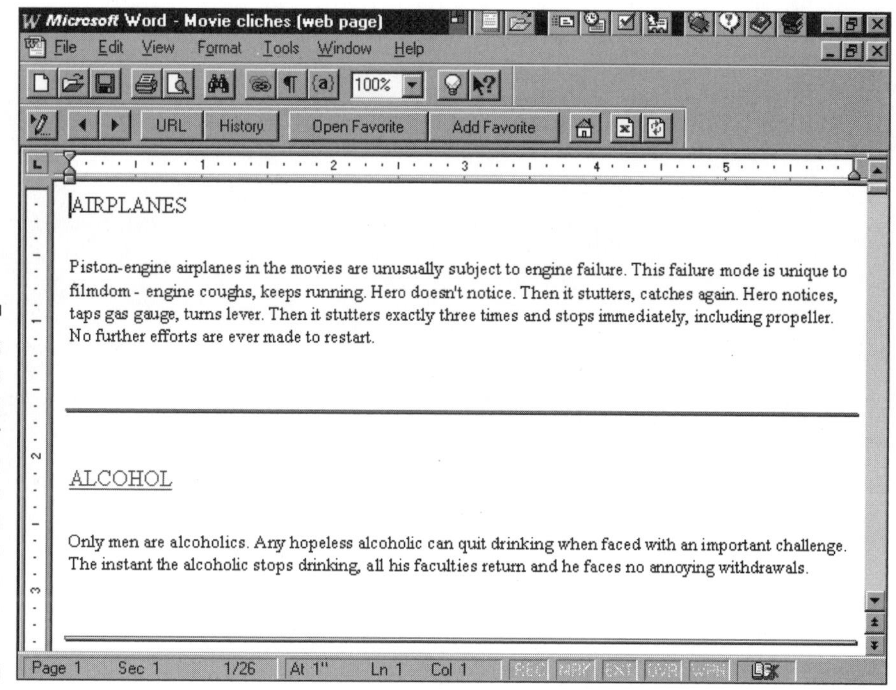

Figure 6-19: The Formatting toolbar helps you navigate through your Web pages on movie cliches.

Part II

Crunching Numbers with Microsoft Excel

"I HEARD THEY WANTED TO FILL OUT THE SHOW A *LITTLE* THIS YEAR."

In this part . . .

Everyone loves money, yet most people hate math (which may explain why most people don't have much money). To turn your computer into a calculating machine, Excel lets you write your own formulas or use one of its many built-in functions to solve complicated calculations.

Functions are simply formulas that someone already has written for you (and verified to make sure that they work correctly). By using built-in functions, you can save yourself time and trouble creating worksheets by yourself.

Because neither computers nor people are perfect, Excel provides auditing features to help you verify that your worksheets actually calculate numbers correctly. This part of the book shows you how to verify the accuracy of your worksheets, as well as how to print your worksheets in pretty pages so that you can impress your boss (even if you don't have the slightest idea what you're doing otherwise).

Chapter 7
Customizing Microsoft Excel

In This Chapter

- Customizing Excel toolbars
- Changing the way Excel works
- Hiding rows and columns of an Excel worksheet
- Freezing rows and columns of an Excel worksheet

Nobody likes being told what to do, which explains why many people don't like school. In the same manner, many software programs provide little flexibility on how the application looks, works, or acts. If you don't like the way your new program works, you may find out the hard way that you just blew several hundred dollars, an hour or two trying to learn the program, and several megabytes of your precious hard disk space.

Fortunately, Microsoft Excel doesn't rely on this fixed-in-stone approach to software usage. Instead, Excel lets you mold program features as if they were Silly Putty. By customizing program features, you can personalize your copy of Excel — which has the added advantage of confusing the living daylights out of someone who tries to use your computer without your permission.

Excel was originally written as a Macintosh spreadsheet program and quickly overtook the spreadsheet competition. Microsoft then wrote a version of Excel for Windows, which soon became even more popular than the mighty Lotus 1-2-3 spreadsheet application. This history lesson has nothing to do with customizing Excel, but it's kind of neat to know this stuff anyway.

Toying with Your Toolbars

Toolbars are sets of related buttons that allow you to perform common tasks. Because Excel has no way of knowing which tasks you perform most often, it provides a wide variety of handy toolbars.

Because Excel has so many built-in toolbars, you may want to take the time to examine which ones you find most useful so that you can display them at all times. Toolbars that you never use can be tucked away out of sight. And because not every toolbar contains the exact commands that you most often use, Excel allows you to customize your favorite toolbars.

Excel provides 13 toolbars, which are shown in Figure 7-1.

Check out *Excel For Windows 95 For Dummies* or *MORE Excel For Windows 95 For Dummies,* both by Greg Harvey (and both published by IDG Books Worldwide, Inc.), for the complete scoop on how to use the Excel toolbars and their buttons.

Making a toolbar appear or disappear

To customize a particular toolbar, you need to first display that toolbar on your screen.

To make a toolbar appear or disappear, follow these steps:

1. **Choose View⇨Toolbars.**

   The Toolbars dialog box appears, as shown in Figure 7-2.

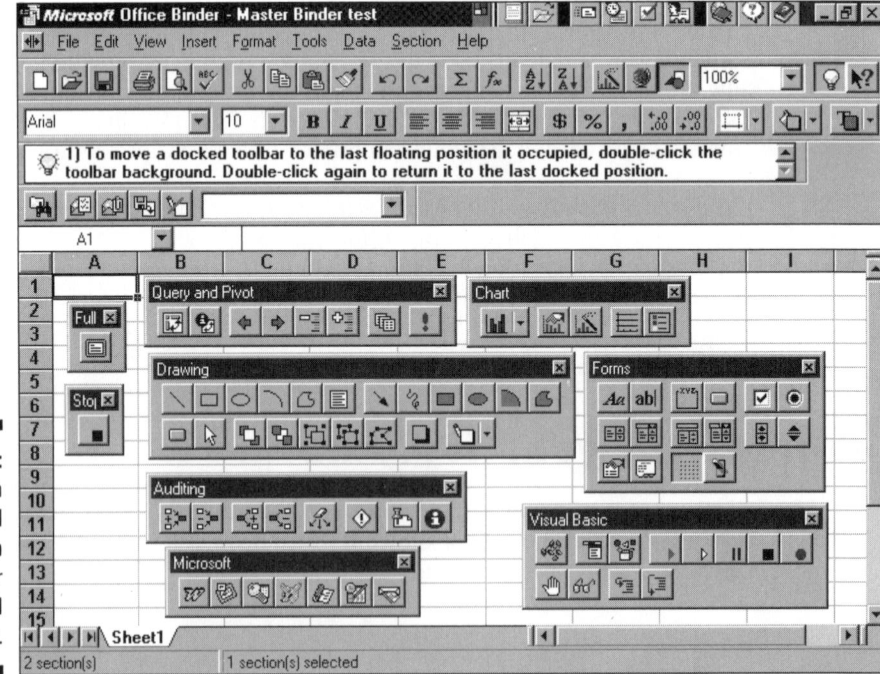

Figure 7-1: Thirteen Excel toolbars in all their splendid glory.

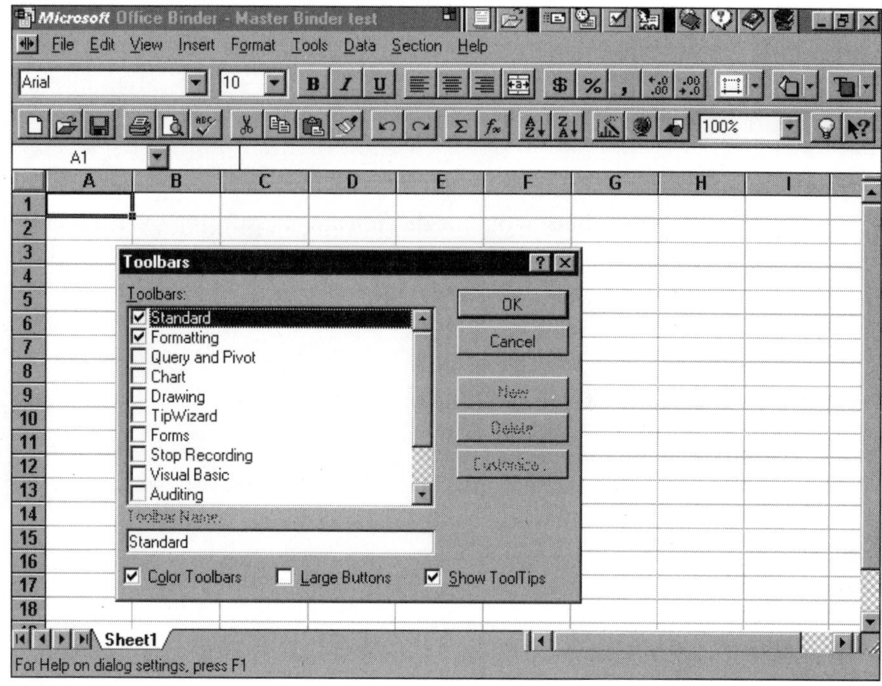

Figure 7-2: Use the Toolbars dialog box to make toolbars appear or disappear.

2. **In the Toolbars dialog box, select the name of the toolbar that you want to modify.**

   To make a toolbar disappear, deselect the toolbar's check box.

3. **Click OK.**

   The toolbar appears on your worksheet as a floating toolbar.

4. **Click OK to close the Toolbars dialog box.**

Removing buttons from a toolbar

The first step to customizing a toolbar is to remove the buttons that you never use. After you eliminate unneeded buttons from a toolbar, you can start cramming your preferred buttons onto the toolbar.

To remove a button from a toolbar, follow these steps:

1. **If you're using Excel in a binder, choose Section⇨View Outside.**

   Skip this step if you're using Excel outside of a binder.

2. **Choose View⇨Toolbars.**

   The Toolbars dialog box appears (refer to Figure 7-2).

3. **Click the button you want to remove from the toolbar, hold down the left mouse button, and drag the button off the toolbar, as shown in Figure 7-3.**

   The button that you drag off the toolbar appears as a gray outline of itself.

4. **Release the left mouse button.**

   The gray button outline disappears as Excel removes the button from the toolbar.

5. **Click Close.**

Adding buttons to a toolbar

After you remove from a particular toolbar all the buttons you don't normally use, you can add your preferred buttons so that you can easily execute the operations you perform most often.

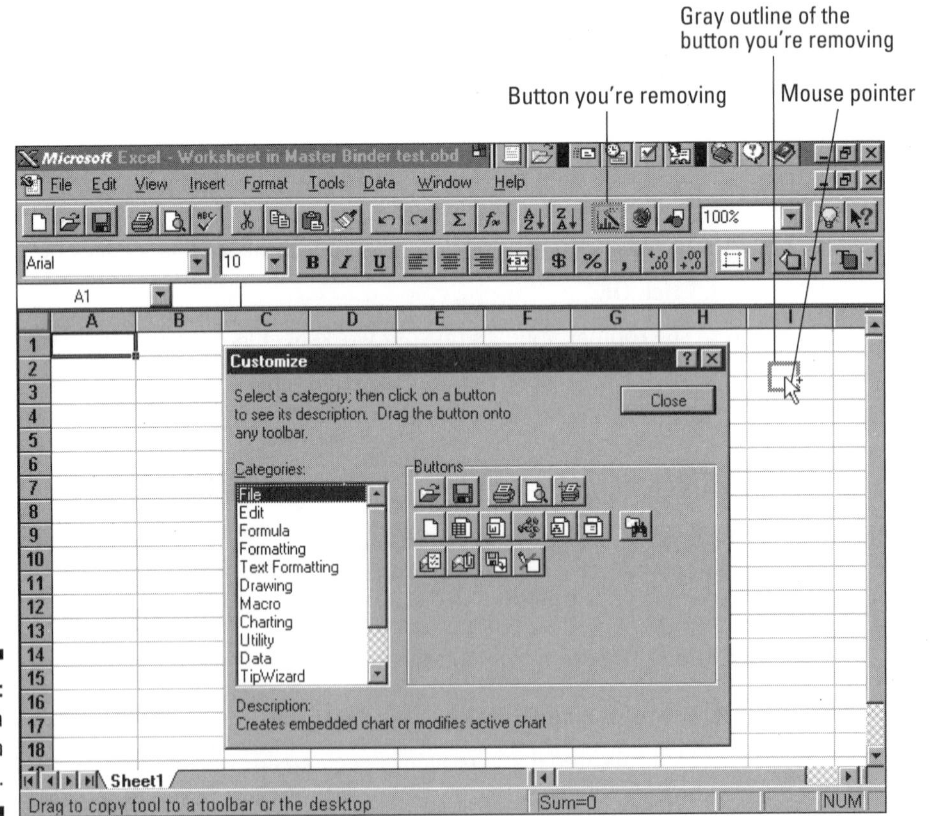

Figure 7-3: Removing a button from a toolbar.

To add a button to a toolbar, follow these steps:

1. **If you're using Excel in a binder, choose Section⇨View Outside.**

   Skip this step if you're using Excel outside a binder.

2. **Choose View⇨Toolbars.**

   The Toolbars dialog box appears (refer to Figure 7-2).

3. **In the Toolbars dialog box, select the name of the toolbar you want to modify.**

   A check mark appears in the check box next to the toolbar name.

4. **Click Customize.**

   Excel displays the toolbar you selected and then displays a Customize dialog box, shown in Figure 7-4.

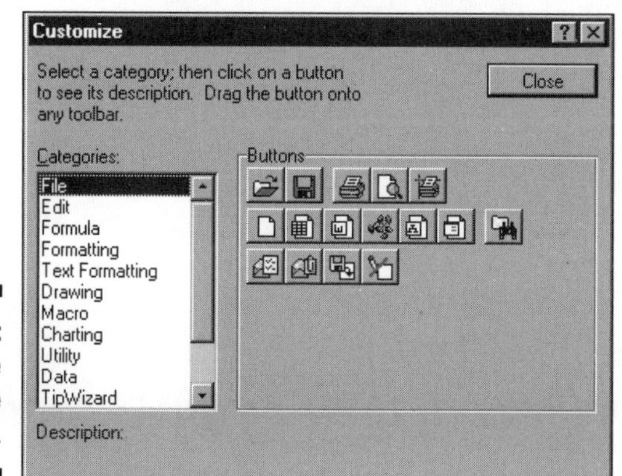

Figure 7-4: The Customize dialog box.

5. **Select a category from the Categories list box.**

   For example, to add a new formatting command to a toolbar, select Format. Excel displays the available formatting buttons in the Buttons group in the Customize dialog box.

6. **From the available buttons shown in the Customize dialog box, select the button you want to add, hold down the left mouse button, and drag the button to the toolbar.**

   Place the mouse pointer where you want the button to appear, as shown in Figure 7-5.

7. **Release the mouse button and click Close.**

   The new button appears on the toolbar.

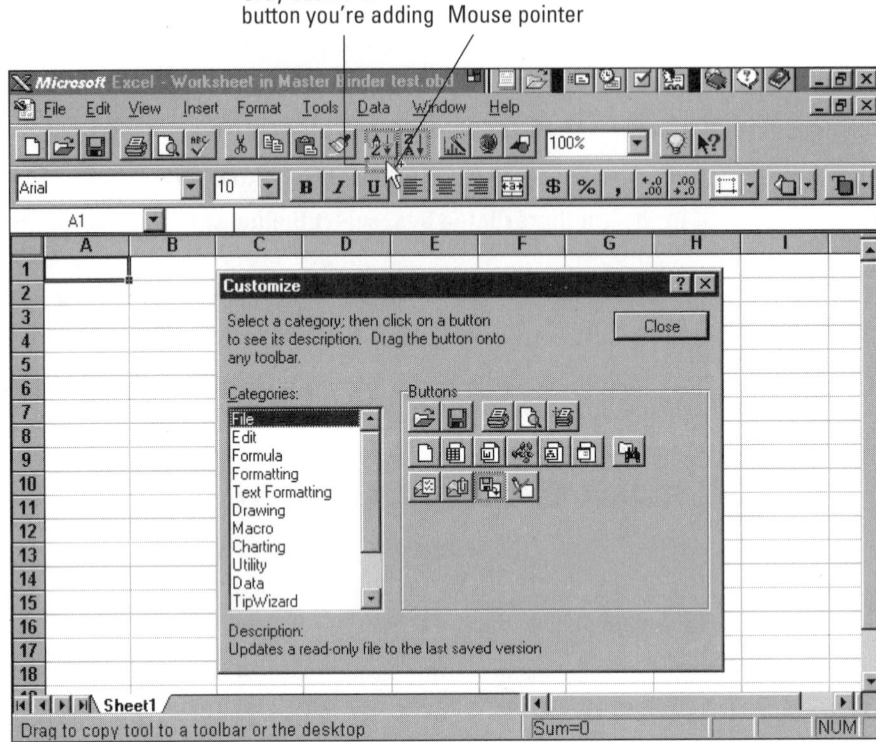

Figure 7-5: Adding a button to a toolbar.

Resetting toolbars to their original condition

If somebody modifies a toolbar and clutters it with a bunch of buttons you never use, you can delete the individual buttons and add the ones you prefer. However, a quicker solution is to reset the toolbar to its original condition and *then* modify the toolbar to your individual tastes.

To reset a toolbar to its original condition, follow these steps:

1. **If you're using Excel in a binder, choose Section➪View Outside.**

   Skip this step if you're using Excel outside a binder.

2. **Choose View➪Toolbars.**

   The Toolbars dialog box appears (refer to Figure 7-2).

3. **In the Toolbars dialog box, select the name of the modified toolbar you want to reset.**

4. **Click Reset.**

   Excel resets the toolbar to its original state.

5. **Click OK to close the Toolbars dialog box.**

   The toolbar now appears in its default, fresh-from-the-factory condition.

Creating your own toolbars

Rather than modify an existing toolbar, you may want to create your own custom toolbar. This way, you haven't modified all the standard Excel toolbars, so if you share a copy of Excel with another user, that person won't get confused.

To create your own custom toolbar, follow these steps:

1. **If you're using Excel in a binder, choose Section⇨View Outside.**

   Skip this step if you're using Excel outside a binder.

2. **Choose View⇨Toolbars.**

   The Toolbars dialog box appears (refer to Figure 7-2).

3. **Type a name for your toolbar in the Toolbar name box.**

4. **Click Customize.**

   The Customize dialog box appears (refer to Figure 7-4).

5. **Select a category from the Categories list box.**

   For example, to add an editing command to a toolbar, select Edit. Excel displays the available editing buttons in the Buttons group.

6. **From the available buttons shown in the Customize dialog box, select the one that you want to add, hold down the left mouse button, drag the button off the Customize dialog box and onto the worksheet, and then release the left mouse button.**

7. **Repeat step 5 to add additional buttons to your newly created toolbar.**

   Excel displays your button in its own toolbar, as shown in Figure 7-6.

8. **Click Close when you're done filling your toolbar with buttons.**

   Your newly created toolbar appears on-screen, ready to use.

To move your floating toolbar, click its title bar, hold down the left mouse button, drag the mouse to where you want the toolbar to appear, and release the mouse button.

Changing the shape of your toolbar

After you create a new toolbar, Excel displays the toolbar as a floating box. If you don't like the shape of your new toolbar (or any other Excel toolbar), simply change its shape to resemble a vertical strip or a rectangle, as shown in Figure 7-7.

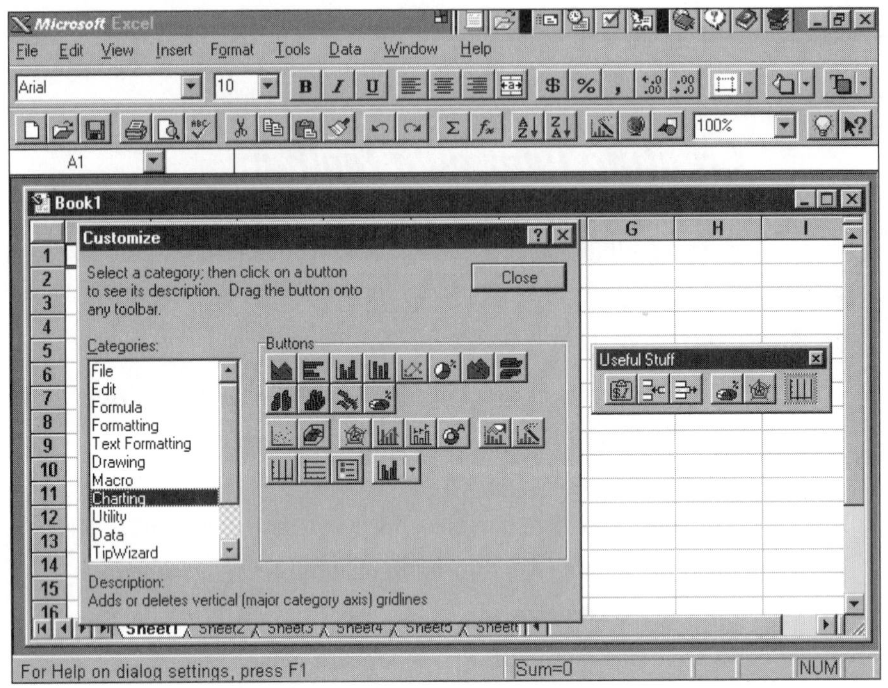

Figure 7-6: Your newly created custom toolbar.

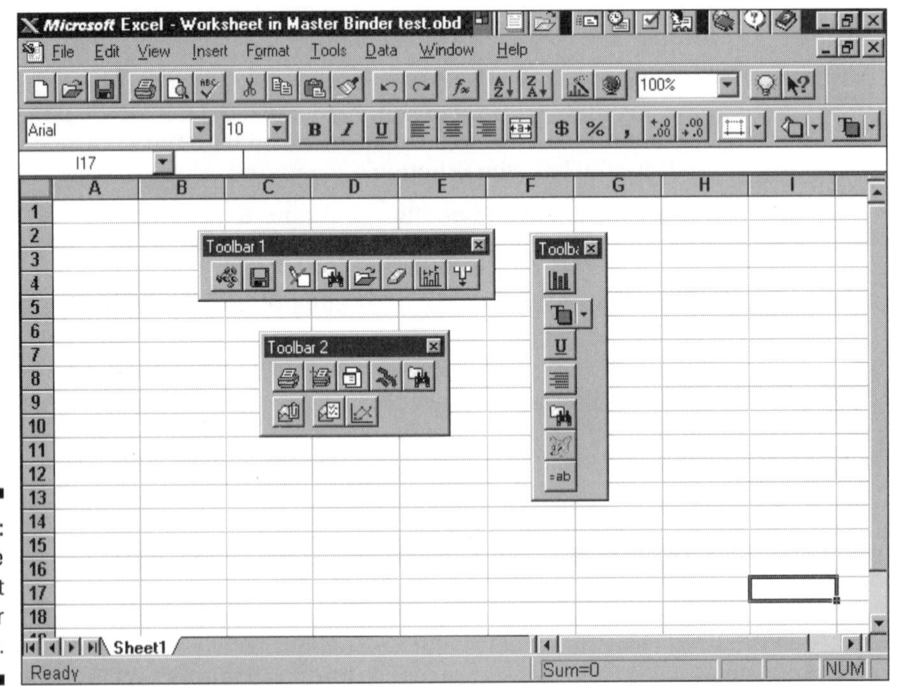

Figure 7-7: Three different shapes for your toolbar.

To change the shape of your toolbar, follow these steps:

1. **Move the mouse pointer to any edge of the toolbar so that the mouse appears as a double-headed arrow pointing left/right or up/down.**
2. **Hold down the left mouse button and drag the mouse until the gray outline of the toolbar changes to a different shape, as shown in Figure 7-8.**
3. **Release the mouse button.**

   The floating toolbar appears with the shape you selected.

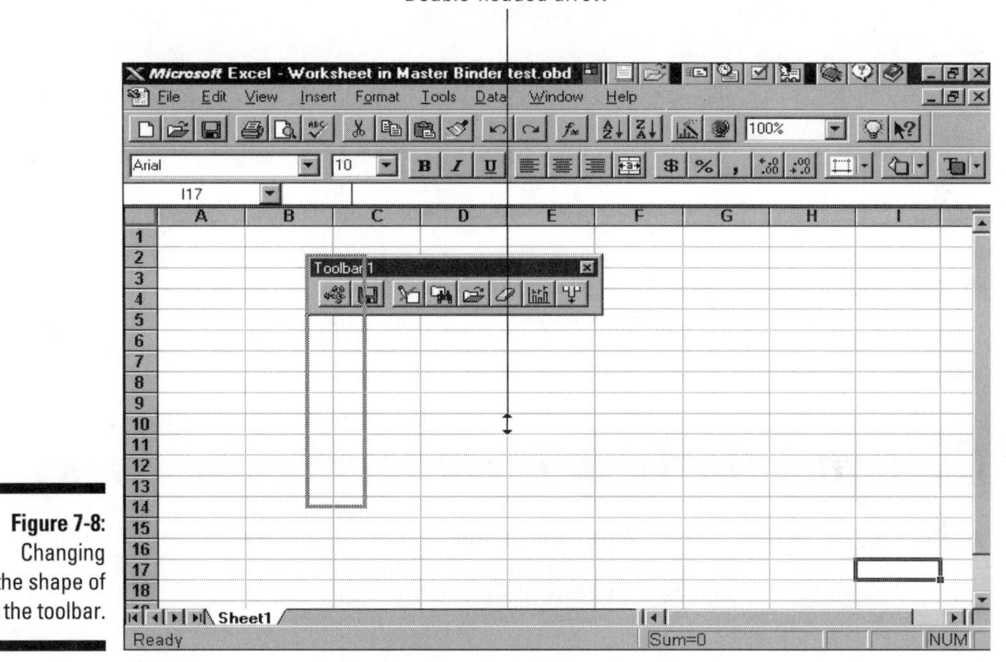

Figure 7-8: Changing the shape of the toolbar.

To change the way a toolbar appears, you can just double-click any gray portion of the toolbar. (Make sure that you don't double-click a button by mistake, or Excel thinks you want it to perform a command.) The moment you double-click the gray portion of a toolbar, it changes its shape from a horizontal strip to a floating toolbar and vice versa.

Deleting your custom toolbars

Because *you* create custom toolbars for your own benefit, you can also wipe them out when you no longer want them around.

You can delete only the toolbars you create; you can never delete any of the built-in Excel toolbars. You can hide built-in toolbars so that Excel doesn't display them, however.

To delete one of your custom toolbars, follow these steps:

1. **If you're using Excel in a binder, choose Section⇨View Outside.**

   Skip this step if you're using Excel outside a binder.

2. **Choose View⇨Toolbars.**

   The Toolbars dialog box appears (refer to Figure 7-2).

3. **In the Toolbars dialog box, select the name of the toolbar you want to delete.**

4. **Click Delete.**

   A dialog box appears, asking whether you *really* want to delete your toolbar.

5. **Click OK.**

   This action deletes your custom toolbar.

6. **Click OK to close the Toolbars dialog box.**

Make sure that you really know what you're doing before you delete one of your custom toolbars. After you delete a custom toolbar, you can't undelete it.

Changing the Way Excel Works and Looks

Because the way Excel works and looks can affect the way you use the program, take a little time to customize some of the more obscure features in Excel. That way you can make your copy of Excel more comfortable to use.

Saving your work

Obviously, if you don't save your work, you'll lose it — which might come in handy if you need to eliminate incriminating evidence. Most users, however, need to save their work. Because saving your work is one of the most important tasks you perform, Excel provides four ways to save your files:

- Click the Save button in the Standard toolbar.
- Choose File⇨Save.
- Press Ctrl+S.
- Use the AutoSave feature so that Excel saves your files for you.

Saving files automatically

To make saving your files easier, Excel can periodically save your files without your having to even think about it. If you forget to save your file, Excel shrugs its shoulders, rolls its eyes, and saves the file for you — all on its own.

To make Excel save your files automatically, follow these steps:

1. **Choose Tools⇨Add-Ins.**

   The Add-Ins dialog box appears, as shown in Figure 7-9.

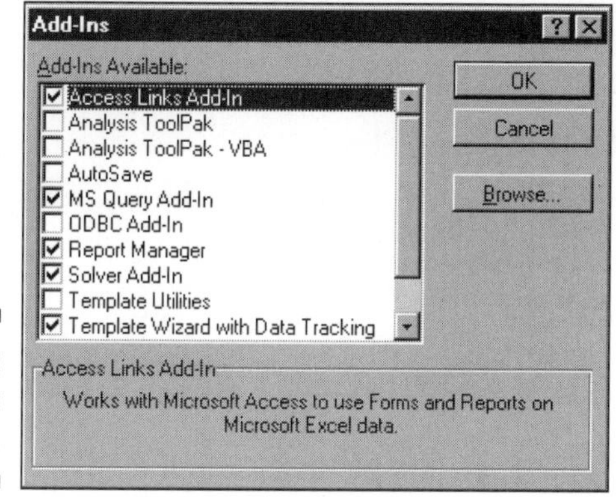

Figure 7-9: The Add-Ins dialog box.

2. **Select the AutoSave check box and click OK.**

   A check mark appears in the the AutoSave check box.

3. **Choose Tools⇨AutoSave.**

   An AutoSave dialog box appears, as shown in Figure 7-10.

Figure 7-10: The AutoSave dialog box.

4. **Select the Automatic Save Every check box so that a check mark appears.**

5. **In the Minutes text box, enter the time interval for Excel to automatically save your file.**

   In this example, Excel will automatically save your file every 13 minutes.

6. Click OK.

If you want Excel to save all open workbooks, click the Save All Open Workbooks option button. If you just want to save the workbook you're using at the time, click the Save Active Workbook Only option button.

Where did I put that file?

Microsoft Office normally saves your files in the `C:\Mydocuments` directory. So, the next time you forget where you stored your file, first look in that directory. However, you may want to store your files in a different directory.

To store your files in a different directory, follow these steps:

1. **Choose Tools⇨Options.**
2. **Click the General tab, as shown in Figure 7-11.**
3. **Click the Default File Location box and type the name of the directory where you want Excel to store your files.**

   For example, type **c:\secret stuff** in the Default File Location box.
4. **Click OK.**

   Excel saves your files in the new default file location.

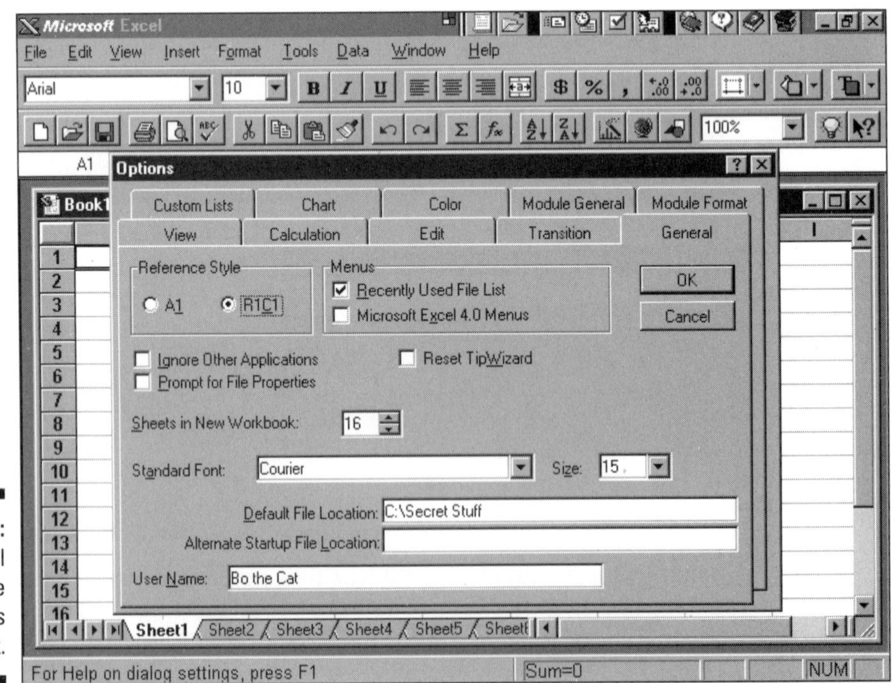

Figure 7-11: The General tab in the Options dialog box.

Messing around with the appearance of Excel

To help you adapt to Excel (and to encourage users of rival spreadsheets to defect to Excel), Microsoft makes it easy to customize the look of Excel. You can modify the font and text size to make your screens easier to read, and you can customize the way Excel labels its columns. You can even make Excel screens mimick screens from other spreadsheet programs with which you may be more familiar.

Playing with fonts

Unless you specify otherwise, Excel displays text in the Arial font at 10-point size. While this font is fine for most people, you may want to choose a different font (for aesthetic reasons) or a different point size (to make your numbers easier to see, in case the tiny 10-point size is too small for you).

To change the font and point size of text displayed in Excel, follow these steps:

1. **Choose Tools➪Options.**
2. **Click the General tab (refer to Figure 7-11).**
3. **Click the Standard Font list box and select the font you want to use.**

   For example, choose Courier in the Standard Font list box.
4. **Click the Size list box and select the point size you want to use.**

   For example, choose 15 in the Size list box.
5. **Click OK.**

You may have to experiment to find the font and point size that looks best to you; Excel won't actually display your new font and point size until you click OK and exit the Options dialog box. To set your new font as the default font, you may have to exit the program and then reload Excel. Aren't computers doing a wonderful job of making your life easier?

Labeling columns by number

Excel labels its columns with letters and its rows with numbers. For example, cell A3 is located in the first column (A) and the third row (3). However, some other spreadsheets (with which you may be more familiar) may label both columns *and* rows with numbers. If you prefer to label your columns with numbers, simply customize the label.

TOOTORIAL

To label columns with numbers instead of letters, follow these steps:

1. **Choose Tools➪Options.**
2. **Click the General Tab (refer to Figure 7-11).**

3. **Click the R1C1 radio button in the Reference Style group.**

   The R1C1 radio button tells Excel, "I want all my columns to be labeled with numbers from now on."

4. **Click OK.**

   Excel immediately labels all your columns with numbers instead of letters.

Mimicking Excel 4.0

It may seem silly that different versions of the same program should look and act differently, but that's the way the software industry works. If you were using Excel Version 4.0 and have switched to Excel 7.0 (because you upgraded to Windows 95), you may notice that the pull-down menus in Version 7.0 look a little different from the pull-down menus in Version 4.0.

In case you're wondering, there was never an Excel Version 6.0. After Excel Version 4.0, Microsoft changed the pull-down menu structure for Excel 5.0, which was the last version designed for Windows 3.1. Then they skipped to Excel 7.0, which was the first version designed for Windows 95. It just goes to show that even with all the computational power of Excel, a simple job like counting from one to seven can still be tough.

You can make the Excel Version 7.0 menus look more like the menus found in Version 4.0. To modify the appearance of your Excel menus, follow these steps:

1. **Choose Tools➪Options.**
2. **Click the General Tab (refer to Figure 7-11).**
3. **In the Menus group, select the Microsoft Excel 4.0 Menus check box.**

   A check mark appears in the check box.

4. **Click OK.**

   Your menus now look just like the Excel Version 4.0 menus.

In case you get tired of using the Excel Version 4.0 pull-down menus, you can easily switch back to the Version 7.0 pull-down menus. To switch back to Excel Version 7.0 menus, choose Options➪New Menus.

Lotus 1-2-3 help

Way back when, the most popular spreadsheet program in the world was Lotus 1-2-3. After Microsoft introduced Windows, the world flocked to programs like Excel, which took over the spreadsheet market and has slaughtered Lotus 1-2-3 in popularity ever since.

If you're a Lotus 1-2-3 veteran who has recently switched to Excel, you'll be glad to know that Excel provides special help for former Lotus 1-2-3 users.

Excel can mimic Lotus 1-2-3 in four ways:

- Displaying explanations on how to perform a command in Excel by using Lotus 1-2-3 commands
- Letting you use Lotus 1-2-3 navigation keys to move the cursor around in Excel
- Evaluating formulas exactly like Lotus 1-2-3
- Letting you enter formulas just like Lotus 1-2-3

To modify Excel to work more like Lotus 1-2-3, follow these steps:

1. **Choose Tools➪Options.**
2. **Click the Transition tab, shown in Figure 7-12.**

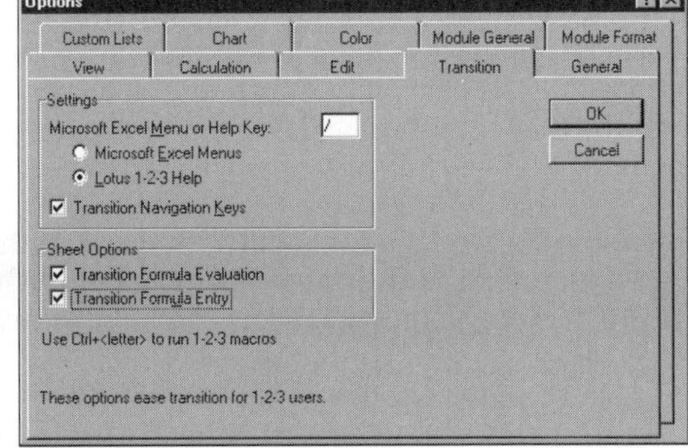

Figure 7-12: The Transition tab in the Options dialog box.

3. **In the Settings group, select the Lotus 1-2-3 Help radio button.**

   This option displays the equivalent commands of Lotus 1-2-3 and Excel whenever you press the slash (/) key.

4. **Select the Transition Navigation Keys check box so that a check mark appears.**

   This option allows you to use Lotus 1-2-3 navigation keys. For example, pressing Ctrl+Home in Excel moves the cursor to cell A1; if you are using Lotus 1-2-3 navigation keys, you simply press Home to do the same thing.

5. **Select the Transition Formula Evaluation check box so that a check mark appears.**

   Select this option if you want Excel to evaluate formulas just like Lotus 1-2-3 does. For example, Lotus 1-2-3 evaluates the formula =–2^4 as –16 because it multiples 2 four times. But Excel multiples –2 four times to calculate that same formula as 16.

6. **Select the Transition Formula Entry check box so that a check mark appears.**

   Check this option if you want to enter formulas like you do with Lotus 1-2-3. With Lotus 1-2-3, for example, you can specify a range of cells by using two periods, such as A1..A5; Excel specifies that same range as A1:A5.

7. **Click OK.**

Changing Your Point of View

How you view something can affect how well you learn from it. You can stare at a wall-sized listing of financial numbers that are scattered all over the place, and you may not learn anything at all. But if you look only at a small portion of that same listing of numbers, you may be able to get a better handle on your company's financial picture.

Excel gives you the option to view worksheets in different ways. At the simplest level, this option enables you to read your worksheets more easily. On a more advanced level, flexibility in viewing your worksheets can help you evaluate what your numbers really mean.

Hiding rows and columns on a worksheet

Unless you create simple worksheets that can fit onto a single computer screen, you can't normally see an entire worksheet at one time. Rather than force you to tediously scroll up, down, right, or left (and risk missing some important connections among your numbers), Excel can selectively hide and display rows and columns. Figure 7-13 and Figure 7-14 show how hiding rows can help you evaluate the data on your worksheet more easily.

The whole purpose of hiding rows or columns is to display only those numbers that are most important. For example, you don't want to wade through endless rows of numbers when you just need to look at the bottom line to find out whether your company is making a profit.

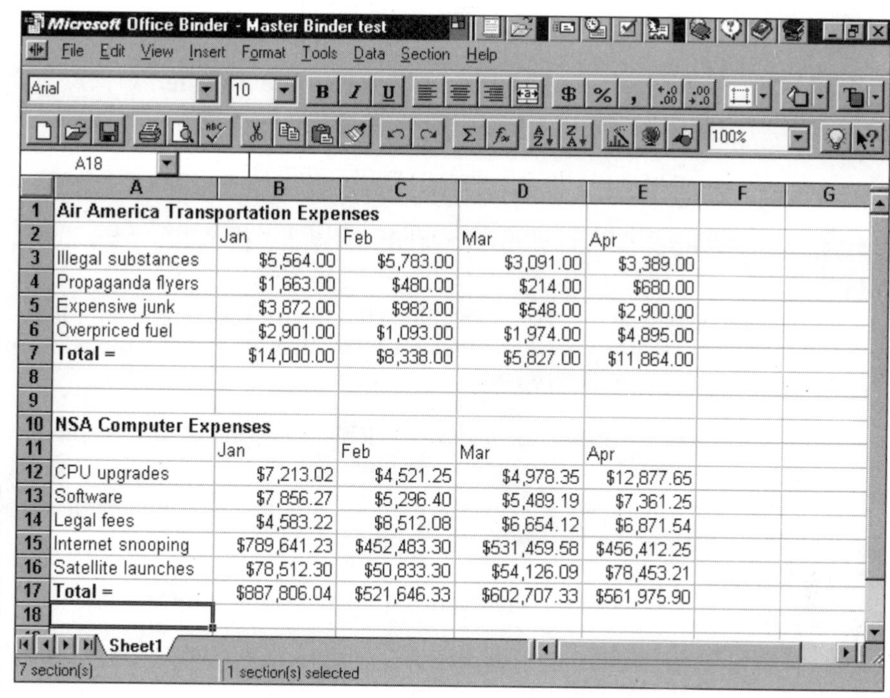

	A	B	C	D	E
1	**Air America Transportation Expenses**				
2		Jan	Feb	Mar	Apr
3	Illegal substances	$5,564.00	$5,783.00	$3,091.00	$3,389.00
4	Propaganda flyers	$1,663.00	$480.00	$214.00	$680.00
5	Expensive junk	$3,872.00	$982.00	$548.00	$2,900.00
6	Overpriced fuel	$2,901.00	$1,093.00	$1,974.00	$4,895.00
7	**Total =**	$14,000.00	$8,338.00	$5,827.00	$11,864.00
8					
9					
10	**NSA Computer Expenses**				
11		Jan	Feb	Mar	Apr
12	CPU upgrades	$7,213.02	$4,521.25	$4,978.35	$12,877.65
13	Software	$7,856.27	$5,296.40	$5,489.19	$7,361.25
14	Legal fees	$4,583.22	$8,512.08	$6,654.12	$6,871.54
15	Internet snooping	$789,641.23	$452,483.30	$531,459.58	$456,412.25
16	Satellite launches	$78,512.30	$50,833.30	$54,126.09	$78,453.21
17	**Total =**	$887,806.04	$521,646.33	$602,707.33	$561,975.90
18					

Figure 7-13: A hideous worksheet with lots of numbers.

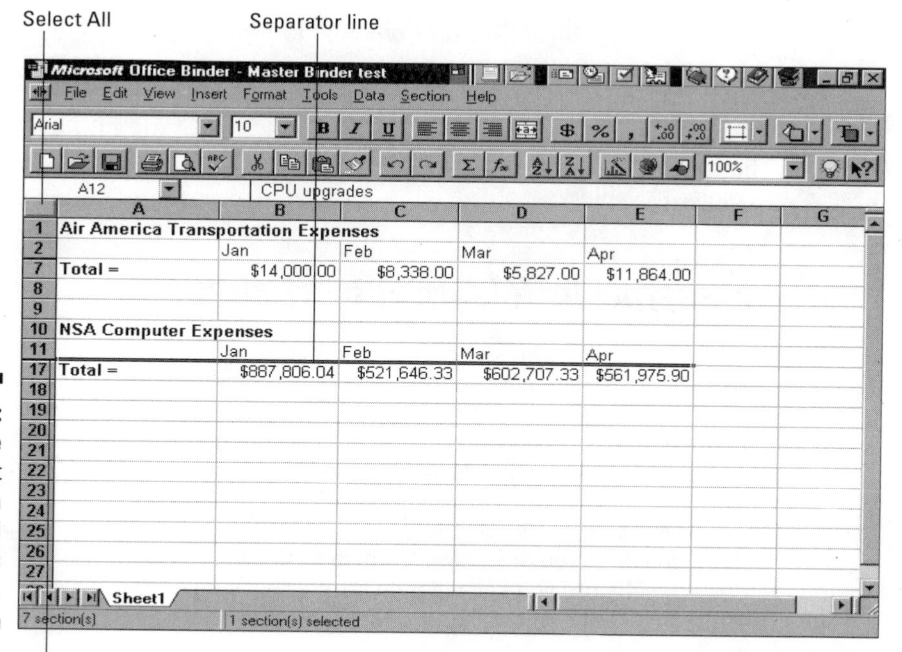

	A	B	C	D	E
1	**Air America Transportation Expenses**				
2		Jan	Feb	Mar	Apr
7	**Total =**	$14,000.00	$8,338.00	$5,827.00	$11,864.00
8					
9					
10	**NSA Computer Expenses**				
11		Jan	Feb	Mar	Apr
17	**Total =**	$887,806.04	$521,646.33	$602,707.33	$561,975.90

Figure 7-14: The same worksheet with unneeded rows hidden.

To hide a row or a column on a worksheet, follow these steps:

1. **Highlight the rows or columns you want to hide.**
2. **Choose Format⇨Row (or Column)⇨Hide.**

   Excel hides the selected rows or columns.

Hiding a row or column does not delete it. Hiding a row or column simply tucks it conveniently out of sight.

You may wonder, "How can I find a hidden row or column after if it's hidden?" Fortunately, when Excel hides rows or columns, it marks them in two distinct ways (refer to Figure 7-14):

- The worksheet displays a thick black line in the row or column labels where rows or columns are hiding.
- The worksheet skips the numbering in row or column labels to show how many rows or columns are hidden.

To unhide a row or column on a worksheet, follow these steps:

1. **Highlight the range of cells containing the hidden rows or columns you want to unhide.**

   For example, if you want to unhide rows 3–6, you select rows 2–7.
2. **Choose Format⇨Row (or Column)⇨Unhide.**

   Excel displays your previously hidden rows or columns.

To unhide all hidden rows or columns on a worksheet, click the Select All button (refer to Figure 7-14) and then choose Format⇨Row (or Column)⇨Unhide.

Freezing labels on a worksheet

If you clutter up a worksheet with endless rows and columns filled with numbers, the worksheet may not make sense to anyone. To help identify what certain numbers mean, write descriptive labels next to your rows or columns of numbers so that anyone can see what those numbers represent. Some examples of descriptive labels are *Total amount, January sales,* or *Quantity sold.*

Unfortunately, if you scroll too far up/down or right/left, your descriptive labels also scroll up/down or right/left, which means they disappear out of sight altogether. Before you know it, you are staring at unlabeled rows and columns of numbers that don't make any sense.

For example, Figure 7-15 shows a worksheet with labels that identify your numbers. The moment you start scrolling, however, the labels scroll out of sight, as shown in Figure 7-16.

Descriptive labels

Microsoft Office Binder - Master Binder test

F2

	A	B	C	D	E	F
1	**Monthly Expenses for the University of Timbuktu**					
2		**Jan**	**Feb**	**Mar**	**Apr**	
3	Athletic scholarships	$5,564.00	$5,783.00	$3,091.00	$3,389.00	
4	Recruitment brochures	$2,356.00	$4,125.00	$2,145.00	$4,587.00	
5	Landscaping	$3,872.00	$982.00	$4,521.00	$2,900.00	
6	President's salary	$2,901.00	$1,093.00	$1,974.00	$4,895.00	
7	Unnecessary travel	$1,555.21	$4,253.21	$1,258.63	$2,115.98	
8	Alcohol	$5,564.00	$5,783.00	$3,091.00	$3,389.00	
9	Expensive gifts	$1,663.00	$5,487.00	$2,561.00	$5,875.00	
10	Maid service	$3,872.00	$7,856.00	$4,758.00	$2,964.00	
11	Limousine service	$2,901.00	$1,093.00	$1,974.00	$4,895.00	
12	Personal chef salary	$1,555.21	$4,253.21	$1,258.63	$2,115.98	
13	Clothing allowance	$5,789.00	$5,783.00	$3,091.00	$3,389.00	
14	Spending money	$1,663.00	$45,216.00	$8,752.00	$1,456.00	
15	Money for new toys	$3,872.00	$7,894.00	$4,566.00	$2,900.00	
16	Classroom supplies	$0.58	$0.38	$1.05	$0.32	
17	Teacher salaries	$1.20	$2.45	$3.21	$1.02	
18	Research	$1.25	$2.50	$1.12	$1.48	

Sheet1

7 section(s) | 1 section(s) selected

Figure 7-15: A worksheet with easy-to-see labels.

Microsoft Office Binder - Master Binder test

A11 Limousine service

	A	B	C	D	E	F
11	Limousine service	$2,901.00	$1,093.00	$1,974.00	$4,895.00	
12	Personal chef salary	$1,555.21	$4,253.21	$1,258.63	$2,115.98	
13	Clothing allowance	$5,789.00	$5,783.00	$3,091.00	$3,389.00	
14	Spending money	$1,663.00	$45,216.00	$8,752.00	$1,456.00	
15	Money for new toys	$3,872.00	$7,894.00	$4,566.00	$2,900.00	
16	Classroom supplies	$0.58	$0.38	$1.05	$0.32	
17	Teacher salaries	$1.20	$2.45	$3.21	$1.02	
18	Research	$1.25	$2.50	$1.12	$1.48	
19	Computers for students	$0.25	$0.14	$0.14	$0.36	
20	Computers for staff	$0.45	$0.12	$0.02	$0.38	
21	Computers for President	$4,587.00	$2,154.00	$3,659.00	$5,586.00	
22	Football equipment	$3,872.00	$4,554.00	$3,566.00	$2,900.00	
23	Laboratory equipment	$0.45	$0.12	$0.09	$0.70	
24	Grocery allowance	$1,555.21	$4,253.21	$1,258.63	$2,115.98	
25	Restaurant tab	$5,564.00	$5,783.00	$3,091.00	$3,389.00	
26	Dormitory maintenance	$0.01	$0.01	$0.01	$0.01	
27	Janitorial services	$0.20	$0.06	$0.07	$0.11	
28	Pet food for President	$2,901.00	$1,093.00	$1,974.00	$4,895.00	

Sheet1

7 section(s) | 1 section(s) selected

Figure 7-16: The same worksheet after the descriptive labels have scrolled out of sight.

To offset the problem of losing descriptive labels as you scroll through a large worksheet, Excel lets you *freeze,* or anchor, labels in specific rows or columns. When you freeze a row or column containing a label, that particular row or column never moves no matter how much you scroll through your worksheet (see Figure 7-17).

To freeze a row or column, follow these steps:

1. **If you are using Excel in a binder, choose Section⇨View Outside.**

   Skip this step if you're using Excel outside a binder.

2. **Click the row number directly below the row that you want to freeze. (Or click the column letter to the right of the column you want to freeze.)**

   If you want to freeze row 2, for example, click the row 3 label to select the entire row. Or if you want to freeze column C, click the column D label to select the entire column.

3. **Choose Windows⇨Freeze Panes.**

   Excel displays a dark gray line to show where you froze your row or column (refer to Figure 7-17).

Frozen line

Microsoft Excel - Worksheet in Master Binder test.o

File Edit View Insert Format Tools Data Window Help

F10

	A	B	C	D	E
1	**Monthly Expenses for the University of Timbuktu and its President**				
2		**Jan**	**Feb**	**Mar**	**Apr**
9	Expensive gifts	$1,663.00	$5,487.00	$2,561.00	$5,875.00
10	Maid service	$3,872.00	$7,856.00	$4,758.00	$2,964.00
11	Limousine service	$2,901.00	$1,093.00	$1,974.00	$4,895.00
12	Personal chef salary	$1,555.21	$4,253.21	$1,258.63	$2,115.98
13	Clothing allowance	$5,789.00	$5,783.00	$3,091.00	$3,389.00
14	Spending money	$1,663.00	$45,216.00	$8,752.00	$1,456.00
15	Money for new toys	$3,872.00	$7,894.00	$4,566.00	$2,900.00
16	Classroom supplies	$0.58	$0.38	$1.05	$0.32
17	Teacher salaries	$1.20	$2.45	$3.21	$1.02
18	Research	$1.25	$2.50	$1.12	$1.48
19	Computers for students	$0.25	$0.14	$0.14	$0.36
20	Computers for staff	$0.45	$0.12	$0.02	$0.38
21	Computers for President	$4,587.00	$2,154.00	$3,659.00	$5,586.00
22	Football equipment	$3,872.00	$4,554.00	$3,566.00	$2,900.00
23	Laboratory equipment	$0.45	$0.12	$0.09	$0.70
24	Grocery allowance	$1,555.21	$4,253.21	$1,258.63	$2,115.98

Sheet1

Ready Sum=0 NUM

Figure 7-17: The same worksheet after the descriptive labels have been frozen in place.

To freeze both a row and a column at the same, follow these steps:

1. **If you're using Excel in a binder, choose Section➪View Outside.**

   Skip this step if you're using Excel outside a binder.

2. **Click the cell directly to the right of the column and below the row that you want to freeze.**

   If you want to freeze column A and row 2, for example, click the cell in column B and row 3.

3. **Choose Window➪Freeze Panes.**

   Excel displays a dark gray line to show where you froze your row and column.

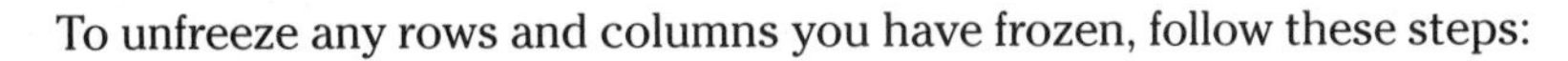

To unfreeze any rows and columns you have frozen, follow these steps:

1. **If you're using Excel in a binder, choose Section➪View Outside.**

   Skip this step if you're using Excel outside a binder.

2. **Choose Window➪Unfreeze Panes.**

Splitting screens on a worksheet

If you want to see two or more parts of your worksheet at one time, you can split your screen into miniature views of your worksheet, known as *panes.* Each pane acts as an independent window that you can scroll separately from the rest of your worksheet. To show you where one pane begins and another pane ends, Excel displays thick pane lines, as shown in Figure 7-18.

To split a screen in half horizontally, follow these steps:

1. **If you're using Excel in a binder, choose Section➪View Outside.**

   Skip this step if you're using Excel outside a binder.

2. **Select the row directly below the row where you want to split your worksheet.**

   For example, if you want to split your worksheet between rows 8 and 9, click the row 9 label.

3. **Choose Windows➪Split.**

   Excel displays a horizontal pane line to show you where you split your worksheet (refer to Figure 7-18).

Microsoft Excel - Worksheet in Master Binder test.o

	A	B	C	D	E	F
1	Monthly Expenses for the University of Timbuktu and its President					
2		Jan	Feb	Mar	Apr	
3	Athletic scholarships	$5,564.00	$5,783.00	$3,091.00	$3,389.00	
4	Recruitment brochures	$2,356.00	$4,125.00	$2,145.00	$4,587.00	
5	Landscaping	$3,872.00	$982.00	$4,521.00	$2,900.00	
6	President's salary	$2,901.00	$1,093.00	$1,974.00	$4,895.00	
7	Unnecessary travel	$1,555.21	$4,253.21	$1,258.63	$2,115.98	
8	Alcohol	$5,564.00	$5,783.00	$3,091.00	$3,389.00	
9	Expensive gifts	$1,663.00	$5,487.00	$2,561.00	$5,875.00	
17	Teacher salaries	$1.20	$2.45	$3.21	$1.02	
18	Research	$1.25	$2.50	$1.12	$1.48	
19	Computers for students	$0.25	$0.14	$0.14	$0.36	
20	Computers for staff	$0.45	$0.12	$0.02	$0.38	
21	Computers for President	$4,587.00	$2,154.00	$3,659.00	$5,586.00	
22	Football equipment	$3,872.00	$4,554.00	$3,566.00	$2,900.00	
23	Laboratory equipment	$0.45	$0.12	$0.09	$0.70	
24	Grocery allowance	$1,555.21	$4,253.21	$1,258.63	$2,115.98	
25	Restaurant tab	$5,564.00	$5,783.00	$3,091.00	$3,389.00	

Sheet1 — Ready — Sum=0 — NUM

Figure 7-18: A worksheet split into two separate panes.

To split a screen in half vertically, follow these steps:

1. **If you're using Excel in a binder, choose Section⇨View Outside.**

   Skip this step if you're using Excel outside a binder.

2. **Select the column directly to the right of where you want to split your worksheet.**

   For example, if you want to split your worksheet between columns B and C, click the gray label named C to select column C.

3. **Choose Windows⇨Split.**

   Excel displays a vertical pane line to show you where you split your columns.

You can also split your worksheet into four different panes to give you yet another view of your numbers.

To split your worksheet into four panes, follow these steps:

1. **If you're using Excel in a binder, choose Section⇨View Outside.**

   Skip this step if you're using Excel outside a binder.

2. **Click the cell directly to the right of the column and below the row where you want to split.**

   For example, if you want to split your worksheet between columns B and C, and between rows 9 and 10, click the cell in column C and row 10.

3. **Choose Windows➪Split.**

   Excel splits your worksheet into four panes as shown in Figure 7-19.

To remove your splits, follow these steps:

1. **If you're using Excel in a binder, choose Section➪View Outside.**

   Skip this step if you're using Excel outside a binder.

2. **Choose Windows➪Remove Split.**

   The worksheet window returns to its normal configuration.

Zooming in for a closer look

In case your eyesight is poor or if you like looking at your entire worksheet at one time, you can make the numbers on your worksheet appear larger (called *zooming* in) or smaller (called *zooming* out). Normally, Excel displays your worksheet on-screen exactly as it appears when you print it.

Microsoft Excel - Worksheet in Master Binder test.obd

File Edit View Insert Format Tools Data Window Help

C10 982

	A	B	C	D	E	F
1	Intelligence Agency Expenses					
2		Jan	Feb	Mar	Apr	
3	Illegal substances	$5,564.00	$5,783.00	$3,091.00	$3,389.00	
4	Guns and ammo	$1,663.00	$480.00	$214.00	$680.00	
5	Missiles	$3,872.00	$982.00	$548.00	$2,900.00	
6	Atom bombs	$2,901.00	$1,093.00	$1,974.00	$4,895.00	
7	Agent Orange	$1,555.21	$4,253.21	$1,258.63	$2,115.98	
8	Land mines	$5,564.00	$5,783.00	$3,091.00	$3,389.00	
9	Propaganda	$1,663.00	$480.00	$214.00	$680.00	
10	Pesticides	$3,872.00	$982.00	$548.00	$2,964.00	
11	Bribe money	$2,901.00	$1,093.00	$1,974.00	$4,895.00	
12	Poltical favors	$1,555.21	$4,253.21	$1,258.63	$2,115.98	
13	Assassins	$5,789.00	$5,783.00	$3,091.00	$3,389.00	
14	Bounty money	$1,663.00	$487.00	$632.00	$680.00	
15	Salaries	$3,872.00	$982.00	$548.00	$2,900.00	
16	Training	$2,901.00	$1,093.00	$1,974.00	$4,895.00	
17	Aircraft	$1,555.21	$4,253.21	$1,258.63	$2,115.98	
18	Research	$8,754.00	$5,745.00	$3,985.00	$3,389.00	

Sheet1

Ready Sum=$982.00 NUM

Figure 7-19: A worksheet split into four separate panes.

To make your worksheet numbers appear bigger, select a higher magnification such as 200%. To make your worksheet numbers appear smaller, select a lower magnification, like 50%. To make your worksheet appear normal size again, select 100%.

To change the zoom magnification on your worksheet, follow these steps:

1. **Click the Zoom Control list box in the Standard toolbar.**
2. **Click the downward pointing arrow, select a magnification (such as 200%) from the drop-down list box, and press Enter.**

   Excel displays your worksheet in your chosen magnification, as shown in Figure 7-20. You also can enter a specific magnification, such as 145%. Excel displays your worksheet using the magnification that you entered.

Microsoft Excel - Worksheet in Master Binder test.obd

	A	B	C
1	Intelligence Agency Expenses		
2		Jan	Feb
3	Illegal substances	$5,564.00	$5,783
4	Guns and ammo	$1,663.00	$480
5	Missiles	$3,872.00	$982
6	Atom bombs	$2,901.00	$1,093
7	Agent Orange	$1,555.21	$4,253
8	Land mines	$5,564.00	$5,783
9	Propaganda	$1,663.00	$480

Figure 7-20: Displaying your worksheet at a higher magnification.

Chapter 8

Having Fun with Formulas and Functions

In This Chapter

- Creating formulas to perform tasks in Excel
- Editing your formulas
- Using the Function Wizard to create formulas

Microsoft Excel's entire reason for existence is to calculate formulas that are too complicated or too boring for you to do yourself. Type a few numbers and create a formula, and within seconds Excel can display the results.

In addition to the standard addition, subtraction, multiplication, and division options, Excel also lets you create more complicated calculations, in case you need statistical results, mathematical calculations, or financial formulas to determine to what extent your bank is ripping you off.

Making Your Own Formulas

Excel is similar to a fancy calculator that lets you calculate any type of result — if you know what you're doing, of course. To create a formula, you have to

- Choose the cell in which to display the calculation
- Type a formula to perform the calculation

To choose a cell in which to display your calculation, just click an empty cell.

To create a formula to perform a calculation, type an equal sign (=) and then your formula, such as **=23*4**, and then press Enter, which displays the number 92 in your cell. Table 8-1 shows the most common calculations you can perform by using a formula.

Table 8-1 Operators for Creating Formulas

Operator	*What It Means*	*Example of What You Type*	*Result*
+	Addition	=5+3.4	8.4
–	Subtraction	=54.2-2.1	52.1
*	Multiplication	=1.2*4	4.8
/	Division	=25/5	5
%	Percentage	=42%	0.42
^	Exponentiation	=4^3	64
=	Equals	=6=7	FALSE
>	Greater than	=7>2	TRUE
<	Less than	=9<8	FALSE
>=	Greater than or equal to	=45>=3	TRUE
<=	Less than or equal to	=40<=2	FALSE
<>	Not equal to	=5<>7	TRUE
&	Text concatenation	="Bo the"&" Cat"	Bo the Cat

Typing both numbers and operators in a cell can be tedious. The real power of Excel comes when you can type numbers in different cells and then create a formula (in another cell) that uses those numbers to calculate a result. To create a formula that can use numbers stored in other cells, you have to use references.

What the heck are references?

In the working world, references are people you can call to get (you hope!) recommendations to help you get a job. In the world of Excel, *references* are cell names a formula uses to calculate a result.

Suppose that you have two numbers stored in cells B4 and C4, as shown in Figure 8-1. In this example, cell D4 contains this formula:

```
=B4*C4
```

The cell references are B4 and C4 in this formula, which tells Excel, "Find the number stored in cell B4 and then multiply it by the number stored in C4."

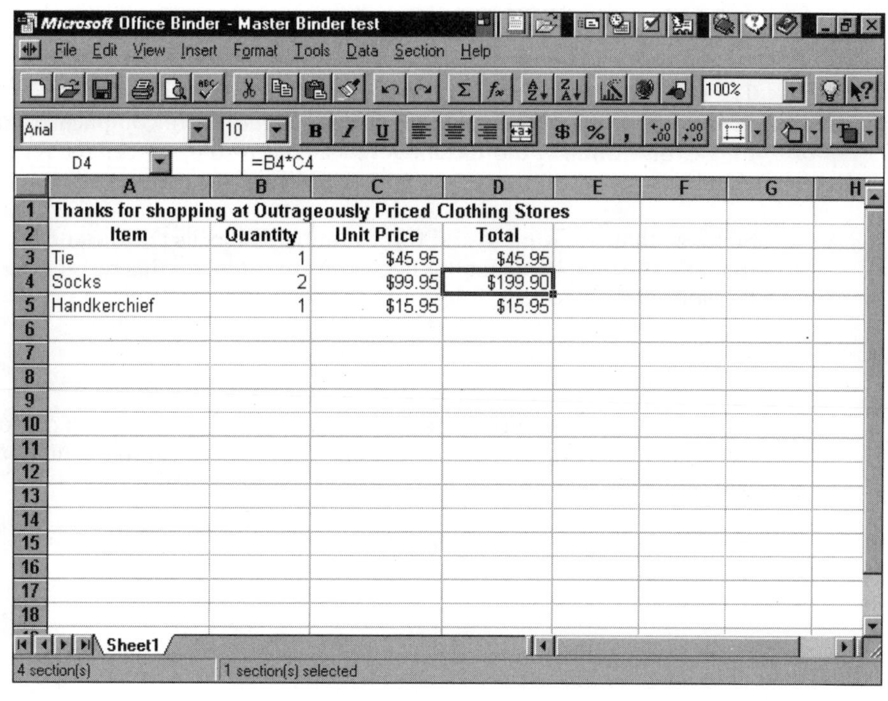

Figure 8-1: Using cell references to calculate a result.

To create a formula using cell references, follow these steps:

1. **Click the cell in which you want the formula to appear.**
2. **Type = (an equal sign).**
3. **Click the cell that contains the number you want to use in your formula (cell B2, for example).**
4. **Type an operator, such as + (a plus sign).**
5. **Repeat steps 3 and 4 as often as necessary.**

   For short formulas, such as those that add two numbers, you need only one operator, such as +. For long formulas, such as those that add two numbers and then subtract the result from a third number, you may need to type the + operator once and the - operator once.

6. **Press Enter.**

   Excel shows the results of your calculations in the worksheet cell where the formula is stored.

The magic of parentheses

The simplest formulas can use two cell references and one operator, such as =B4*C4. However, you'll probably have to create more complicated formulas that involve three or more cell references. With so many cell references, you should use parentheses to organize everything.

Suppose that you want to add three numbers; in cells D3, D4, and D5; and then multiply the total by a number in cell D6. To calculate this result, you can use this formula:

```
=D3+D4+D5*D6
```

Unfortunately, Excel interprets this formula to mean, "Hey, stupid! Multiply the number in D5 by the number in D6. Then add this result to the numbers in D3 and D4."

If you have the following values stored in the corresponding cells:

```
$45.95      D3
$199.90     D4
$15.95      D5
7.75%       D6
```

the formula =D3+D4+D5*D6 calculates the number 247.0861 (or $247.09 if you format the cell to display numbers as currency), which definitely isn't the result you want.

What you really want is for all the numbers in cells D3, D4, and D5 to be added and then the total multiplied by the number in D6. To tell Excel to complete this action, you have to use parentheses as shown in Figure 8-2.

```
=(D3+D4+D5)*D6
```

The parentheses tell Excel, "Hey, stupid! First add all the numbers stored in cells D3, D4, and D5, and then multiply this total by the number stored in D6." Using the same values for D3, D4, D5, and D6, Excel calculates 20.2895 (or $20.29 if you format the cell to display numbers as currency), which is the result you want.

If you remember nothing else from this section (or from high school algebra), just remember this: You must always organize multiple cell references in parentheses to make sure that Excel calculates the references in the correct order.

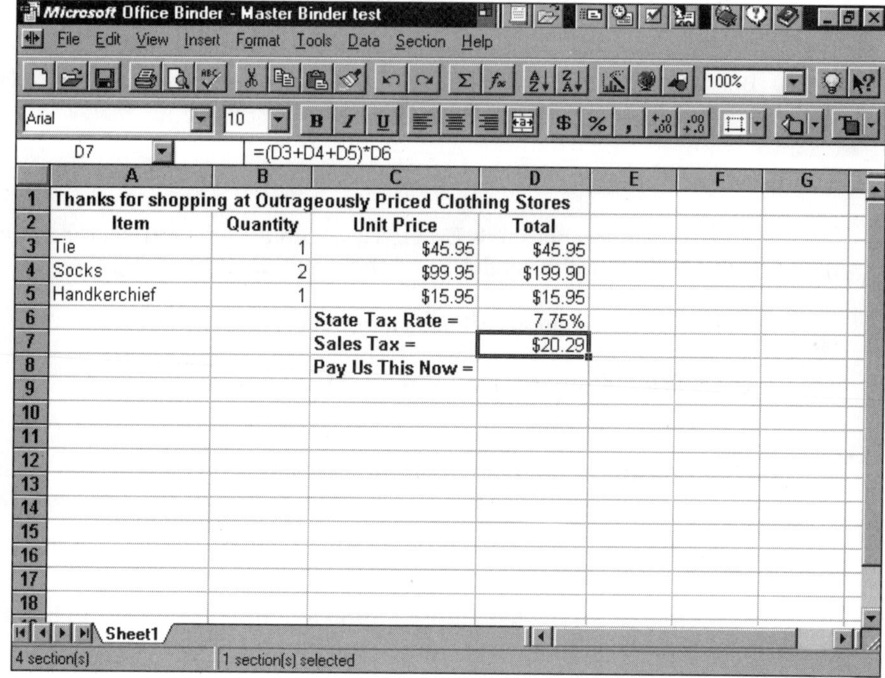

Figure 8-2: Using parentheses in cell references to calculate a result.

Home on the cell range

Despite the parentheses that organize the formula `=(D3+D4+D5)*D6`, referencing multiple cells can be cumbersome and unwieldy. Rather than type a long formula of multiple cells, such as D3+D4+D5, make things easy on yourself by specifying a range.

Two types of cell ranges exist:

- **Contiguous ranges:** D3+D4+D5, for example
- **Noncontiguous ranges:** D3+E4+H9, for example

To use cell ranges in a formula, you must also use a built-in function, such as SUM, which adds all the numbers stored in the cell range you specify. For example, `=SUM(D2:D6)` adds all the numbers stored in cells D2 through D6. Some other built-in functions that work with contiguous and noncontiguous ranges include AVERAGE, MAX, MIN, and COUNT.

Specifying a contiguous range

A *contiguous range* of cells is nothing more than a rectangular bunch of cells touching one another, such as cells stacked one on top of the other or side by side. Suppose that you want to use the following formula:

```
=(D3+D4+D5)*D6
```

Because cells D3, D4, and D5 are a contiguous range of cells, you can enter the formula by simply typing this line:

```
=SUM(D3:D5)*D6
```

The `D3:D5` references tells Excel, "Hey, stupid! Sum (add) all the numbers stored in cells D3 through D5 and then multiply the result by the number in D6."

To specify a contiguous range in a formula, follow these steps:

1. **Click the cell in which you want the formula to appear.**
2. **Type = (an equal sign).**
3. **Type the built-in function, such as SUM or AVERAGE, you want to apply to your contiguous range, and then type a left parenthesis (().**
4. **Click the first cell that contains the number you want to use in your formula (cell D3, for example).**
5. **Hold down the left mouse button and drag the mouse to highlight the entire cell range you want to include.**

   Excel highlights your selected cell range with a dotted line, as shown in Figure 8-3.
6. **Let go of the mouse button and type a right parenthesis ()).**
7. **Type the rest of your formula (if necessary) and then press Enter.**

Specifying (what else?) a noncontiguous range

In case certain numbers are stored in cells that aren't touching one another, you have to create a noncontiguous range. For example, consider the following formula:

```
=SUM(D3,G5,X7)
```

This formula tells Excel, "Add the number stored in cell D3 to the number stored in cell G5, and add the total to the number stored in cell X7."

To specify a noncontiguous range in a formula, follow these steps:

1. **Click the cell in which you want the formula to appear.**
2. **Type = (an equal sign).**
3. **Type the built-in function you want to apply to your noncontiguous range, such as SUM or AVERAGE, and then type the left parenthesis (().**

4. **Click the first cell that contains the number you want to use in your formula (cell D3, for example).**
5. **Type a comma (,).**
6. **Click the next cell that contains the number you want to use in your formula (cell D7, for example).**
7. **Repeat steps 5 and 6 as often as necessary.**

   For example, you may need to repeat steps 5 and 6 for each additional cell reference you want to include in your formula.

8. **Type a right parenthesis ()), and then press Enter.**

You can combine contiguous and noncontiguous ranges in the same formula, such as

```
=SUM(D3:D5,D7)
```

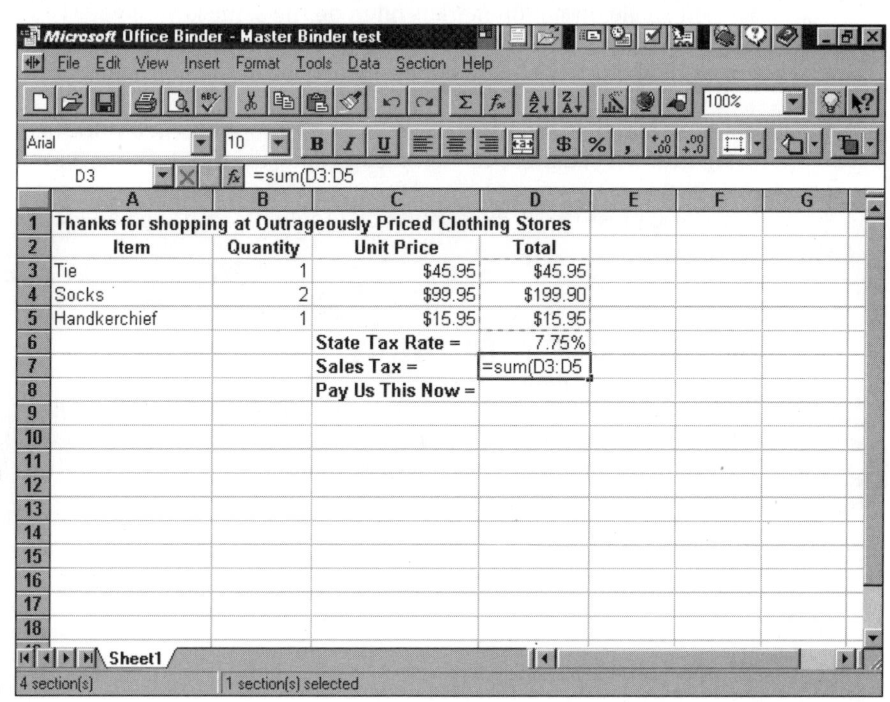

Figure 8-3: Highlighting a contiguous range of cells.

Editing Formulas

After you type a formula in a cell, you can always edit it later. This feature comes in handy when you type a formula incorrectly (when you forget to use parentheses, for example).

Displaying formulas

Before you can edit a formula, you have to find it. Because formulas display numbers in the same way as cells that contain only numbers, finding which cells contain your formulas and which cells contain plain numbers can be difficult.

To display all your formulas in a worksheet at one time, just press Ctrl+‘ (Ctrl+left single quotation mark).

The left single quotation mark is often on the same key on your keyboard as the tilde symbol (~). On some keyboards, this key is to the left of the 1 key on the top row; on other keyboards, this key may be at the bottom, near the spacebar.

When you press Ctrl+‘, Excel displays all your formulas in a worksheet, as shown in Figure 8-4. If you press Ctrl+‘ a second time, Excel hides your formulas again.

When you press Ctrl+‘, Excel turns off number formatting and changes column widths.

Wiping out a formula

If you don't need a formula any more, you can wipe it out completely. In case you want to exercise your destructive urges and delete a formula for good, click the cell that contains the formula you want to delete. Press Delete or Backspace, and Excel wipes out your formula.

If you delete a formula by mistake, you can recover it if you immediately press Ctrl+Z.

Editing a formula

To edit a formula (to type a parenthesis or add another cell reference, for example), you use the Formula Bar (refer to Figure 8-4). Every time you click a cell that contains a formula, the Formula Bar displays the formula so that you can view the entire thing and edit it.

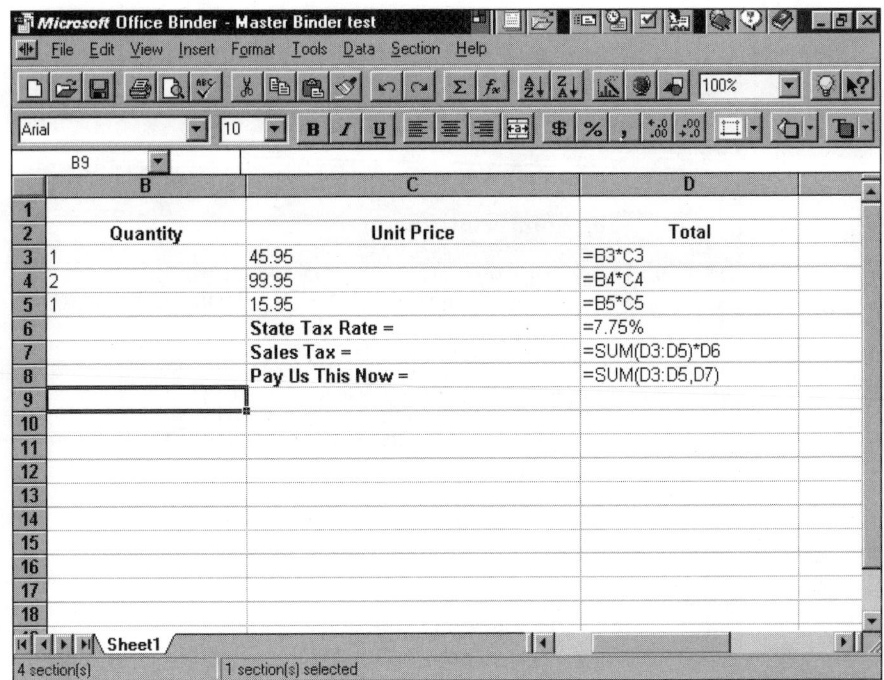

Figure 8-4: Displaying a formula in Formula Bar.

To edit a formula, follow these steps:

1. **Click the cell that contains the formula you want to edit.**

   Excel dutifully displays that formula on the Formula Bar, as shown in Figure 8-5.

2. **Click the Formula Bar to display a cursor.**
3. **Press Backspace or Delete to erase part of your formula.**
4. **Press the left- and right-arrow keys to move the cursor around, and type any corrections.**
5. **Press Enter.**

   Excel calculates a new result based on your modified formula.

Function Wizard to the Rescue!

Quick! Write the formula to calculate the depreciation of an asset for a specified period by using the fixed declining-balance method. If you have absolutely no idea what the preceding sentence means, you're not alone. Even if you do know what it means, however, you may still have no idea how to create a formula to calculate this result.

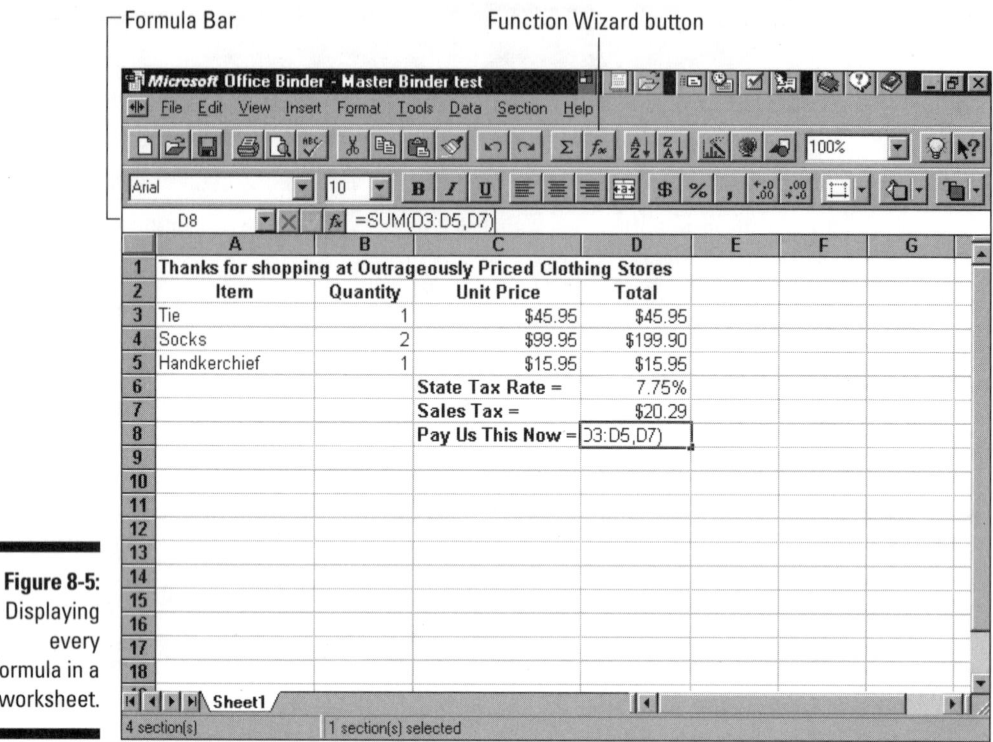

Figure 8-5: Displaying every formula in a worksheet.

Rather than force you to rack your brain and create cumbersome and complicated formulas on your own, Excel comes with a list of predefined formulas, called *functions.*

The main difference between a function and a formula is that a function just asks you which cell references (numbers) to use whereas a formula forces you to choose your cell references and tell Excel whether to add, subtract, multiply, or divide. For simple calculations, create your own formulas; for complicated calculations, use a built-in function instead.

In case you're wondering, you can create a formula that uses a function. For example, the following formula uses the SUM function but also uses the multiplication operator:

```
=SUM(D4:D5)*D7
```

If you happen to read spreadsheet-comparison advertisements, one feature every spreadsheet publisher mentions is the number of functions its spreadsheet contains. The hope is that the more built-in functions that are available, the less time you have to waste creating your own formulas.

Excel contains nine types of functions:

- **Financial:** Calculates interest payments and rate of return, for example
- **Date & Time:** Displays dates and times in various formats
- **Math & Trig:** Calculates cosine and logarithms, for example
- **Statistical:** Calculates frequency distributions and most common values, for example
- **Lookup & Reference:** Returns values such as the number of columns in a reference or returns the row number of a reference
- **Database:** Returns the average or maximum value from chosen database entries
- **Text:** Converts numbers into text or returns the leftmost characters from a text string
- **Logical:** Tests whether the value of something is True or False
- **Information:** Returns the formatting of a cell or the data type of its value

Do you have to understand what 99 percent of these function categories mean? Nope. Most people rarely use any of these function categories, but in case you have to do some heavy-duty number-crunching, just remember that Excel probably has a built-in function that can make your job easier. For math students, poke around long enough and you may even find functions to help you do your homework faster.

To help you choose the correct function, Excel comes with the Function Wizard, which guides you step-by-step through the process of choosing a function and filling it with cell references so that you don't have to do it all yourself.

To use the Function Wizard, follow these steps:

1. **Click the cell in which you want to use a function.**
2. **Click the Formula Bar.**
3. **Click the Function Wizard button (refer to Figure 8-5).**

   A Function Wizard dialog box appears, as shown in Figure 8-6.
4. **In the Function Category list box, click the category that contains the type of function you want to use (Financial or Statistical, for example).**
5. **In the Function Name list box, click the function you want to use.**

   Note: Every time you highlight a function, Excel displays a brief explanation at the bottom of the dialog box.

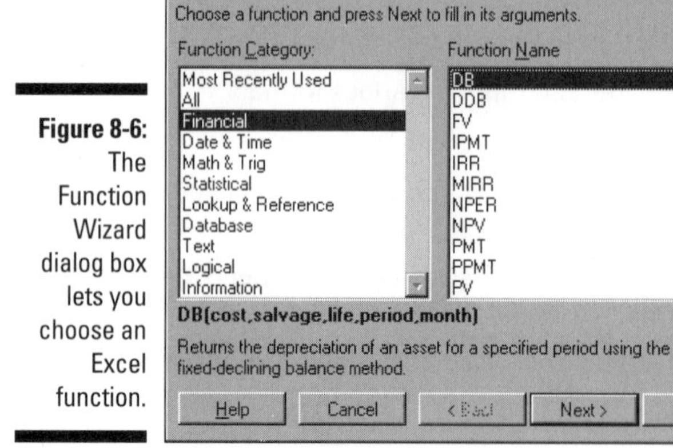

Figure 8-6: The Function Wizard dialog box lets you choose an Excel function.

6. **Click Next>.**

   The Function Wizard displays a second dialog box, which asks for specific cell references, as shown in Figure 8-7.

7. **Click the cells that contain the numbers you want to use, such as cell B3 for the rate.**

   You may have to move the Function Wizard dialog box out of the way to see your worksheet.

8. **Click Finish.**

   Excel calculates a value based on the function you chose and the numbers you told it to use in step 7.

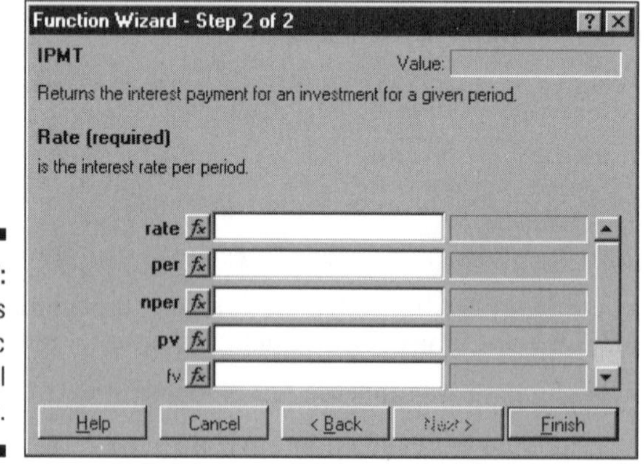

Figure 8-7: Excel asks for specific cell references.

Chapter 9

Verifying that Your Worksheets Really Work

In This Chapter

- Tracing your formulas for problems
- Dealing with error messages
- Examining your cells in detail
- Looking for an oddball formula
- Correcting spelling errors

After you spend some time typing labels, numbers, and formulas into a worksheet, your job still isn't over. Now you have to make sure that your formulas calculate the correct answer. After all, you can create the best-looking spreadsheet in the world with fancy fonts, but if it consistently calculates wrong answers, no one can use it (except for the United States government's budget accountants).

To make sure that your spreadsheet calculates its formulas correctly, you may need to spend time examining each formula. Naturally this can be a pain in the neck, but spending time checking your formulas is much easier than making a big mistake and going bankrupt because of your spreadsheet's faulty calculations.

How Excel Helps Verify Your Formulas

To help you verify that your formulas are working correctly, Excel comes with a special auditing feature that can identify:

- Where a formula gets its data (so that you can see whether a formula is getting all the data it needs)
- How one formula may depend on the (possibly incorrect) calculation from another formula

If a formula isn't getting all the right data, it obviously can't calculate the correct results. Likewise, calculations from one formula can be used as data by another formula; if one formula calculates wrong answers, any formulas that depend on that first formula are messed up as well.

Most of Excel's auditing features are hidden on the Auditing toolbar. To display the Auditing toolbar, follow these steps:

1. **Choose View➪Toolbars.**

   The Toolbars dialog box appears.

2. **Click the Auditing check box so that a check mark appears and then click OK.**

   The Auditing toolbar appears (see Figure 9-1).

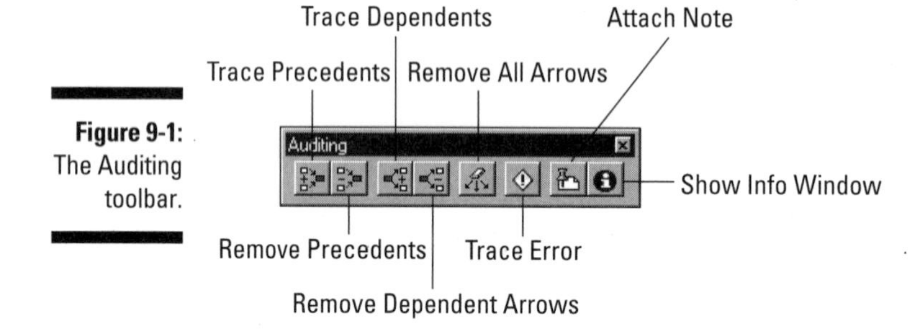

Figure 9-1: The Auditing toolbar.

Tracing Your Formulas

In case you're wondering, a *precedent* is a cell that contains data used by a formula. A *dependent* is a cell that contains a formula. Suppose that a formula in cell B7 looks like this:

```
=B5+B6
```

In this example, the cells B5 and B6 are called the precedents, and the cell B7 is the dependent. As long as you remember these definitions, you won't get confused between the Trace Precedents and the Trace Dependents buttons.

Understanding where a formula gets its data

A formula is only as good as the data it receives. Feed a formula the wrong data, and you always get the wrong answer. (This law of nature explains why governments are perpetually clueless: As long as they keep asking the wrong questions, they never come up with the correct answers.)

If you want to know where your formula is getting its data, click the cell that contains the formula you want to examine and then click the Trace Precedents button on the Auditing toolbar. Excel draws one or more arrows to show all the cells from which your formula, chosen in step 1, is getting its data (see Figure 9-2).

If a formula uses data stored in an individual cell, that cell is marked by a dot. If a formula doesn't use data in a cell, no dot appears even if the arrow is drawn over it.

Knowing which formulas a cell affects

The beauty of spreadsheets is that you can change one number in a cell and watch that change ripple throughout the rest of your spreadsheet as it recalculates formulas from top to bottom. In case you want to know how the data stored in one cell may affect your formulas stored in other cells, you can use Excel's auditing features to show you all the formulas that depend on a particular cell.

If you want to know which formulas a cell affects, click the cell you want to examine and then click the Trace Dependents button on the Auditing toolbar. Excel draws one or more arrows that show which formulas your cell will change (see Figure 9-3).

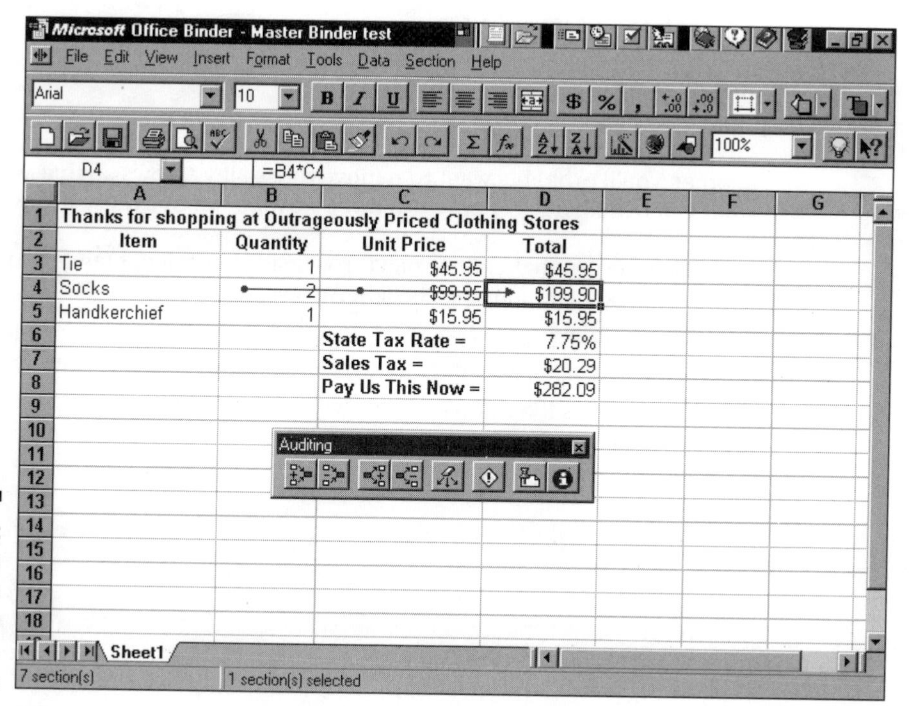

Figure 9-2: Tracing where a formula gets its data.

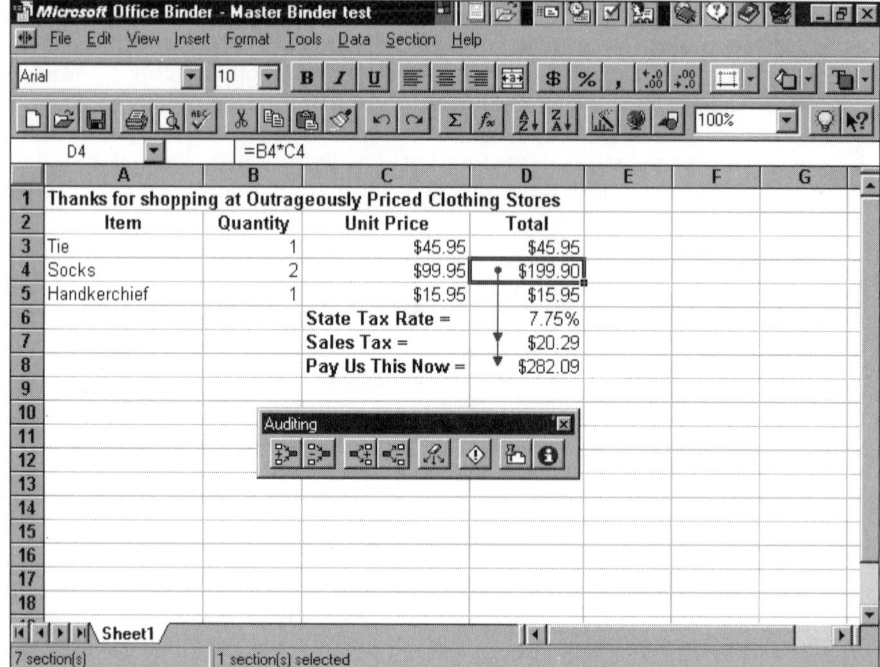

Figure 9-3: Tracing to see which formulas a cell affects.

Getting rid of those precedent and dependent arrows

After you trace your cells and formulas so that you know how they affect one another, you'll probably want to remove those silly arrows so that you can see what you're doing. Excel provides three ways to remove these arrows:

- Click the cell that contains an arrowhead (the cell containing a formula), and click the Remove Precedent Arrows button.
- Click the cell that contains a dot, and click the Remove Dependent Arrows button. (You have to complete this step for each cell that contains a dot in the same arrow.)
- Click the Remove All Arrows button.

Knowing What to Do When a Formula Displays an Error Message

Sometimes you may create a formula and, rather than display a result, the cell displays an error message (#VALUE!, for example). Table 9-1 shows some of the most common error messages and a description of how you messed up.

Table 9-1 Common Error Messages in Excel Formulas

Error Value	*What It Means*
#DIV/0!	Your formula is trying to divide by zero.
#VALUE!	Your formula isn't receiving the type of data it expects. For example, a formula might get a text string when it expects an integer.
######	The cell width is too small to display the entire number. (To fix this problem, simply widen your cell.)

Whenever your formula displays an error message rather than an actual result, you have to hunt down and correct the mistake right away by following these steps:

1. **Click the cell that contains the error message.**
2. **Click the Trace Error button on the Auditing toolbar.**

   Excel draws a line that shows you all the cells which feed data to your formula, as shown in Figure 9-4. In this example, Excel is telling you that you're trying to add the text string "Total" stored in cell D2. Because you can't add a string to a number, Excel displays an error message in cell D8.

Digging into the Guts of Your Cells

In case you want to examine one of your cells in minute detail to understand which data it contains, how it's formatted, or which formula may be stored in it, you can display all this information and more by using the Show Info Window button on the Auditing toolbar.

To examine a single cell in great detail, follow these steps:

1. **If you're using Excel in a binder, choose Section⇨View Outside.**

   Skip this step if you're using Excel outside a binder.

2. **Click the cell you want to examine.**

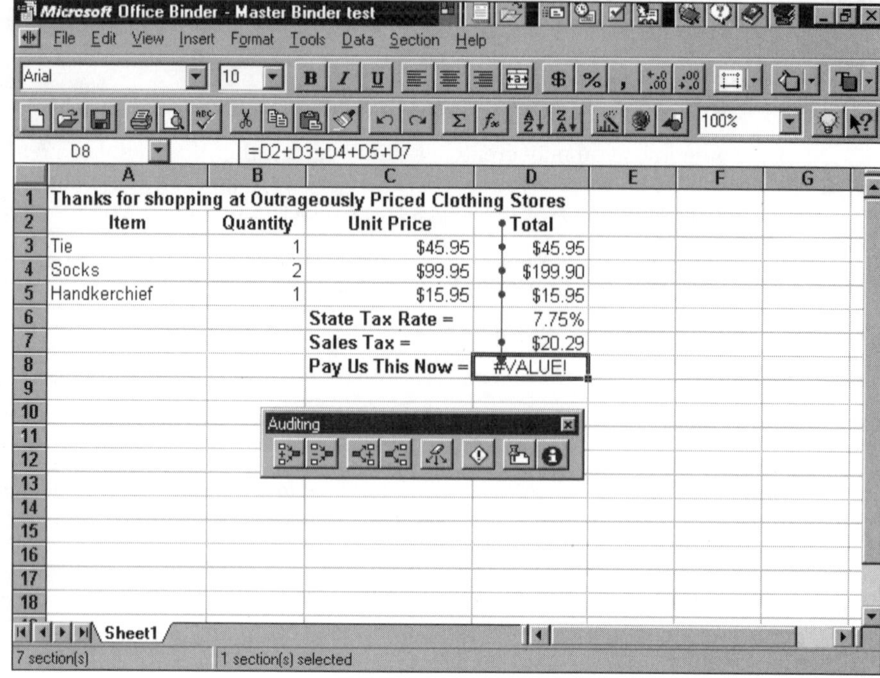

Figure 9-4: Tracing an error message to see which cells may be to blame.

3. **Click the Show Info Window button on the Auditing toolbar.**

   Excel displays the cell info, as shown in Figure 9-5. ***Note:*** To hide or display additional information, use the Info menu and choose what you want to see or hide.

4. **Choose File⇨Close.**

   Excel displays your worksheet again.

Finding the Oddball Formula

Often you need a row or column of nearly identical formulas, such as row 7, as shown in Figure 9-6. In this example, all the cells in row 7 should add the contents of the cells in rows 3, 4, 5, and 6.

How do you know whether all the formulas in that row are adding up all the rows they're supposed to? Unless you relish the idea of examining each formula, one by one, Excel has an easier method that lets you quickly find in a row or column a formula that doesn't fit the other formulas in the same row or column.

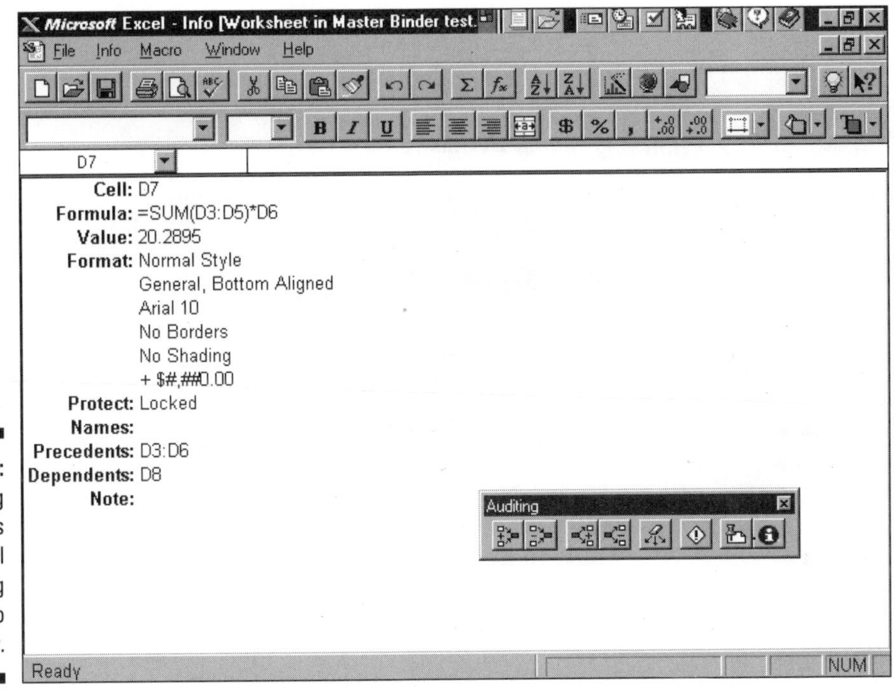

Figure 9-5: Examining the contents of a cell using the Info Window.

Microsoft Office Binder - Master Binder test

File Edit View Insert Format Tools Data Section Help

B7 =SUM(B3:B6)

	A	B	C	D	E	F	G
1	**Air America Transportation Expenses**						
2		Jan	Feb	Mar	Apr		
3	Illegal substances	$5,564.00	$5,783.00	$3,091.00	$3,389.00		
4	Guns and ammo	$1,663.00	$480.00	$214.00	$680.00		
5	Missiles	$3,872.00	$982.00	$548.00	$2,900.00		
6	Atom bombs	$2,901.00	$1,093.00	$1,974.00	$4,895.00		
7	**Total =**	$14,000.00	$7,245.00	$5,827.00	$11,864.00		
8							
9							
10	**NSA Computer Expenses**						
11		Jan	Feb	Mar	Apr		
12	Pentium upgrades	$7,213.02	$4,521.25	$4,978.35	$12,877.65		
13	Microsoft Office 95	$7,856.27	$5,296.40	$5,489.19	$7,361.25		
14	PGP legal fees	$4,583.22	$8,512.08	$6,654.12	$6,871.54		
15	Internet snooping	$789,641.23	$452,483.30	$531,459.58	$456,412.25		
16	Satellite launches	$78,512.30	$50,833.30	$54,126.09	$78,453.21		
17	**Total =**	$887,806.04	$521,646.33	$602,707.33	$561,975.90		
18							

Sheet1

4 section(s) 1 section(s) selected

Figure 9-6: A row of nearly identical formulas.

To find an oddball formula in a row or column, follow these steps:

1. **Highlight the row or column that contains the formulas you want to check.**
2. **Choose Edit⇨Go To (or press Ctrl+G).**

   The Go To dialog box appears, as shown in Figure 9-7.

Figure 9-7: The Go To dialog box.

3. **Click Special.**

   The Go To Special dialog box appears, as shown in Figure 9-8.

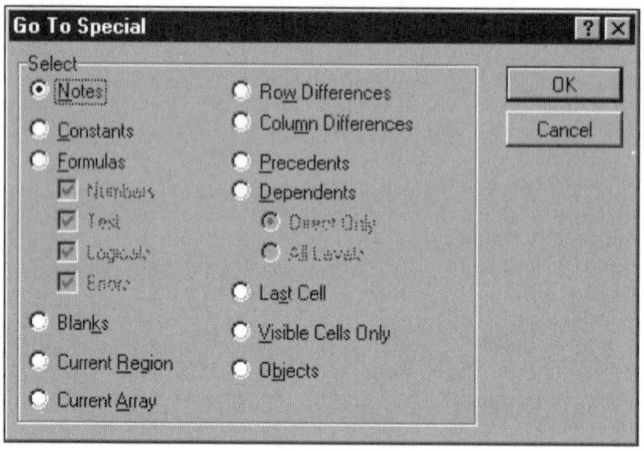

Figure 9-8: Use the Go To Special dialog box to look for row or column differences in your formulas.

4. **Click either the Row Differences or Column Differences radio button and then click OK.**

   Excel highlights the cell or cells that contain formulas which are not similar to their neighboring cells.

Checking Your Spelling

Just because you don't know how to spell doesn't mean that you're stupid. Unfortunately, though, misspellings and typos can make you look stupid even if your data is 100 percent accurate and up-to-date. Unless you want to prevent your boss from giving you a raise just because you titled your spreadsheet "Our 1997 Anual Budgett Report," rest assured that Excel can check your spelling before you print your spreadsheet for other people to see.

To check your spelling, follow these steps:

1. **Press F7.**

   The Spelling dialog box appears and highlights the first word that Excel suspects is misspelled, as shown in Figure 9-9.

Spelling

Not in Dictionary: NSA

Change To: NCI

Suggestions: NCI

Ignore | Ignore All | Change | Change All | Add | Suggest | AutoCorrect

Add Words To: CUSTOM.DIC

Cell Value: NSA Computer Expenses

Always Suggest

Ignore UPPERCASE

Undo Last | Cancel

Figure 9-9: The Spelling dialog box.

2. **Choose one of the following:**

   - **Ignore:** If you know that the word is spelled correctly
   - **Ignore All:** If you want Excel to ignore all additional occurrences of the word
   - **Change:** If you want Excel to correct your spelling with the word displayed in the Change To box
   - **Change All:** If you want Excel to correct all additional occurrences of the word
   - **Add:** To add the word to Excel's dictionary
   - **Suggest:** If you want to look up variations of a word displayed in the Suggestions list box. For example, if you highlight the word he in the Suggestions list box and click Suggest, Excel displays a list of similarly spelled words such as hoe, has, ho, and hen.

- **AutoCorrect:** If you want to add a misspelled word (along with its correct spelling) to Excel's list of words that are corrected automatically
- **Undo Last:** If you want to undo the last word Excel's spell checker replaced for you

3. **Repeat step 2 for each word that Excel highlights as being misspelled.**

   Click Cancel if you want to stop checking before the spell checker is finished. Otherwise, Excel displays a dialog box to let you know when the spelling in your entire worksheet has been checked.

Chapter 10
Printing Pretty Pages

In This Chapter

- Fitting your work on a single page
- Messing with margins
- Placing headers and footers on a page
- Choosing paper size and changing its orientation
- Deciding whether to print gridlines, headings, and page orders

After you type all your text and numbers, make sure that your formulas work properly, and format it all to look nice, your next headache (if you choose to accept the assignment) is to make your pages look presentable when you print them.

You could waste your time and paper, of course, by adjusting the format of your worksheet, printing it, readjusting your worksheet, and printing it again until you finally get it right. If everyone who uses Excel did that, however, global deforestation would occur at a much faster rate. In the interest of ecology and your own patience, you should adjust the appearance of your worksheet and print it only when it's absolutely ready.

Squeezing (or Blowing Up) Your Work

Nothing is more frustrating than creating a spreadsheet in which everything fits on one page — except for one line that prints on a second page, as shown in Figure 10-1. Rather than print your spreadsheet on two pages and leave the second page mostly blank, you can tell Excel to squeeze all your work on a single page.

To shrink or expand your spreadsheet, follow these steps:

1. **If you're using Excel within a binder, choose Section➪View Outside.**

   Skip this step if you're using Excel outside a binder.

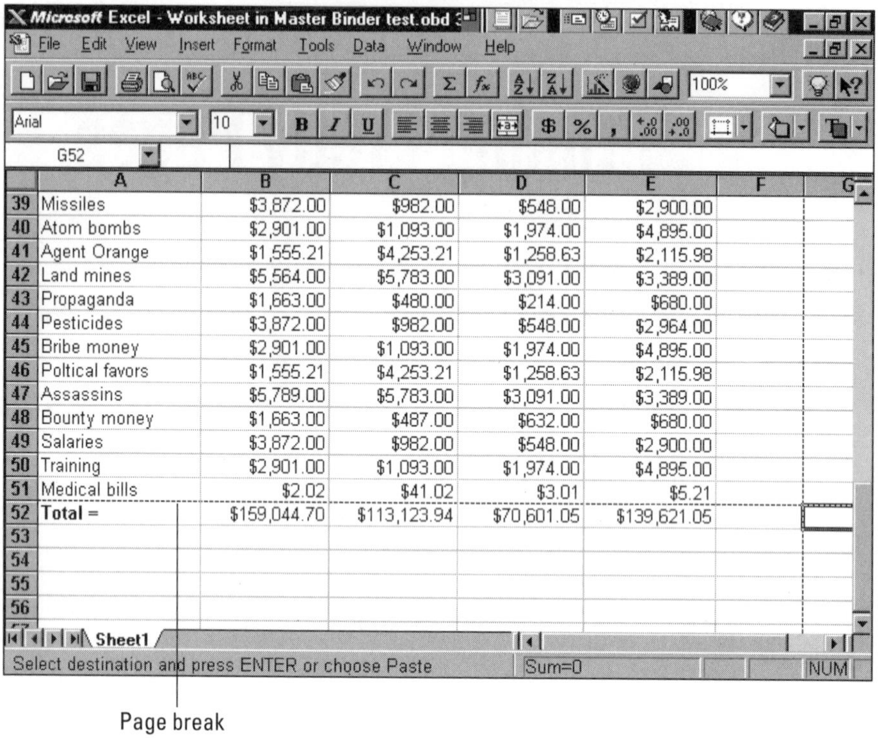

	A	B	C	D	E
39	Missiles	$3,872.00	$982.00	$548.00	$2,900.00
40	Atom bombs	$2,901.00	$1,093.00	$1,974.00	$4,895.00
41	Agent Orange	$1,555.21	$4,253.21	$1,258.63	$2,115.98
42	Land mines	$5,564.00	$5,783.00	$3,091.00	$3,389.00
43	Propaganda	$1,663.00	$480.00	$214.00	$680.00
44	Pesticides	$3,872.00	$982.00	$548.00	$2,964.00
45	Bribe money	$2,901.00	$1,093.00	$1,974.00	$4,895.00
46	Poltical favors	$1,555.21	$4,253.21	$1,258.63	$2,115.98
47	Assassins	$5,789.00	$5,783.00	$3,091.00	$3,389.00
48	Bounty money	$1,663.00	$487.00	$632.00	$680.00
49	Salaries	$3,872.00	$982.00	$548.00	$2,900.00
50	Training	$2,901.00	$1,093.00	$1,974.00	$4,895.00
51	Medical bills	$2.02	$41.02	$3.01	$5.21
52	Total =	$159,044.70	$113,123.94	$70,601.05	$139,621.05

Page break

Figure 10-1: A typical worksheet inconveniently separated by a page break.

2. **Choose File⇨Print Preview.**

   Excel displays your worksheet exactly as it will look when you print it (see Figure 10-2).

3. **Click Setup.**

   The Page Setup dialog box appears, as shown in Figure 10-3.

4. **Click the Fit to option button and then click the page(s) wide by list box and the tall list box to specify how you want Excel to squeeze your spreadsheet on your pages.**

5. **Click OK.**

   Excel displays your newly scaled worksheet.

6. **Click Close when you're happy with the way your worksheet will look when it's printed.**

As an alternative to clicking the Fit to option button in step 4, you can click the Adjust to option button and then click the % normal size list box to change the scaling of your worksheet.

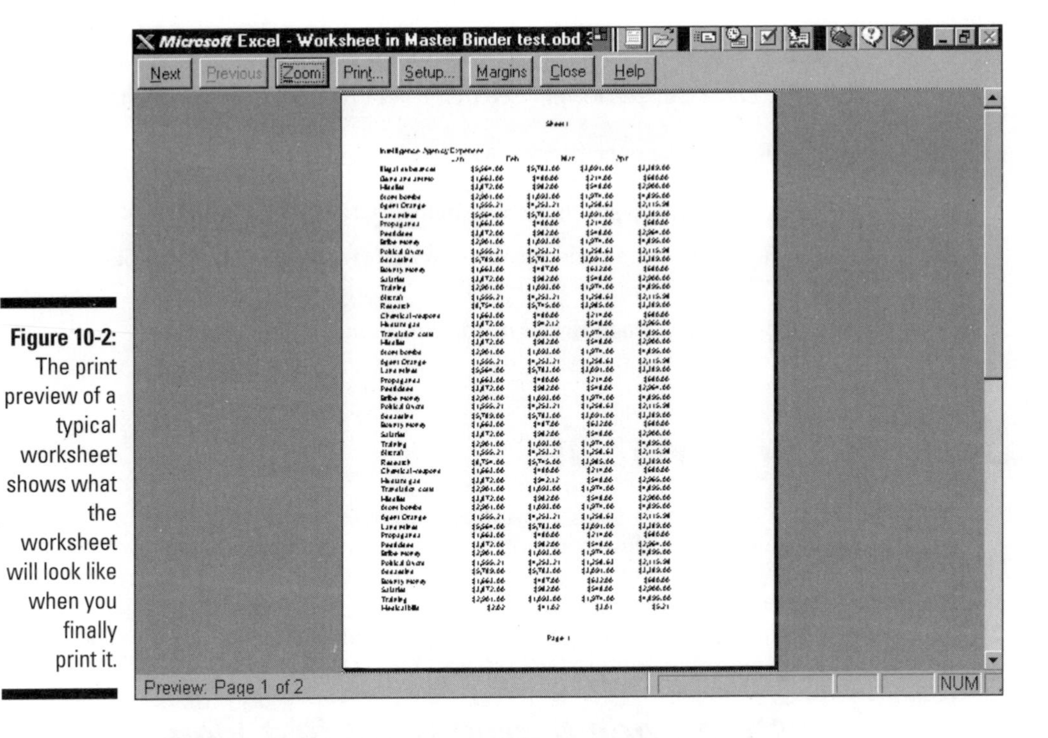

Figure 10-2: The print preview of a typical worksheet shows what the worksheet will look like when you finally print it.

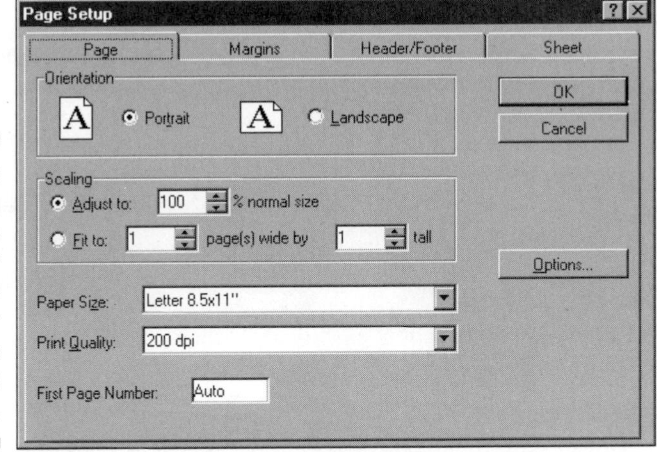

Figure 10-3: Specifying some of the options for the way your document's pages are set up.

This option lets you specify an exact percentage to shrink or expand your worksheet. To shrink your worksheet, choose a percentage less than 100 (90, for example). To expand your worksheet, choose a percentage larger than 100 (120, for example).

Shrinking or expanding your worksheet lets you change the way page breaks separate your worksheet. If you already know where you want to put a page break, you can easily tell Excel, "See that row? Put a page break right there."

To place or remove a page break, follow these steps:

1. **Click a row you want to display below the page break.**

   If you want to put a page break between rows 6 and 7, for example, click any cell in row 7.

2. **Choose Insert⇨Page Break or Insert⇨Remove Page Break.**

Setting Page Margins

Nothing is more annoying than printing your entire worksheet, binding it together, and then suddenly realizing that your margins are so narrow that you have to pry apart the binding just to see your entire worksheet. To prevent this problem and to give you another way to make your worksheets look aesthetically pleasing, Excel lets you adjust its top, bottom, right, and left margins.

Adjusting page margins the fast way

If you're in a hurry and want to adjust your page margins quickly, using your mouse is the easiest route. Using your mouse isn't precise, but it's fast and easy, which is a rare commodity in anything involving personal computers.

To adjust your page margins quickly, follow these steps:

1. **If you're using Excel within a binder, choose Section⇨View Outside.**

   Skip this step if you're using Excel outside a binder.

2. **Choose File⇨Print Preview.**

   Excel displays your worksheet exactly as it will look when you print it (refer to Figure 10-2).

3. **Click Margins.**

   Excel displays your document's margins, as shown in Figure 10-4.

4. **Move the mouse pointer over any of the page margins so that the pointer turns into a double-headed arrow (refer to Figure 10-4).**

5. **Hold down the left mouse button and drag the mouse to where you want the new margin to appear.**

   The original page margin line remains visible, and a new dotted line appears under the mouse pointer so that you know where the new page margin will appear.

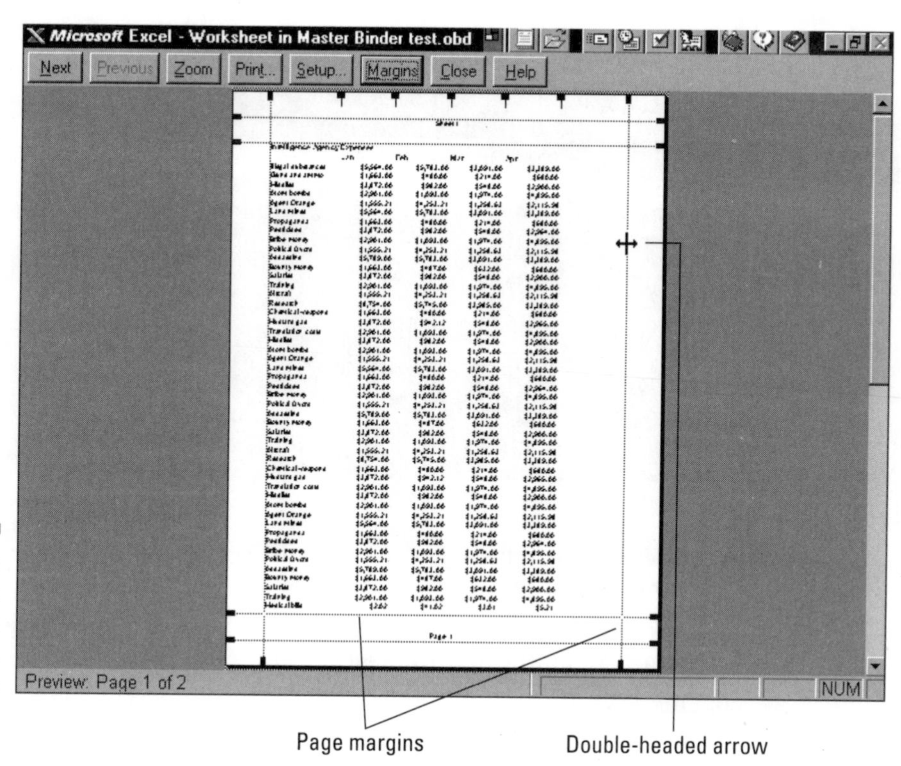

Figure 10-4: Excel shows your page margins.

6. **When you're happy with the page margin position, release the left mouse button.**

Adjusting page margins the slower, more precise way

In case you absolutely must have page margins narrowed to two decimal places, you can specify exact values rather than just move the page margins around and guess where they should appear.

To adjust your page margins by typing values, follow these steps:

1. **If you're using Excel within a binder, choose Section⇨View Outside.**

   Skip this step if you're using Excel outside a binder.

2. **Choose File⇨Page Setup.**

   The Page Setup dialog box appears.

3. **Click the Margins tab, as shown in Figure 10-5.**

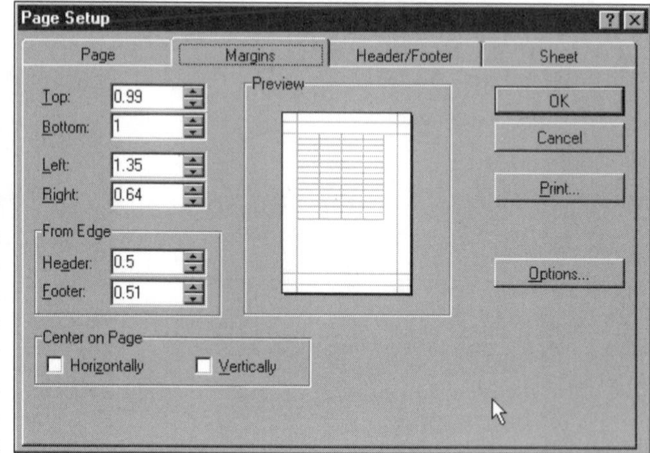

Figure 10-5: Excel lets you choose the margins for your documents. How nice.

4. **Click the Top, Bottom, Left, or Right list boxes and choose a value for your page margins.**
5. **Click the Horizontally and Vertically check boxes in the Center on Page group if you want your worksheet neatly centered on the page.**
6. **Click OK.**

Playing with Headers and Footers

A *header* consists of text that appears at the top of every page in your worksheet, but only when you print it. Here are some typical examples of headers:

- Annual 1996 Report
- Prepared by John Doe (who deserves a fat raise)
- Top Secret: Destroy after reading

A *footer* consists of text that appears at the bottom of every page in your worksheet, but only when you print it. Here are some typical examples of footers:

- Page 5
- Copyright(c) 1996
- Warning: Profit margins seem larger than they really are.

To help make the process of choosing a header or footer as mindless as possible, Excel provides a list box that contains some common types of headers and footers. You can also create your own headers and footers and get as creative as you want.

Choosing a header and footer

If you don't want to think for yourself, the easiest way to go is to choose a header or footer that Excel has already created for you.

To choose one of the default headers or footers, follow these steps:

1. **If you're using Excel within a binder, choose Section⇨View Outside.**

   Skip this step if you're using Excel outside a binder.

2. **Choose File⇨Print Preview.**

   Excel displays your worksheet exactly as it will look when you print it (refer to Figure 10-2).

3. **Click Setup.**

   The Page Setup dialog box appears (see Figure 10-6).

4. **Click the Header list box and then choose a header.**
5. **Click the Footer list box and then choose a footer.**
6. **Click OK.**

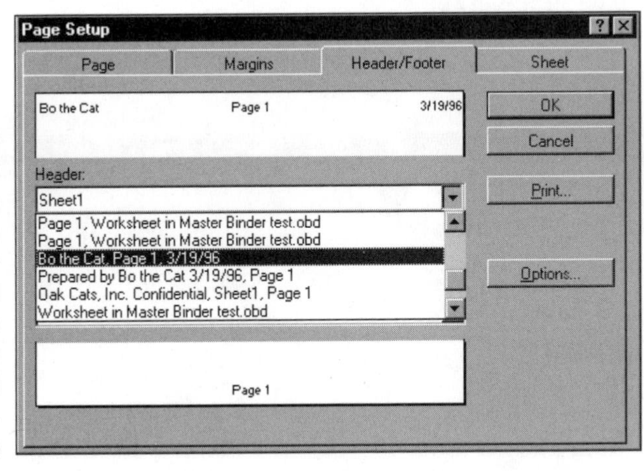

Figure 10-6: Specifying the way you want your headers and footers to look on a printed page.

Making your own headers and footers

Unfortunately, being forced to choose from one of Excel's default headers or footers can seem as limiting as choosing between two equally obnoxious and unappealing politicians. To give you even greater freedom, Excel lets you create your own custom headers and footers.

To create a custom header or footer, follow these steps:

1. **If you're using Excel within a binder, choose Section⇨View Outside.**

   Skip this step if you're using Excel outside a binder.

2. **Choose File⇨Print Preview.**

   Excel displays your worksheet exactly as it will look when you print it (refer to Figure 10-2).

3. **Click Setup.**

   The Page Setup dialog box appears (refer to Figure 10-6).

4. **Click the Header/Footer tab.**

5. **Click Custom Header.**

   The Header dialog box appears, as shown in Figure 10-7.

6. **Click the text displayed in the Left Section, Center Section, or Right Section box.**

   After you finish typing text in the Left Section box, you can click the Center Section box and type more text and then click in the Right Section box and type even more text, if you want.

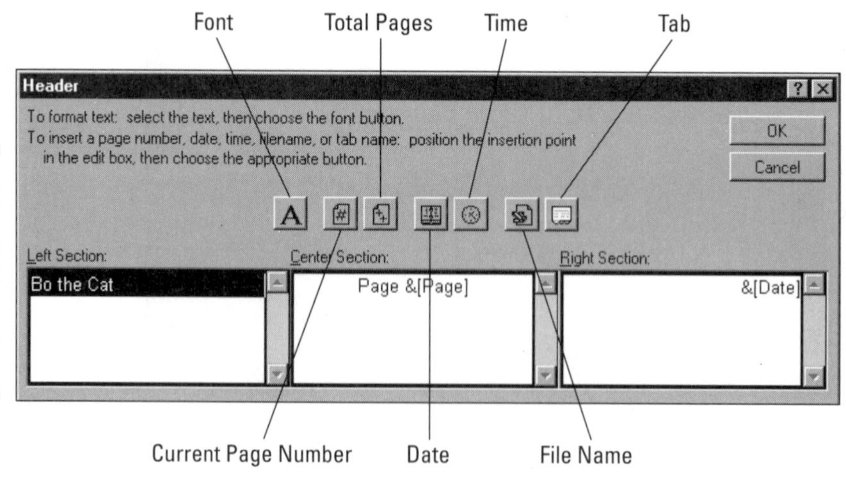

Figure 10-7: This helpful dialog box lets you set up a document's header.

7. **Type the new text you want to display (such as** Chapter 11**). If you want Excel to insert or format text for you, click one of the following buttons:**
   - **Font:** Lets you change your document's font and font size
   - **Current Page Number:** Displays the current page number
   - **Total Pages:** Displays the total number of pages in your worksheet
   - **Date:** Inserts the date on which you print the worksheet
   - **Time:** Inserts the time at which you print the worksheet
   - **File Name:** Inserts the filename of your worksheet
   - **Tab:** Inserts the worksheet name
8. **Click OK.**

   The Page Setup dialog box appears again.
9. **Click Custom Footer.**

   The Footer dialog box that appears looks suspiciously similar to the Header dialog box (refer to Figure 10-7).
10. **Repeat steps 5 and 6 and fill in the information for a footer.**
11. **Click OK.**

    The Page Setup dialog box appears again.
12. **Click OK.**

Changing the Paper Size and Orientation

Sometimes a worksheet doesn't fit within the confines of a typical piece of paper. When this situation occurs, you can tell Excel to print your worksheets sideways or on legal-size paper so that everything fits on a single page.

Changing the page orientation

The two types of page orientation are portrait and landscape. In *portrait orientation,* a page is taller than it is wide. Think about how you would orient a canvas to paint someone's portrait. Because most people are taller than they are wide, height is more important.

In *landscape orientation,* a page is wider than it is tall. If you paint a landscape, width is more important than height, so you should use landscape orientation when you want to print your worksheets sideways on a sheet of paper.

To change the page orientation of your worksheet, follow these steps:

1. **If you're using Excel within a binder, choose Section⇨View Outside.**

   Skip this step if you're using Excel outside a binder.

2. **Choose File⇨Print Preview.**

   Excel displays your worksheet exactly as it will look when you print it (refer to Figure 10-2).

3. **Click Setup.**

   The Page Setup dialog box appears (refer to Figure 10-6).

4. **Click the Page tab.**
5. **Click the Portrait or Landscape option button.**
6. **Click OK.**

Choosing the size of your paper

Many people use paper that measures 8 1/2 × 11 inches. If you want to cram more of your worksheet on a single page, you can, of course, stuff your printer with different sizes of paper. Immediately after you load your printer with a different size of paper, you also have to tell Excel the size of the new paper so that it prints your worksheets on the paper correctly.

To tell Excel the size of the paper on which to print, follow these steps:

1. **If you're using Excel within a binder, choose Section⇨View Outside.**

   Skip this step if you're using Excel outside a binder.

2. **Choose File⇨Page Setup.**

   The Page Setup dialog box appears (refer to Figure 10-6).

3. **Click the Paper Size list box and then choose a paper size.**
4. **Click OK.**

Printing Gridlines, Headings, and Page Orders

The entire purpose of displaying gridlines and headings is to help you place your labels, numbers, and formulas. Normally, when you print a worksheet, you don't want your gridlines and row or column headings to appear, because they can be as distracting as the wires holding up a marionette during a puppet show.

Because Excel gives you options for practically everything imaginable, you can also choose to print your gridlines and headings. Then you can see exactly which cells contain labels, numbers, and formulas.

One good time to print gridlines and headings is when you're printing a worksheet with all its formulas revealed (you can reveal your formulas by pressing Ctrl+'). Then you can see exactly which cells contain the data a formula uses.

If you have a particularly large worksheet (three pages or more), you can even tell Excel in which order you want to print everything. Then you don't have to re-sort your worksheets by hand after printing them. The two choices for printing your worksheets are

- Down, then Across
- Across, then Down

Which method you choose depends on your personal preferences and how you organized your data in a worksheet. For example, you may want to print Down, then Across if your data were organized as follows:

1st Quarter sales				***2nd Quarter sales***			
	Jan.	Feb.	Mar.		Apr.	May	Jun.
Cat food				Cat food			
Dog food				Dog food			
Fish food				Fish food			

3rd Quarter sales				***4th Quarter sales***			
	Jul.	Aug.	Sep.		Oct.	Nov.	Dec.
Cat food				Cat food			
Dog food				Dog food			
Fish food				Fish food			

If your worksheets were organized in this way, you would probably want to print Down, then Across so your data prints in order. However, suppose your worksheets were organized in this way:

1st Quarter sales

	Jan.	Feb.	Mar.
Cat food			
Dog food			
Fish food			

3rd Quarter sales

	Jul.	Aug.	Sep.
Cat food			
Dog food			
Fish food			

2nd Quarter sales

	Apr.	May	Jun.
Cat food			
Dog food			
Fish food			

4th Quarter sales

	Oct.	Nov.	Dec.
Cat food			
Dog food			
Fish food			

In this case, you would probably want to print Across, then Down to make sure your data appeared in the right order.

To change the print order of your worksheet or to make Excel print gridlines and headings, follow these steps:

1. **If you're using Excel within a binder, choose Section⇨View Outside.**

   Skip this step if you're using Excel outside a binder.

2. **Choose File⇨Print Preview.**

   Excel displays your worksheet exactly as it will look when you print it (refer to Figure 10-2).

3. **Click Setup.**

   The Page Setup dialog box appears (refer to Figure 10-6).

4. **Click the Sheet tab.**

5. **If you want to print gridlines, click the Gridlines check box so that a check mark appears.**

6. **If you want to print row and column headings, click the Row and Column Headings check box so that a check mark appears.**
7. **Click either the Down, then Across option button or the Across, then Down radio button in the page Order group.**
8. **Click OK.**

Chapter 11

Sharing Your Excel Files

In This Chapter

- Converting files into a different format for use with another program
- Adding notes to your worksheets
- Experimenting with different scenarios
- Protecting your worksheets from other people
- Making your own Web pages with Excel and the Internet Assistant

The three dominant spreadsheets on the market are Microsoft Excel, available for both Windows and the Macintosh; Lotus 1-2-3, available on both Windows and OS/2 — the Macintosh version got dumped years ago; and Quattro Pro, which is a clone of Lotus 1-2-3.

Because Quattro Pro (and many lesser known spreadsheets) can use Lotus 1-2-3, if you ever want to convert an Excel file for someone else's use, you can — nine times out of ten — just convert your file to a Lotus 1-2-3 file.

The process of converting Excel files into Lotus 1-2-3 files isn't difficult. If you're fortunate enough to share your Excel files with someone else who also uses Excel, you can use all sorts of neat features to add comments without printing a copy on paper and marking it up by hand. When your worksheets look perfect, you can print them for the world to see. In fact, you can even post them as Web pages on the World Wide Web by using the Internet Assistant.

Converting Files from or for Other Spreadsheets

When you convert an Excel file into another file format, you "export" the file. When you *export* a file, you make a copy of your original Excel document and save the second copy in a different file format, such as Lotus 1-2-3.

Sharing Excel files with the Excel Viewer

Excel is the number-one spreadsheet in the universe, but not everyone has a copy of the program buried on his or her hard disk. Since many people refuse to buy Microsoft programs, the easiest way to share your Excel files with others is to hand them to people along with a copy of a special program called the Excel Viewer.

The Excel Viewer is a free program that only lets you view and print Excel files (hey, what do you want for nothing?); you cannot edit an Excel file within the Excel Viewer program.

By giving all the people you know a copy of Excel Viewer, you can freely share your files with them without converting your Excel files to a strange file format, such as Lotus 1-2-3. To get a free copy of Excel Viewer, download it from CompuServe or America Online or directly from Microsoft's Web site, at `http://www.microsoft.com`.

Here are two reasons that you may have to convert a file:

- You used Excel to create a file, but you want to give the file to someone who uses a different spreadsheet program.
- Someone gives you a file created by using another spreadsheet program, and you want to view and edit the spreadsheet in Excel.

When someone gives you a file created by a different spreadsheet and you want to edit it in Excel, you import the file. When you *import* a file, Excel loads the file and lets you save a copy of it as an Excel worksheet.

When you convert a file from Excel 7.0 to another file format, you may lose cell formatting, formulas, and features available only in Excel 7.0. In other words, if you convert an Excel 7.0 file to a Lotus 1-2-3 file, be careful: The conversion may not be 100 percent accurate, but you're probably used to nothing working the way it should if you've been using personal computers long enough.

Exporting an Excel file

Excel knows how to save files for older versions of Excel as well as various versions of Lotus 1-2-3. In case you want to save a file for use in an obscure spreadsheet that should have been yanked off the market decades ago, you can also save your Excel files as text or in dBASE or another oddball format, which virtually guarantees that anyone in the universe with a computer can use your Excel files.

Just to numb your mind with all the possibilities, Excel can save a file in any of these formats:

- **Excel versions 2.1, 3.0, and 4.0:** Exports an Excel 7.0 file into an older version of Excel. Because many programs can import Excel files, this method may be the simplest and most reliable way to transfer Excel files to another program.
- **Lotus 1-2-3 versions 1.0 to 4.0:** Exports an Excel 7.0 file into an older version of Lotus 1-2-3. Because most programs can import either Excel or Lotus 1-2-3 files, this format and the Excel format may be the only formats you ever have to use.
- **dBASE II, III, and IV:** Exports an Excel 7.0 file into a dBASE data file. This format is especially handy if you want to transfer an Excel file to a database program (Alpha Five, dBASE, FoxPro, or Paradox, for example).
- **DIF (Data Interchange Format) and SYLK (Symbolic Link format):** Exports an Excel 7.0 file into a DIF or SYLK file, two older formats once touted as "standards" that most everyone ignored, anyway. Still, if you want to transfer an Excel file to an older spreadsheet, such as SuperCalc, choose this option.
- **WQ1 (QuattroPro/DOS):** Exports an Excel 7.0 file into an ancient WQ1 file format originally used by Quattro Pro Version 1.0 for DOS. If you need to transfer your Excel 7.0 files to someone using any version of Quattro Pro, save your Excel 7.0 in this format.
- **CSV (Comma Separated Values format):** Exports an Excel 7.0 file into a special text file that's most useful for exporting an Excel file to a Macintosh, OS/2, or non-spreadsheet Windows program.
- **Text:** Exports an Excel 7.0 file into a text file any program can use, even programs running on obscure computers such as the Amiga or Atari.

Practically every program in the world knows how to use an Excel, Lotus 1-2-3, or dBASE file. To retain all your formatting, try saving your file as an older version of an Excel file first. If that doesn't work, try Lotus 1-2-3. Ninety-nine percent of the time, these two file formats are the only ones you ever need, so you can ignore all the weird formats, such as DIF, SYLK, or CSV.

To export an Excel file and save it in a different file format, follow these steps:

1. **If you're using Excel within a binder, choose Section⇨View Outside.**

   Skip this step if you're using Excel outside a binder.

2. **Choose File⇨Save As. (If you're using Excel within a binder, choose File⇨Save Copy As.)**

   The Save As dialog box appears, as shown in Figure 11-1.

3. **Click the Save as type list box and then choose a file format.**

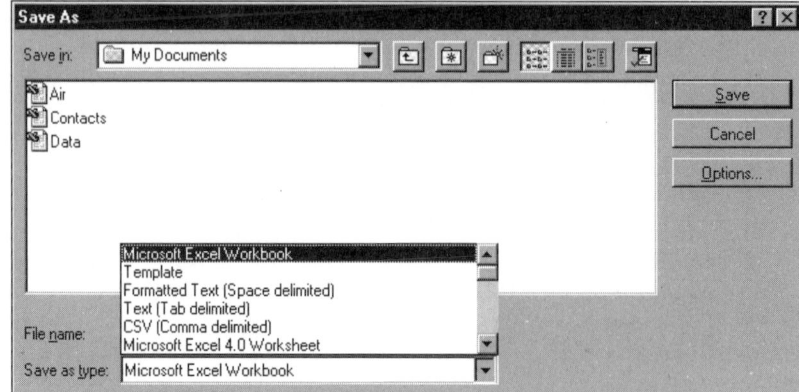

Figure 11-1: Saving a file in a different format in the Save As dialog box.

4. **Type a name for your file in the File name box.**

   To avoid any confusion between your original Excel file and the exported file, save your exported file under a different name.

5. **Click Save.**

Importing a file into Excel

Excel knows how to import files created by a variety of programs, including Works, Quattro Pro, Lotus 1-2-3, dBASE, and older versions of Excel.

To import a file into Excel, follow these steps:

1. **Load Excel as a separate program (not within an Office binder).**
2. **Choose File⇨Open.**

   The Open dialog box appears.

3. **Click the Files of type list box and choose the file format you want to import (Lotus 1-2-3 Files, Excel Files, or dBASE Files, for example).**
4. **Click the file you want to import and then click Open.**

   If all goes well, Excel displays the data exactly as it appears in its original file format. Most likely, though, you have to go through your imported file and edit it slightly.

If you have a foreign file format you want to add to an Office binder, you first have to convert that foreign file into an Excel file. After you convert it into an Excel file, you can add it to your Office binder.

To import a file into an Office binder, follow these steps:

1. **Repeat steps 1 through 4 in the preceding steps for importing a file.**
2. **Choose File⇨Save to save your newly imported file as a genuine, 100 percent authentic Excel file.**
3. **Open the Office binder in which you want to add your newly converted file.**
4. **Choose Section⇨Add from File.**

   The Add from File dialog box appears.
5. **Click the Excel file you saved in step 5 and then click Add.**

Tacking on Notes to the Cells in Your Worksheet

When you share your Excel files with other people, you may want to add notes to your worksheets to ask for more help, question certain formula assumptions, or tell your co-worker what a jerk your boss was last Friday afternoon. You can print your worksheets on paper and attach notes to them with a paper clip, but Excel has a neat feature that lets you instead attach notes directly to your individual worksheet cells.

Attaching notes

Notes can come in handy when you want to remind yourself about the contents of a certain cell ("January sales were down because Bob messed up") or if you're sharing Excel worksheets with others ("Jane, verify that this figure is accurate; if it's not, you'll be suspected of embezzlement").

To attach a note to a cell, follow these steps:

1. **Click the cell to which you want to attach your note.**
2. **Choose Insert⇨Note.**

   The Cell Note dialog box appears, as shown in Figure 11-2.

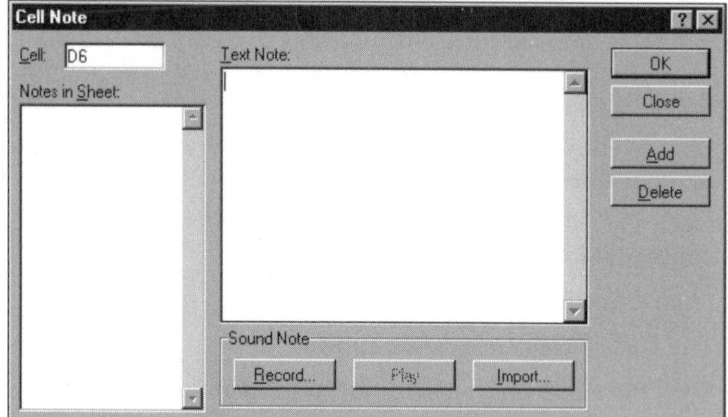

Figure 11-2: Attaching a note to a cell.

3. **Type your comment in the Text Note box.**
4. **Click OK.**

   Excel draws a little, red dot in the upper-right corner of the cell, to let you know that the cell contains a note, as shown in Figure 11-3.

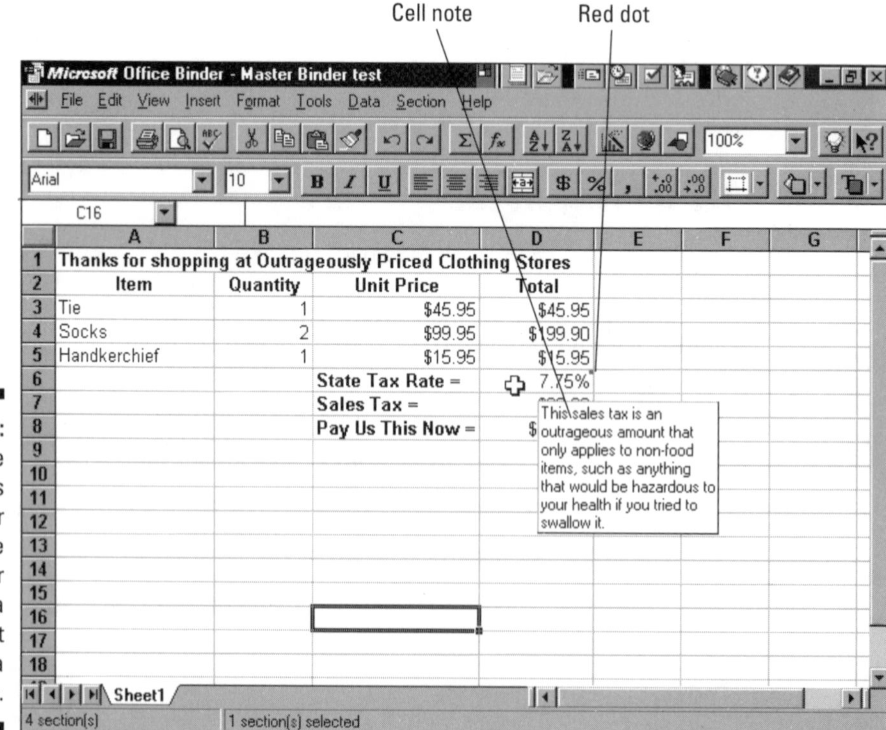

Figure 11-3: A cell note appears whenever you move the cursor over a cell that contains a red dot.

Finding your notes again

After you or someone else has scattered various notes in different cells, the hard part may be finding them so that you can read them. If you want, you can look for every red dot that appears in a cell, but if you have that much time on your hands, you probably need a hobby to soak up your free time. For an easier method, just have Excel show you a list of all the cell notes in a worksheet.

To find all the cell notes buried throughout a worksheet, follow these steps:

1. **Choose Insert⇨Note.**

   The Cell Note dialog box appears, listing all the cell notes in the Notes in Sheet box, as shown in Figure 11-4.

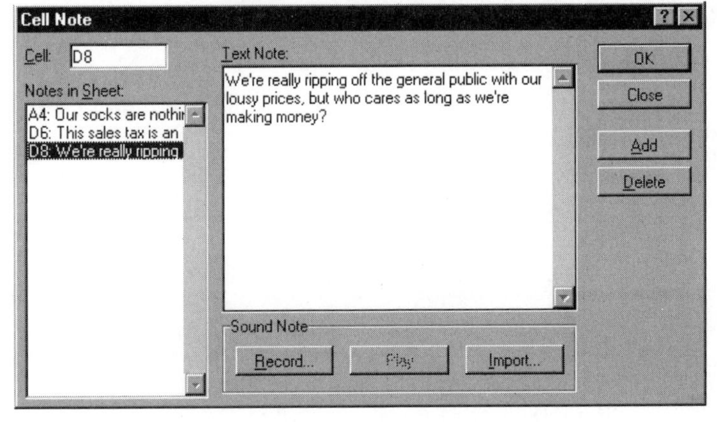

Figure 11-4: The Cell Note dialog box lists all the cell notes stored in a worksheet.

2. **Click the cell note, stored in the Notes in Sheet box, that you want to read.**

   Excel displays the contents of that cell note in the Text Note box.

3. **Click OK.**

4. **Press Ctrl+G to move the cursor to the cell that contains a cell note.**

   The Go To dialog box appears.

5. **Type the cell reference (such as A5 or H19) in the Reference box, and then click OK.**

   Excel moves the cursor to your chosen cell.

6. **Move the mouse pointer over the cell.**

   Excel displays the cell note.

Printing notes

When you print your worksheets, Excel normally refuses to print your cell notes. In case you want (or need) to print your cell notes along with your worksheets, you can do so, by following these steps:

1. **If you're using Word within a binder, choose Section⇨View Outside.**

   Skip this step if you're using Word outside a binder.

2. **Choose File⇨Page Setup.**

   The Page Setup dialog box appears.

3. **Click the Sheet tab, shown in Figure 11-5.**

Figure 11-5: Using the Sheet tab to specify options for printing notes in an Excel worksheet.

4. **Click the Notes check box so that a check mark appears in it.**

5. **Click OK.**

Deleting notes

After littering a worksheet with notes, you'll eventually want to get rid of them so that they don't keep sprouting messages whenever you move the mouse pointer over them.

Make sure that you really do want to delete your notes, because after you delete them, you can never undelete or retrieve them again, no matter how hard you cry or scream.

To delete a note, follow these steps:

1. **Choose Insert⇨Note.**

   The Cell Note dialog box appears with a list of all the cell notes in the Notes in Sheet box (refer to Figure 11-4).

2. **In the Notes in Sheet box, click the cell note you want to delete.**

   Excel displays the contents of that cell note in the Text Note box.

3. **Click Delete.**

   Excel displays a frantic dialog box which lets you know that the note will be permanently deleted.

4. **Click OK.**

   The Cell Note dialog box appears again.

5. **Click OK.**

   Excel deletes your note so thoroughly that not even your local computer guru will ever be able to recover it again.

Playing with Scenarios

Creating a worksheet and plugging in numbers can give you an accurate calculation, but what if you aren't sure which values you should use? Suppose that you're creating a report that lists how much money your company has lost in the past year and that not all the sales results for the fourth quarter are available yet.

Rather than just give up and go home (which is probably the more appealing option), Excel lets you create your worksheet anyway and then create separate scenarios. A *scenario* is just an identical copy of your worksheet with slightly different numbers plugged in to it.

One scenario may contain numbers that show a highly optimistic possibility, and another scenario may contain numbers that show a more pessimistic result. By letting you plug in different numbers to the same worksheet and store separate copies of them, you can forecast the range of possible outcomes that might occur. If fourth quarter sales are high, for example, you can pay off your bills; if fourth quarter sales are lower than expected, you can start looking for another job tomorrow.

Creating a scenario

Before you create a scenario, you have to create your worksheet. Then you have to specify which cells (as many as 32 different cells) will contain different numbers between your scenarios. The cells you choose are called *changing cells* because the contents of these cells will — obviously — vary between your multiple scenarios.

To create a scenario, follow these steps:

1. **Choose Tools⇨Scenarios.**

   The Scenario Manager dialog box appears, as shown in Figure 11-6.

Figure 11-6: The Scenario Manager dialog box lets you create your wildest fantasies about your worksheets.

2. **Click Add.**

   The Add Scenario dialog box appears.

3. **In the Scenario Name box, type a descriptive name for your scenario (Best-Case Scenario if Bob Doesn't Ruin Our Latest Deal, for example).**
4. **Click in the Changing Cells box.**
5. **Hold down the Ctrl key and click all the cells that will contain varying data.**

   You may have to move the Add Scenario dialog box out of the way in order to see your worksheet. (You have to do this step only the first time you create a scenario.)

6. **Click OK.**

   The Scenario Values dialog box appears, as shown in Figure 11-7.

Figure 11-7: The Scenario Values dialog box.

7. **Type a value for each of your changing cells and then click OK.**
8. **Repeat steps 2 through 6 for each scenario you want to create.**

Viewing a scenario

After you create two or more scenarios, you can view them and see how the different numbers may affect the rest of your worksheet.

To view your scenarios, follow these steps:

1. **Choose Tools⇨Scenarios.**

   The Scenario Manager dialog box appears (refer to Figure 11-6).

2. **Click the scenario name you want to view and then click Show, as shown in Figure 11-8.**

   Excel shows you how the numbers stored in your chosen scenario affect the rest of your worksheet.

3. **Click Close.**

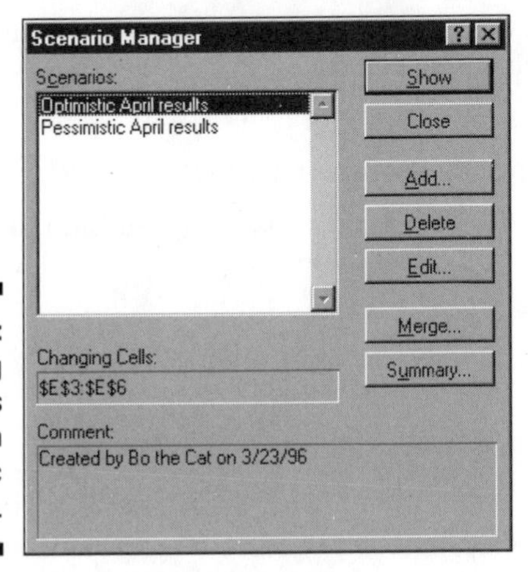

Figure 11-8: Displaying numbers stored in an optimistic scenario.

Editing a scenario

A scenario contains numbers you can always change later, just in case your first guess was wrong or if you eventually get more accurate numbers. If that happens, just edit your scenario and plug in your new numbers. Another reason you may want to change your scenario is to change the number of changing cells in a scenario.

To edit a scenario, follow these steps:

1. **Choose Tools⇨Scenarios.**

   The Scenario Manager dialog box appears (refer to Figure 11-6).

2. **Click the scenario name you want to edit and then click Edit.**

   The Edit Scenario dialog box appears, as shown in Figure 11-9.

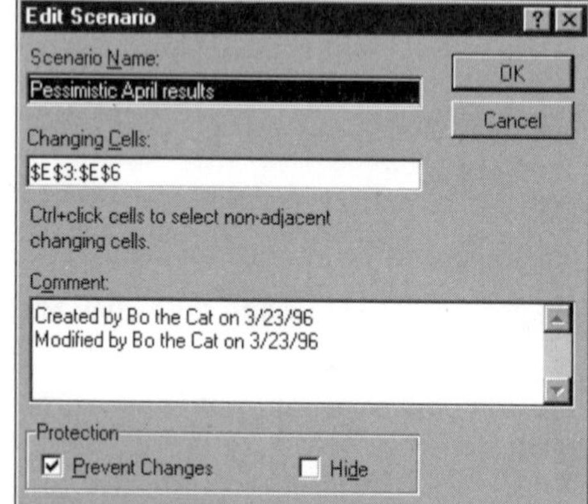

Figure 11-9: Self-esteem problems can show up in the Edit Scenario dialog box.

3. **If necessary, hold down the Ctrl key and click the cell you want to add to or delete from your changing cell list.**

4. **Click OK.**

   The Scenario Values dialog box appears (refer to Figure 11-7).

5. **Type the new values for your scenario's changing cells and then click OK.**

6. **Click Close.**

Deleting a scenario

Scenarios are great for playing around with different numbers, but you probably won't want to keep your scenarios around forever.

If you delete a scenario, you cannot undelete it. Make sure that you really want to delete a scenario, because when it's gone, it's gone for good.

To delete a scenario, just choose Tools➪Scenarios. When the Scenario Manager dialog box appears (refer to Figure 11-6), click the scenario name you want to delete, and then click Delete.

Protecting Your Worksheets from the Harm Others May Do

If you plan to share your Excel files with others, you probably don't want people to type different values, edit your labels, or mess around with your formulas. To keep others from messing up your carefully crafted worksheets, Excel gives you two ways to protect them from modification:

- Protect individual sheets
- Protect an entire workbook

A workbook consists of one or more sheets. If you protect only one sheet in your workbook, other people can still modify the other sheets.

When you protect an individual sheet, no one can modify the contents of that sheet. When you protect an entire workbook, no one can add or delete a sheet in the workbook. People can still edit the contents of your individual sheets, however. If you want complete protection from modifications, protect your individual sheets and your entire workbook.

Protecting your work

Protecting your work is a good idea whenever you plan to let anyone else look at your Excel files.

To protect a sheet or workbook, follow these steps:

1. **Choose Tools➪Protection and then either Protect Sheet or Protect Workbook.**

   The Protect Sheet or Protect Workbook dialog box appears, as shown in Figure 11-10.

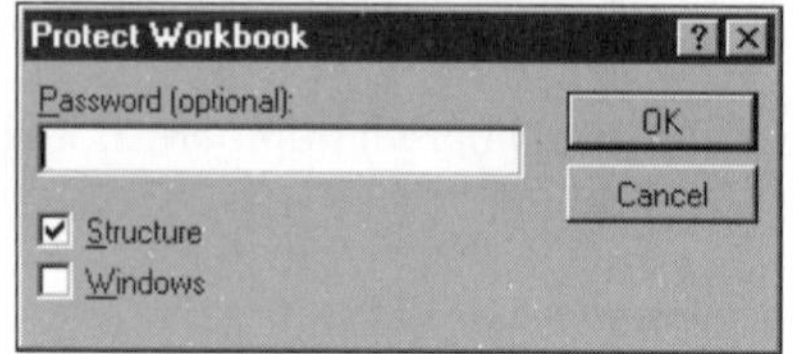

Figure 11-10: Protecting your work from bad guys.

2. **Type a password in the Password box to password-protect your sheet or workbook.**

   Typing a password is optional, but I highly recommend it. If you don't type a password, anyone can use the Unprotect command to unprotect your work and modify your worksheet. Ideally, you should pick a password that's easy for you to remember but difficult for someone else to guess. For example, using your name as a password wouldn't be smart (although it might keep your boss from guessing it). A combination of letters and numbers may be best, such as the initials of your name mixed with your favorite numbers, such as S6C6O6T6T.

3. **Click OK.**

   The Confirm Password dialog box appears, asking you to type your password again, as shown in Figure 11-11.

4. **Type your password again and then click OK.**

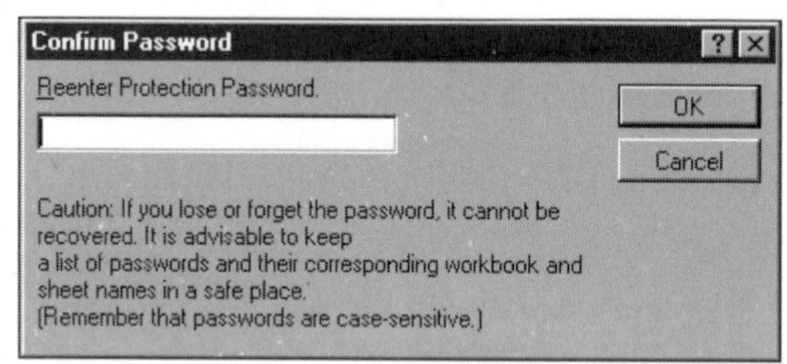

Figure 11-11: Excel tries to makes sure that no one illicitly swipes your information.

If you have multiple sheets in a workbook, you can protect each sheet with a different password. Then you can share your passwords with other people so that only certain people can edit specific sheets.

If you password-protect your sheet or workbook and forget your password, you're locked out from editing your own work. The good news is that many third-party programs can crack a protected Excel file and retrieve your password. The bad news is that thieves can use these same programs to find your password and modify your Excel files. So don't expect a simple password to keep out determined intruders.

Unprotecting your work

After you let hordes of other people paw over your work, you can unprotect your files so that you can edit them again.

To unprotect a sheet or workbook, follow these steps:

1. **Choose Tools⇨Protection and then either Unprotect Sheet or Unprotect Workbook.**

   An Unprotect Sheet or Unprotect Workbook dialog box appears, as shown in Figure 11-12.

2. **Type your password in the Password box and then click OK.**

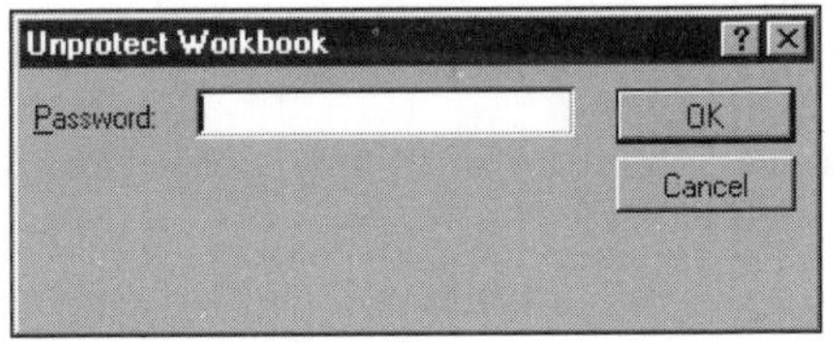

Figure 11-12: Before you can unprotect a sheet or workbook, Excel forces you to type the password.

Excel at Converting Worksheets into Web Page Tables

Microsoft Office can't create Web pages right out of the box; you have to get a free copy of the Internet Assistant for each program. To create Web pages using Word, for example, you need to use the Internet Assistant for Word. Likewise, to create Web pages by using Excel, you need a copy of the Internet Assistant for Excel.

You can get a free copy of these Internet Assistant programs for Word, Excel, PowerPoint, Access, and Schedule+ by downloading them from CompuServe, America Online, the Microsoft Network, or directly from Microsoft's own Web page at `http://www.microsoft.com`. After you get a copy of these Internet Assistant programs and install them on your computer, you can start creating Web pages by using Microsoft Office.

The Internet Assistant for Excel is an add-on file called HTML.XLA that you must copy into your Excel Library directory (such as C:\MSOFFICE\EXCEL\LIBRARY). After you copy the HTML.XLA file to your hard disk, you can start creating Web pages.

Because a typical Excel worksheet consists of rows and columns, the Internet Assistant for Excel is ideally suited for creating tables for your Web pages (and horrible at creating general purpose Web pages that require only text).

Excel can create a Web page with your worksheet neatly formatted as a table, or it can just create a table that you can insert into an existing Web page. To create a table and insert it into an existing Web page, you have to put the `##Table##` string in your existing Web page where you want the table to appear. If you don't understand HTML (HyperText Markup Language) codes, simply use Excel to create Web pages with your tables on them.

To convert a worksheet into a Web-page table, follow these steps:

1. **Load Excel as a separate program (not within a binder).**
2. **Choose File⇨Open and load the HTML.XLA file.**
3. **Choose File⇨Open and load the file you want to convert into a Web-page table.**
4. **Highlight the part of your worksheet that you want to convert into a Web page.**
5. **Choose Tools⇨Internet Assistant Wizard.**

   The Internet Wizard dialog box appears, as shown in Figure 11-13.
6. **Click Next>.**

   Step 2 of the Internet Assistant Wizard dialog box appears, as shown in Figure 11-14, giving you a choice between creating a separate Web page or inserting your table into an existing Web page. Unless you know what you're doing, it's easier to use the default setting that creates a separate Web page.
7. **Click Next>.**

   Step 3 of the Internet Assistant Wizard dialog box appears, as shown in Figure 11-15.
8. **Type a title, header, name, and so on that you want to appear on your Web page and click Next> when you're done.**

   Step 4 of the Internet Assistant Wizard dialog box appears, asking how you want to convert your data. For most purposes, it's best to convert your formatting as well.

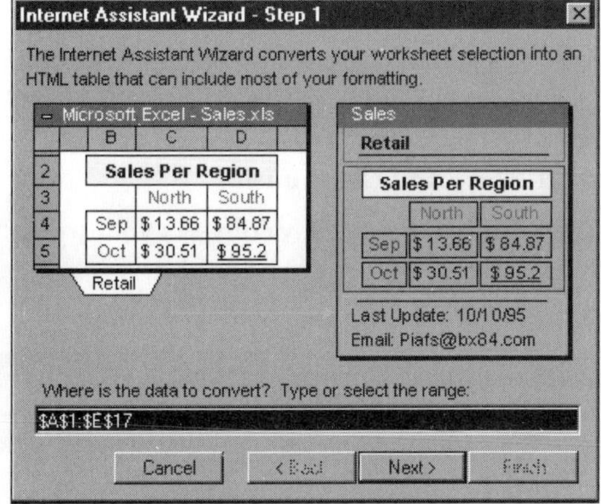

Figure 11-13: The first step toward converting your worksheet data into a table.

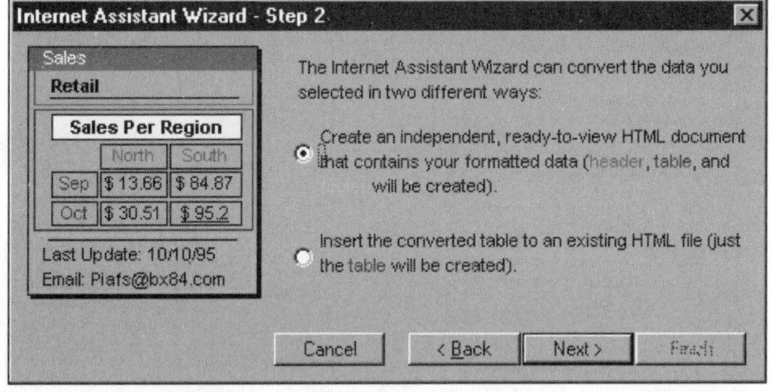

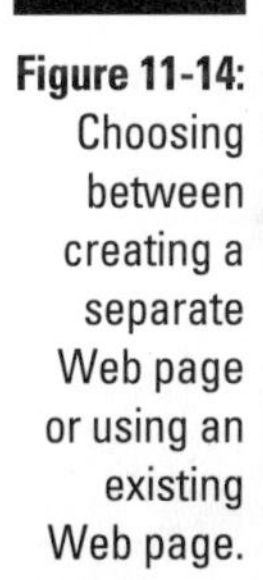

Figure 11-14: Choosing between creating a separate Web page or using an existing Web page.

Figure 11-15: Customizing the look of your Web page.

9. **Click Next>.**

   Step 5 of the Internet Assistant Wizard dialog box appears, asking you to choose a name for your Web page along with a directory where you want to store it.

10. **Type a name and directory and click Finish.**

    The Internet Assistant for Excel magically converts your worksheet into a genuine Web page, ready for posting (see Figure 11-16).

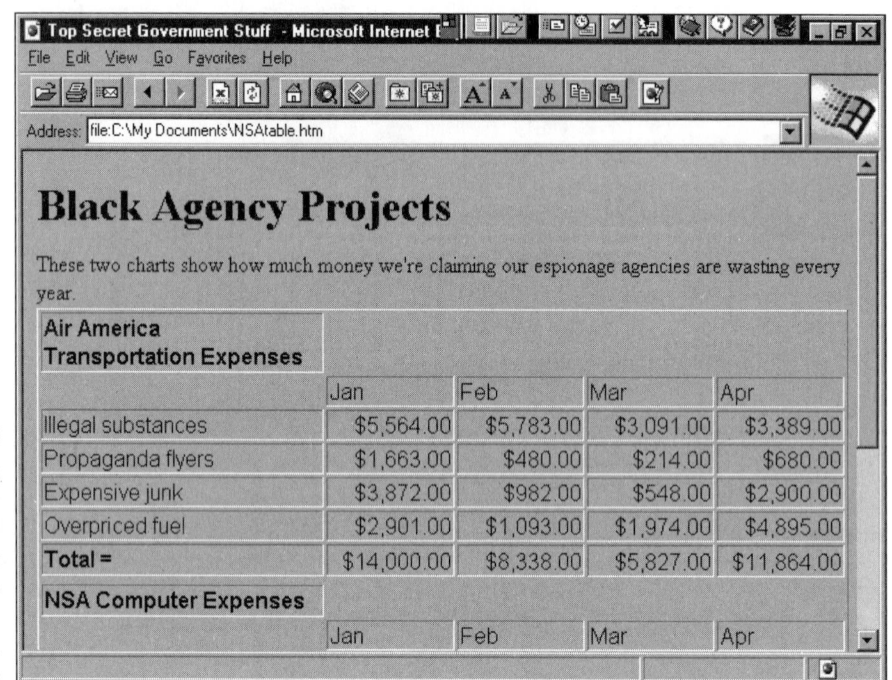

Black Agency Projects

These two charts show how much money we're claiming our espionage agencies are wasting every year.

Air America Transportation Expenses				
	Jan	Feb	Mar	Apr
Illegal substances	$5,564.00	$5,783.00	$3,091.00	$3,389.00
Propaganda flyers	$1,663.00	$480.00	$214.00	$680.00
Expensive junk	$3,872.00	$982.00	$548.00	$2,900.00
Overpriced fuel	$2,901.00	$1,093.00	$1,974.00	$4,895.00
Total =	$14,000.00	$8,338.00	$5,827.00	$11,864.00
NSA Computer Expenses				
	Jan	Feb	Mar	Apr

Figure 11-16: A typical Excel worksheet displayed as a table in a Web page.

Part III

The Microsoft PowerPoint Dog-and-Pony Show

"For further thoughts on that subject, I'm going to download Leviticus and go through the menu to Job, chapter 2, verse 6, file 'J.' It reads..."

In this part . . .

The number one fear of most Americans is speaking in public. However, the number one fear of most audiences is wasting their time and being bored to death during a presentation.

Fortunately, Microsoft PowerPoint can tackle both ends of the problem by helping you create dazzling presentations so that you don't have to say a word and your audience doesn't have to do anything but stare mindlessly at your slide show. By learning how to add neat slide-transition effects, you can give your slide-show presentation that feeling of importance when you may really have nothing of substance to offer.

To help you create and give your slide show presentation, PowerPoint can create notes (so you know what you're supposed to be talking about at any give time) and handouts (so your audience doesn't have to take notes themselves, which frees them to daydream instead of paying attention to what you're saying).

With PowerPoint as your presentation tool, you'll never be at a loss for words again. Unless, of course, the power goes out during your presentation.

Chapter 12

Customizing PowerPoint

In This Chapter

- Changing PowerPoint's toolbars
- Changing the colors on a presentation
- Using the Slide Master

In case you haven't noticed the latest trend, almost every program lets you customize it to some extent. Although the idea of customizing a program may seem as foreign as the idea of customizing your own private jet, doing so is not as hard as you may think. Even better, after you customize PowerPoint, you may find using it even easier than before.

So should you bother customizing PowerPoint? Maybe. If you use PowerPoint regularly, only you know which commands are most important to you. By taking time to read this chapter, you can figure out how to mold PowerPoint so that it works the way you do, not the other way around.

If you customize PowerPoint, other people may not be familiar with the way you customized it. That can be a problem if two people share the same computer and same copy of PowerPoint, or it can be a blessing if it keeps people from using your computer without your knowledge.

Changing PowerPoint Toolbars

PowerPoint provides toolbars that contain buttons. By clicking a button, you can quickly choose a command without memorizing obscure keystroke commands or wading through confusing pull-down menus.

To provide some semblance of organization, PowerPoint organizes related buttons into each of its seven toolbars. You can display up to seven toolbars at once, although if you display all of them, they tend to clutter up the screen and get in the way, as shown in Figure 12-1.

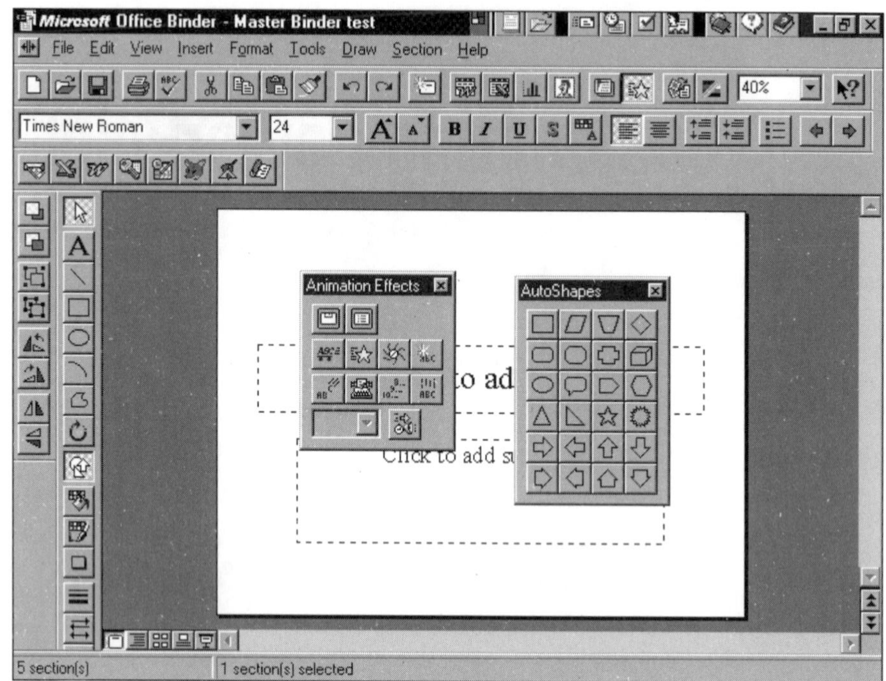

Figure 12-1: PowerPoint with every possible toolbar displayed.

So which toolbars should you display and which ones should you hide? Unlike a high school quiz, this question has no one simple answer that you can memorize (or copy from someone else). The two most commonly used toolbars are the Standard and Formatting toolbars. If you plan to draw graphics, however, you may want to hide these toolbars and display the Drawing or Drawing+ toolbars. So the only toolbars you need to display at any given time are the ones that contain the commands you need to use at that particular moment.

Most likely, you won't need all seven toolbars at the same time, so you can make one or more of Word's toolbars appear or disappear, depending on what you need at the time.

To make a toolbar appear or disappear, follow these steps:

1. **Choose View⇨Toolbars.**

   The Toolbars dialog box appears, as shown in Figure 12-2.

2. **For each toolbar you want displayed, click its check box so that a check mark appears. For each toolbar you want hidden, make sure that the toolbar's check box is empty.**

3. **Click OK.**

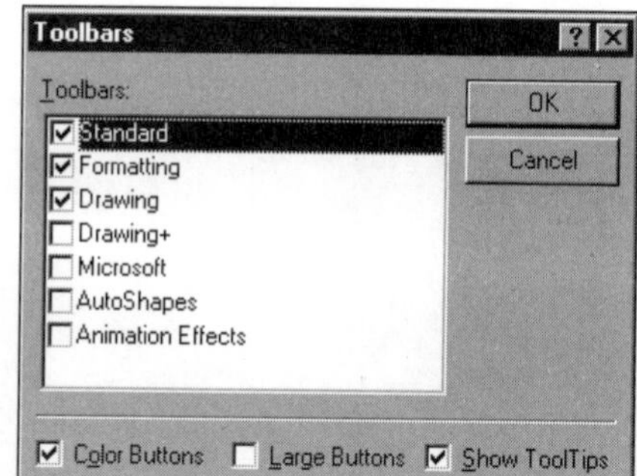

Figure 12-2: The Toolbars dialog box.

Modifying the existing toolbars

PowerPoint provides the most common commands in its toolbars so that you don't have to dig through pull-down menus. Not everyone uses the exact same commands, so PowerPoint may provide some buttons that you don't need. Just get rid of the buttons that represent commands that you never use and keep only the buttons for the commands you want to keep.

Because the PowerPoint toolbars are already crowded with buttons, you may want to modify your toolbars by removing the buttons you don't want.Feel free to experiment with your toolbars; you can always restore them back to their original, pristine condition later.

To remove a button from a toolbar, follow these steps:

1. **If you're using PowerPoint in a binder, choose Section⇨View Outside.**

   Skip this step if you're using PowerPoint outside a binder.

2. **Choose View⇨Toolbars.**

   The Toolbars dialog box appears (refer to Figure 12-2).

3. **Click Customize.**

   The Customize Toolbars dialog box appears, as shown in Figure 12-3.

4. **Point to the toolbar button you want to remove, hold down the left mouse button, and drag the button off the toolbar, as shown in Figure 12-4.**

5. **Release the left mouse button.**

   PowerPoint immediately removes your chosen button from the toolbar.

6. **Click Close.**

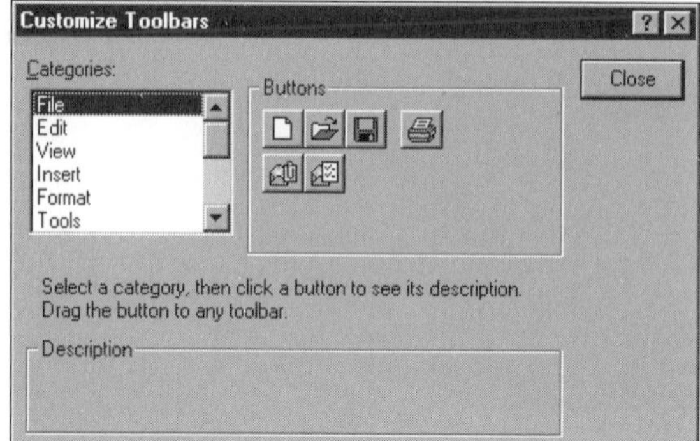

Figure 12-3: The Customize Toolbars dialog box.

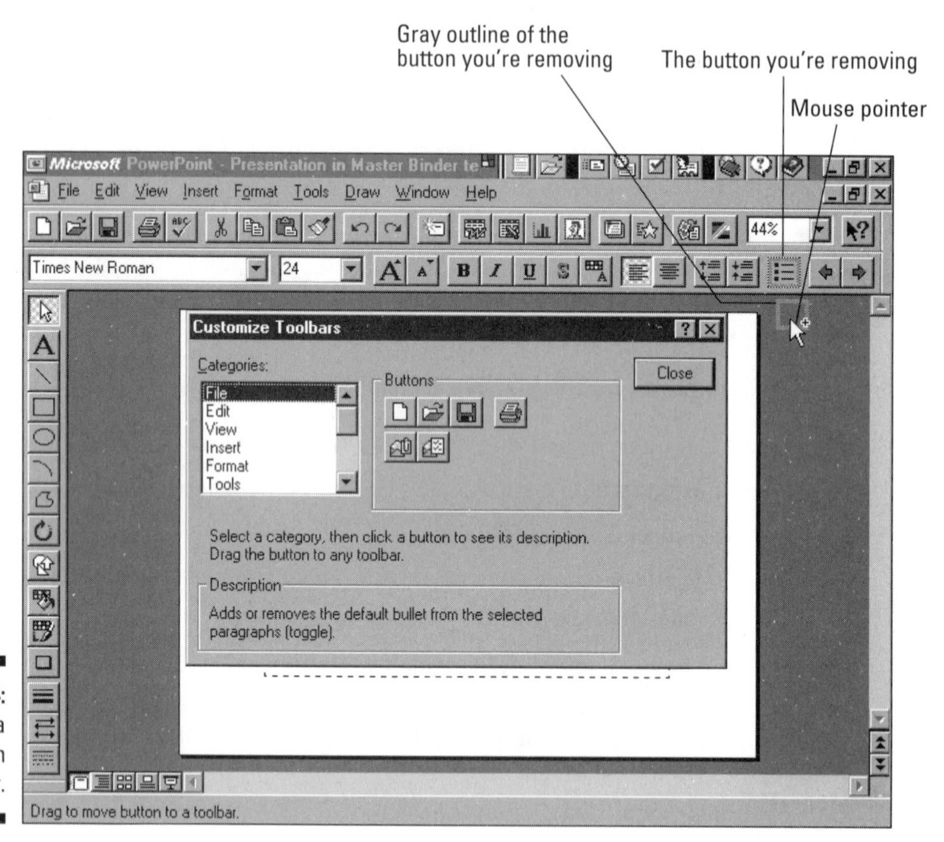

Figure 12-4: Removing a button from a toolbar.

You can add a button to any toolbar at any time, but because most toolbars are already crowded with buttons, you may want to make room for your new buttons by removing some buttons that you know you'll never use in a million years. After you remove one or more buttons from a toolbar, you will have more room to start adding your own buttons to the toolbar.

If you need to add three or more buttons to a toolbar, you might find it more convenient to create a new toolbar, as described in the upcoming section "Making your own toolbars."

To add a button to a toolbar, follow these steps:

1. **If you are using PowerPoint in a binder, choose Section⇨View Outside.**

   Skip this step if you're using PowerPoint outside a binder.

2. **Choose View⇨Toolbars.**

   The Toolbars dialog box appears (refer to Figure 12-2).

3. **Click Customize.**

   The Customize Toolbars dialog box appears, as shown in Figure 12-5.

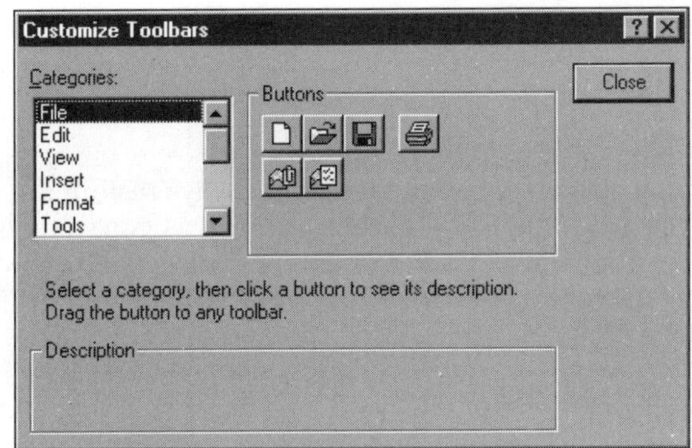

Figure 12-5: The Customize Toolbars dialog box.

4. **Click a category displayed in the Categories list box.**

   To add a formatting command to a toolbar, for example, click Format in the Categories list box. PowerPoint displays some buttons under the Buttons group.

5. **Point to the button you want to add, hold down the left mouse button, and drag the chosen button to the location on the toolbar where you want it to appear, as shown in Figure 12-6.**

6. **Release the mouse button and click Close.**

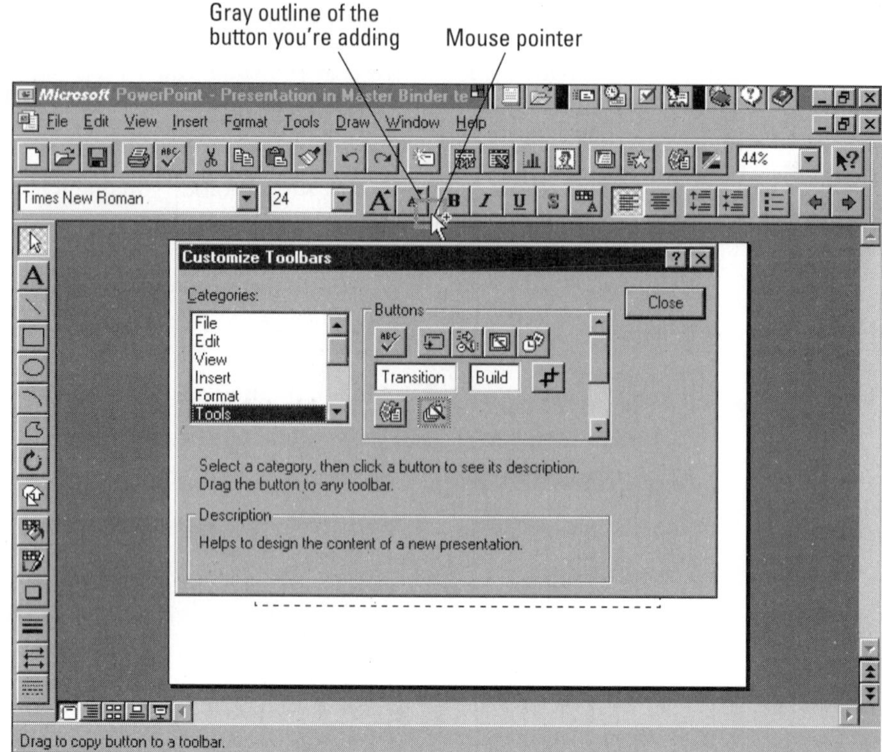

Figure 12-6: Adding a button to a toolbar.

PowerPoint provides a special command that can always restore the toolbars to their original state, so add and delete buttons as much as you want. If you totally rearrange your toolbars beyond recognition, you can tell PowerPoint, "Hey, I goofed. Fix all my toolbars so they look the way Microsoft originally designed them to look."

To reset a toolbar, follow these steps:

1. **If you are using PowerPoint in a binder, choose Section⇨View Outside.**

   Skip this step if you're using PowerPoint outside a binder.

2. **Choose View⇨Toolbars.**

   The Toolbars dialog box appears (refer to Figure 12-2).

3. **Highlight the toolbar you want to reset.**

4. **Click Reset.**

   PowerPoint resets your toolbar to its original state.

5. **Click OK in the Toolbars dialog box.**

Making your own toolbars

Instead of modifing your existing toolbars, you can have more fun by creating custom toolbars. You can combine your personal favorite commands in a toolbar designed just for you.

Creating your own toolbars has another advantage as well. If you create your own toolbars and don't modify other PowerPoint toolbars, someone else can use your copy of PowerPoint without getting confused.

To make your own toolbar, follow these steps:

1. **If you are using PowerPoint in a binder, choose Section⇨View Outside.**

   Skip this step if you're using PowerPoint outside a binder.

2. **Choose View⇨Toolbars.**

   The Toolbars dialog box appears (refer to Figure 12-2).

3. **Click New.**

   The New Toolbar dialog box appears, as shown in Figure 12-7.

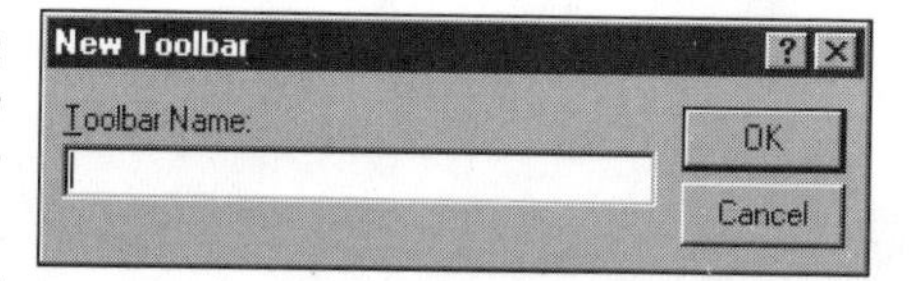

Figure 12-7: The New Toolbar dialog box.

4. **Type a name for your toolbar in the Toolbar Name box and click OK.**

   The Customize dialog box appears next to your toolbar, which now appears as a floating toolbar, as shown in Figure 12-8.

5. **Click a category displayed in the Categories list box.**

   To add an editing command to a toolbar, for example, click Edit in the Categories list box. PowerPoint displays some buttons under the Buttons group.

6. **Point to the button you want to add, hold down the left mouse button, drag the button to the location on the toolbar where you want it to appear, and release the mouse button, as shown in Figure 12-9.**

7. **Click Close when you're done filling your toolbar with buttons.**

   Your newly created toolbar appears on-screen, ready to use.

To move your floating toolbar, point to the title bar of the toolbar, hold down the left mouse button, drag the toolbar with the mouse to wherever you want it to appear, and release the mouse button.

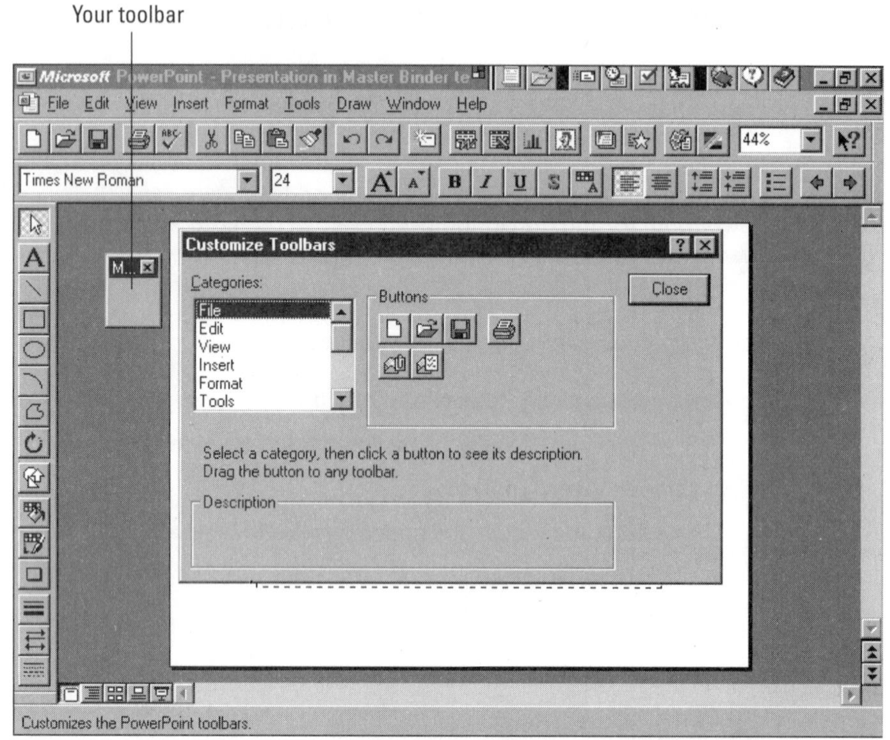

Figure 12-8: Your newly created toolbar.

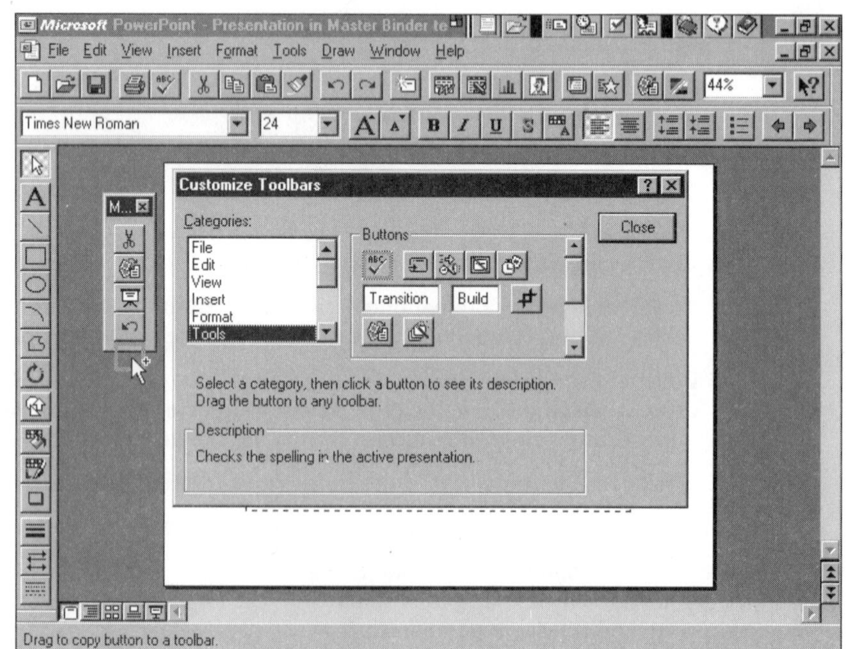

Figure 12-9: Your newly created toolbar with some buttons on it.

If you don't like the shape of your toolbar, you can change it to resemble a skinny floating toolbar, a rectangle, or a toolbar stretched vertically or horizontally. Changing the shape of a toolbar just makes it look nice; the shape of a toolbar does not affect the function of the toolbar.

To change the shape of your toolbar, follow these steps:

1. **Move the mouse pointer to the left, right, top, or bottom edge of the toolbar so that the mouse pointer turns into a double-pointing arrow, pointing left and right or up and down.**
2. **Hold down the left mouse button and drag the mouse until the gray outline of the toolbar turns in the shape that you want, as shown in Figure 12-10.**

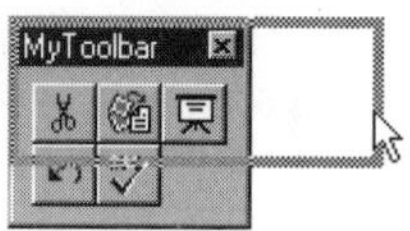

Figure 12-10: Changing the shape of the toolbar.

3. **Release the mouse button.**

If you double-click the title bar of your floating toolbar, PowerPoint squashes your toolbar horizontally across the top of your screen. If you double-click anywhere in the gray space on the toolbar again, PowerPoint displays your toolbar as a floating toolbar once more.

You can delete any toolbar that you create, but you can never delete any built-in PowerPoint toolbars. When you delete a toolbar of your own creation, you (naturally) also delete all the buttons stored on that toolbar. So any time you decide that you've created a toolbar that's totally worthless and deserves to be wiped out from the face of the earth, just delete it so that the toolbar doesn't continually haunt you with its existence.

To delete one of your toolbars, follow these steps:

1. **If you're using PowerPoint in a binder, choose Section⇨View Outside.**

   Skip this step if you're using PowerPoint outside a binder.

2. **Choose View⇨Toolbars.**

   The Toolbars dialog box appears (refer to Figure 12-2).

3. **Highlight the toolbar you want to delete.**
4. **Click Delete.**
5. **Click OK in the Toolbars dialog box.**

If you suddenly change your mind and want to undelete your newly deleted toolbar, click Undelete right away before clicking OK in step 5. The moment you delete a toolbar and click OK in step 5, you're telling PowerPoint, "I really want to wipe that toolbar so completely out of existence that it will be impossible for me to recover it again, even if I scream and cry really loud."

Just in case you're wondering, pressing Ctrl+Z will not undo any toolbars you've deleted. So make sure that you really want to delete a toolbar before you actually tell PowerPoint to get rid of it, or you may be sorry.

Playing with Pretty Colors

The whole purpose of PowerPoint is to create visually stunning presentations. No one will question the validity of your data if they're too busy admiring your creation. This same principle that looks are more important than substance is the reason why so many Hollywood actors and actresses can get paid millions of dollars a year without having one coherent thought in their lives.

When people first see your PowerPoint presentation, the first part they'll notice is the colors you chose. If the colors are pleasing, they may even read any text displayed. But if your colors are hard to read or just plain awful, this slight distraction can keep even your most ardent supporter from reading, let alone understanding, any text or charts you may be trying to present.

Changing the background colors

Each slide can have its own background color, or all the slides can share a single background color. Varying the background color once in a while is a good idea; because it gives you that all-important feeling of independence and creativity in a job that's probably stifling your future anyway, and it may prevent your audience from falling asleep during your presentation.

To change the background color of your slides, follow these steps:

1. **Choose Format⇨Custom Background.**

   The Custom Background dialog box appears, as shown in Figure 12-11.

2. **Click in the list box that appears in the Background Fill group.**

   A pop-up menu appears, as shown in Figure 12-12.

3. **Click a color that you want to use for your background.**

   The Background Fill box displays a sample slide with your chosen color.

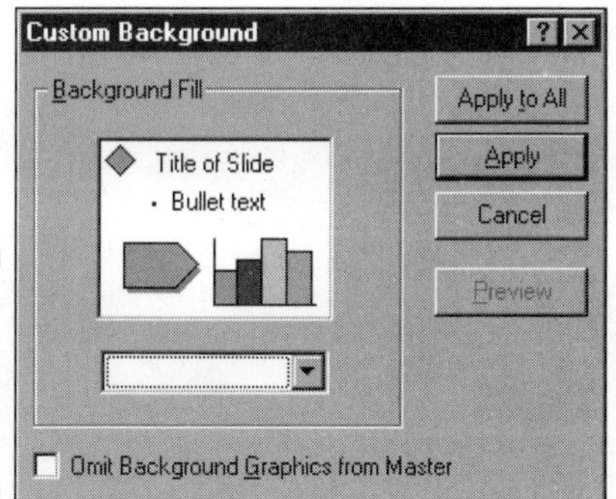

Figure 12-11: The Custom Background dialog box.

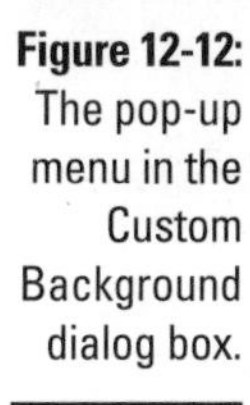

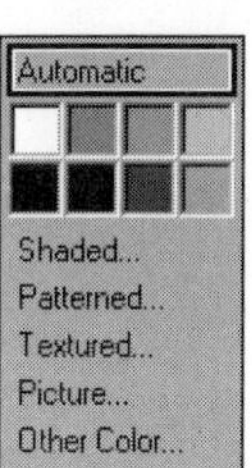

Figure 12-12: The pop-up menu in the Custom Background dialog box.

4. **Click Apply (if you want to change the background color of the current slide) or click Apply to All (if you want to change the background color of all your slides).**

Altering your background patterns

Not only can you change the background color of your slides, but you can get even more flamboyant and alter the background patterns as well. PowerPoint gives you four ways to change the background pattern:

- **Shaded:** Displays the background in gradual variations of one or two colors, as shown in Figure 12-13.
- **Patterned:** Displays a background pattern, such as vertical stripes, diagonal lines, or the appearance of a brick background, as shown in Figure 12-14.
- **Textured:** Displays wood-grained, tile, or marble background, as shown in Figure 12-15.
- **Picture:** Lets you insert a picture for the background or your slides.

REMEMBER

You can choose only one of the preceding four options. For example, if you choose Shaded, then you can't choose Textured, and vice versa.

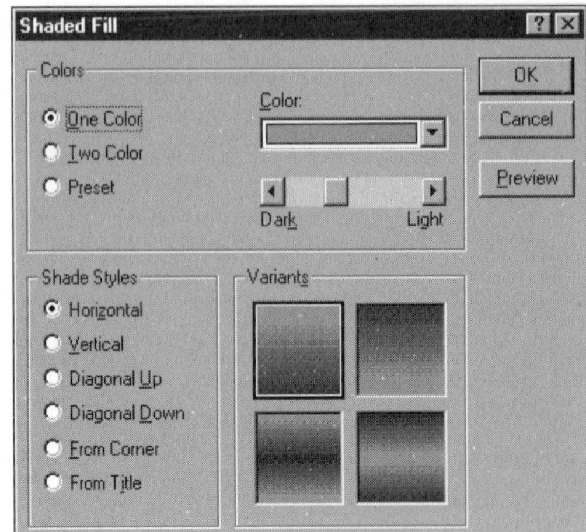

Figure 12-13: The Shaded Fill dialog box where you can choose a different shading.

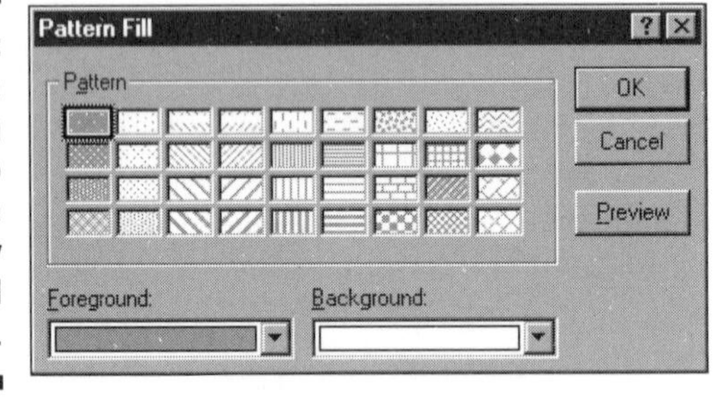

Figure 12-14: The Pattern Fill dialog box to choose a fancy background pattern.

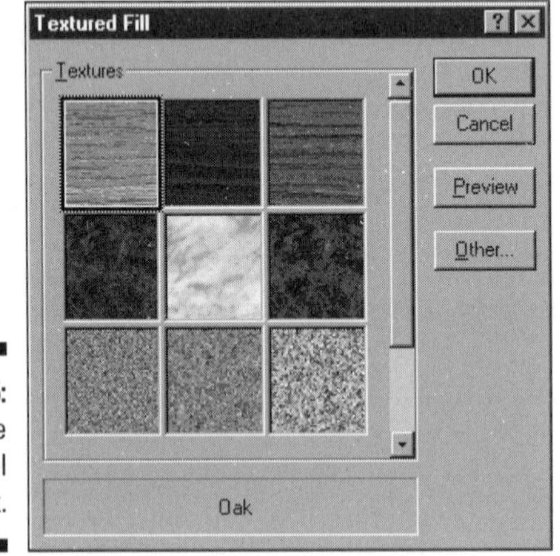

Figure 12-15: The Textured Fill dialog box.

To change the background pattern for your slides, follow these steps:

1. **Choose Format⇨Custom Background.**

   The Custom Background dialog box appears (refer to Figure 12-11).

2. **Click in the list box that appears in the Background Fill group.**

   A pop-up menu appears (refer to Figure 12-12).

3. **Click in the list box that appears in the Background Fill group and choose Shaded, Patterned, Textured, or Picture.**

4. **Click Apply (if you want to change the background pattern of the current slide) or click Apply to All (if you want to change the background pattern of all your slides).**

Picking your own background colors

The folks at Microsoft want you to be happy, so they make sure that their programs come loaded with so many options to give you the feeling of absolute freedom. As part of this goal, Microsoft designed PowerPoint so that you could pick your own background colors. That way, you can display your slides in a psychedelic color or something equally unappealing, if you want.

To choose your own background color, follow these steps:

1. **Choose Format⇨Custom Background.**

   The Custom Background dialog box appears (refer to Figure 12-11).

2. **Click in the list box that appears in the Background Fill group.**

   A pop-up menu appears (refer to Figure 12-12).

4. **Click in the list box that appears in the Background Fill group and choose Other Color.**

   The Colors dialog box appears, as shown in Figure 12-16.

5. **Click a color that you want to use and click OK.**

   In case you want to create your own colors, click the Custom tab and go wild defining your own background color.

6. **Click Apply (if you want to change the background pattern of the current slide) or click Apply to All (if you want to change the background pattern of all your slides).**

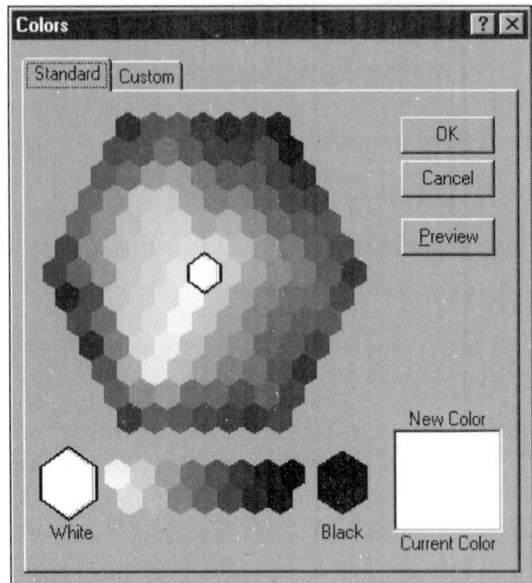

Figure 12-16: The Colors dialog box.

Certain colors, textures, or patterns may interfere or completely nullify other colors, textures, or patterns you may choose. For example, trying to display black text against a black bacground will be as futile as trying to introduce an honest government into a Third World country.

Changing the color scheme

Besides changing the background color of your slides, PowerPoint also lets you change the color of your slide text, titles, lines, and other features. Just to give the colors of these parts of your slides a name, Microsoft calls these color options the *color scheme*.

Whenever you want to sound important, use long-winded, mysterious sounding terms like "color scheme." That way nobody will question your authority on any subject, even for those subjects you know nothing about.

PowerPoint comes with several color schemes built-in, but you can always define your own color schemes if you want. To change the color scheme of your slide, follow these steps:

1. **Choose Format⇨Slide Color Scheme.**

   A Color Scheme dialog box appears, as shown in Figure 12-17.

2. **Click a color scheme from the Color Schemes group.**
3. **Click Apply to use your chosen color scheme for the current slide. (Or click Apply to All to use your chosen color scheme for all your slides.)**

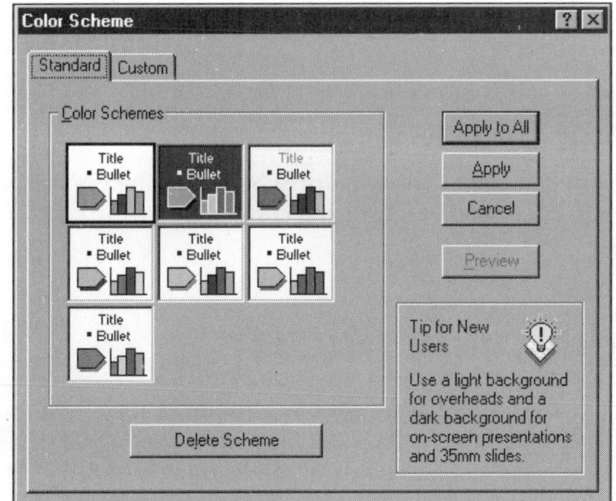

Figure 12-17: The Color Scheme dialog box

For you more creative and adventurous souls, you can create and use your own color schemes. To make your own color scheme, follow these steps:

1. **Choose Format⇨Slide Color Scheme.**

   The Color Scheme dialog box appears (refer to Figure 12-17).

2. **Click the Custom tab as shown in Figure 12-18.**

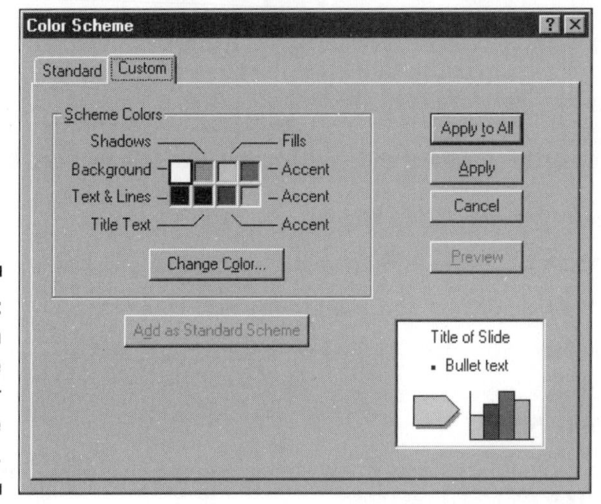

Figure 12-18: The Custom tab in the Color Scheme dialog box.

3. **Double-click an item, such as Background or Text & Lines, whose color you want to change.**

   The Colors dialog box appears (refer to Figure 12-16).

4. **Click a color and click OK.**
5. **Click Apply to use your chosen color scheme for the current slide. (Or click Apply to All to use your chosen color scheme for all your slides.)**

Take Me to Your Slide Master

The Slide Master is a fancy term that sounds more exciting than it really is. Essentially, the Slide Master acts like a cookie cutter, letting you design the format and layout of your slides. That way when you create a new slide, you can just type your text without worrying about the formatting.

You can define three common items on a Slide Master:

- Formatting for your titles and text
- Pictures to appear on all your slides
- Text to appear on all your slides

Defining the formatting of titles and text

Text usually appears on a slide in two forms: as a title or as text. The title usually appears at the top of the slide to grab your attention, while the text underneath provides greater detail, explanation, or excuses.

To define the formatting for your slide's titles and text, follow these steps:

1. **Choose View⇨Master⇨Slide Master.**

   The Slide Master appears, as shown in Figure 12-19.

2. **Highlight the title or text you want to format.**
3. **Change the font, font size, alignment, underlining, and so on for your chosen text.**
4. **Choose View⇨Slides.**

   All your current slides and any new slides you add will follow the format you defined on your Slide Master.

If you want specific text to appear on all your slides, you have to add a separate text box and type the text in it. See the section "Making text appear on all your slides" later in this chapter.

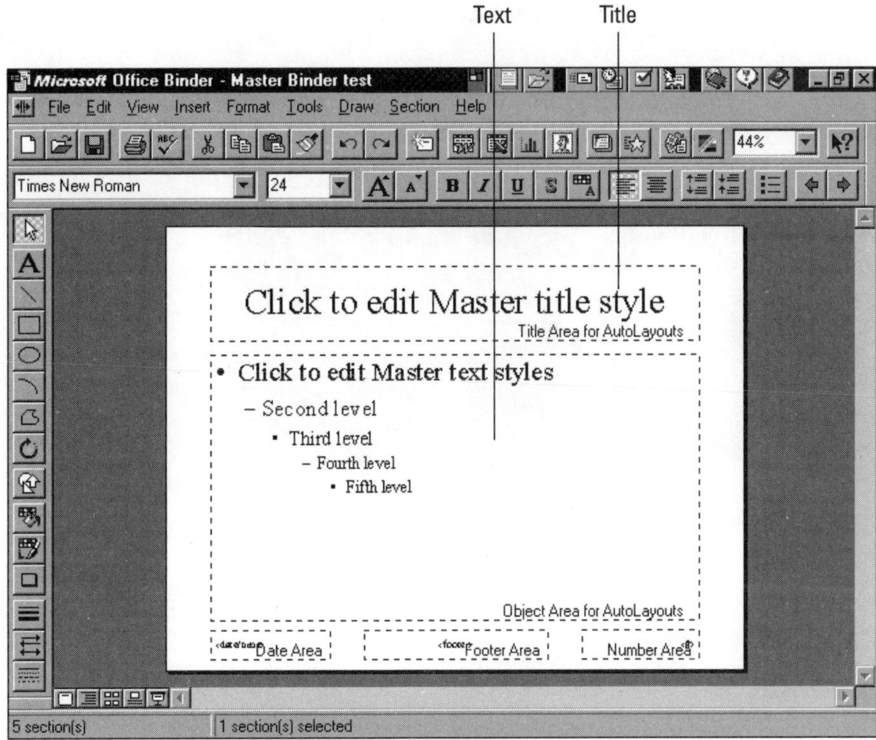

Figure 12-19: A typical Slide Master.

Putting in pictures to appear on all your slides

A picture is worth a thousand words, which usually means people prefer looking at pictures rather than using their minds to read and think for themselves. For example, you may want to include your company logo on each slide so that your audience doesn't forget about your company.

To place a picture that you want to appear on all your slides, follow these steps:

1. **Choose View⇨Master⇨Slide Master.**

   The Slide Master appears (refer to Figure 12-19).

2. **Choose Insert⇨Clip Art.**

   The Microsoft ClipArt Gallery 2.0 dialog box appears, as shown in Figure 12-20.

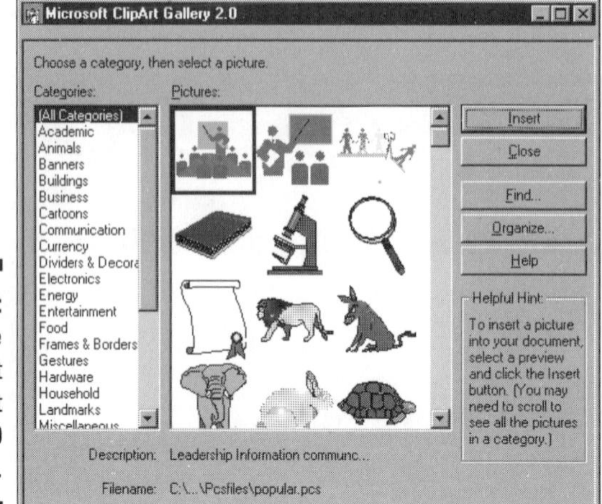

Figure 12-20: The Microsoft ClipArt Gallery 2.0 dialog box.

3. **Click the picture you want to include on your Master Slide and click Insert.**

   The picture you chose appears on your Master Slide, as shown in Figure 12-21.

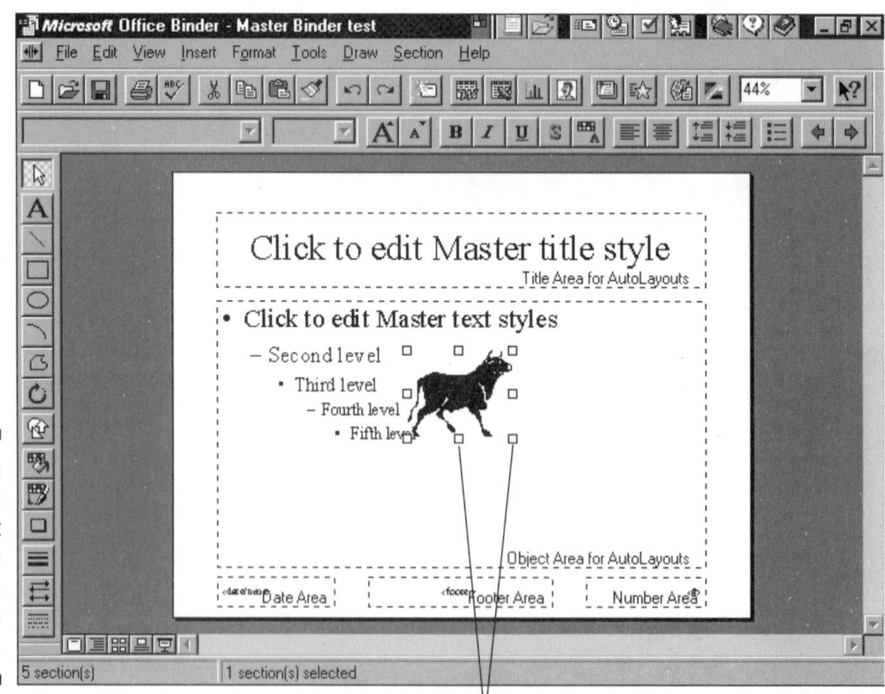

Figure 12-21: A typical clip art image displayed on the Slide Master.

4. **Point to the image, hold the left mouse button down, and move the mouse to place your clip art image where you want it. Then let go of the mouse button.**

   To stretch or shrink the image, click the handle, hold down the left mouse button, and drag the image to change its size.

5. **Choose View⇨Slides.**

   All your current slides and any new slides you add will display your chosen clip art you defined on your Slide Master, as shown in Figure 12-22.

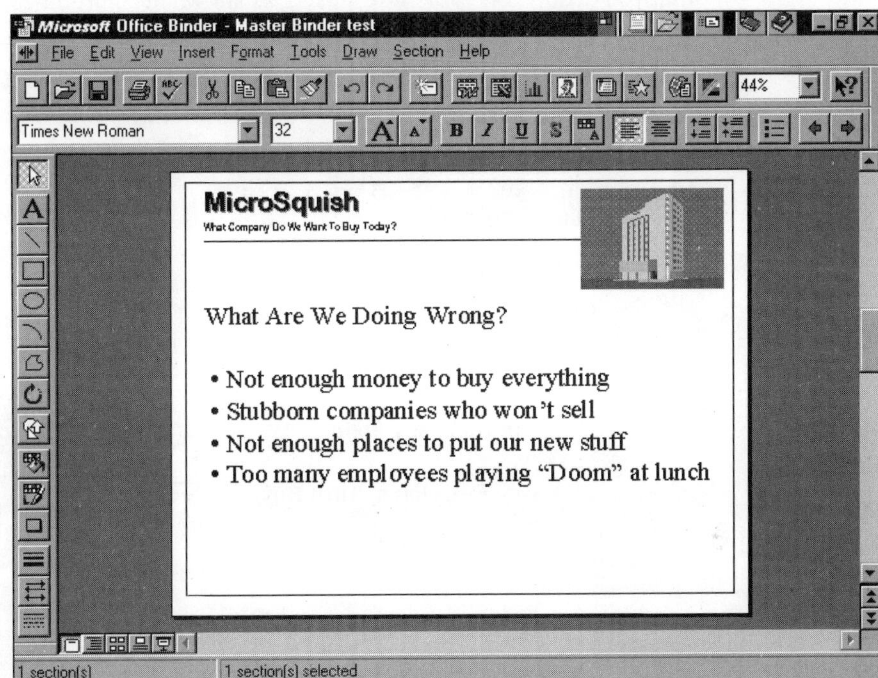

Figure 12-22: How text from the Slide Master appears on your slides.

Making text appear on all your slides

In addition to having the same pictures appear on all of your slides, you may also want text to appear on all your slides. For example, you may want to display a caption at the top or bottom of each slide that reads, "Classified Information (Just joking!)."

To make repetitive text appear on all of your slides, follow these steps:

1. **Choose View⇨Master⇨Slide Master.**

   The Slide Master appears (refer to Figure 12-19).

2. **Click the Text Tool button, which is located on the Drawing toolbar.**
3. **Move the mouse pointer to where you want a text box to appear on your Master Slide, hold down the left mouse button, move the mouse, and then release the mouse button to draw your text box.**

   PowerPoint displays your text box as a square or rectangle.
4. **Type the text you want to appear on all of your slides.**
5. **Choose View⇨Slides.**

   All your current slides and any new slides you add will display your text that you defined on your Slide Master, as shown in Figure 12-23.

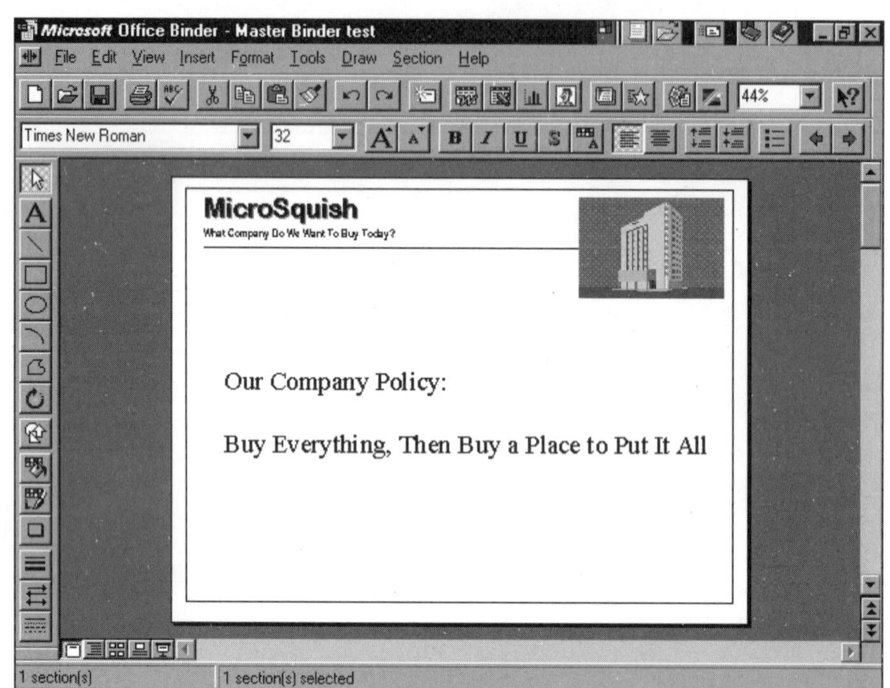

Figure 12-23: How a clip art image appears on your slides.

Chapter 13

Making Notes and Handouts

In This Chapter

- Jotting down notes for yourself
- Making notes for yourself or recording comments from audience members
- Giving handouts to your audience

In addition to helping you make slides, PowerPoint lets you create notes and handouts. *Notes* are for your benefit so that you can jot down ideas, statistics, or alibis that you can see while you're making a presentation. *Handouts* let you pass out printed copies of your presentation so that members of your audience can jot down their ideas or questions.

Neither notes nor handouts are necessary. By creating notes to yourself, you can avoid looking foolish during that all-important business meeting most people don't pay attention to anyway. By creating handouts, you can give your audience members something to remember (or throw away) after they leave your presentation.

Making a Generic Notes Page

Before writing any notes or handouts, take some time to design their layout. Then you can ensure that your notes and handouts look consistent (even if the text that's written on them doesn't make any sense).

PowerPoint provides a Note Master that lets you design a uniform layout and appearance for your notes. A note typically contains one slide along with any explanatory text underneath it. By printing your notes and keeping them nearby while you're giving a presentation, you can use them to make sure that you don't forget any relevant points.

Because your notes will likely be seen only by you, you can be as wildly creative and outrageous or as sparse and minimal as you want, without worrying about annoying other people.

To design the Note Master, follow these steps:

1. **Choose View⇨Master⇨Notes Master.**

   PowerPoint displays your notes page, as shown in Figure 13-1.

2. **Choose View⇨Zoom.**

   The Zoom dialog box appears.

3. **Click an option button to choose a resolution (such as 100%) and then click OK.**

4. **Draw any borders, lines, or shapes you want to insert on all your notes pages.**

5. **Highlight and format any text styles, such as the Master text style or the Second level style, as shown in Figure 13-2.**

6. **Choose View⇨Notes Pages.**

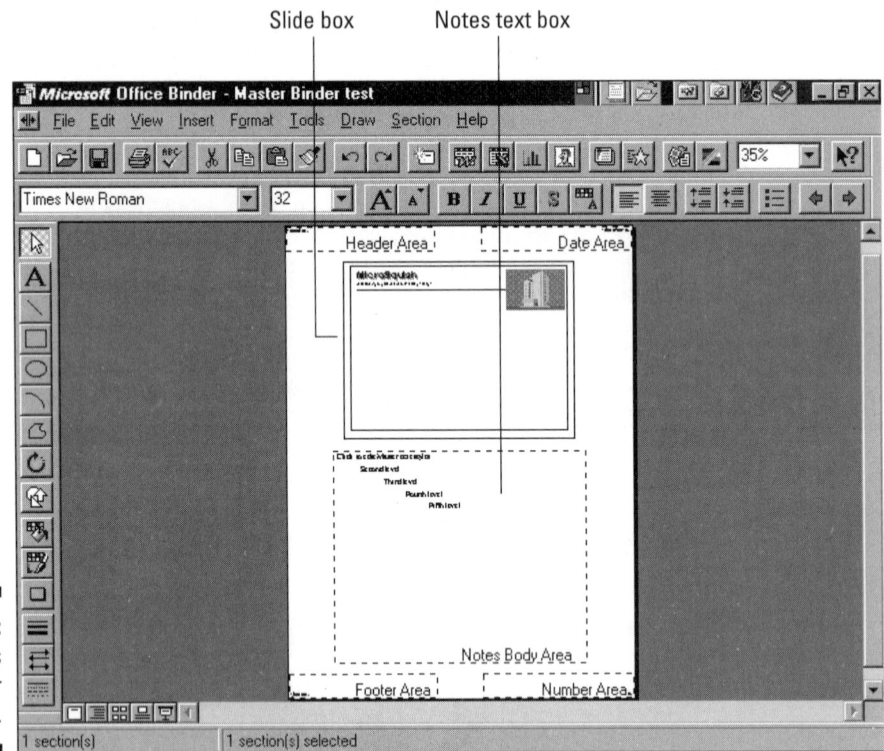

Figure 13-1: The notes Master page.

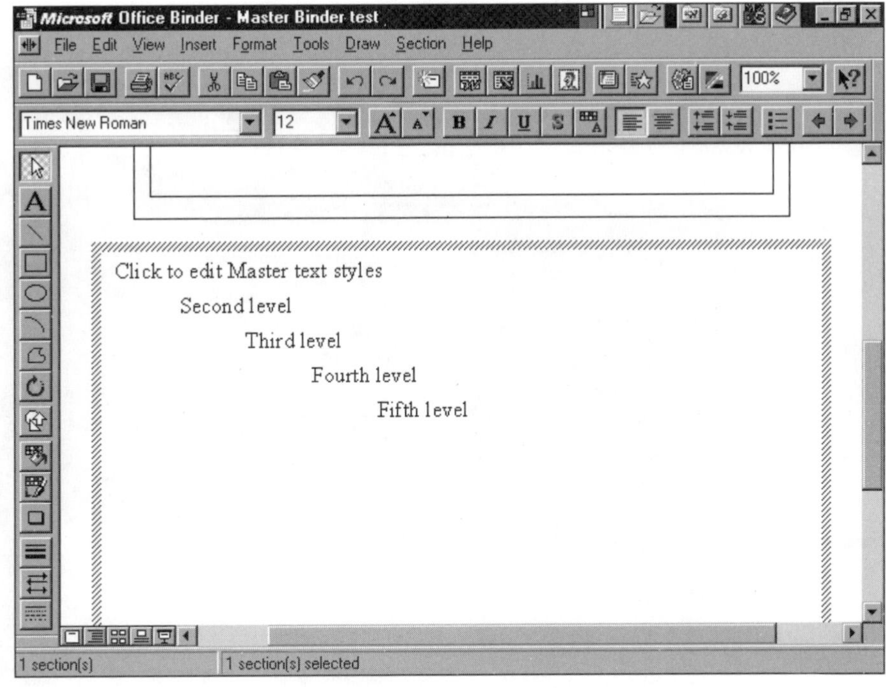

Figure 13-2: The Notes page displays different text styles.

Jotting Down Notes for Posterity

Because you're the only one who will see your notes, you can write anything on them you want (points you want to make during your presentation, stories or statistics to support a particular slide, or tasteless jokes to keep yourself amused while you're giving a presentation to a captive audience).

You can create a separate notes page for each slide in your presentation either before you present your PowerPoint slides to an audience (so that you can jot down notes ahead of time) or during your presentation (so that you can write comments from audience members who are paying attention).

Creating notes for yourself

To create a note before giving a presentation, follow these steps:

1. **Choose View⇨Notes Pages.**

   PowerPoint displays your slide and note, as shown in Figure 13-3.

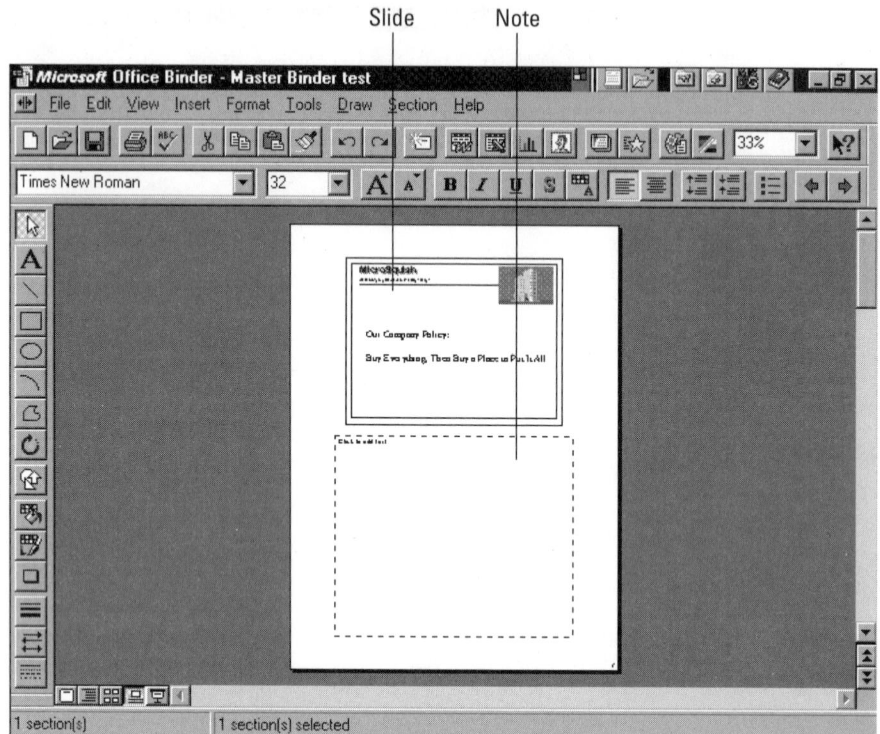

Figure 13-3: A typical notes page connected to a slide.

2. **Choose View⇨Zoom.**

   The Zoom dialog box appears.

3. **Click a radio button (such as 100%) to change the resolution of your notes page so that you can really see something, and then click OK.**

   PowerPoint displays your notes page so that you see what you're writing, as shown in Figure 13-4.

4. **Click the notes page text box and type any ideas, stories, statistics, or funny jokes you want.**

5. **Highlight any text and click the Promote or Demote buttons if you want to indent blocks of text.**

Writing notes during a presentation

The notes page is also a great place to jot down any comments, questions, or ideas you may get from the audience. For example, you may show a slide which proves that your company really isn't going bankrupt, and then someone will

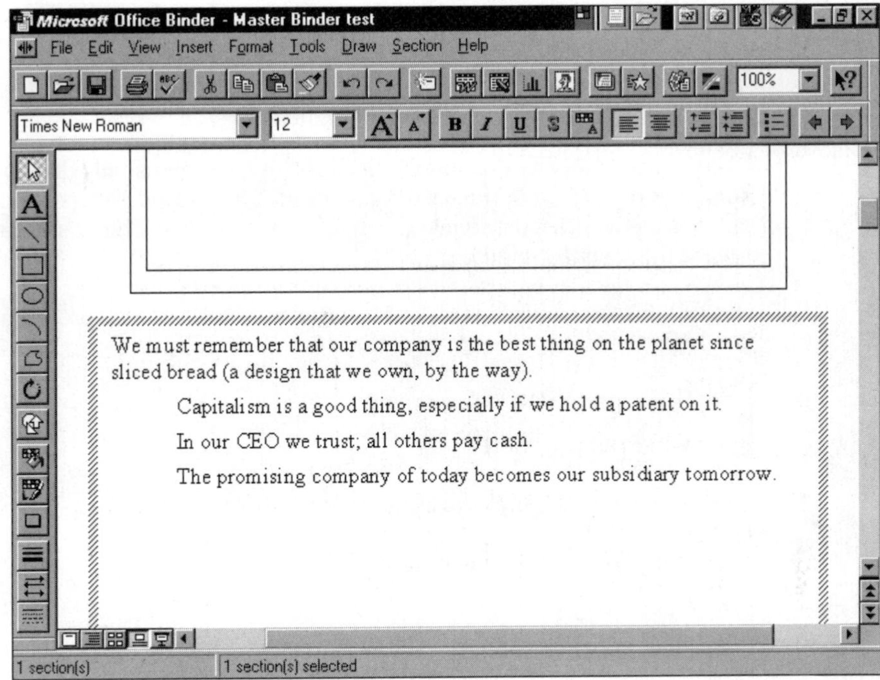

Figure 13-4: A typical notes page blown up to 100 percent resolution.

ask for facts. Rather than jot down this request on a separate piece of paper, you can jot it on your notes page instead. That way you won't risk losing any audience comments (unless, of course, you lose your computer).

When you're writing comments during a presentation, you can store them in one of three places:

- On the notes page
- On a temporary page called the Meeting Minutes page
- As a separate slide titled Action Items

Typing text on the notes page

To type text on the notes page during a presentation, follow these steps:

1. **Click the right mouse button.**

   A pop-up menu appears.

2. **Click Meeting Minder.**

   The Meeting Minder dialog box appears.

3. **Click the Notes Pages tab.**

4. **Type on your notes page any text you want to store for future reference.**
5. **Click OK.**

Typing meeting minutes

Every boring meeting that won't affect society one bit usually demands that someone keep track of the meeting minutes. That way, if anyone really cares about what was discussed in a meeting three weeks ago, he or she can just review the meeting minutes.

PowerPoint lets you keep track of meeting minutes during a presentation. After you type them, you have to store them in one of two places:

- As a separate Word document
- As part of your notes page

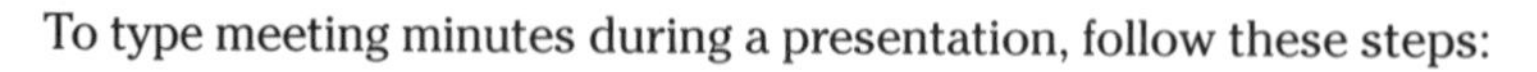

To type meeting minutes during a presentation, follow these steps:

1. **Click the right mouse button.**

   A pop-up menu appears.
2. **Click Meeting Minder.**

   The Meeting Minder dialog box appears.
3. **Click the Meeting Minutes tab.**
4. **Type any text you want to save as part of your meeting minutes.**
5. **Click Export when you're done.**

   Another Meeting Minder dialog box appears.
6. **Click one of the following check boxes so that a check mark appears:**
   - Send Meeting Minutes and Action Items to Microsoft Word
   - Add Meeting Minutes to Notes Pages
7. **Click Export Now.**

Creating an Action Items slide

While you're giving a presentation, some bozo (your boss, for example) will probably want to know what type of action he or she can assign someone else to do. For these types of unwelcome comments, PowerPoint provides a special Action Items text box.

To type text in the Action Items box during a presentation, follow the steps in the preceding section, "Typing meeting minutes." When you get to steps 3 and 4, however, click the Action Items tab instead, type any text you want to save as part of your Action Items, and continue following the rest of the steps.

Whenever you type any text in the Action Items text box, PowerPoint automatically creates a special Action Items slide that appears at the end of your presentation, as shown in Figure 13-5.

Printing your notes pages

After you write and save text on your notes pages, you may well want to print them so that you don't have to use your computer every time you want to read them.

To print your notes pages, follow these steps:

1. **If you're using Power Point within a binder, Choose Section⇨View Outside.**

   Skip this step if you're using PowerPoint outside a binder.

2. **Choose File⇨Print.**

   The Print dialog box appears.

3. **Click the Print what list box and then choose Notes Pages.**

4. **Click OK.**

MicroSquish
What Company Do We Want To Buy Today?
Action Items
• Remember to ask the CEO for a raise after this presentation.
• Don't forget to take your computer home.

Figure 13-5: PowerPoint automatically creates the Action Items slide.

Providing Distracting Handouts to Your Audience

Unlike notes, handouts are meant for others to see. If you want to be taken seriously (professionally), you had better make your handouts neat, organized, and presentable.

Handouts can contain these items:

- Slides from your presentation
- Additional text that you think others may find useful
- Additional pictures that may supplement or clarify your slides

To create a handout, follow these steps:

1. **Choose Tools⇨Write-Up.**

   The Write-Up dialog box appears.

2. **Click one of the following option buttons:**

   - **Notes Next to Slides**
   - **Blank Lines Next to Slides**
   - **Notes Below Slides**
   - **Blank Lines Below Slides**

   Note: If you want to provide space for people to write their own comments, choose one of the Blank Lines options. If you want to include your own notes on a handout, choose one of the Notes options.

3. **Click one of the following option buttons:**

   - **Paste**
   - **Paste Link**

   Note: If you want your handouts to change automatically whenever you change a slide, click the Paste Link option button.

4. **Click OK.**

   Your handout appears in a separate Word window, as shown in Figure 13-6.

5. **Choose File⇨Save.**

   The Save As dialog box appears.

6. **In the File name box, type a name for your handout file.**

7. **Click Save.**

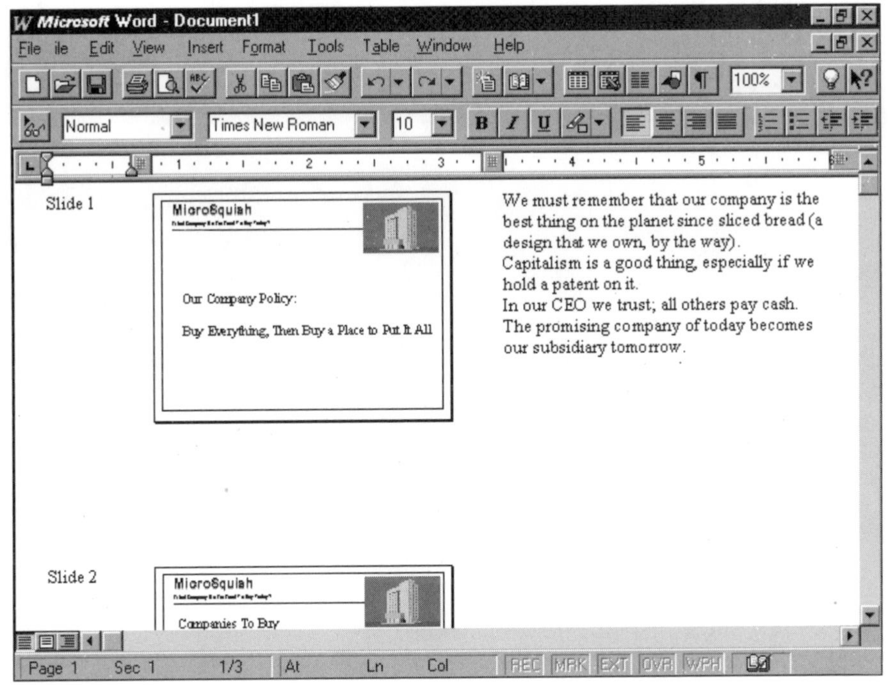

Figure 13-6: Word displays a typical handout.

8. **Choose File⇨Exit to exit from Word.**

   If you're using PowerPoint as a separate program, stop here. If you're using PowerPoint as part of an Office binder, continue to step 9.

9. **Choose Section⇨Add from File.**

   The Add from File dialog box appears.

10. **Click the filename you chose in step 6 and then click Add.**

    Your handouts are now part of your Microsoft Office binder.

The only reason to store your handouts as part of your Office binder is so that you can keep track of everything in a single binder file.

After PowerPoint stores your handout as a separate Word file, you can print them at any time by using Word.

Chapter 14

Showing Off Your PowerPoint Presentations

In This Chapter

- Using text or visual effects for your slide show
- Changing the order of your slides
- Avoiding having to rearrange your slides by hiding and inserting them
- Copying your presentation for portable presentations
- Using the Internet Assistant to post your presentation on the World Wide Web

PowerPoint makes it easy to create your own slide show presentations. After you create your slide show, of course, you eventually have to show it to someone.

Because first impressions are often more important than substance, PowerPoint provides all sorts of ways to spice up your slide show, including Hollywood-style transitions from one slide to another, sound effects to accompany each slide, and scrolling text to make your slides more entertaining to watch.

Just remember that the fancier you make your slide show, the more memorable it will be. Naturally, you can go too far with special effects and make your slide show memorable because it was obnoxious, so choose your slide show presentation features carefully.

Making Neat Transitions

If you've ever seen a slide show at school or in someone's living room, you know how boring they can be. One slide appears, everyone yawns, and then a new slide appears, and everyone secretly looks at his or her watch.

To break up the tedium of one slide after another appearing in an endless parade of monotony, PowerPoint lets you create special transitions between your slides. Now your slide can dissolve on-screen, wipe itself away from left to right, slide up from the bottom of the screen to cover the preceding slide, or split in half to reveal a new slide underneath.

PowerPoint lets you create two types of transitions for your slides:

- Visual transitions
- Text transitions

A *visual transition* determines how your slide looks when it is first displayed. A *text transition* determines how the text on your slide looks.

Creating your slide's visual transition

To create a visual transition for each of your slides, follow these steps:

1. **Choose Tools⇨Slide Transition.**

   The Slide Transition dialog box appears, as shown in Figure 14-1.

Figure 14-1: The Slide Transition dialog box for creating Hollywood-style special effects.

2. **Click the Effect list box and choose an effect (Cut, Dissolve, or Wipe Right, for example).**

   PowerPoint shows you the effect in the picture box.

3. **Click either the Slow, Medium, or Fast option button in the Speed group.**

   PowerPoint uses the picture box to show you how quickly your slide will change.

4. **In the Advance group, click the Only on mouse click option button or the Automatically after option button.**

   If you click the Only on mouse click option button, you can display a new slide by clicking the mouse. If you use the Automatically after option button, PowerPoint displays a new slide after a few seconds, whether you like it or not.

5. **Click the Sound list box and choose a sound you want to play whenever your slide appears.**

6. **If you want the sound to play continuously until another slide appears with a different sound assigned to it, click the Loop until next sound check box.**

7. **Click OK.**

Creating your slide's text transition

The whole idea behind creating text transitions is so that after your slide first appears in view, each click of the mouse causes your text to slide into view. This type of dramatics can keep your audience interested in watching your slides if only to see what unusual effects you may have created for their amusement.

To create a transition for the text on your slides, follow these steps:

1. **Choose Tools⇨Build Slide Text.**

   A pop-up menu appears.

2. **Choose a text transition, such as Fly from Left or Wipe Right.**

Sorting Your Slides

You can spend hours creating the perfect PowerPoint slide show and then suddenly discover that one slide would look better if it appeared earlier or later in your presentation. Rather than tear your hair out in fear that you can't rearrange your slides, relax; you can simply move the slide to another position.

To sort your slides, follow these steps:

1. **Choose View⇨Slide Sorter.**

   PowerPoint displays all your slides in the order in which they will appear, as shown in Figure 14-2.

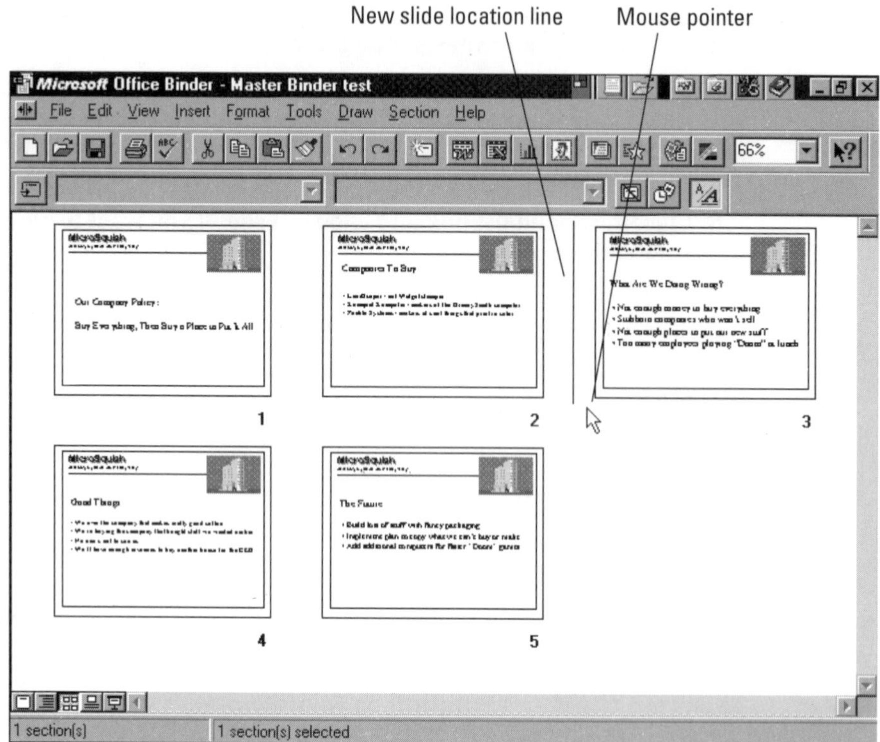

Figure 14-2: In Slide Sorter view, all your slides line up in order, ready to march.

2. **Click the slide you want to move so that the outer edges appear as a black border.**
3. **Hold down the left mouse button.**

   A little gray box appears on the stem of the mouse pointer (see Figure 14-2).
4. **Drag the mouse to the new location at which you want the slide to appear.**

   PowerPoint displays a vertical gray line to show you where the new slide will appear.
5. **Release the mouse button.**

   PowerPoint moves your slide to its new location.

Hiding and Inserting Slides

Feel free to create your slides in any order you want, because you can always rearrange them afterward. PowerPoint lets you, at any time, insert a new slide (in case you forgot to include vital information) or hide an existing slide (in case you want to hide vital information).

Hiding an existing slide

Sometimes you may create a slide but, for some reason, not want to show it during your next presentation. Rather than delete it, you can just hide it temporarily from your slide show. That way, the slide still exists but no one (except you) can see it.

To hide an existing slide, follow these steps:

1. **Choose View⇨Slide Sorter.**

   PowerPoint displays all your slides in the order in which they will be displayed (refer to Figure 14-2).

2. **Click the slide you want to hide so that the outer edges appear as a black border.**

3. **Choose Tools⇨Hide Slide. (Or click the Hide Slide button, which is located on the Slide Sorter toolbar.)**

   PowerPoint displays a slash through your chosen slide number, as shown in Figure 14-3.

To unhide a slide, just repeat the preceding steps.

Inserting a new slide

You can insert a new slide into an existing slide show at any time. Then if you get a sudden inspiration to add something new to your presentation, you can pop in a new slide quickly and easily.

To insert a new slide, follow these steps:

1. **Choose View⇨Slide Sorter.**

   PowerPoint displays all your slides in the order in which they will appear (refer to Figure 14-2).

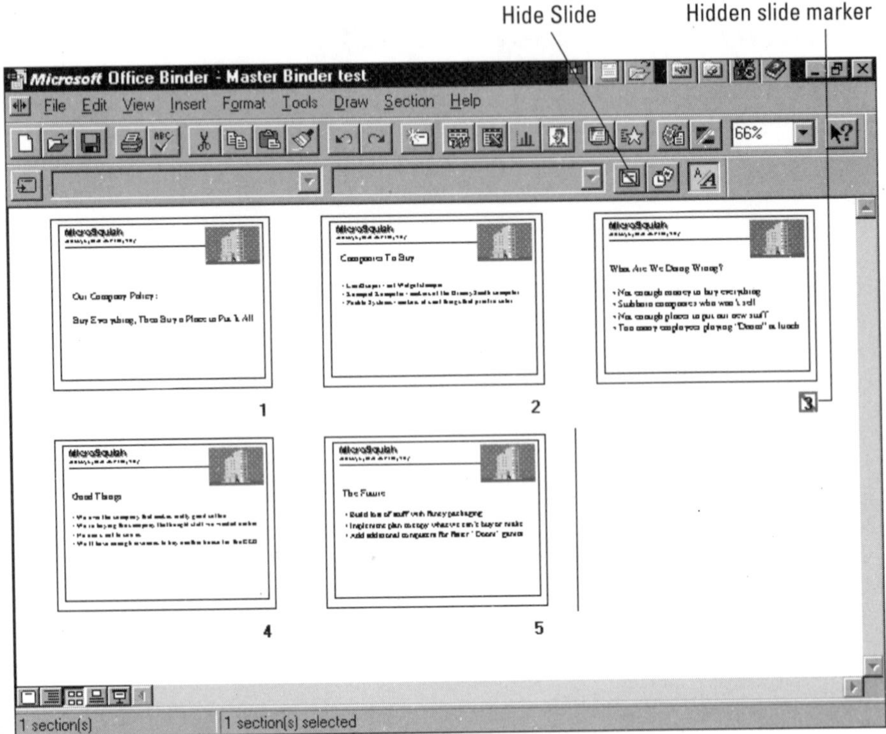

Figure 14-3: Using Slide Sorter view to mark a slide so that it will disappear during your next presentation.

2. **Click between the two slides where you want to insert your new slide so that a vertical line is displayed, as shown in Figure 14-4.**

   If you want to add a new slide after your second slide, for example, click between slides 2 and 3.

3. **Choose Insert⇨New Slide. (Or click the Insert New Slide button.)**

   The New Slide dialog box appears.

4. **Click the slide layout you want to use and then click OK.**

   PowerPoint adds your new slide in your chosen location.

5. **Double-click your newly created slide to edit it.**

Packing Up Your Presentation for the Road

When you finally have your entire slide show perfectly organized, complete, and ready to show, you have two choices: Herd everyone around the computer you used to create your PowerPoint presentation (or drag your computer to another room), or copy your PowerPoint presentation to floppy disks so that you can show it on another computer.

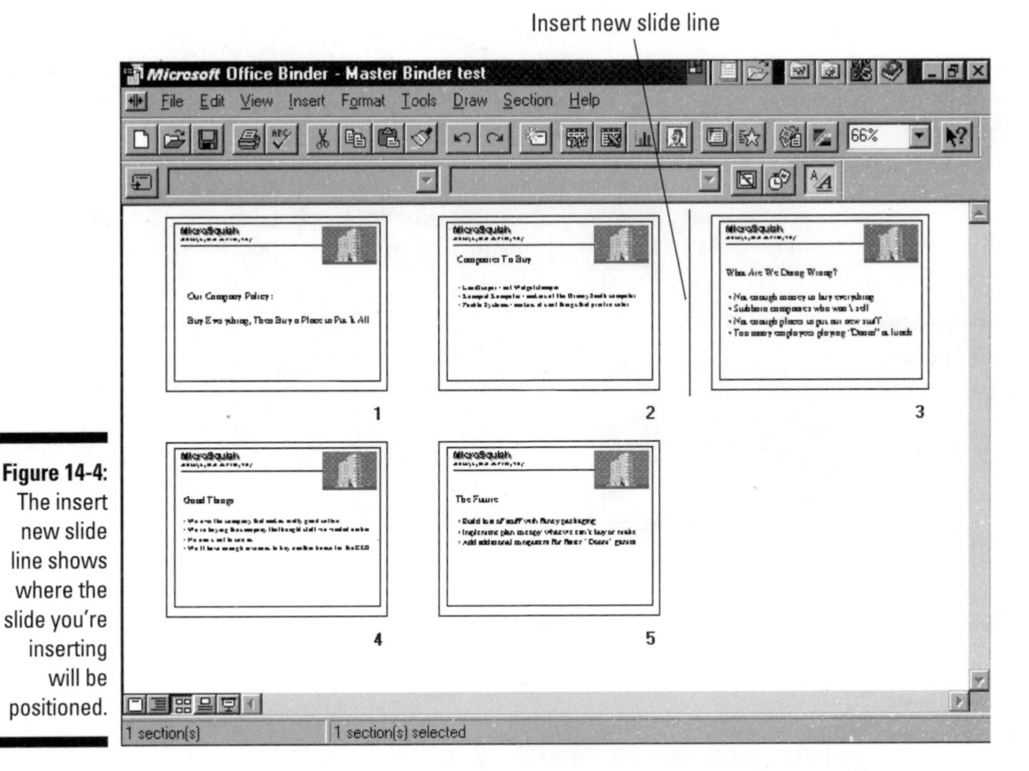

Figure 14-4: The insert new slide line shows where the slide you're inserting will be positioned.

Unless you're fortunate enough to have a laptop computer that you can easily drag around with you, copying your PowerPoint presentation to one or more floppy disks and then running them on another computer is usually much simpler.

Testing your slide show

Before you show your presentation during that crucial business meeting, you should first test your slide show. Then you can see whether you used too many obnoxious sound effects or annoying visual effects that detract from your presentation.

To test your slide show, follow these steps:

1. **Choose View➪Slide Show.**

   The Slide Show dialog box appears.

2. **Click the Rehearse New Timings option button.**

3. **Click Show.**

   PowerPoint displays a Rehearsal dialog box, which shows the time used to show each slide, as shown in Figure 14-5.

4. **Click the mouse to see each slide in your entire presentation.**

   At the end of your presentation, the PowerPoint dialog box appears, telling you how much time your presentation took and asking whether you want to record the amount of time in Slide Sorter view, as shown in Figure 14-6.

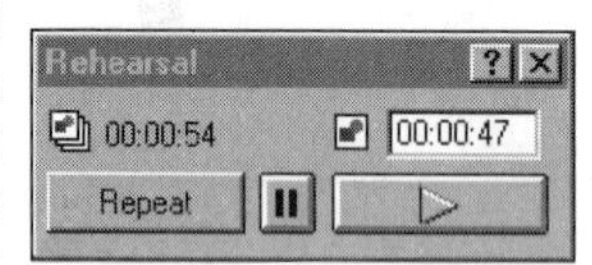

Figure 14-5: The Rehearsal dialog box tells you how much time your slide show is wasting.

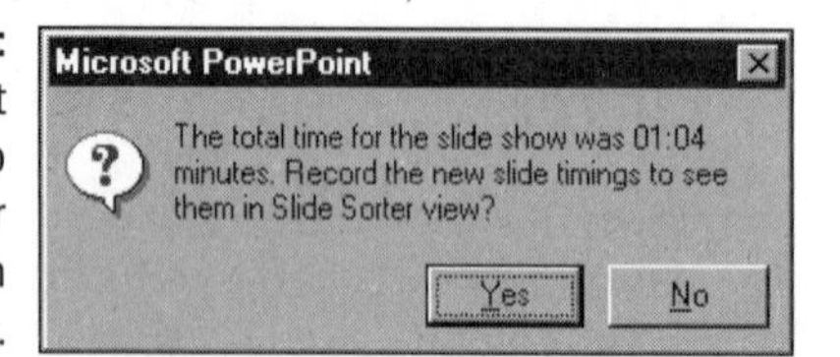

Figure 14-6: PowerPoint wants to record your presentation time.

5. **Click Yes if you want to save the timing or No if you don't want to save the timing.**

   If you click Yes, PowerPoint exhibits the Slide Sorter view with the time for each slide displayed, as shown in Figure 14-7.

To view your slide show presentation with the stored timing, follow these steps:

1. **Choose View⇨Slide Show.**

   The Slide Show dialog box appears.

2. **Click the Use Slide Timings option button.**

3. **Click Show.**

   PowerPoint displays your entire slide show by using the stored times for each slide.

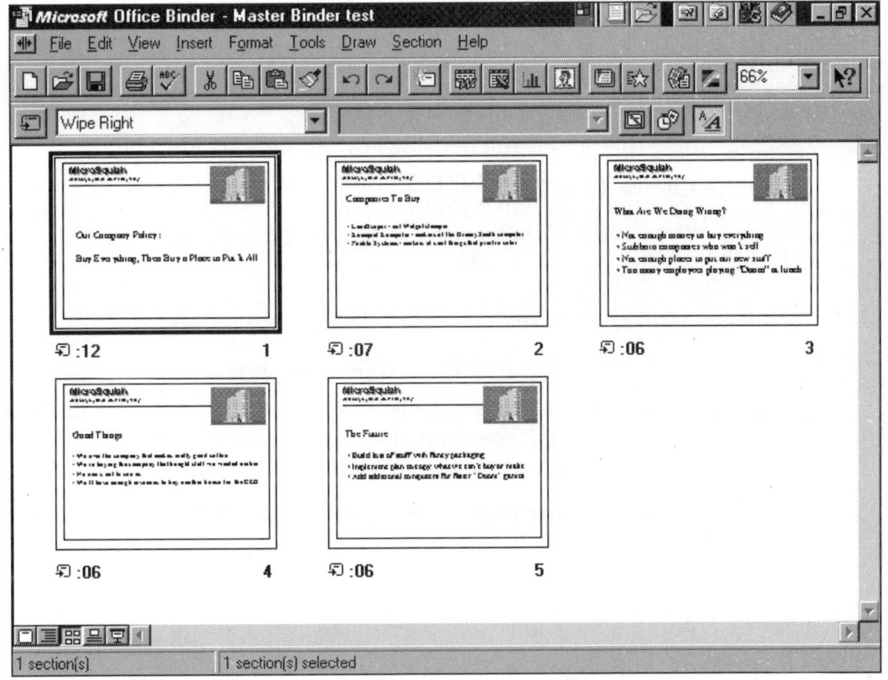

Figure 14-7: Slide Sorter view displays your record-breaking presentation time.

Copying your presentation to floppy disks

When you decide that your slide show is ready for public eyes (or when you just don't feel like working on it anymore), you can keep it on your computer to be displayed later. If you want to show your presentation on another computer, however, PowerPoint lets you copy your presentation to one or more floppy disks. So what happens if you want to show your presentation on another computer? If the other computer also has a copy of PowerPoint and Windows 95, you can just copy your PowerPoint file and run it on this other computer.

But if the other computer only has Windows 95 (but no copy of PowerPoint), you have to store your presentation on a floppy disk along with a special PowerPoint viewer and installation program.

After you copy your PowerPoint presentation to floppy disks, you can run your presentation on another computer.

If you want to run your PowerPoint presentation on another computer, make sure that the other computer is also running Windows 95. If you try to copy your Windows 95 PowerPoint presentation to a computer running Windows 3.1, your presentation won't work.

To copy your presentation to a floppy disk, follow these steps:

1. **If you're using PowerPoint within a binder, choose Section⇨View Outside.**

   Skip this step if you're using PowerPoint outside a binder.

2. **Choose File⇨Pack And Go.**

   The Pack and Go Wizard dialog box appears.

3. **Click Next.**

   Another Pack and Go Wizard dialog box appears.

4. **Click one of the following option buttons:**

   - **Untitled Presentation:** To package your currently displayed presentation in PowerPoint. (If you have saved your PowerPoint presentation to disk, the filename appears instead of Untitled Presentation.)
   - **Other presentations:** To package a different presentation created with PowerPoint

5. **Click Next.**

   Another Pack and Go Wizard dialog box appears.

6. **Click one of the following option buttons:**

   - **Drive A**
   - **Choose Destination** (to store your presentation on a different drive or directory)

7. **Click Next.**

   One more Pack and Go Wizard dialog box appears.

8. **Make sure that a check mark appears in the Include Linked Files check box if linked files are a part of your PowerPoint presentation and in the Embed TrueType fonts check box if you want to make sure that all your fonts are kept with your PowerPoint presentation.**

9. **Click Next.**

   Not surprisingly, still another Pack and Go Wizard dialog box appears.

10. **Make sure that a check mark appears in the Include PowerPoint Viewer check box if you want to be certain that you can run your PowerPoint presentation on another computer that runs Windows 95.**

11. **Click Next.**

    The final Pack and Go Wizard dialog box appears.

12. **Click Finish.**

    PowerPoint copies your presentation to your chosen disk and directory (drive A, for example).

After you store your PowerPoint presentation on floppy disks, you can take those disks to any computer and run the PNGSETUP.EXE program to install and run your presentation on another computer.

The PNGSETUP.EXE file is a special installation program that PowerPoint creates when you choose the Pack and Go command. Don't erase this file by mistake or you won't be able to copy and display your PowerPoint presentation to another computer.

Making Great Web Pages From PowerPoint Presentations

PowerPoint seems a natural for creating Web pages, since it already lets you create visually stunning presentations without much work. So not surprisingly, Microsoft has released an Internet Assistant for PowerPoint that lets you convert your presentations into Web pages.

The Internet Assistant for PowerPoint comes packed in a file called PPTIA.EXE. When you run this file, it expands into several other files, one of which contains the Internet Assistant program installation program called IA4PPT95.EXE. Running the IA4PPT.EXE installs the Internet Assistant for PowerPoint program on your computer.

To convert a presentation into a Web page, follow these steps:

1. **Load PowerPoint as a separate program (not within a binder).**
2. **Choose File⇨Open and load the file you want to convert into a Web page.**
3. **Choose File⇨Export as HTML.**

   The HTML Export Options dialog box appears, as shown in Figure 14-8. The Grayscale and Color option buttons let you choose whether to create a Web page in black and white or color.

   The JPEG and GIF option buttons let you choose the bitmap format for your graphics. GIF files are slightly larger than JPEG files. If you choose to save your graphics as JPEG files, you also can use the horizontal scroll bar to determine the image quality (Low to High) versus the file size (Smaller to Larger).
4. **Type a name and directory for your Web page and click OK.**

   The Internet Assistant for PowerPoint magically converts your slides into genuine Web pages, ready for posting, as shown in Figure 14-9.

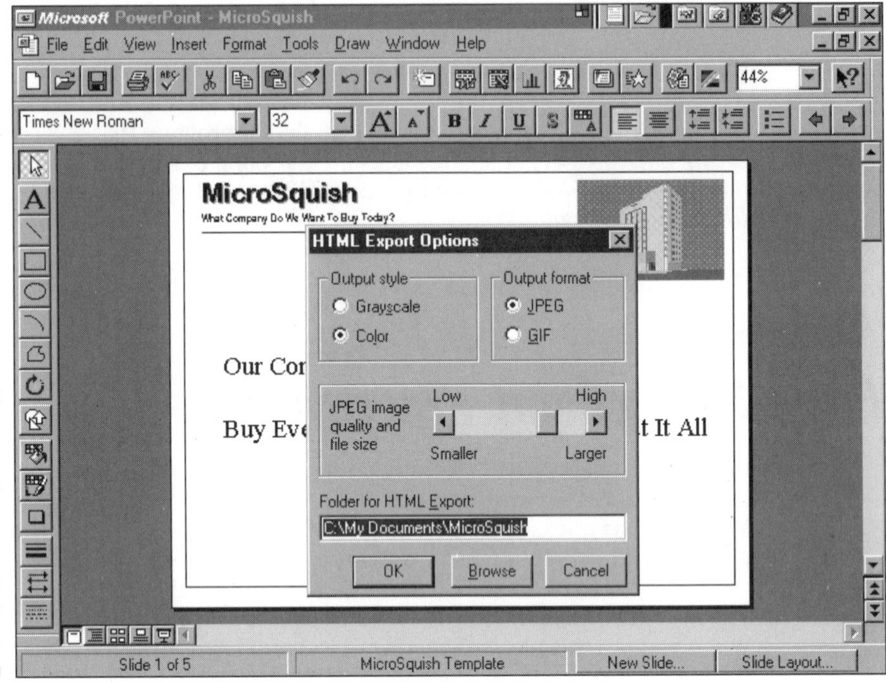

Figure 14-8: Choosing options for converting your presentation into a Web page.

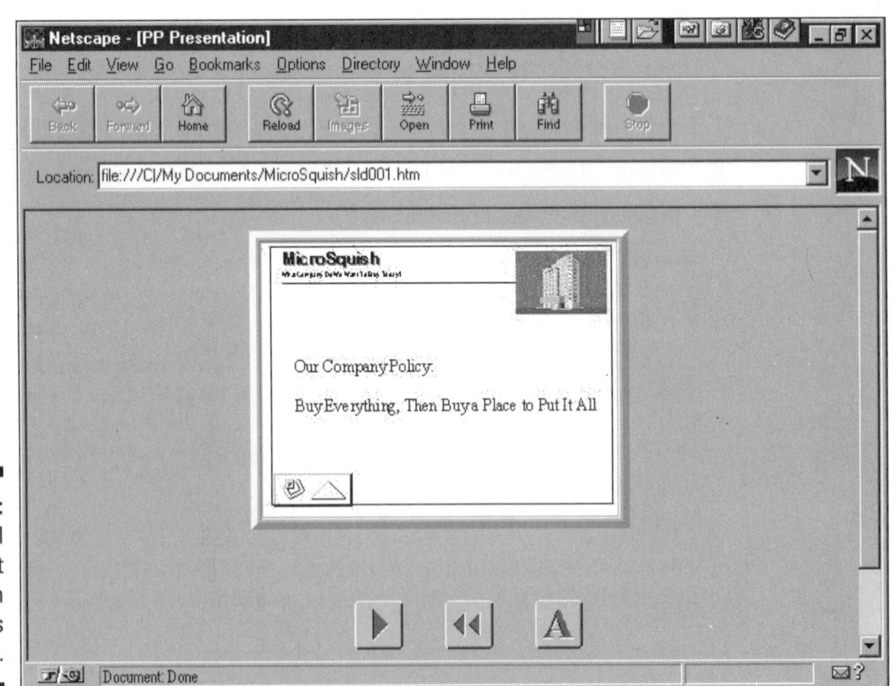

Figure 14-9: A typical PowerPoint presentation displayed as a Web page.

Part IV
Staying Organized with Microsoft Schedule+

"ALL THIS STUFF? IT'S PART OF A SUITE OF INTEGRATED SOFTWARE PACKAGES DESIGNED TO HELP UNCLUTTER YOUR LIFE."

In this part . . .

Time is money, which means that if you use your time wisely, you can make more money than someone who squanders their hours everyday until they're left wondering why they're not getting anything important done in their lives.

To help you become one of those few people who actually take time to plan their day and work toward long-term goals, this part of the book unlocks the secrets to using Schedule+ for organizing your day.

By using Schedule+, you can take responsibility for your own life and pursue the goal of your dreams, which immediately puts you in the minority of the population that knows what they want out of life.

Chapter 15
Customizing Schedule+

In This Chapter

- Playing with different days and times
- Changing the way your reminders and tasks work
- Modifying the way Schedule+ displays your data
- Changing time zones
- Adding and removing tabs

Microsoft Schedule+ can help you keep track of appointments, anniversaries, names, addresses, phone numbers, and goals for yourself or your job. Although Microsoft tried to make Schedule+ appeal to as many people as possible, you may not want to accept the way it works, looks, or acts.

Rather than suffer, take some time to customize Schedule+ so that it works more like the way you want. It probably still won't work exactly the way you want, but at least you can change it to make it more acceptable to your own personal habits.

Playing with Different Days and Times

Not everyone works Mondays through Fridays, begins the day at 8:00 a.m., or schedules appointments in neat, 30-minute blocks. If you fit into this way of working, you can skip the rest of this chapter. If you would rather modify Schedule+ so that it works the way you do, however, take heart: You can modify the Schedule+ weekly and time settings whenever you want.

To change the Schedule+ day and time settings, follow these steps:

1. **Choose Tools⇨Options.**

   The Options dialog box appears, as shown in Figure 15-1.

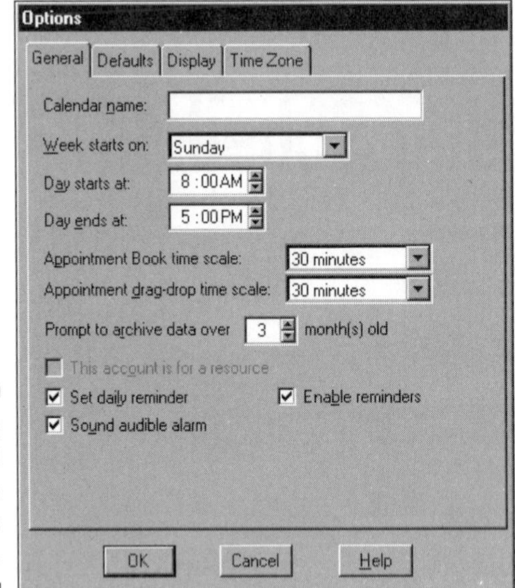

Figure 15-1: The General tab in the Options dialog box.

2. **Click the General tab.**
3. **Click the Week starts on list box and choose the day on which you want your week to begin (such as Sunday or Monday).**
4. **Click the Day starts at list box to choose a time for each day's appointments to begin (such as 8:00 a.m. or 5:30 a.m.).**
5. **Click the Day ends at list box and choose a time for each day's appointments to end (such as 5:00 p.m. or 6:30 p.m.).**
6. **Click the Appointment Book time scale list box and choose the way you want Schedule+ to divide up your time (such as in 5-minute or 30-minute time blocks).**
7. **Click the Appointment drag-drop time scale and choose the way you want Schedule+ to let you drag around appointments (such as in 10-minute or 30-minute time blocks).**
8. **Click OK.**

Schedule+ lets you set appointments 24 hours a day, beginning at 12:00 midnight until 11:59 p.m. Changing the times for Day starts at and Day ends at simply highlights your working day in a lighter shade of yellow, as shown in Figure 15-2.

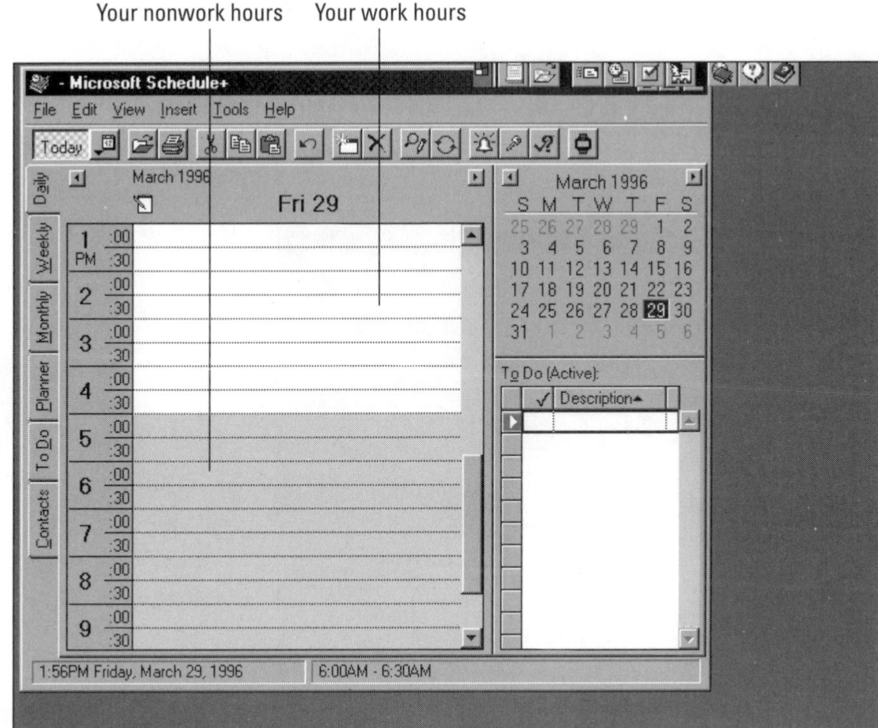

Figure 15-2: Schedule+ displays different shades for your designated work hours and the rest of your day.

Changing the Way Your Reminders and Tasks Work

When you set an appointment, you can ask Schedule+ to remind you of your appointment so that you don't forget it. (Of course, if you're afraid that you might forget an appointment, you probably don't care about that appointment in the first place.) Depending on how much you procrastinate, you can ask Schedule+ to remind you a few minutes before your appointment.

Likewise, when you define a task you want to complete, you can ask Schedule+ to remind you of an approaching deadline a few days in advance. You can also specify default settings for the priority, duration, and estimated length of time required to complete a task.

To tell Schedule+ how to set your reminders and tasks, follow these steps:

1. **Choose Tools⇨Options.**

   The Options dialog box appears (refer to Figure 15-1).

2. **Click the Defaults tab, shown in Figure 15-3.**

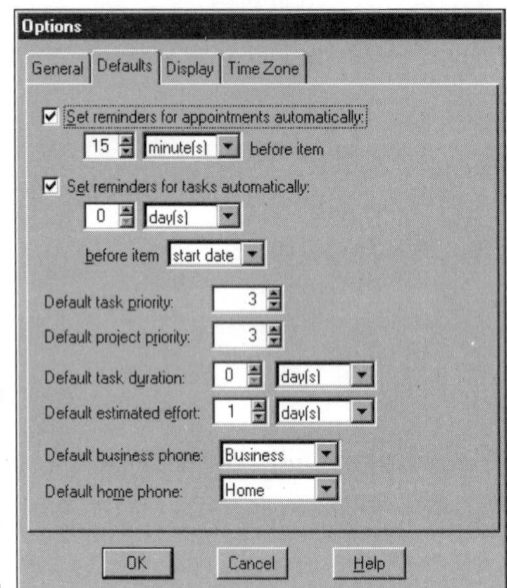

Figure 15-3: The Defaults tab in the Options dialog box.

3. **If you want Schedule+ always to remind you of upcoming appointments, make sure that a check mark appears in the check box labeled Set reminders for appointments automatically.**

4. **Click the two list boxes directly underneath to define how soon you want Schedule+ to remind you of an upcoming appointment (such as 15 minutes or one hour before your appointment).**

5. **If you want Schedule+ always to remind you of an upcoming task's start date or deadline, make sure that a check mark appears in the Set reminders for tasks automatically check box.**

6. **Click the two list boxes directly underneath to define how soon you want Schedule+ to remind you of an upcoming task (such as 15 minutes or one hour before your task).**

7. **Click the before item list box to define whether you want Schedule+ to remind you of a task's start date or deadline.**

8. **Click the Default task priority list box and choose a priority for most of your tasks (such as 1 for high priority or 3 for medium priority).**

9. **Click the Default project priority list box and choose a priority for most of your projects (such as 1 for high priority or 3 for medium priority).**
10. **Click the two Default task duration list boxes, and choose the average length of your tasks in days, weeks, or months.**
11. **Click the two Default estimated effort list boxes, and choose the average length of time it takes to complete your tasks in minutes, hours, days, weeks, or months.**
12. **Click OK.**

After you create a task or project, you can always raise or lower its priority later. Setting the default settings for tasks and projects simply lets you choose the most common priority for your tasks and projects (so that you don't have to keep changing it every time you create a new task or project).

Modifying the Way Schedule+ Displays Your Data

Not everyone may like the way Schedule+ displays information on-screen. Some people may prefer to use different colors to highlight their appointments, display larger-size fonts to make appointments easier to read, or hide gridlines when they're viewing names.

If you want to change the way Schedule+ displays information, follow these steps:

1. **Choose Tools⇨Options.**

   The Options dialog box appears (refer to Figure 15-1).
2. **Click the Display tab, shown in Figure 15-4.**
3. **To change the colors Schedule+ uses, click the Appointment Book, Planner, Grid, and Page list boxes in the Backgrounds group.**
4. **To change the colors Schedule+ uses in the Planner portion, click the Owner, Required, Optional, and Resource list boxes in the Planner group.**
5. **If you want tooltips to appear when you point to an icon, make sure that a check mark appears in the Show ToolTips check box.**
6. **If you want gridlines to appear when you view your list of contacts, make sure that a check mark appears in the Show gridlines check box.**
7. **If you want to see week numbers when you view your calendar (so that you'll know how many weeks are left in the year), make sure that a check mark appears in the Show week numbers in the calendar check box.**

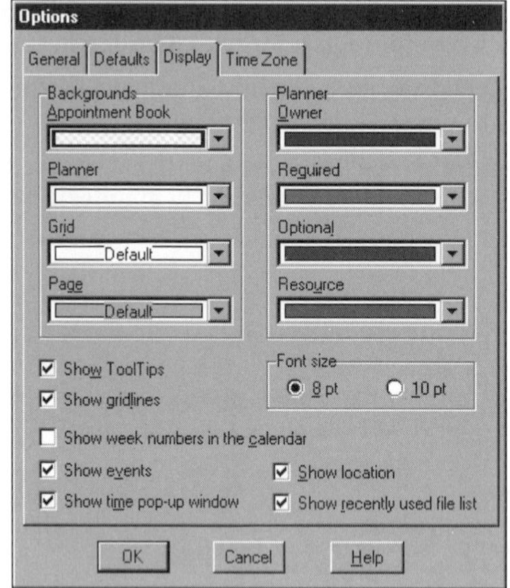

Figure 15-4: The Display tab in the Options dialog box.

8. **If you want to see events displayed in Schedule+, make sure that a check mark appears in the Show events check box.**
9. **If you want Schedule+ to pop up a window that lists the starting and stopping time of an appointment when you click it, make sure that a check mark appears in the Show time pop-up window.**
10. **If you want to make sure that Schedule+ shows the location of your appointments (assuming that you've defined a location for them), make sure that a check mark appears in the Show location check box.**
11. **If you want Schedule+ to display (at the bottom of the File menu) the last files you opened, make sure that a check mark appears in the Show recently used file list.**
12. **Click either the 8 pt or 10 pt radio button in the Font size group.**
13. **Click OK.**

Changing Time Zones

Schedule+ can keep track of your daily, weekly, and monthly appointments, tasks, and projects, so it's usually a good idea to keep your copy of Schedule+ with you wherever you go. Because most people don't change times zones on a daily basis, storing Schedule+ on a desktop computer doesn't require worrying about time zones.

If you're one of those jet-setters who keeps Schedule+ on your laptop computer and crosses time zones so often that you sometimes have trouble remembering which city you're in (let alone what time or day it may be), you may have to modify your time zone occasionally so that Schedule+ doesn't remind you of an appointment you had two hours ago.

To change the time zone Schedule+ uses, follow these steps:

1. **Choose Tools⇨Options.**

   The Options dialog box appears (refer to Figure 15-1).

2. **Click the Time Zone tab, shown in Figure 15-5.**

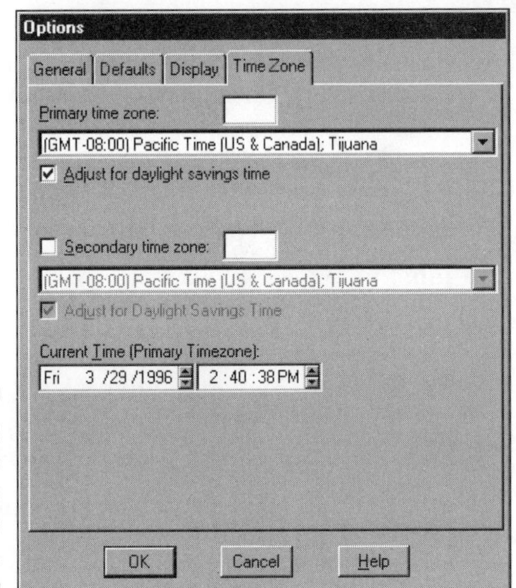

Figure 15-5: The Time Zone tab in the Options dialog box.

3. **Click the Primary time zone list box and choose your current time zone.**
4. **Make sure that a check mark appears in the Secondary time zone check box if you want to define a second time zone you visit frequently.**
5. **Click the two Current Time list boxes to set the current date and time.**
6. **Click OK.**

Adding and Removing Tabs

To help organize the different parts your life, Schedule+ provides separate pages organized by tabs that appear on the left side of the screen. Clicking the Daily tab displays your daily appointments, clicking the Monthly tab displays your monthly appointments, and so on.

What happens if you use certain portions of Schedule+ more than other parts? In that case, you can add and remove tabs so that you see only the ones you use most often.

Removing a tab

The first step in customizing your tabs is to remove the ones you don't need, don't like, or don't want to see because they get in the way. To remove a tab, follow these steps:

1. **Click the tab you want to remove.**

   Schedule+ displays the information stored on that tab.

2. **Choose View⇨Remove Tab.**

   The dialog box asks whether you really want to remove the current tab, shown in Figure 15-6.

3. **Click Yes.**

   Your chosen tab disappears.

When you remove a tab, you're simply tucking it out of sight. Any information displayed on the tab is still stored on your hard disk.

Figure 15-6: The Microsoft Schedule+ dialog box wants you to make sure that you want to remove a tab.

Adding a tab

After clearing your copy of Schedule+ of tabs you don't need, you can take some time to add the tabs you want displayed. To add a tab, follow these steps:

1. **Choose View⇨Tab Gallery.**

   The Tab Gallery dialog box appears, as shown in Figure 15-7.

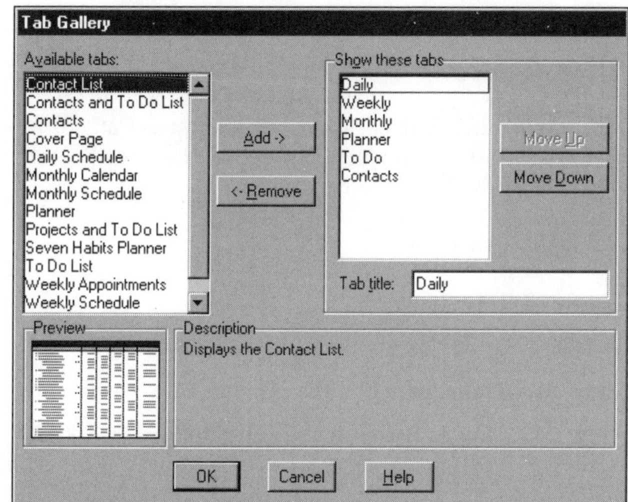

Figure 15-7: The Tab Gallery dialog box.

2. **In the Available tabs list box, click a tab you want to appear in your copy of Schedule+.**
3. **Click the Add button.**

   Schedule+ displays your chosen tab in the Show these tabs list.
4. **Repeat steps 2 and 3 for each tab you want to add.**
5. **Click OK.**

Moving a tab

Every time you add a tab, Schedule+ blindly inserts it above the currently selected tab in the Show these tabs box (refer to Figure 15-7). Because this placement isn't always the most convenient one for your tabs, you can rearrange your tabs to suit your own sense of organization.

To move a tab, follow these steps:

1. **Choose View⇨Tab Gallery.**

   The Tab Gallery dialog box appears (refer to Figure 15-7).

2. **In the Show these tabs list, click the tab you want to move.**
3. **Click Move Up or Move Down until the tab is in the position you want.**
4. **Click OK.**

Renaming a tab

Tabs usually display a dull but descriptive label, such as Daily or Monthly. In case you want to use more creative labels, such as My Daily Schedule or Hopeless Projects, you can just rename a tab.

To rename a tab, follow these steps:

1. **Choose View⇨Tab Gallery.**

   The Tab Gallery dialog box appears (refer to Figure 15-7).

2. **In the Show these tabs list, click the tab you want to rename.**
3. **Type a new name for your tab in the Tab title box.**
4. **Click OK.**

Chapter 16

The Seven Habits of Successful People

In This Chapter

- Learn the seven habits successful people use in their lives
- Define your life's mission
- Identify the roles you play
- Focus on your goals
- Gain wisdom from others

If you have ever read the book *The Seven Habits of Highly Successful People,* by Stephen R. Covey, you may wonder how you can use the book's success techniques in your own life. Fortunately, Microsoft has licensed the book's techniques and added them directly to Schedule+. Now you can apply the book's techniques on your computer so that you can stop suffering and do something with your life that you truly enjoy.

Learning the Seven Habits of Success

For people who haven't read *The Seven Habits of Highly Successful People,* the book claims that people are successful not because they're lucky, genetically superior, or smarter than anyone else. Instead, it says that people are successful because they follow certain habits that anyone can learn. These habits are shown in this list:

- **Be proactive.** Don't sit on your butt and complain. Instead, take action to change your life for the better.
- **Begin with the end in mind.** Set goals you can measure objectively rather than abstract goals such as "I just want to be happy."
- **Put first things first.** After you know which goals you want to achieve, always work toward your goals and ignore trivial distractions that won't get you closer to your goals.

- **Think win–win.** Find a way to help others to succeed while you succeed as well.
- **Seek first to understand and then to be understood.** Spend more time listening to others before talking yourself.
- **Synergize.** Combine ideas from others to create even better solutions.
- **Sharpen the saw.** Always take time to improve your skills and learn new ones.

If you consistently follow these seven habits, the odds are in your favor that you'll reach your goals and achieve greater success than people who do nothing but whine all day, try to destroy others in their pursuit of success, or spend most of the day doing trivial tasks that have nothing to do with their goals.

Now that you know the seven habits successful people use to achieve their goals, you may be wondering how to apply those principles in your own life. Fortunately, Schedule+ can help you by asking you to define the following:

- Your mission statement
- The roles you want to play
- The goals you want to achieve

Your *mission statement* helps you define the direction in which you want to take your life. Your employer may even have a mission statement, such as "Provide nutritious, tasty meals at reasonable prices" or "Increase corporate profits at the expense of the environment." Think of a mission statement as a guideline. If your mission statement is "Save the planet" but your job requires you to bury toxic waste in Third World countries for international oil companies, you can check your mission statement and realize that you're off track.

Each one of us plays different roles in life, such as spouse, parent, worker, and boss. By choosing the roles most important to you, you can determine the goals you want to achieve for each role.

If your most important role is to be a loving parent, for example, one of your goals may be to spend a certain amount of time with your children. If another one of your roles is as an employee, one of your goals may be to complete all projects ahead of schedule. After you know the most important roles in your life, you can better define the goals you want to achieve.

Choosing Your Mission

Now that you realize the importance of having a mission statement, you may have no idea how to create one for yourself. Because this process can be intimidating, Microsoft Schedule+ provides a special Wizard to guide you through it, step-by-step.

To create your mission statement, follow these steps:

1. **Choose Tools⇨Seven Habits Tools.**

   The Seven Habits Tools dialog box appears, as shown in Figure 16-1. Click the up- and down-arrow buttons to read different leading questions to help you clarify your mission statement.

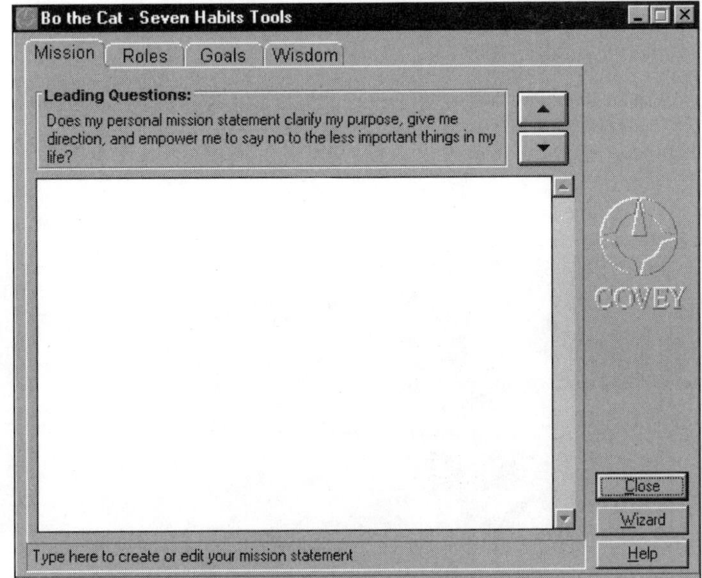

Figure 16-1: The Seven Habits Tools dialog box asks you leading questions to help you clarify your mission statement.

2. **Click the Wizard button.**

   The Seven Habits Wizard dialog box appears, shown in Figure 16-2.

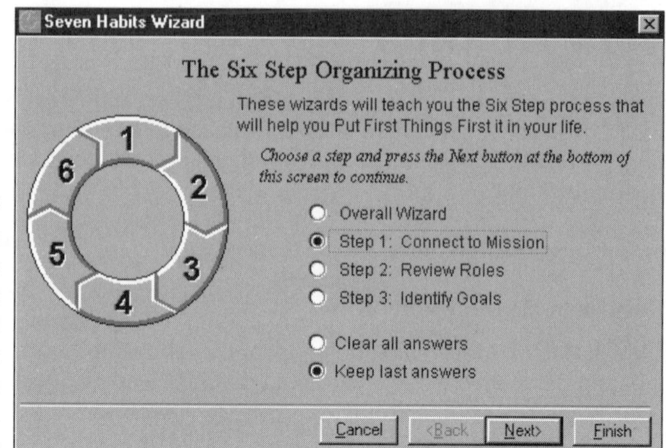

Figure 16-2: Taking the first steps toward putting first things first in your life.

3. **Click the Next> button.**

   A dialog box appears that describes the purpose of a personal mission statement, as shown in Figure 16-3.

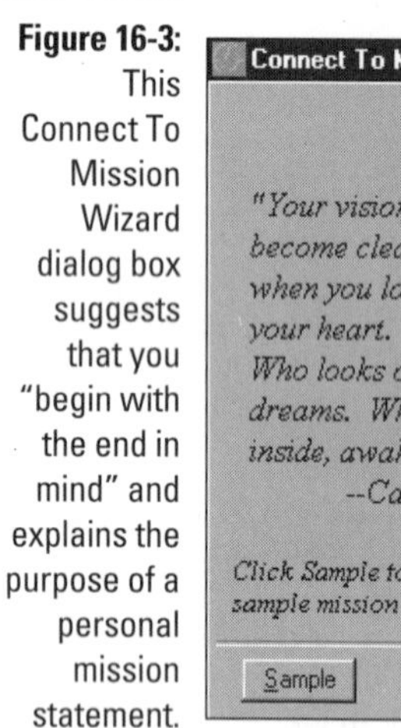

Figure 16-3: This Connect To Mission Wizard dialog box suggests that you "begin with the end in mind" and explains the purpose of a personal mission statement.

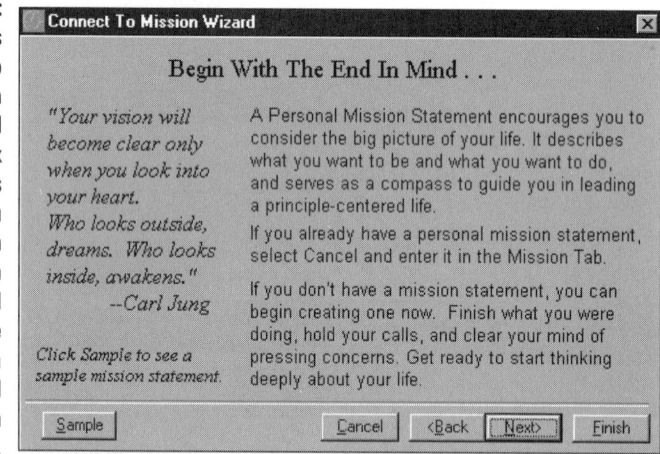

4. **Click the Sample button to see a sample mission statement, shown in Figure 16-4.**

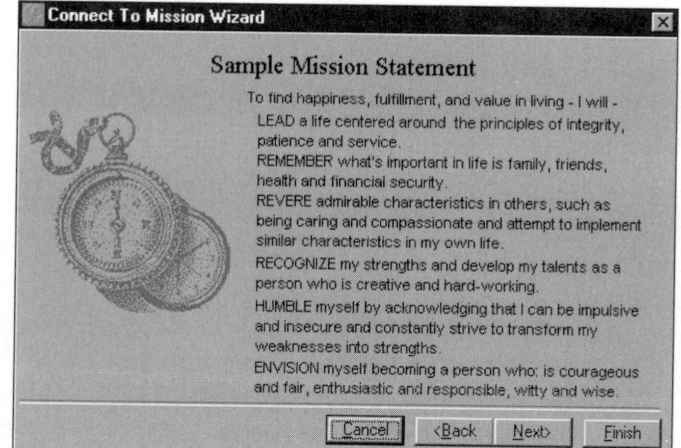

Figure 16-4: A sample mission statement.

5. **Click Next>.**

   Another Connect To Mission Wizard dialog box appears, as shown in Figure 16-5.

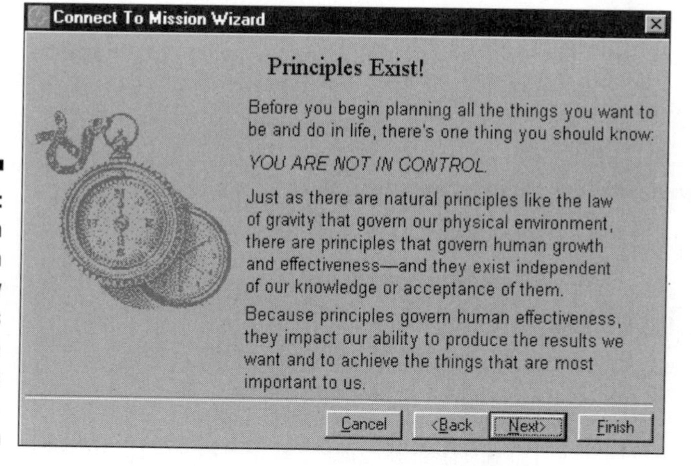

Figure 16-5: An explanation of how principles can help you govern your life.

6. **Click Next>.**

   A message asking what you value appears in the Connect To Mission Wizard dialog box, shown in Figure 16-6.

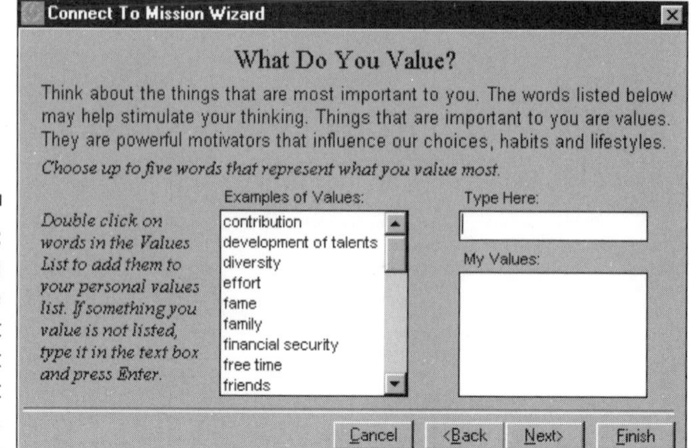

Figure 16-6: Thinking about the things that are most important to you.

7. **Double-click the important values listed in the Examples of Values list box, or type a value in the Type Here box and press Enter.**

   Schedule+ displays your chosen values in the My Values box. You can choose as many as five values.

8. **Click Next>.**

   A message that explains the difference between values and principles appears in the Connect To Mission Wizard dialog box, shown in Figure 16-7.

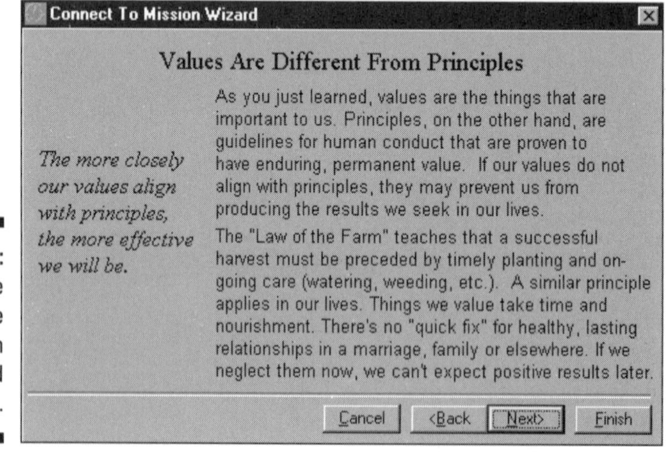

Figure 16-7: The difference between values and principles.

9. **Click Next>.**

   A message about aligning your life to your principles appears in the Connect To Mission Wizard dialog box.

10. **Double-click the important principles listed in the Examples of Principles list box, or type a value in the Type Here box and press Enter.**

    Schedule+ displays your chosen values in the My Principles box. You can choose as many as four principles.

11. **Click Next>.**

    A message about considering the life of someone else appears in the Connect To Mission Wizard dialog box.

12. **Click in the two list boxes and choose one or two people who have influenced your life, such as a friend, historical figure, or teacher.**

13. **Click Next>.**

    A message asking what you admire about those influential people appears in the Connect To Mission Wizard dialog box.

14. **Double-click a word listed in the Descriptive Words list box, or type a word in the Type Here box and press Enter.**

    Schedule+ displays your chosen values in the Admirable Qualities box. You can choose as many as six descriptive words.

15. **Click Next>.**

    A message about considering your strengths and talents appears in the Connect To Mission Wizard dialog box.

16. **Double-click a word listed in the Strengths and Talents list box, or type a word in the Type Here box and press Enter.**

    Schedule+ displays your chosen values in the My Strengths box. You can choose as many as six strengths.

17. **Click Next>.**

    A message asking what you believe is in your way appears in the Connect To Mission Wizard dialog box.

18. **Double-click a word listed in the Descriptive Words list box, or type a word in the Type Here box and press Enter.**

    Schedule+ displays your chosen values in the My Obstacles box. You can choose as many as three obstacles.

19. **Click Next>.**

    A message suggesting that you think in terms of relationships appears in the Connect To Mission Wizard dialog box.

20. **Type as many as four important relationships in your life, such as your spouse or companion or family member.**

21. **Click Next>.**

    A message that describes how to project yourself forward in time appears in the Connect To Mission Wizard dialog box, shown in Figure 16-8.

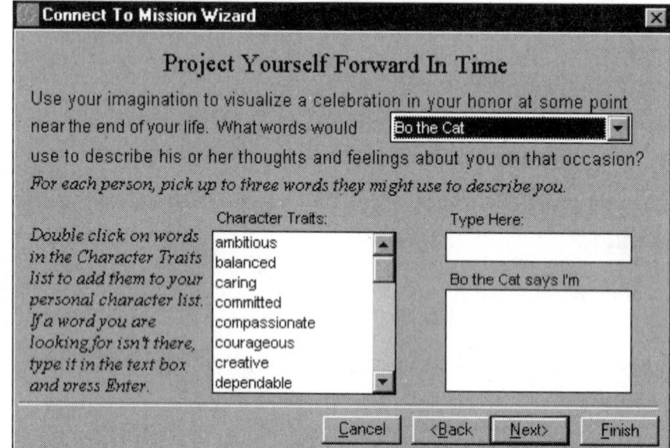

Figure 16-8: Using your imagination to project yourself forward in time.

22. **Click the list box in the upper right corner of the dialog box, and select one of the people you chose in step 20.**

23. **Double-click a word listed in the Character Traits list box, or type a word in the Type Here box and press Enter.**

    Schedule+ displays your chosen values in the text box in the bottom right corner. You can choose as many as three words per person.

24. **Repeat steps 22 and 23 for each person you chose in step 20.**

25. **Click Next>.**

    A message about your personal mission statement appears in the Connect To Mission Wizard dialog box.

26. **Click Finish.**

    The Seven Habits Wizard dialog box appears (refer to Figure 16-2).

27. **Click Finish.**

    Schedule+ displays the personal mission statement it automatically created for you, as shown in Figure 16-9.

28. **Click Close.**

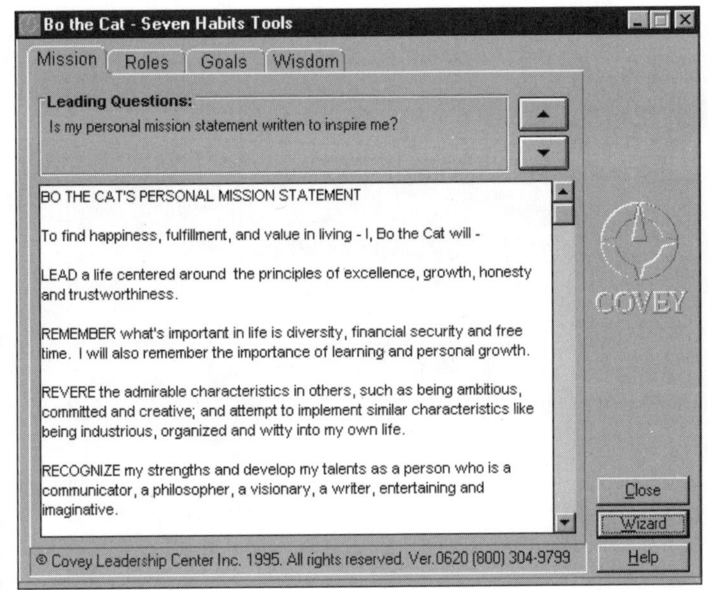

Figure 16-9: A typical mission statement in the Seven Habits Tools dialog box.

After you've created your mission statement, it's a good idea to review it daily and modify it periodically if necessary. After all, a mission statement is useless if you never use it.

Role-Playing Your Way to Success

The roles you play in your life can determine which parts of your life (the ones they never teach you about in public school!) that you think are most important for your own sense of happiness, well-being, and satisfaction. If you don't identify the most important roles in your life, you're likely to neglect them. You may, for example, neglect a spouse or child in favor of pursuing more mundane tasks, such as getting a raise or a promotion in a dead-end job in a corporation that doesn't care about you anyway.

To define your roles, follow these steps:

1. **Choose Tools⇨Seven Habits Tools.**

   The Seven Habits Tools dialog box appears (refer to Figure 16-1).

2. **Click the Roles tab, shown in Figure 16-10.**
3. **Click Wizard.**

   The Seven Habits Wizard dialog box appears.

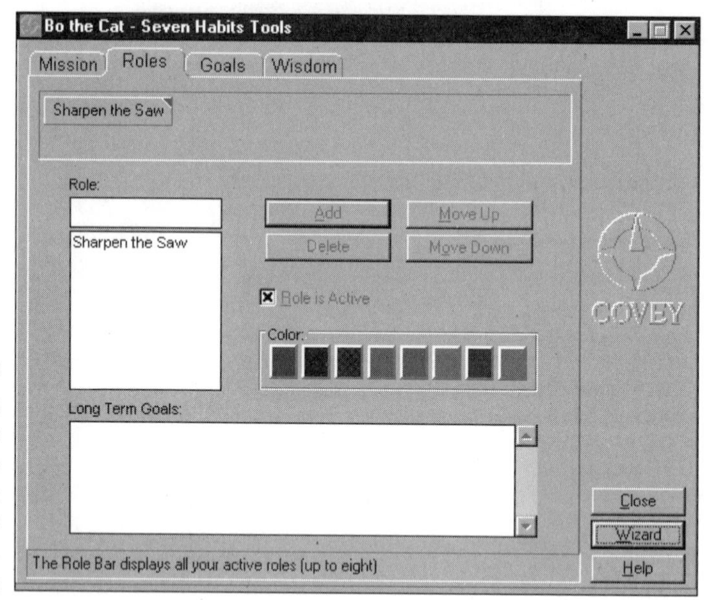

Figure 16-10: The Roles tab in the Seven Habits Tools dialog box.

4. **Click Next>.**

   The Review Roles Wizard dialog box appears.

5. **Click Next>.**

   A message about identifying your personal roles appears in the Review Roles Wizard dialog box, as shown in Figure 16-11.

6. **Double-click a word listed in the Examples of Personal Roles list box, or type a word in the Type Here box and press Enter.**

   Schedule+ displays your chosen values in the Your Personal Roles text box. You can choose as many as ten roles.

7. **Click Next>.**

   A message about identifying your work roles appears in the Review Roles Wizard dialog box.

8. **Double-click a word listed in the Examples of Work Roles list box, or type a word in the Type Here box and press Enter.**

   Schedule+ displays your chosen values in the Your Work Roles text box. You can choose as many as ten roles.

9. **Click Next>.**

   A message about identifying your social roles appears in the Review Roles Wizard dialog box.

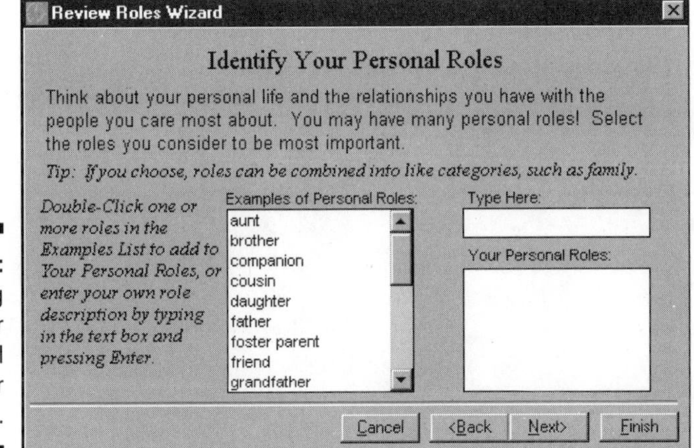

Figure 16-11: Identifying your personal roles in your relationships.

10. **Type any social role in the Type Here box and press Enter.**

    Schedule+ displays your chosen values in the Your Social Roles text box.

11. **Click Next>.**

    A message about refining your roles appears in the Review Roles Wizard dialog box, shown in Figure 16-12.

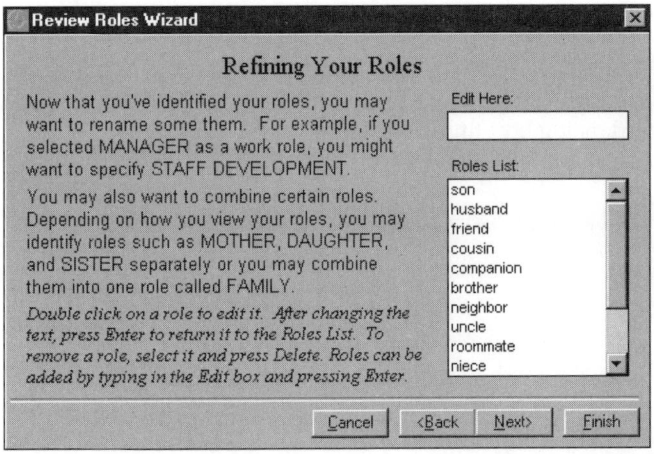

Figure 16-12: Refining the roles you play in life.

12. **Double-click any of the roles listed in the Roles List list box, type a new word or phrase in the Edit Here box, and then press Enter.**

13. **Click Next>.**

    A message about choosing the roles that are most important to you appears in the Review Roles Wizard dialog box, shown in Figure 16-13.

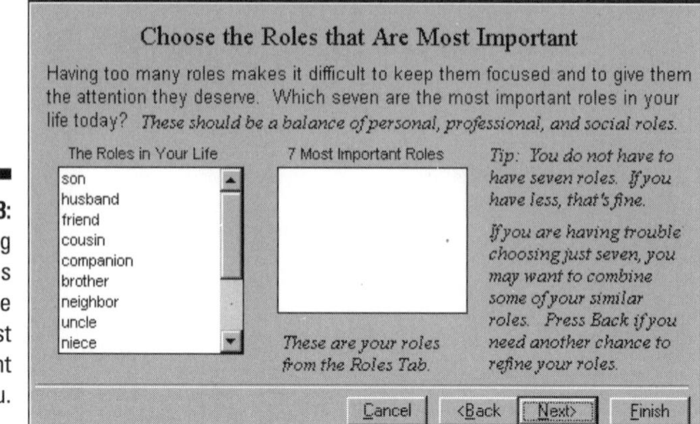

Figure 16-13: Choosing the roles that are most important to you.

14. **Double-click as many as seven of the roles listed in The Roles in Your Life list box.**
15. **Click Next>.**

    A message about sharpening the saw appears in the Review Roles Wizard dialog box, shown in Figure 16-14.
16. **Click Story.**

    A story appears in the Review Roles Wizard dialog box.
17. **Click Next>.**

    A message asking "Why sharpen the saw?" appears in the Review Roles Wizard dialog box, shown in Figure 16-15.

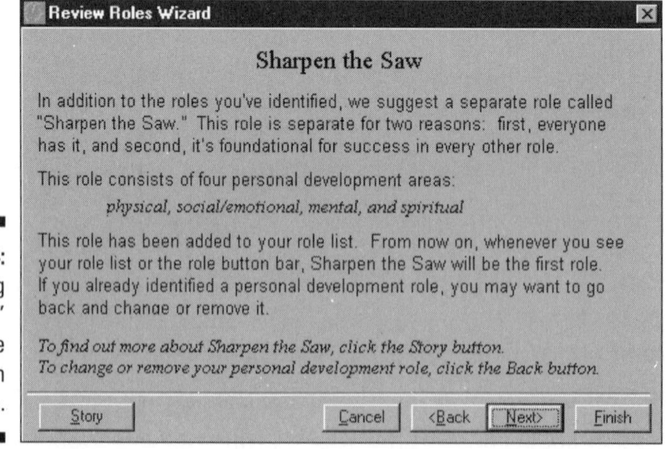

Figure 16-14: "Sharpening the saw" is the foundation for success.

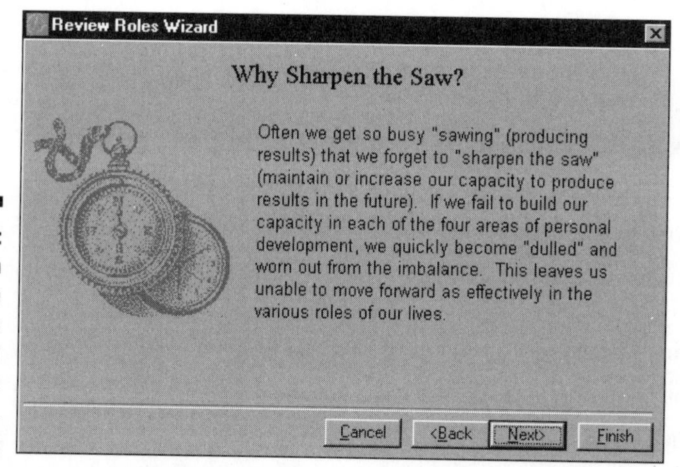

Figure 16-15: An explanation of why you should sharpen the saw.

18. **Click Next>.**

    An example of how one person sharpens the saw appears in the Review Roles Wizard dialog box, shown in Figure 16-16.

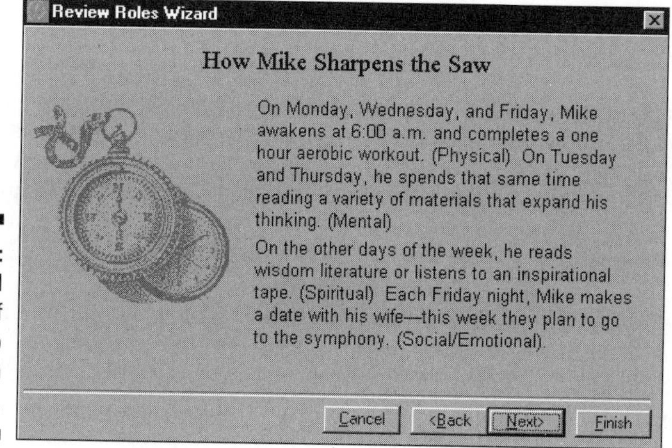

Figure 16-16: A practical example of how to sharpen the saw.

19. **Click Next>.**

    A message about long-term goals for your roles appears in the Review Roles Wizard dialog box.

20. **Click the My Roles list box and choose a role.**
21. **Type a goal in the Long Term Goals for this Role box.**
22. **Repeat steps 20 and 21 for each of the roles listed in the My Roles list box.**

23. **Click Next>.**

    A message about assigning role colors appears in the Review Roles Wizard dialog box.

24. **Click a role and then click a color listed in the Color group.**

    Make sure that you choose a different color for each role.

25. **Click Next>.**

    A message congratulating you for identifying your first set of roles appears in the Review Roles Wizard dialog box.

26. **Click Finish.**

    The Seven Habits Wizard dialog box appears.

27. **Click Finish.**

    Schedule+ displays your roles in the Seven Habits Tools dialog box.

28. **Click each of the roles displayed at the top of the dialog box and type a goal in the Long Term Goals box for each of your roles.**

29. **Click Close.**

Aiming For Your Goals

Goals help you decide what's important to you (your job probably isn't at the top of the list) and what steps you need to take to achieve your goals. Obviously, if you don't know what you want from life, you're probably never going to achieve what you want. Rather than wait until it's too late, take the time now to plan your goals so that you can do what you want with your life regardless of what other people think you should be doing instead.

To plan and view your goals, follow these steps:

1. **Choose Tools⇨Seven Habits Tools.**

    A Seven Habits Tools dialog box appears (refer to Figure 16-1).

2. **Click the Goals tab, shown in Figure 16-17.**

3. **Click Wizard.**

    The Seven Habits Wizard dialog box appears.

4. **Click Next>.**

    A message asking "Why set weekly goals?" appears in the Identify Goals Wizard dialog box.

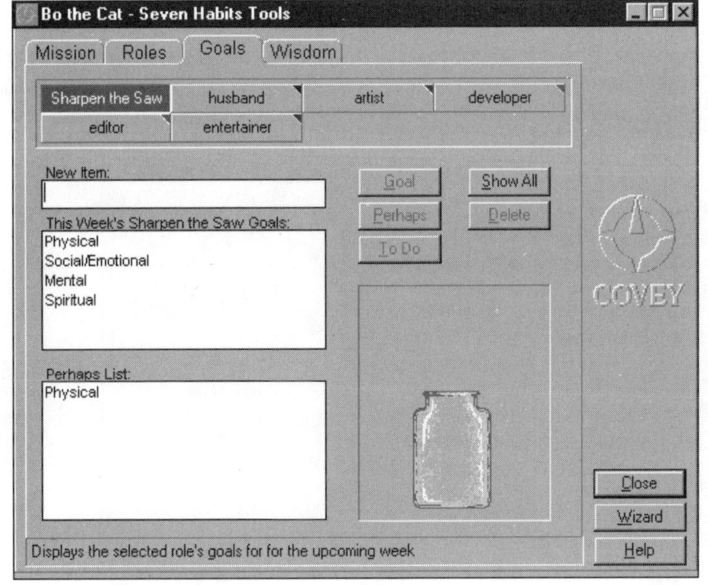

Figure 16-17: The Goals tab in the Seven Habits Tools dialog box.

5. **Click Next>.**

   The message that appears in the Identify Goals Wizard dialog box suggests that you consider the one thing that will have the most positive effect on your life, shown in Figure 16-18.

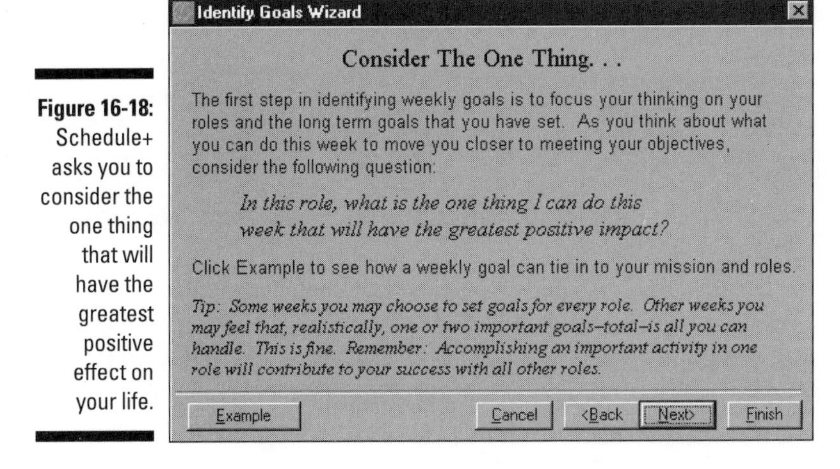

Figure 16-18: Schedule+ asks you to consider the one thing that will have the greatest positive effect on your life.

6. **Click Example.**

   An example of a weekly goal appears in the Identify Goals Wizard dialog box, shown in Figure 16-19.

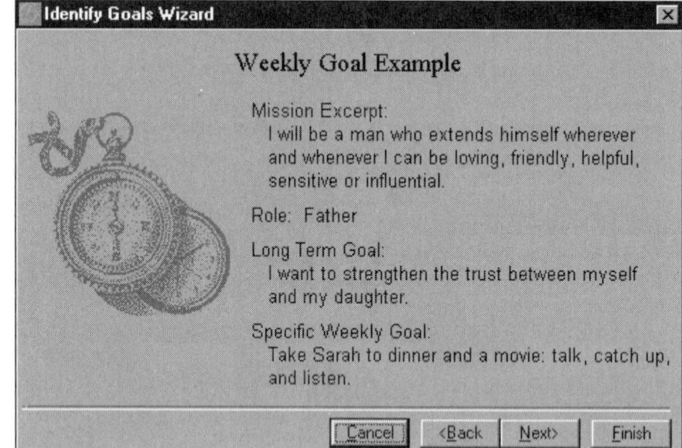

Figure 16-19: An example of a weekly goal.

7. **Click Next>.**

   The "Consider the one thing" message appears again.

8. **Click Next>.**

   A message about your weekly goals for sharpening the saw appears in the Identify Goals Wizard.

9. **Click Example.**

   A message about being creative appears in the Identify Goals Wizard dialog box.

10. **Click Next>.**

11. **Type a goal in the Physical, Social/Emotional, Mental, and Spiritual box and then click Next>.**

    A message asking you to specify the one most important action you can take appears in the Identify Goals Wizard dialog box, shown in Figure 16-20.

12. **Type a goal for the role displayed in the This Week's Goal box and click Next Role.**

    Repeat this step for each of your defined roles.

13. **Click Next>.**

    An explanation of "big rocks" appears in the Identify Goals Wizard dialog box, shown in Figure 16-21.

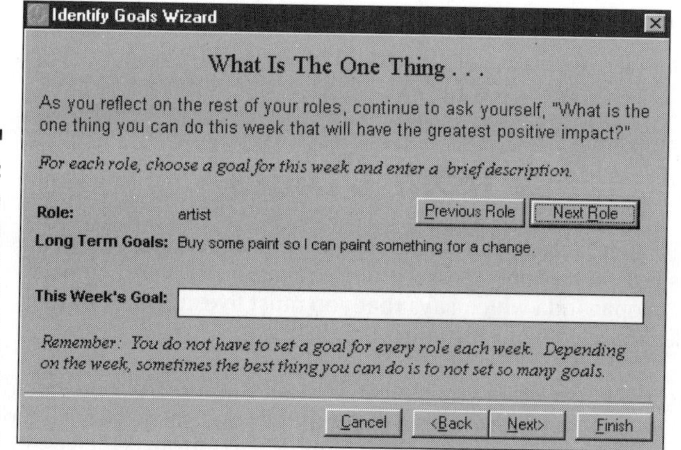

Figure 16-20: Specify one thing you can do this week to have a positive effect on your life.

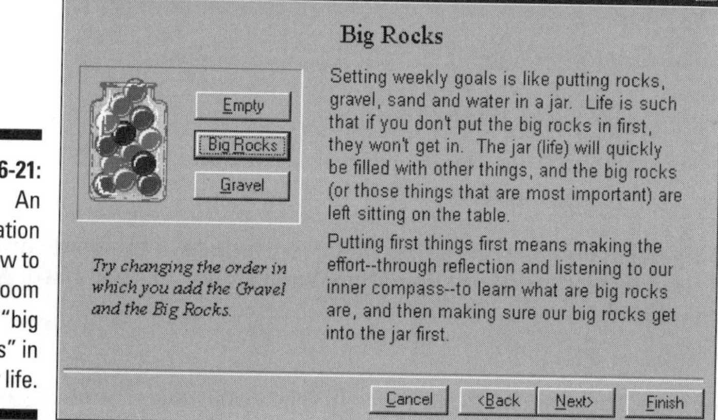

Figure 16-21: An explanation of how to make room for the "big rocks" in your life.

14. **Click Next>.**

    A message about the fourth step, weekly organization, appears in the Identify Goals Wizard dialog box.

15. **Click Next>.**

    An explanation of how to put your big rocks first appears in the Identify Goals Wizard dialog box.

16. **Click Finish.**

    The Seven Habits Wizard dialog box appears again.

17. **Click Finish.**

    Schedule+ shows you your weekly goals in the This Week's Goals box.

18. Click Close.

Schedule+ displays your weekly goals in the To Do (Active) box.

Gaining Wisdom from Others

Albert Einstein's elementary-school teacher believed that Albert was retarded. Thomas Edison had only a third-grade education. Rather than believe the societal propaganda which says that you must live, act, and work in a certain way, take charge of your own direction instead.

Because it's unlikely that you'll receive much support from society in support of your goals, Schedule+ provides a list of quotes and stories from famous people throughout history. By reading these quotes and stories, you'll realize that "idiots" and "imbeciles" have dominated society throughout history and that wisdom and insight have guided people to greatness no matter which period of time in which they live.

To read an inspirational quote or story, follow these steps:

1. **Choose Tools⇨Seven Habits Tools.**

   The Seven Habits Tools dialog box appears (refer to Figure 16-1).

2. **Click the Wisdom tab.**
3. **Double-click a book icon button that corresponds to the quote or story you want to read, such as "Franklin: Doing Good" or "Hubbard: A Declaration."**

   Your chosen selection appears.

4. **Click New Topic to choose another inspirational story, or click Close to return to Schedule+.**

Part V
Storing Information in Microsoft Access

AFTER SPENDING 9 DAYS WITH 12 DIFFERENT VENDORS AND READING 26 BROCHURES, DAVE HAD AN ACUTE ATTACK OF TOXIC OPTION SYNDROME.

In this part . . .

The Professional edition of Microsoft Office 95 comes with Microsoft Access, the most popular relational database program in the world. If you don't have the slightest idea what a relational database is, don't worry. Just remember that Access is a database that lets you store and retrieve information ranging from names and addresses to part numbers and inventory bar codes.

This part of the book shows you how to automate Access and customize it for your own purposes. Need a specialized program for tracking information but don't feel like shelling out hundreds of dollars to buy one? Then learn to customize and program Access to make it obey your commands.

Who knows? With enough practice, you can find out enough about programming Access that you can start creating your own custom programs to sell or give away. And then you can get a better job, thanks to the power of Access.

Chapter 17

Customizing Microsoft Access

In This Chapter

- Customizing the appearance of your toolbars
- Understanding how Access works with your keyboard
- Adjusting the way Access prints your documents

Microsoft Access is a powerful database program; in computer terms, "powerful" means that a program can be difficult to use and understand. To make Access easier to use, take some time to modify the way it looks and works. By changing the Access toolbars and menus to display only the commands you need and use most often, you can make the program seem friendlier than it really is.

Modifying Your Toolbars

Toolbars give you one-click access to common program commands. Because no one at Microsoft knows which commands you want to see on your toolbars, Access simply displays toolbars with the most likely commands shown as icons. Access provides 19 different toolbars that display icons for such tasks as designing tables and drawing forms.

Unless you have absolutely no idea what you're doing, it's unlikely that you'll ever want to display — let alone use — all 19 toolbars in your entire lifetime. Because you may need one or more of the Access toolbars, you can make them appear or disappear, depending on what you need at the time.

To make a toolbar appear or disappear, follow these steps:

1. **Choose View⇨Toolbars.**

   The Toolbars dialog box appears, as shown in Figure 17-1.

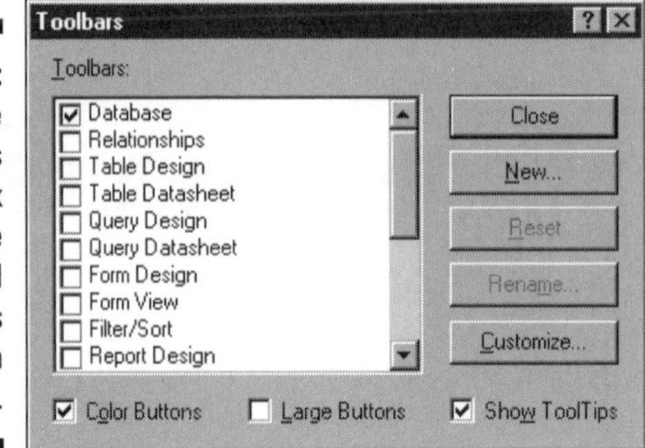

Figure 17-1: The Toolbars dialog box lists the standard toolbars available in Access.

2. **For each toolbar you want displayed, click its check box so that a check mark appears. For each toolbar you want hidden, make sure that the toolbar's check box is empty.**
3. **Click Close.**

Modifying existing toolbars

The quickest way to customize your toolbars is to add, delete, and rearrange the buttons on the existing Access toolbars. By modifying your toolbars, you can cram them full of the buttons you use most often and get rid of the ones you won't use even if your life depended on it.

Because the Access toolbars already contain more buttons than you probably need, you should first remove the ones you don't want. That way, you can make room for adding your own buttons later.

To remove a button from a toolbar, follow these steps:

1. **Choose View⇨Toolbars.**

   The Toolbars dialog box appears (refer to Figure 17-1).
2. **Click Customize.**

   Access displays the Customize Toolbars dialog box, shown in Figure 17-2.
3. **Highlight the toolbar you want to modify and click its check box so that a check mark appears.**
4. **Point to the button you want to remove from the toolbar, hold down the left mouse button, and drag the icon anywhere off the toolbar, as shown in Figure 17-3.**
5. **Release the left mouse button.**

   Access immediately removes the button from the toolbar.
6. **Click Close.**

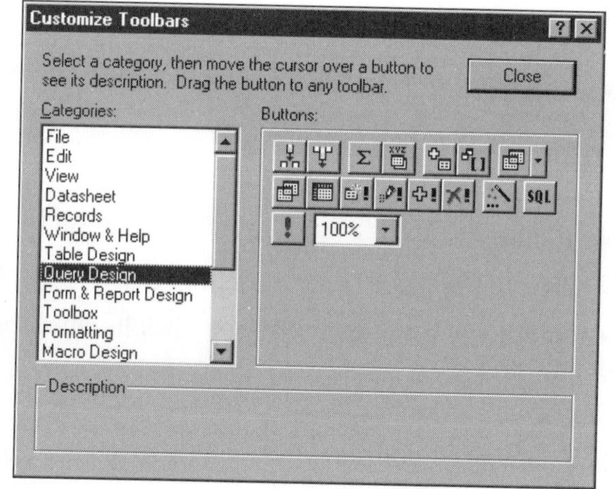

Figure 17-2: The Customize Toolbars dialog box.

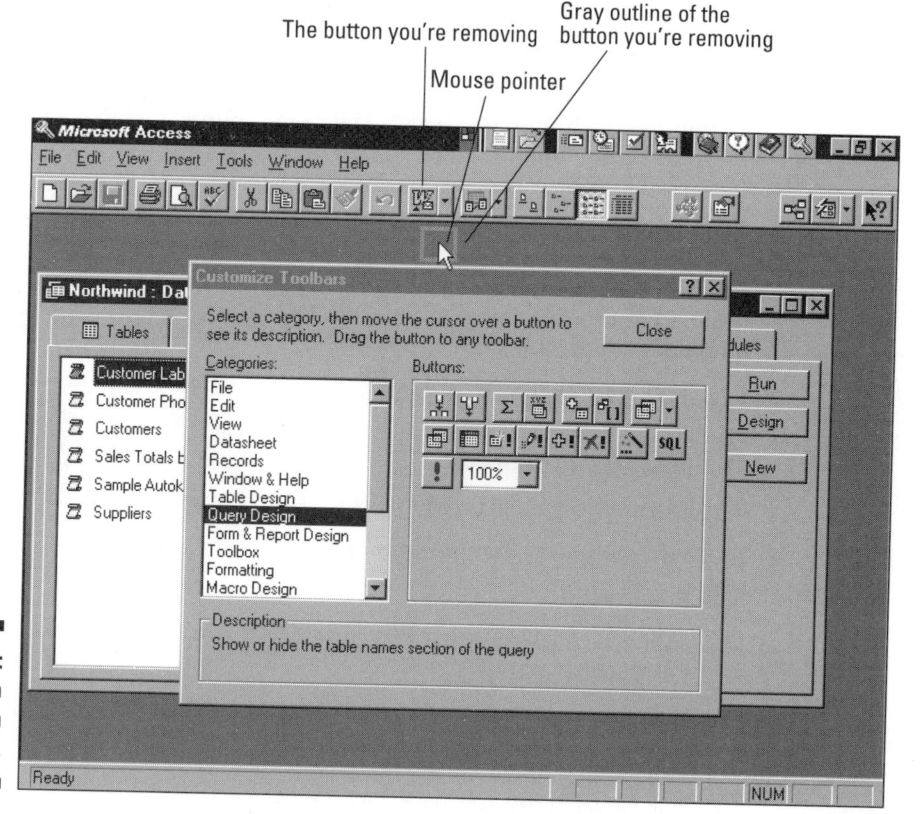

Figure 17-3: Removing a button from a toolbar.

You can add your own buttons to a toolbar, but if a toolbar is already full of buttons, it may already look pretty crowded. As a general rule, you should remove all the useless buttons from a toolbar before you begin adding your own buttons to the toolbar.

To add a button to a toolbar, follow these steps:

1. **Choose View⇨Toolbars.**

   The Toolbars dialog box appears (refer to Figure 17-1).

2. **Highlight the toolbar you want to modify and click its check box so that a check mark appears.**

3. **Click Customize.**

   Access displays the toolbar you chose and then displays a Customize Toolbars dialog box (refer to Figure 17-2).

4. **Click a category displayed in the Categories list box.**

   To add a datasheet command to a toolbar, for example, click Datasheet in the Categories list box. Access displays some buttons in the Buttons group.

5. **Point to the button you want to add, hold down the left mouse button, and drag the button to the toolbar on which you want it to appear, as shown in Figure 17-4.**

6. **Release the mouse button and click Close.**

If you mess up your toolbars beyond recognition, don't panic: You can reset them to their original state. Because you can always reset a toolbar, feel free to experiment and customize your toolbars as much as you want.

To reset a toolbar, follow these steps:

1. **Choose View⇨Toolbars.**

   The Toolbars dialog box appears (refer to Figure 17-1).

2. **Highlight the toolbar you want to reset.**

3. **Click Reset.**

   A dialog box asks whether you're sure that you want to reset the toolbar, as shown in Figure 17-5.

4. **Click Yes.**

   Access resets your toolbar to its original state.

5. **Click Close in the Toolbars dialog box.**

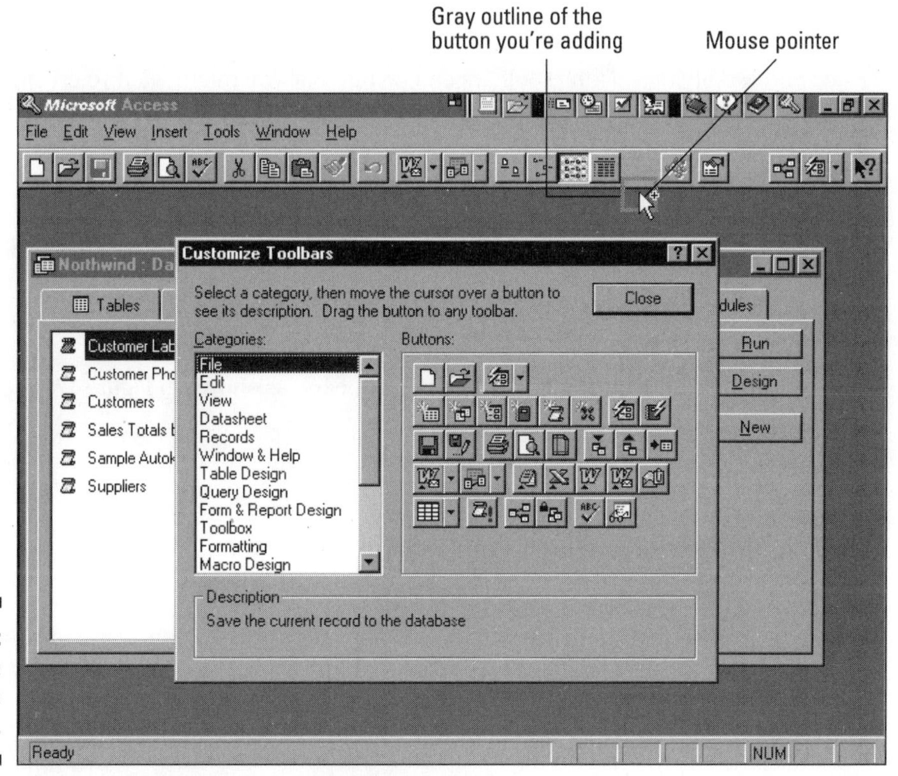

Figure 17-4: Adding a button to a toolbar.

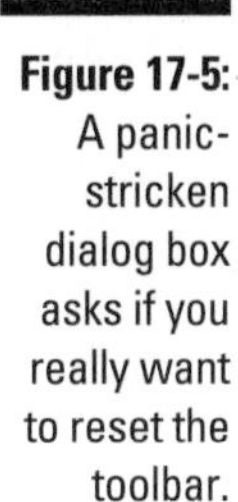

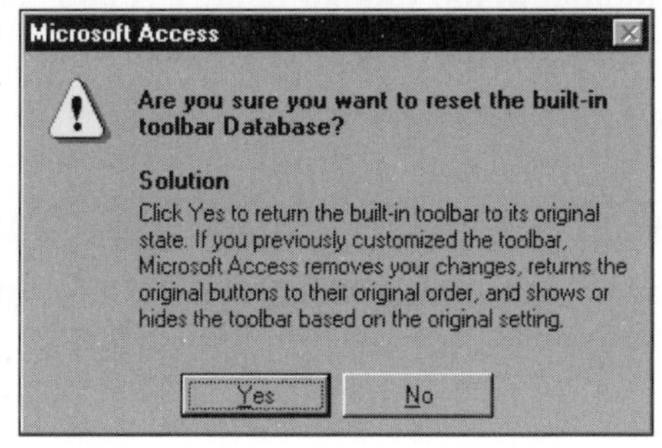

Figure 17-5: A panic-stricken dialog box asks if you really want to reset the toolbar.

If you reset a toolbar, Access dumps any buttons you added and replaces any buttons you deleted. So before you reset a toolbar, make sure that you really want to take such drastic action; adding or deleting buttons individually may be easier in the long run.

Making your own toolbars

Modifying existing toolbars can be fun, but you might want to create your own custom toolbars instead. That way, you can combine your favorite commands in a toolbar that's custom designed just for you.

To make your own toolbar, follow these steps:

1. **Choose View⇨Toolbars.**

   The Toolbars dialog box appears (refer to Figure 17-1).

2. **Click New.**

   The New Toolbar dialog box appears, as shown in Figure 17-6.

Figure 17-6: You can choose a new name for your toolbar in this dialog box.

3. **Type a name for your toolbar in the Toolbar name box and click OK.**

   The Toolbars dialog box is displayed next to your toolbar, which appears as a floating toolbar, as shown in Figure 17-7.

4. **Click Customize.**

   The Customize Toolbars dialog box appears (refer to Figure 17-2).

5. **Click a category displayed in the Categories list box.**

   To add an editing command to a toolbar, for example, click Edit in the Categories list box. Access displays some buttons in the Buttons group.

6. **Point to the button you want to add, hold down the left mouse button, drag the button to the toolbar on which you want it to appear, and release the mouse button, as shown in Figure 17-8.**

7. **Click Close when you finish filling your toolbar with buttons.**

   Your newly created toolbar appears on-screen, ready to use.

To move your floating toolbar, point to its title bar, hold down the left mouse button, drag the mouse to where you want the toolbar to appear, and release the mouse button.

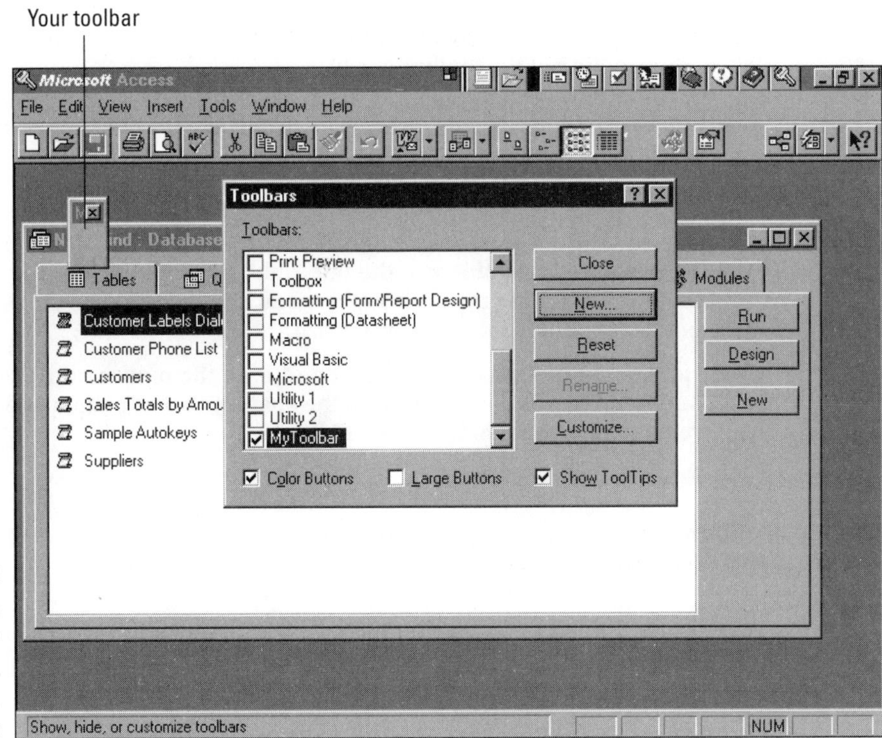

Figure 17-7: Your newly created toolbar.

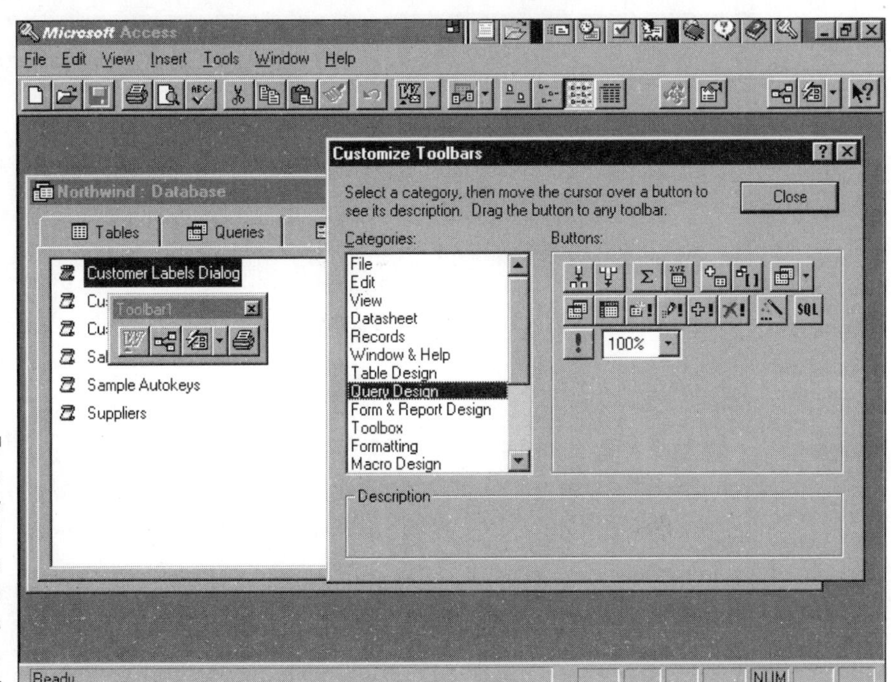

Figure 17-8: Your newly created toolbar with some buttons on it.

Changing the shape of a toolbar simply makes it look nice on-screen; it doesn't affect the function of the toolbar one bit.

If you don't like the shape of your newly created toolbar, just use your mouse to change it.

To change the shape of your toolbar, follow these steps:

1. **Move the mouse pointer to the left, right, top, or bottom edge of the toolbar so that the mouse pointer turns into a double-headed arrow that points left and right or up and down.**
2. **Hold down the left mouse button and drag the mouse until the gray outline of the toolbar turns into the shape you want (such as a wide rectangle), as shown in Figure 17-9.**
3. **Release the mouse button.**

You can delete from the face of the earth any of your own toolbar creations, but you can never delete any of the Access toolbars.

You can never delete any of the original Access toolbars, but you can reset them. Resetting an original Access toolbar wipes out any changes made to it.

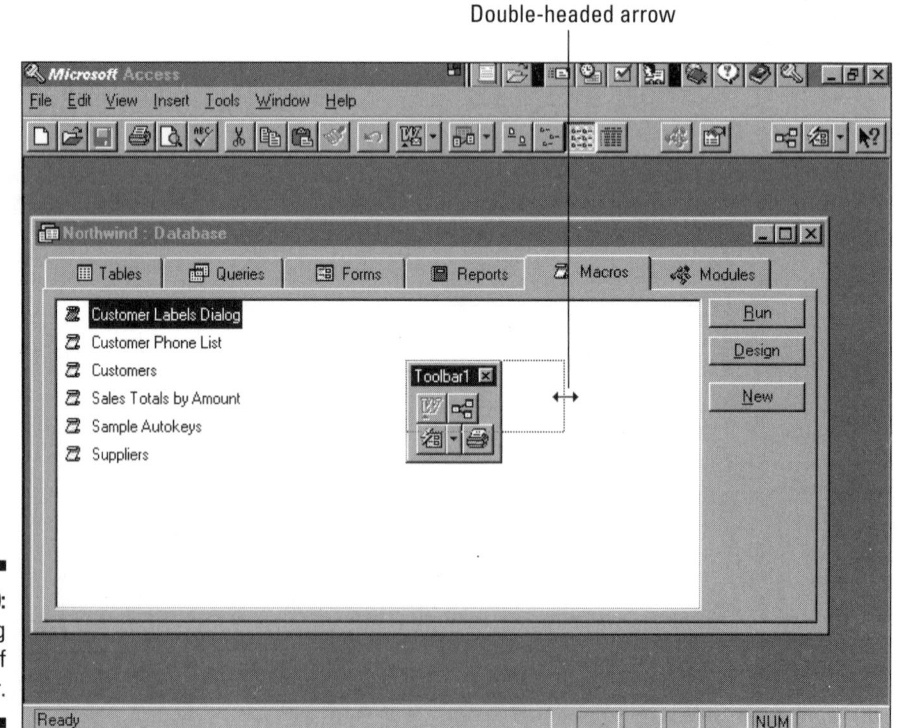

Figure 17-9: Changing the shape of a toolbar.

To delete one of your toolbars, follow these steps:

1. **Choose View⇨Toolbars.**

   The Toolbars dialog box appears (refer to Figure 17-1).

2. **Highlight the toolbar you want to delete.**
3. **Click Delete.**

   If you highlight one of Access's original toolbars, you won't see the Delete button. The Delete button replaces the Reset button the moment you highlight one of your own toolbars that you created.

   A dialog box appears and asks whether you really want to delete your toolbar.

4. **Click Yes.**
5. **Click Close in the Toolbars dialog box.**

Make sure that you really want to delete one of your toolbars. After you delete one, you can't undelete it if you change your mind later.

Displaying toolbars in different ways

For the sheer joy of giving you more options that can clog your mind and make it look like you're doing something productive at your computer when you're really just goofing around, Access gives you different ways to display its toolbars:

- As a long, skinny, horizontal strip at the top of your screen
- As a floating toolbar

You can change the way a toolbar appears just by double-clicking any gray portion of the toolbar. (Don't double-click an button by mistake.) The moment you double-click a toolbar, it changes its shape from a horizontal strip to a floating toolbar and vice versa. Figure 17-10 shows you what the Database toolbar looks like as a floating toolbar.

Making Access Work with Your Keyboard

When someone uses your Access database to type or search for information, their keyboard serves two purposes:

- Lets them type information into a database
- Moves the cursor from one field to another

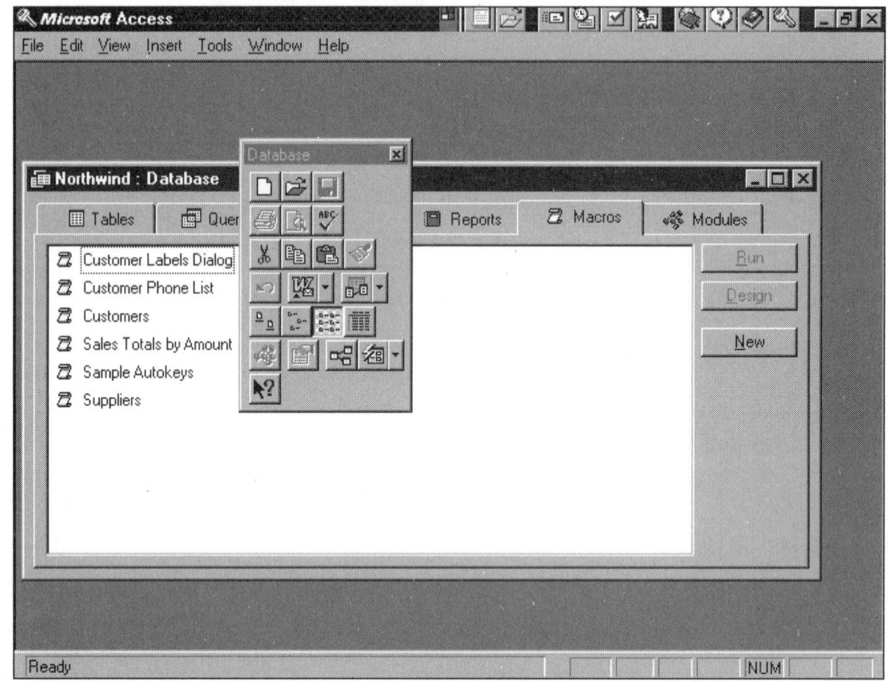

Figure 17-10: The Database toolbar appears as a floating toolbar.

A *field* is simply a box in which you can type information, such as your name, address, phone number, part number, or total quantity.

To give you limited control over the way you can move your cursor, Access lets you customize your keyboard in three ways:

- Whether the arrow key moves the cursor to a different field or within the same field
- Whether pressing the Enter key moves the cursor to a different field or to a different record
- Where Access displays the cursor when it moves to a different field

Many data-entry typists can type rapidly, so they tend to prefer using the keyboard to manuever around a database instead of using the mouse. Make sure that pressing an arrow or Enter key moves the cursor to the next logical field. For example, after someone types their name in a Name field, the next logical step is for them to type an address. Therefore, most users expect that pressing an arrow or Enter key should move the cursor from the Name field to the Address field.

To customize your keyboard, follow these steps:

1. **Choose Tools⇨Options.**

   The Options dialog box appears.

2. **Click the Keyboard tab.**

3. **Click one of the option buttons in the Move After Enter group:**

   - **Don't Move**
   - **Next Field**
   - **Next Record**

   Most database programs usually move the cursor to the next field after the user presses Enter. If your users are accustomed to the Enter key doing something different, however, you can choose either the Don't Move or Next Record option button instead.

4. **Click one of the option buttons in the Arrow Key Behavior group:**

   - **Next Field**
   - **Next Character**

   The Next field option button moves the cursor to the next field if the user presses the right-arrow key. However, this can be annoying if the user is trying to edit a field, because the user can never use the arrow keys to edit a field and must use the mouse instead. If your users complain that editing fields is too clumsy with the mouse, you may want to choose the Next Character option button.

5. **Click one of the option buttons in the Behavior Entering Field:**

   - **Select Entire Field**
   - **Go to Start of Field**
   - **Go to End of Field**

   The Select Entire Field option button simply highlights any data stored in the next field. So if the user even presses one key, all the data previously stored in the field gets wiped out and replaced with the key the user just pressed. If you have large chunks of data stored in your fields and don't trust your users not to accidentally wipe out data at the touch of a button, you may want to choose the Go to Start or Go to End of Field option buttons instead.

6. **Click OK.**

No matter which keyboard options you choose, you can always selectively edit existing data by using your mouse to highlight text.

Changing the Way Access Prints

As with most computer programs, it's not enough to type information and save it on disk for posterity. You eventually have to print your data so that other people can look at it without crowding around your computer screen and getting in your way.

To change the way your database prints, follow these steps:

1. **Choose File⇨Page Preview.**

   Access shows you how your database will look if you decide it print it now, as shown in Figure 17-11.

2. **Choose File⇨Page Setup.**

   The Page Setup dialog box appears.

3. **Click the Margins tab and type any new measurements for your top, bottom, left, and right margins.**
4. **If you don't want Access to print lines and other decorative items, click the Print Data Only check box so that a check mark appears.**
5. **Click the Page tab.**
6. **In the dialog box that's displayed, make any changes to the size or orientation of the paper you use to print your Access data.**
7. **Click the Layout tab.**
8. **In the dialog box that's displayed, make any changes to the way you want Access to print your data on the page.**
9. **Click OK.**

   Access displays your changes in the Print Preview window. Now you're ready to either print or repeat steps 2 through 8 to adjust the way Access prints your data. Have fun!

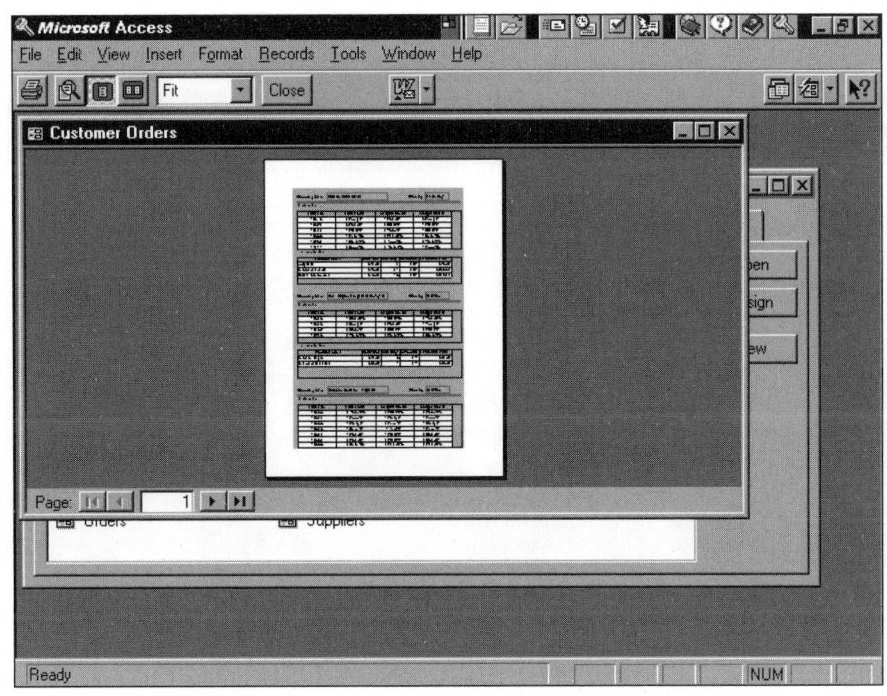

Figure 17-11: The print preview of a typical database.

Chapter 18

Automating Microsoft Access

In This Chapter

- Creating macros to carry out boring or repetitive tasks
- Using command buttons to make Access perform tasks
- Programming Visual Basic to automate Access
- Converting Access databases into Web pages

Why should you work any harder than you have to when you have a $2,000 computer (or a summer intern willing to work for minimum wage) ready to do your work for you automatically? Computers are supposed to make our lives easier, so you'll be happy to know that you can automate Microsoft Access to a limited degree. You can focus on your important work and let Access worry about the trivial details, such as typing state abbreviations and part-number codes.

Depending on how much freedom you want to give Access, you can use three items to automate Access:

- Macros
- Command buttons
- A real-life programming language: Visual Basic

Which one should you choose? If you just want to automate Access for your personal use, create a macro or a command button. If you plan to automate Access for others, use a command button or Visual Basic. If you really need to create something complicated that requires writing your own program, use Visual Basic.

Making Macros

A macro acts like a tape recorder. First, you record your keystrokes on disk. Then you can "play back" those same keystrokes at the touch of a button. Macros let you perform repetitive or complicated tasks one time and then tell

Access, "Remember that really long series of keystrokes I asked you to record three months ago? I want you to perform those keystrokes all over again while I go out to lunch."

Creating a macro

At its simplest level, a macro can automatically type text for you, such as *Massachusetts,* or perform an action such as opening a form and printing it. Access lets you create macros that can perform all types of tasks; here are just a few of the more common macro uses:

- Simulate someone typing at the keyboard
- Choose a command from the Access pull-down menus
- Set the value of another field

Simulating someone typing at the keyboard

Macros that simulate someone's typing at a keyboard are most useful for getting Access to type long, repetitive text for you so that you don't have to do it yourself. For example, if you have to type a long-winded name, such as *The American Corporation for the Creation of Political Dishonesty,* over and over again, you'd probably go slowly mad at your computer. Such a task would be perfectly suited for your computer; your computer can't lose its mind, so it's perfectly happy to perform dull, repetitive tasks.

To create a macro that simulates typing at the keyboard, follow these steps:

1. **Open the database window and click the Macros tab, shown in Figure 18-1.**

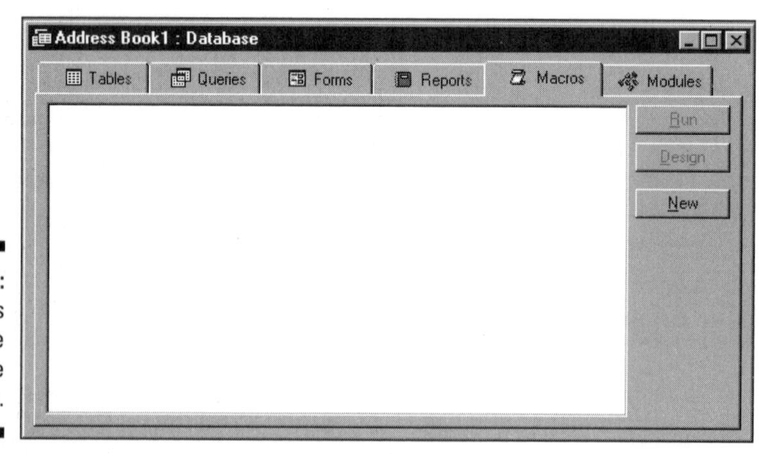

Figure 18-1: The Macros tab in the database window.

2. **Click New.**

   A Macro window appears, as shown in Figure 18-2.

3. **Click the gray downward-pointing arrow in the Action list box and choose SendKeys.**

   A Keystrokes and Wait box appears (see Figure 18-2).

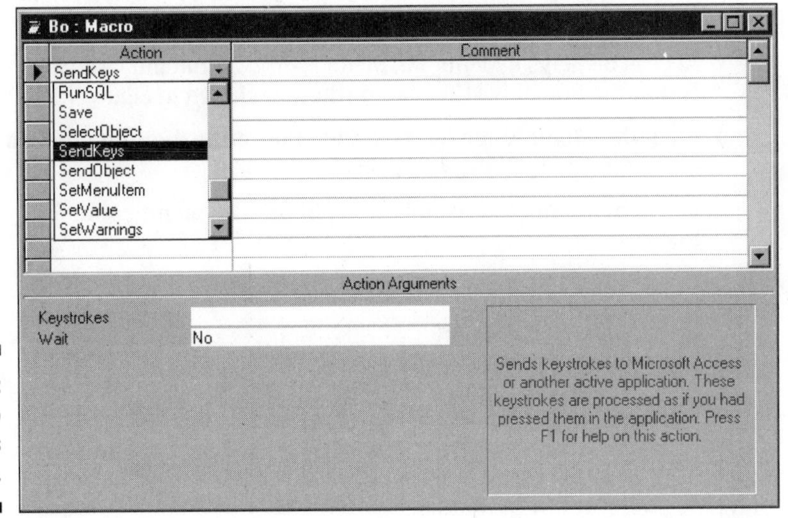

Figure 18-2: The Macro window is ready to go.

4. **In the Keystrokes box, type the text you want the macro to type for you.**

   You can type as many as 256 characters.

5. **Click the Wait list box and choose Yes or No.**

   Choose Yes only if your macro types text too rapidly for your database to handle.

6. **Click the close box in the Macro window.**

Choosing an Access menu command

Sometimes you may need a macro that can choose one or more Access menu commands for you so that you don't have to waste time choosing them yourself. If you want to transfer your Access data to an Excel worksheet, for example, you have to choose Tools➪OfficeLinks➪Analyze It With MS Excel. Clumsy? Yes, so let an Access macro do it for you instead.

To create a macro that chooses menu commands, follow these steps:

1. **Open the database window and click the Macros tab (refer to Figure 18-1).**
2. **Click New.**

   A Macro window appears (refer to Figure 18-2).
3. **Click the gray downward-pointing arrow in the Action list box and choose DoMenuItem.**

   Access displays a Menu Bar, Menu Name, Command, and Subcommand box at the bottom of the macro window, shown in Figure 18-3.
4. **Click the Menu Name list box and choose the menu name you want to use, such as File, Edit, or Tools.**
5. **Click the Command list box and choose the menu command you want to use.**

Figure 18-3: In this window, create a macro that chooses a menu command.

6. **If the menu command you chose displays a submenu, click the Subcommand list box and choose the menu command you want to use.**
7. **Click the close box in the Macro window.**

Setting the value of another field

Data-entry can be the most tedious work in the world, which explains why you see so many classified ads looking for data-entry people. To help make data-entry a little less repetitive (and boring), Access enables you to use macros to set the values of other fields.

For example, many order forms list two addresses: a billing address and a shipping address. Nine times out of ten, the two addresses are identical, yet nine times out of ten, you have to type each address twice. This not only increases the chance of making a mistake but makes you feel as if your job is essentially useless, as well.

To avoid this problem, you can have Access copy the billing address into the shipping address by using a macro. That way, you don't have to keep typing repetitive data.

To create a macro that can set the value of another field based on certain data, follow these steps:

1. **Open the database window and click the Forms tab.**
2. **Click a form and then click Design.**
3. **Click a text box (such as the City text box) in which you want to start your macro.**
4. **Press the right mouse button.**

   A pop-up menu appears, as shown in Figure 18-4.

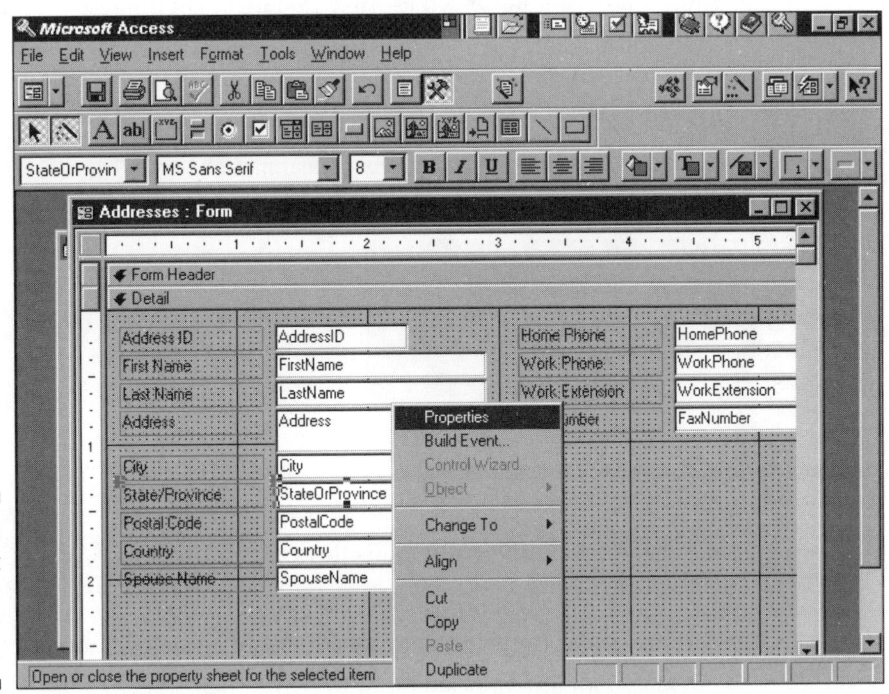

Figure 18-4: The right mouse button pop-up menu.

5. **Click Properties.**

   A Text Box dialog box appears.

6. **Click the Event tab, shown in Figure 18-5.**

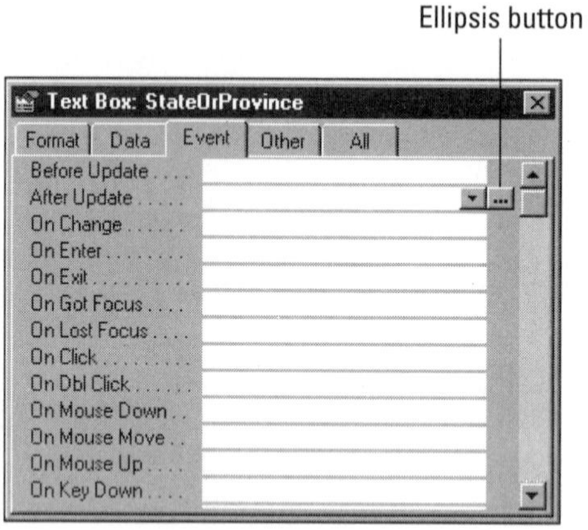

Figure 18-5: The Event tab in the Text Box dialog box.

7. **Click an event box, such as After Update or On Change.**

   Access displays a gray button with an ellipsis (three dots) on it (refer to Figure 18-5).

8. **Click the ellipsis button.**

   The Choose Builder dialog box appears, as shown in Figure 18-6.

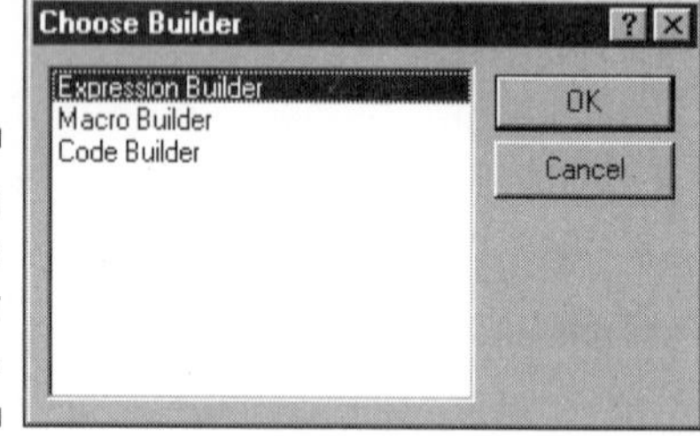

Figure 18-6: The Choose Builder dialog box.

9. **Click Macro Builder and then click OK.**

   The Save As dialog box appears, as shown in Figure 18-7.

10. **Type a name for your macro in the Macro Name box and click OK.**

    A Macro window appears (refer to Figure 18-2).

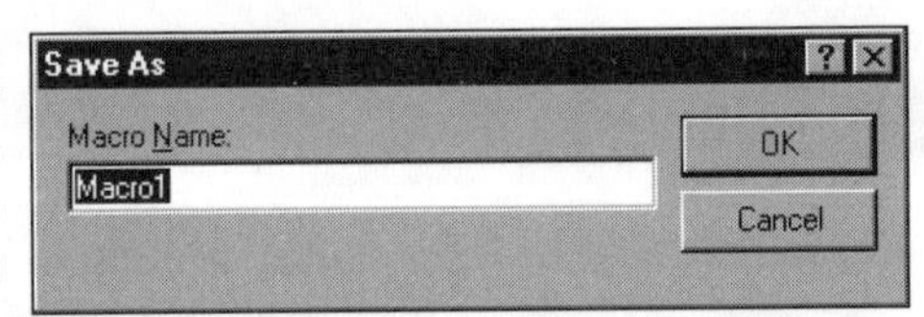

Figure 18-7: Choose a name for your macro in the Save As dialog box.

11. **Click the gray downward-pointing arrow in the Action list box and choose SetValue.**

    Access displays Item and Expression boxes in the middle of the Macro window, as shown in Figure 18-8.

12. **Click the Item box and type the field (surrounded by square brackets) you want the macro to change, such as [ShipFirst], as shown in Figure 18-9.**

13. **Click the Expression box and type the field that contains the data you want to appear in the field you chose in step 12. In Figure 18-9, the data stored in the [FirstName] field will appear in the [ShipFirst] field.**

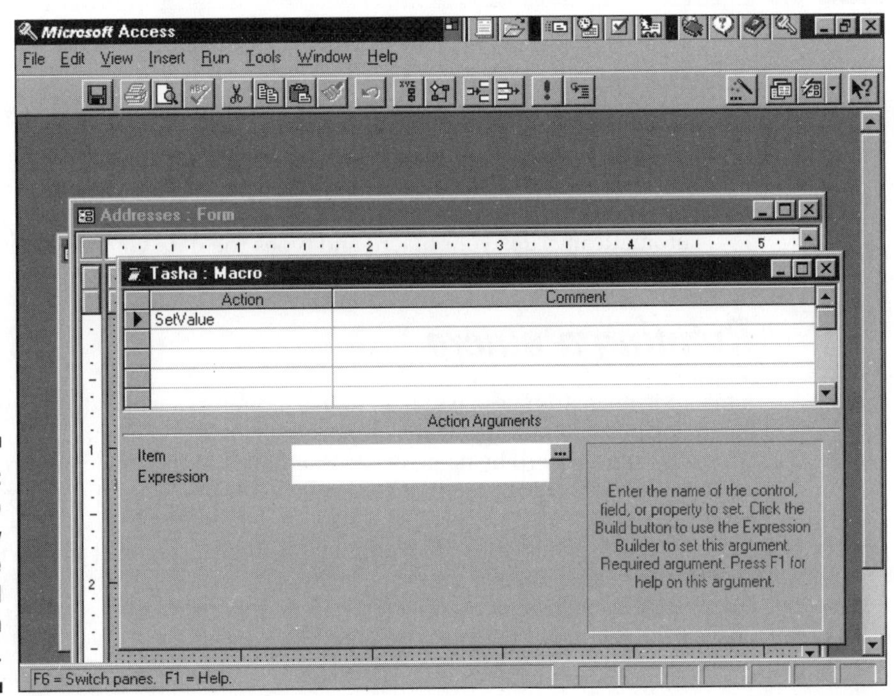

Figure 18-8: The Macro window displays the Item and Expression boxes.

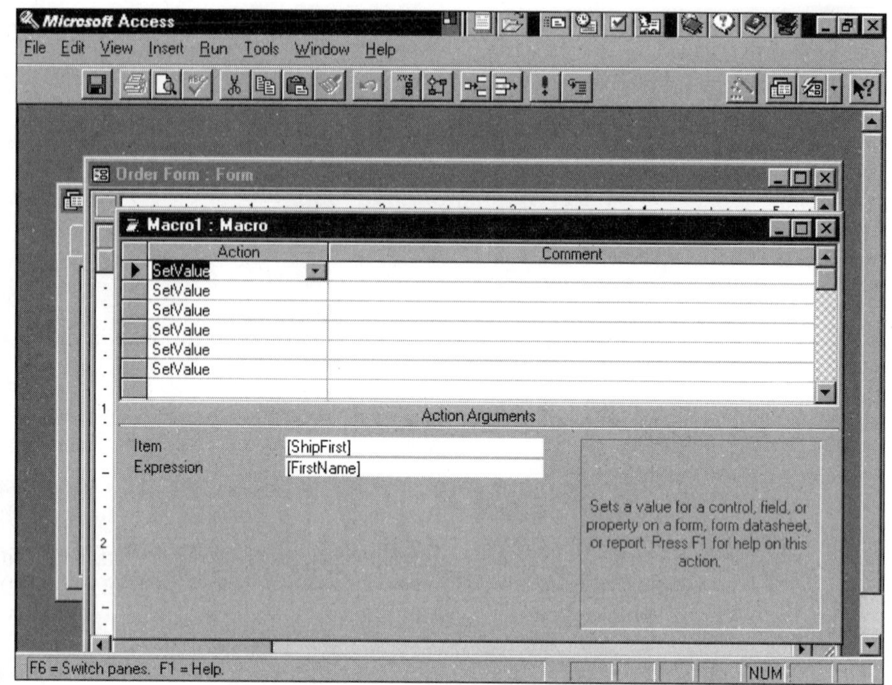

Figure 18-9: Define a field and its data to change.

14. **Click the close box in the Macro window.**
15. **Click the close box in the Text Box window.**
16. **Click the close box in the Form design window.**

    The next time you enter data in the field you chose in step 3, Access automatically runs your macro and types the data you defined in step 13.

Running a macro

A macro is no good unless you plan to use it once in a while. To give you as much flexibility as possible when it comes to running your macro, you can choose to run a macro by name or by assigning it to a specific keystroke (such as Ctrl+3) and then pressing that keystroke when you want the macro to run.

Some macros, such as those that simulate someone typing at the keyboard, require the cursor to be in a specific location before you run them. If you run a macro with the cursor in the wrong location, the macro may run blissfully unaware that it might be typing data in the wrong place.

Choosing a macro to run by name

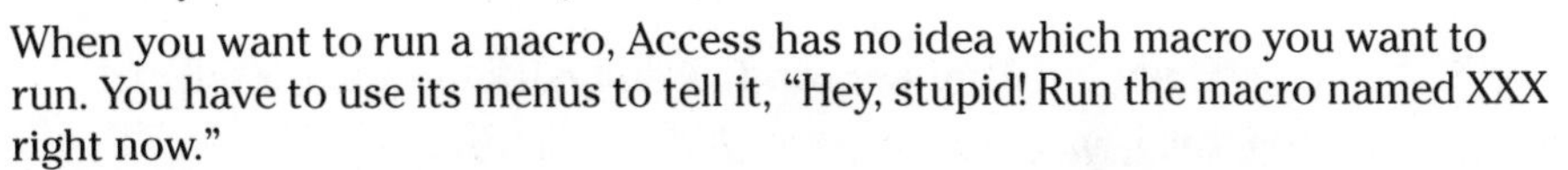

When you want to run a macro, Access has no idea which macro you want to run. You have to use its menus to tell it, "Hey, stupid! Run the macro named XXX right now."

To run a macro by name, follow these steps:

1. **Choose Tools⇨Macro.**

   The Run Macro dialog box appears, as shown in Figure 18-10.

2. **Click the Macro Name list box and choose the macro you want to run.**
3. **Click OK.**

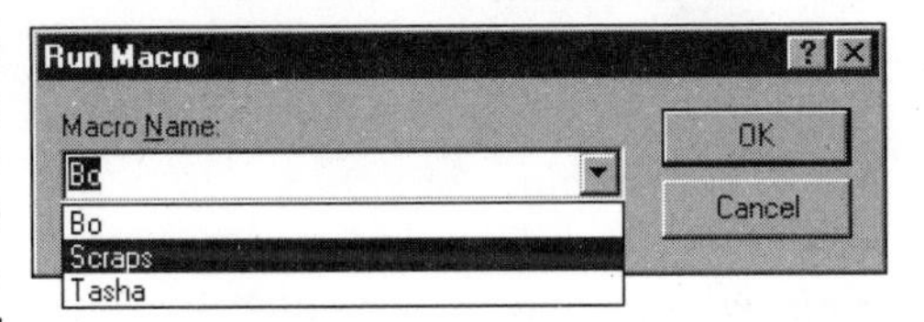

Figure 18-10: In this dialog box, choose a macro to run.

Running a macro from a keystroke combination

Although you can always run a macro by choosing it by name, it may be more convenient to assign the macro to a keystroke combination first. Then you can quickly type the keystroke combination (such as Ctrl+2), and the macro runs right away. The main drawback to running a macro by using a keystroke combination is that you have to remember which keystroke combination you assigned to your macro. Table 18-1 lists some of the more common types of keystrokes you can assign to a macro.

Table 18-1 Common Types of Keystrokes Assigned to Macros

Keystroke Combination	*Example*	*How Access Interprets the Keystroke*
Ctrl+Letter key	Ctrl+Q	^Q
Ctrl+Number key	Ctrl+5	^5
Any function key	F11	{F11}
Ctrl+Any function key	Ctrl+F12	^{F12}
Shift+Any function key	Shift+F4	+{F4}

To assign a keystroke combination to a new macro, follow these steps:

1. **Open the database window and click the Macros tab.**
2. **Click New.**

   The Macro window appears, as shown in Figure 18-11.
3. **Click the Macro Names button in the Macro toolbar.**

   The Macro Name column magically appears, as shown in Figure 18-12.
4. **Click the top of the Macro Name column and type the keystroke combination you want to assign, such as ^4 for Ctrl+4 or +{F3} for Shift+F3.**
5. **Click the Action list box, choose an action (such as SendKeys or DoMenuItem), and then choose any additional options to define your macro.**
6. **Click the close box in the Macro window.**

   A dialog box appears, asking whether you want to save your macro.
7. **Click Yes.**

   A Save As dialog box appears.
8. **Type** AutoKeys **in the Macro Name box and then click OK.**

   Your macro is ready to use.

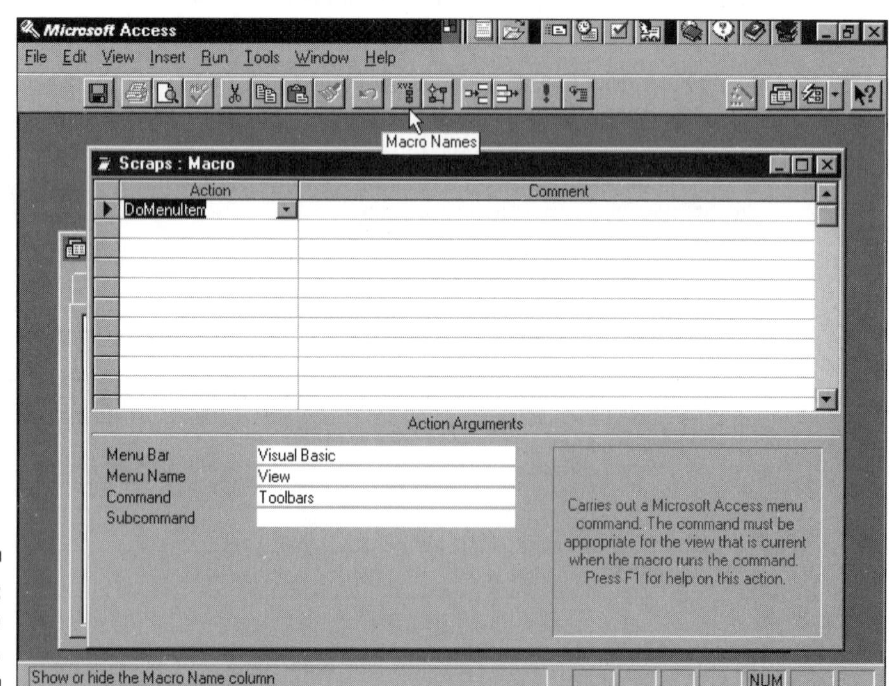

Figure 18-11: The Macro window.

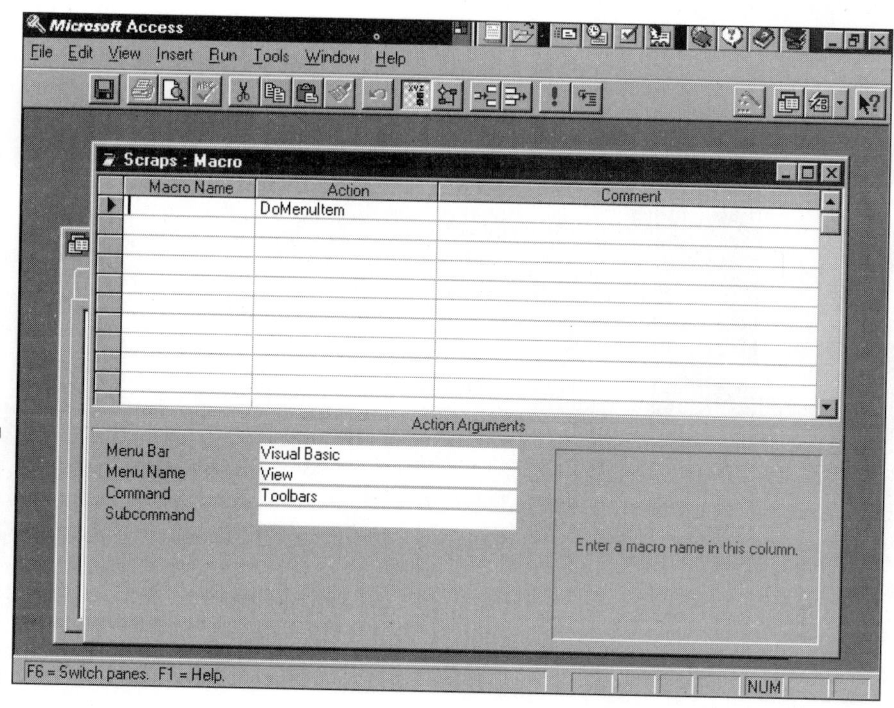

Figure 18-12: The Macro window now displays the Macro Name column.

Every macro assigned to a unique keystroke combination must be stored in the macro group called AutoKeys. The AutoKeys macro group simply stores all your macros that run when you press its keystroke combination. You must separate each macro on its own line in the AutoKeys Macro window, as shown in Figure 18-13.

Deleting a macro

No matter how useful a macro may be, the time comes when you want to delete it. To delete a macro, follow these steps:

1. **Open the database window and click the Macros tab.**
2. **Point to the macro you want to delete and click the right mouse button.**

   A pop-up menu appears, as shown in Figure 18-14.
3. **Click Delete.**

   A dialog box appears, asking whether you really want to delete your macro.
4. **Click Yes.**

If you delete a macro by mistake, immediately press Ctrl+Z to make Access recover it for you.

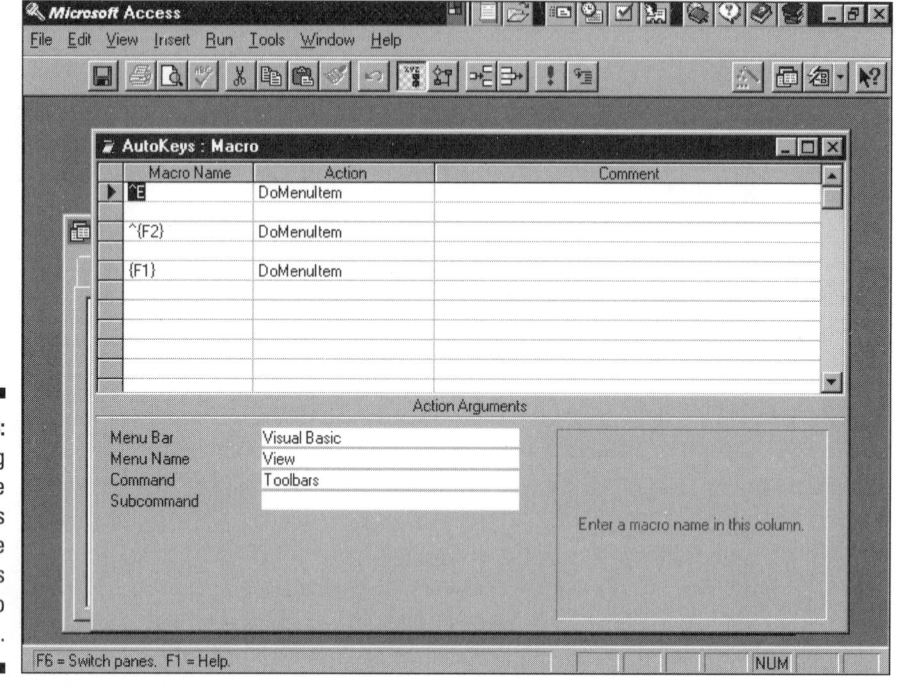

Figure 18-13: Storing multiple macros in the AutoKeys macro group.

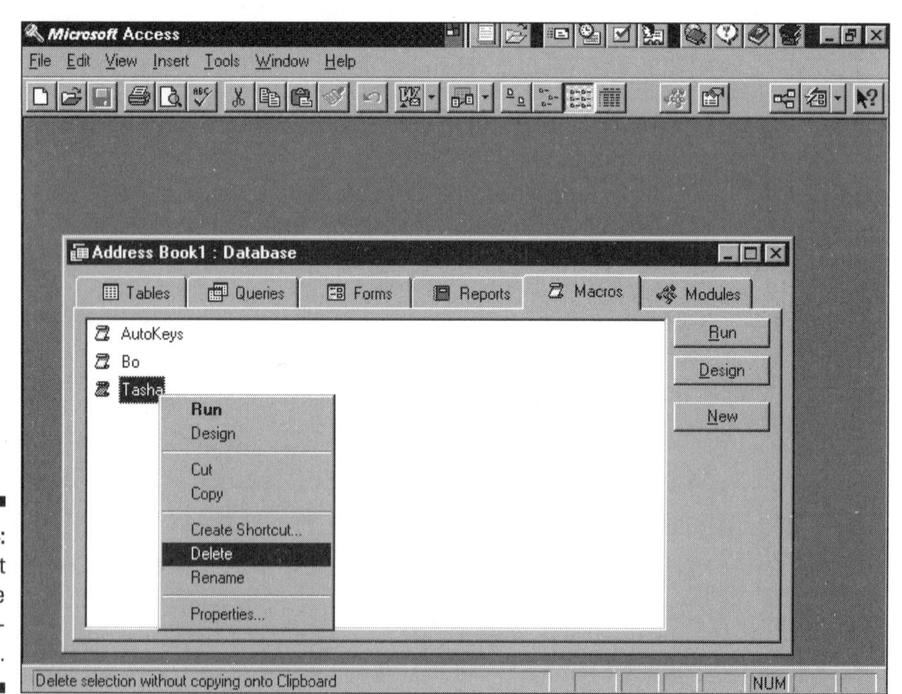

Figure 18-14: The right mouse button pop-up menu.

Using Command Buttons

Command buttons are nothing more than a button you can click. The moment you click a command button, Access does something, such as print a record, delete a record, or run a macro. By sprinkling command buttons on your forms, you can choose a command by clicking the command button instead of wading through pull-down menus and looking for the command you need.

Creating a command button

You can create a command button only while Access is in Form design view. Although you can clutter a form with as many command buttons as you want, it's a good idea to use them sparingly and arrange them neatly so that they look nice.

To create a command button, follow these steps:

1. **Open the database window and click the Forms tab.**
2. **Click the form you want to use and click Design.**

   Access displays your form in design view.
3. **Choose View⇨Toolbox.**

   The Toolbox toolbar appears, as shown in Figure 18-15. (If a check mark appears next to the Toolbox command, skip this step.)
4. **Click the Command Button button.**
5. **Move the mouse to the location at which you want to place your command button. Then hold down the left mouse button, drag the mouse to draw your command button, and release the mouse button.**

   Access draws your command button and displays the Command Button Wizard dialog box, as shown in Figure 18-16.
6. **Click a category in the Categories list box.**
7. **Click an action in the Actions list box.**
8. **Click Next>.**

   Another Command Button Wizard dialog box appears, asking whether you want text or a picture on your command button, as shown in Figure 18-17.
9. **Click either the Text or Picture radio button and choose the text or picture you want to appear on your command button.**

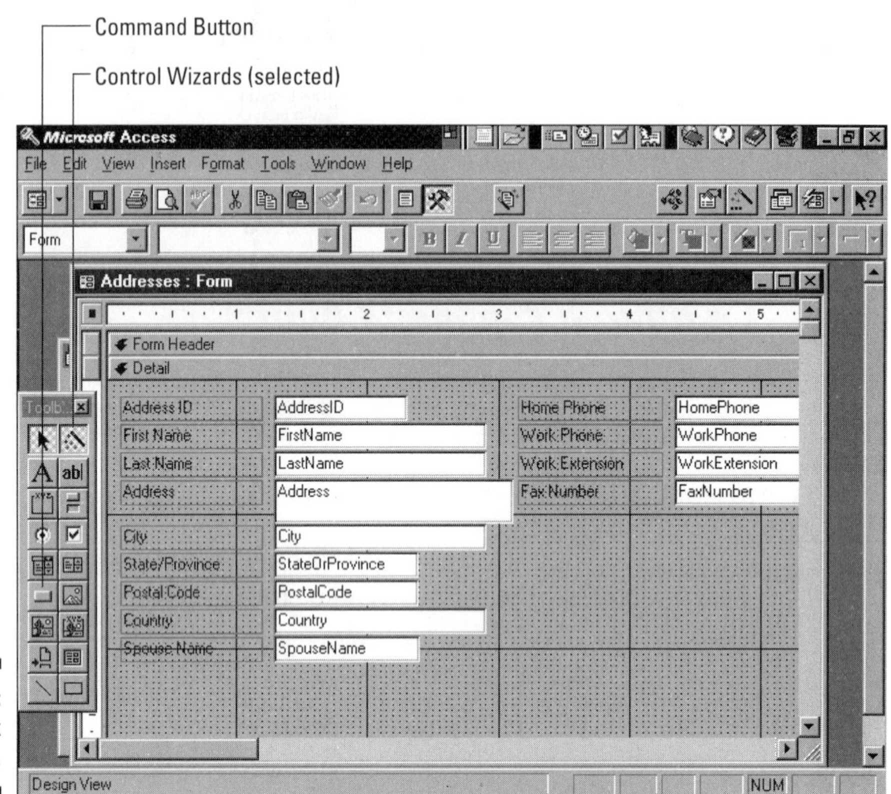

Figure 18-15: The Toolbox toolbar.

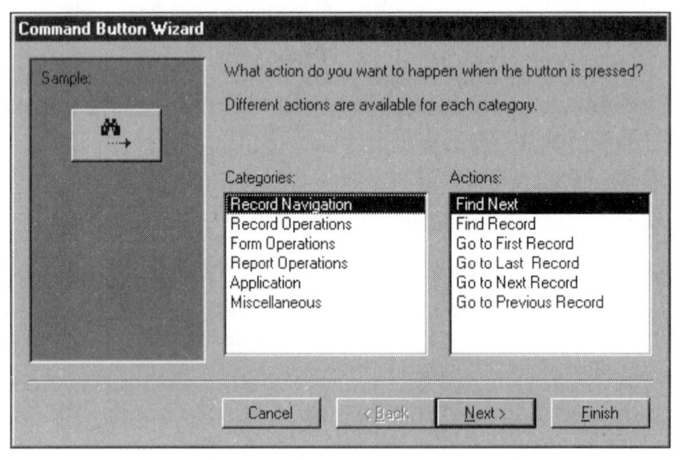

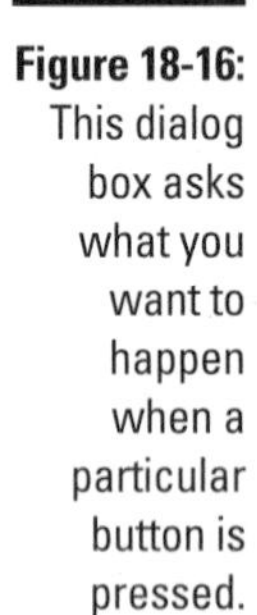

Figure 18-16: This dialog box asks what you want to happen when a particular button is pressed.

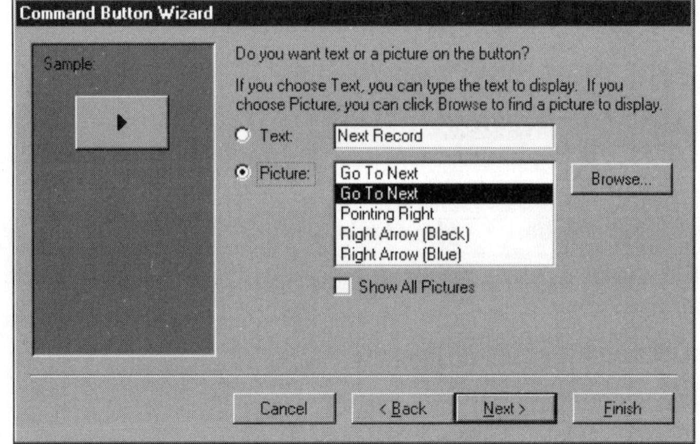

Figure 18-17: Specify whether you want text or a picture displayed on the button.

10. **Click Next>.**

    A third Command Button Wizard dialog box appears, asking for a name to give your command button, as shown in Figure 18-18.

11. **Type a name and click Finish.**

    Access displays the command button on your form.

12. **Click the close box in the Form design window.**

    A dialog box appears, asking whether you want to save your changes.

13. **Click Yes.**

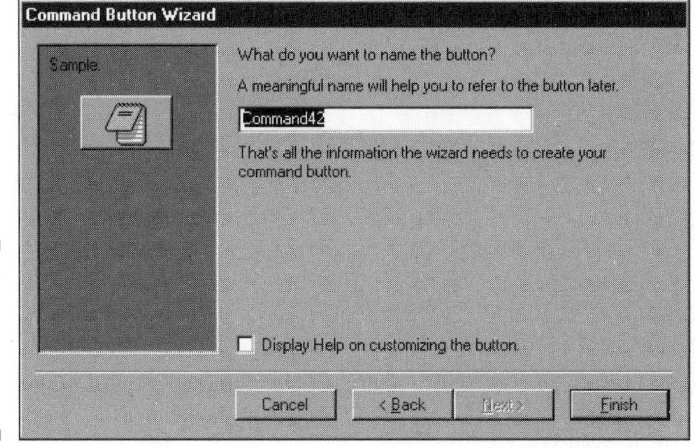

Figure 18-18: Give the button a meaningful name.

Deleting a command button

Because you can always add a command button to a form, it makes sense that you can also delete a command button at any time.

To delete a command button, follow these steps:

1. **Open the database window and click the Forms tab.**
2. **Click the form that contains the command button you want to delete and then click Design.**

   Access displays your form in design view.
3. **Click the command button you want to delete.**

   Access displays gray handles around the command button.
4. **Press Delete.**

   The command button disappears.

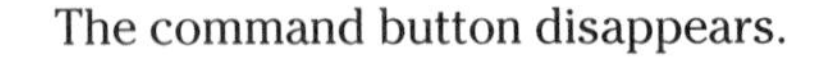

If you delete a command button by mistake, press Ctrl+Z right away to bring it back again.

Real Programming with Visual Basic

Visual Basic is a full-blown programming language. In fact, many people have created commercial-quality programs using Visual Basic and sold them for thousands of dollars to unsuspecting government agencies. For the ultimate in power and flexibility (not to mention frustration and tedium), Visual Basic is the most powerful way to automate Access.

The two faces of Visual Basic

Microsoft sells a separate language compiler called Visual Basic, which lets you write general-purpose programs, such as games, utilities, or even databases. If you want to write different types of programs, you have to buy a copy of Visual Basic.

If you only want to write custom databases, it's easier (not to mention cheaper, especially if you already own a copy of Access) just to use the version of Visual Basic that Microsoft included inside Access.

So when someone mentions "Visual Basic," they could be talking about Visual Basic (the language compiler that you have to buy separately) or Visual Basic (the programming language that comes free inside Access).

When this book uses the term *Visual Basic,* it's referring to the version of Visual Basic inside Access.

Although you can create supercomplicated programs by using Visual Basic, most Visual Basic programs consist of two parts:

- Command buttons
- Event procedures

Command buttons make it easy for someone to use your database without using a single Access menu command. Figure 18-19 shows command buttons that let a user perform various tasks at the click of a button.

Event procedures contain the actual instructions, written in Visual Basic, that tell your command buttons what to do when a user clicks it. Without an event procedure, a command button looks nice but doesn't do anything useful (much like the Vice President of the United States).

Creating a command button (for Visual Basic)

When you create a command button, the Command Button Wizard normally pops its head in the way and guides you through the creation of your command

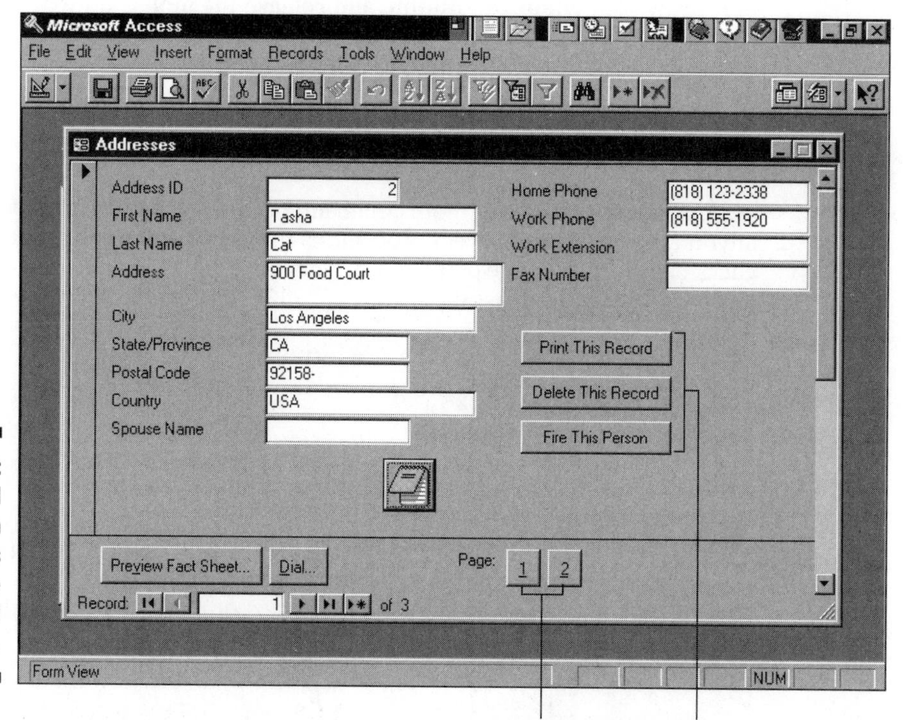

Figure 18-19: A typical form displays multiple command buttons.

button through a series of Command Button Wizard dialog boxes. The Command Button Wizard can be helpful, but it can get in the way if you want to write a Visual Basic event procedure to control your command button instead.

To create a command button so that you can write a Visual Basic event procedure, follow these steps:

1. **Open the database window and click the Forms tab.**
2. **Click the form you want to use and click Design.**

   Access displays your form in design view.
3. **Choose View⇨Toolbox.**

   The Toolbox toolbar appears (refer to Figure 18-15). If a check mark appears next to the Toolbox command, skip this step.
4. **Click the Control Wizards button so that it doesn't appear pressed in.**

   (If it already does not appear pressed in, skip this step.)
5. **Click the Command Button.**
6. **Move the mouse to the location at which you want to place your command button. Then hold down the left mouse button, drag the mouse to draw your command button, and release the mouse button.**

   Access draws your command button.

Writing an event procedure

After you've drawn one or more command buttons on a form, they don't do anything until you write event procedures that tell them what to do if someone clicks one of them. Some of the more common types of Visual Basic commands let you perform these tasks:

- Assign another object, such as a text box, a string, or a value
- Display a message box
- Perform a calculation

Assigning another object a string or value

If you want to change the contents of a field (also known as an *object*), you can use Visual Basic to stuff a text string or number into that field. To do that, you have to know the name of the field and the text or number you want to stuff into it, such as:

```
Private Sub cmdZip_Click()
  PostalCode = "92102"
End Sub
```

If you had a command button named cmdZip and you clicked it, Access would look for an object called PostalCode and replace its contents with the text string "92102".

Displaying a message box

When a user clicks a command button, Access can display a message box. To create a message box, you have to specify the message you want displayed and the title of the message box. Figure 18-20 shows the message box that the following Visual Basic code creates:

```
Private Sub cmdZip_Click()
  MsgBox "Delete everything?", , "Warning!!!"
End Sub
```

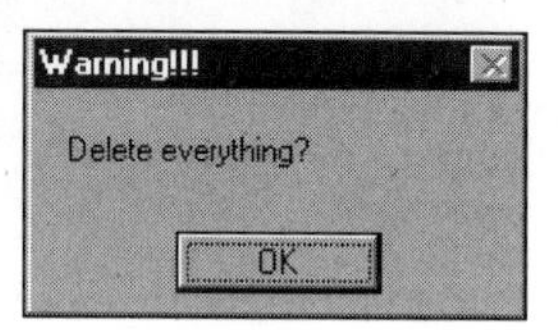

Figure 18-20: A message box created by Visual Basic code.

Performing a calculation

Visual Basic can perform simple addition, subtraction, multiplication, or division by using numbers stored in one or more objects. Table 18-2 shows typical commands for performing a calculation.

Table 18-2 Common Visual Basic Mathematical Operators

Operation	*Operator*	*Real-Life Visual Basic Example*
Addition	+	Total = SalesTax + ProductCost
Subtraction	–	TakeHomePay = Salary – IncomeTax
Multiplication	*	Rabbits = Parents * Days
Division	/	Government = Conservatives /Liberals

The joy of Visual Basic programming

Visual Basic includes all sorts of commands that let you create arrays, perform conditional execution by using If-Then statements, and manipulate the information stored in your Access database. If you have no idea what these terms mean and you don't care, you probably won't ever need to learn more about Visual Basic.

What can Visual Basic do for you, and why should you bother learning how to use it? Access is great for storing information, but unless you know the right commands to choose from its pull-down menus, the information just sits there.

By using Visual Basic, you can create your own programs that need to store and retrieve information, such as a mail-order management program, an inventory-tracking program, a church-management program, a multilevel marketing program, or any other type of program that requires storing lots of different information.

Visual Basic essentially lets you turn your Access databases into custom programs. If you ever have wished that you had a special program to help you store, track, and organize information, writing your own Visual Basic program in Access might be just what you need.

Writing an event procedure

To write an event procedure, follow these steps:

1. **Point to the command button for which you want to write an event procedure.**
2. **Click the right mouse button.**

   A pop-up menu appears, as shown in Figure 18-21.
3. **Click Build Event.**

   The Module window appears, as shown in Figure 18-22.
4. **Write your Visual Basic code to perform a task, such as assigning the contents of a field with a string or number or displaying a message box.**
5. **Click the close box in the Module window.**
6. **Click the close box in the Form design window.**

   A dialog box appears, asking whether you want to save your changes.
7. **Click Yes.**

Obviously, this brief introduction to the Visual Basic programming language barely scratches the surface of how to program Access. If you're intrigued and want to learn more about Visual Basic programming, consider buying a copy of *Access Programming For Dummies,* by Rob Krumm (published by IDG Books Worldwide).

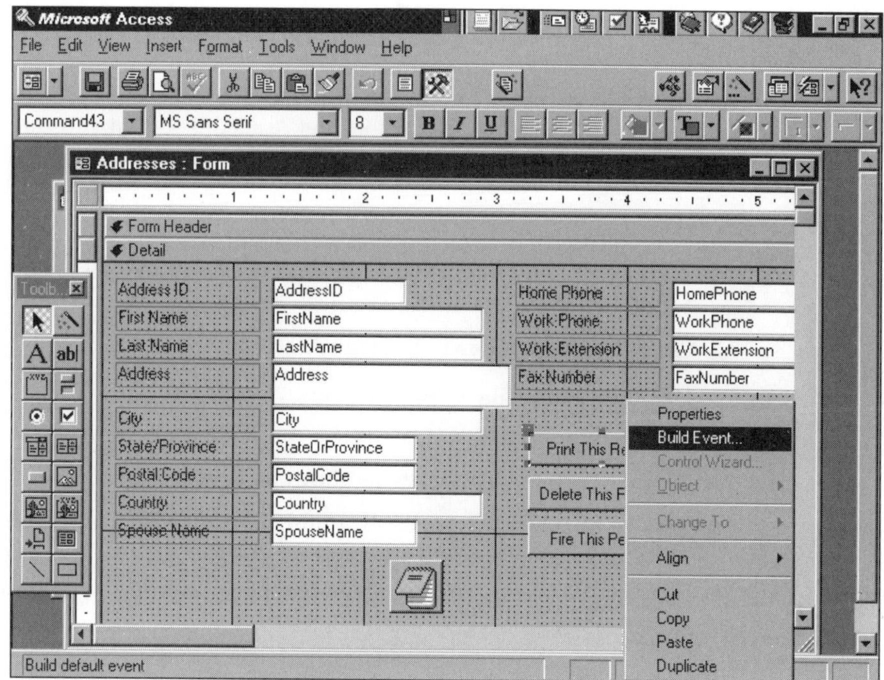

Figure 18-21: The right mouse pop-up menu.

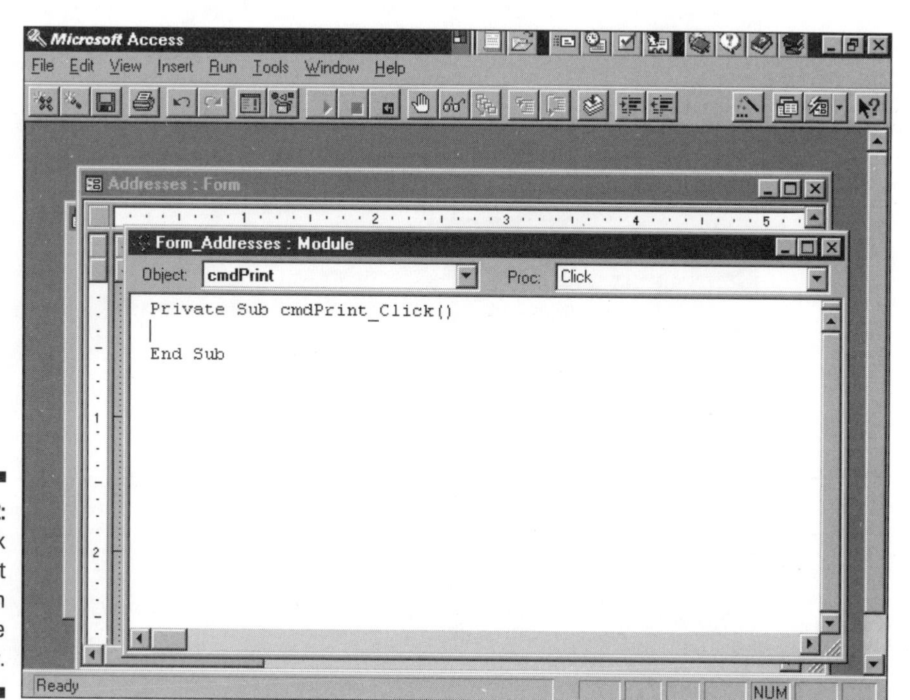

Figure 18-22: A blank event procedure in the Module window.

Putting Access Databases on the Web

The Internet Assistant for Access comes buried in a file called IA95.EXE. Running this program installs the Internet Assistant so that you can convert your Access databases into Web pages as well.

To convert an Access database into a Web page, follow these steps:

1. **Load Access and load a database that you want to convert into a Web page.**
2. **Choose Tools⇨Add-ins⇨Internet Assistant.**

   The Internet Assistant dialog box appears.
3. **Click Next >.**

   Another dialog box appears, as shown in Figure 18-23.
4. **Click in the Object Type list box and choose Table, Query, Form, Report, or All to tell Access what you want to convert into a Web page.**
5. **Click the check box of all the objects listed in the Object Name list box.**

   Make sure a check mark appears in front of all the objects you want to convert into a Web page.

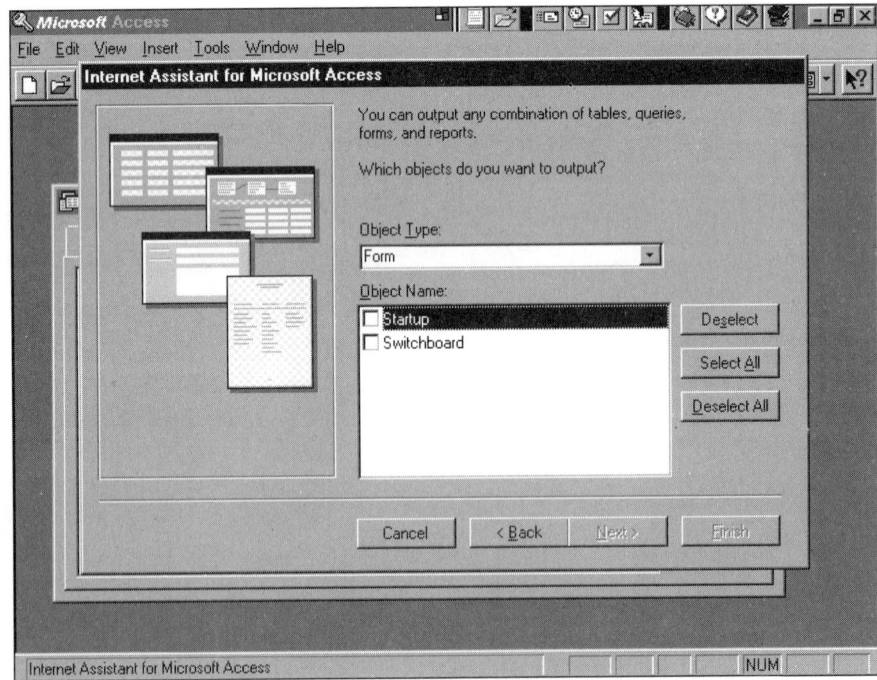

Figure 18-23: The first Internet Assistant dialog box.

6. **Click Next >.**

   Another dialog box appears, asking if you want to use an existing document as a template. A template lets Access create a Web page similar to an existing Web page.

7. **Click the Choose an existing HTML document to use as a template or the Do not use a template radio button and then click Next >.**

   Another dialog box appears, asking where you want to store your Web pages.

8. **Type a file name and directory and click Finish.**

   Access creates your Web pages, shown in Figure 18-24.

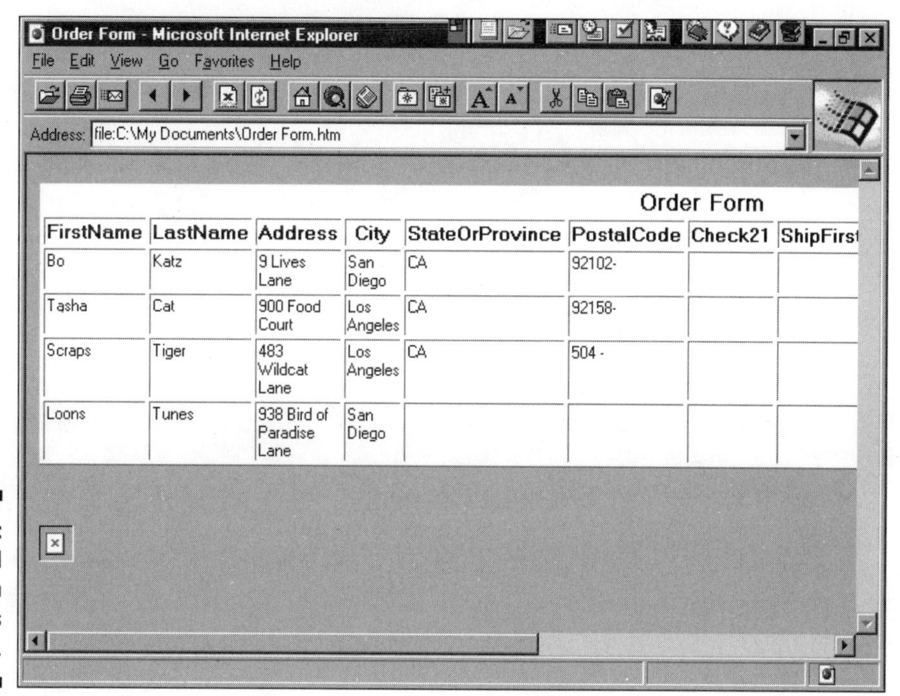

FirstName	LastName	Address	City	StateOrProvince	PostalCode	Check21	ShipFirst
Bo	Katz	9 Lives Lane	San Diego	CA	92102-		
Tasha	Cat	900 Food Court	Los Angeles	CA	92158-		
Scraps	Tiger	483 Wildcat Lane	Los Angeles	CA	504 -		
Loons	Tunes	938 Bird of Paradise Lane	San Diego				

Figure 18-24: A typical Access form displayed as a Web page.

Chapter 19

Sharing Your Microsoft Access Databases

In This Chapter

- Converting databases to and from Access so that you can use information from other programs
- Creating a startup form to provide information to people who use your database
- Using a password to protect your work

Microsoft Access is rapidly becoming the most popular database program running under Windows. Many people who own Access have, unfortunately, no idea how to use it, and even more people don't own Access but use a rival database program with a weird name, such as dBASE, FileMaker Pro, Alpha Five, or Paradox. (Believe it or not, because some people even store data in their spreadsheets, Access can convert Lotus 1-2-3 or Excel files into Access database files. Will wonders never cease?)

What happens if you spend hours creating an Access database that contains valuable names and addresses, but you want to give the list to a co-worker who uses another database program? You can type all the information into the other database program, but that defeats the entire purpose of using Access. Or you can take the easy way out and convert your Access database into another database file format.

This capability works backward, too. Suppose that your company used to store data in a program such as dBASE but has since switched to Access. Go ahead and create your Access database and let Access do the hard work of converting your ancient dBASE files into a real, honest-to-goodness Access database.

To make Access as powerful as powerful can be, make sure that Access can share your valuable data with other people no matter which program or computer they may be using. The goal is to convince the global population to switch eventually to Microsoft products and take over the world in the name of Microsoft and Bill Gates.

Many rival database programs are dBASE clones in disguise, which means that they create and store data in dBASE file formats, just as the original dBASE program does. The most popular dBASE clone programs include FoxPro, Clipper, Approach, and Alpha Four (and its successor, Alpha Five).

Converting Databases to (And from) Access

Access can work with rival database files in three ways. It can

- Convert a foreign database file into an Access database
- Link a foreign database file to an Access database
- Convert an Access database into another file format

Converting a rival database file format (such as a file created in dBASE, Paradox, Approach, or FoxPro) into a real Access database file is handy if you plan to use Access only to update the database file.

It's best to link a database file into Access when you want to use Access but also want to use the original database program, such as dBASE or FoxPro, that created the database file.

Converting an Access database is handy when you want to give your data to someone who uses a different database program. Because two separate copies of the data then exist (one copy in Access and a second copy in a rival database file format, such as dBASE), this method is best if you're abandoning Access and switching to a rival program, such as Paradox.

Identifying your database files

If you have a database file but have no idea which program created it, just look at its file extension, as shown in this table:

File Extension	*Database File Type*
DBF	dBASE
DB	Paradox
WKS, WK1, WK2, WK3	Lotus 1-2-3
XLS	Excel

Just remember that dBASE comes in different versions: dBASE III Plus, dBASE IV, and dBASE 5. If you have a file that doesn't have any of these file extensions, chances are good that it's stored in a proprietary file format created by an obscure oddball database, such as PFS:File, Nutshell, or DataPerfect. In these cases, you'll have to convert the database to a dBASE file first before converting it into an Access database.

A long time ago, dBASE was the most popular database program in the world. As a result, nearly every database program can create dBASE files. When you need to convert database files into Access from a different program, try converting your files into dBASE format first and then converting those dBASE files into Access.

Turning foreign files into an Access database

The easiest way to use Access is, obviously, to force everyone to abandon rival database programs and switch to Access instead. To help you support Microsoft's apparent quest for world software domination, Access can turn foreign database files into a genuine Access database. That way, you never have to use any other database program for the rest of your life.

To convert a foreign database file into an Access database, follow these steps:

1. **Choose File⇨New Database.**

   The New dialog box appears, as shown in Figure 19-1. (Skip to step 4 if you want to convert a foreign database file into an existing Access database.)

2. **Click the General tab, click the Blank Database icon, and click OK.**

   The New Database dialog box appears, as shown in Figure 19-2.

3. **Type a name for your database in the File name box and click Create.**

   Access displays a blank Database window, shown in Figure 19-3.

4. **Choose File⇨Get External Data⇨Import.**

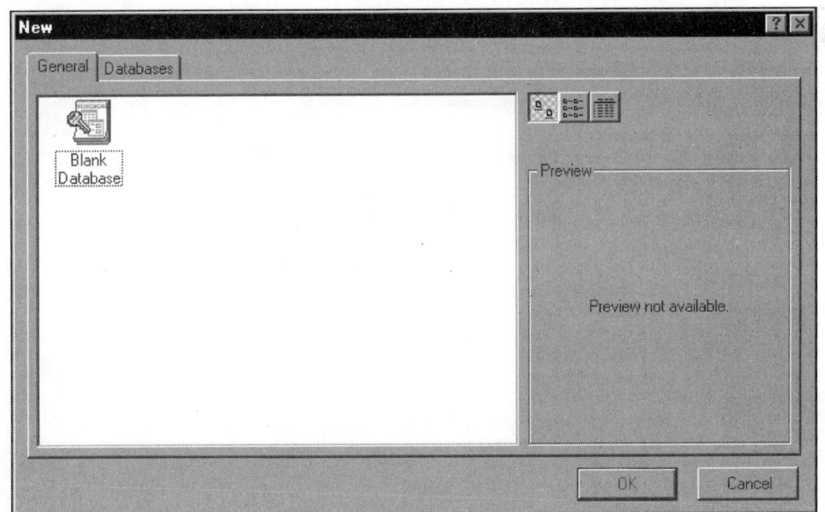

Figure 19-1: The New dialog box.

5. **Click the File of type list box and choose the file format you want to convert.**

   If you have a dBASE III file, for example, choose dBASE III. A list of files that match your criteria appears in the Import dialog box.

6. **Click the file you want to convert and click Import.**

7. **Click Close.**

   Access displays your newly converted database in the Database window.

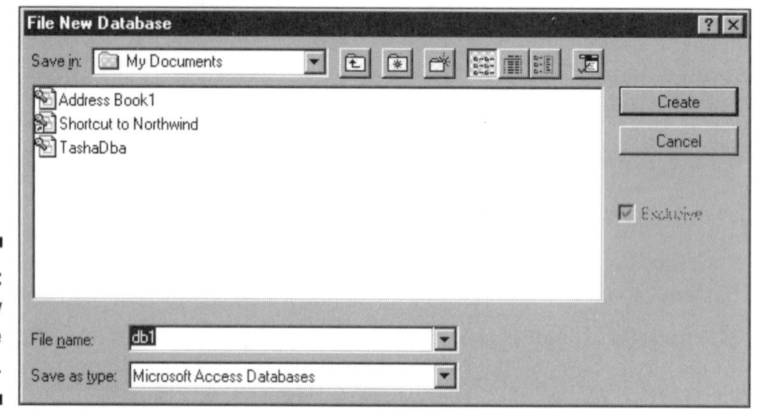

Figure 19-2: The New Database dialog box.

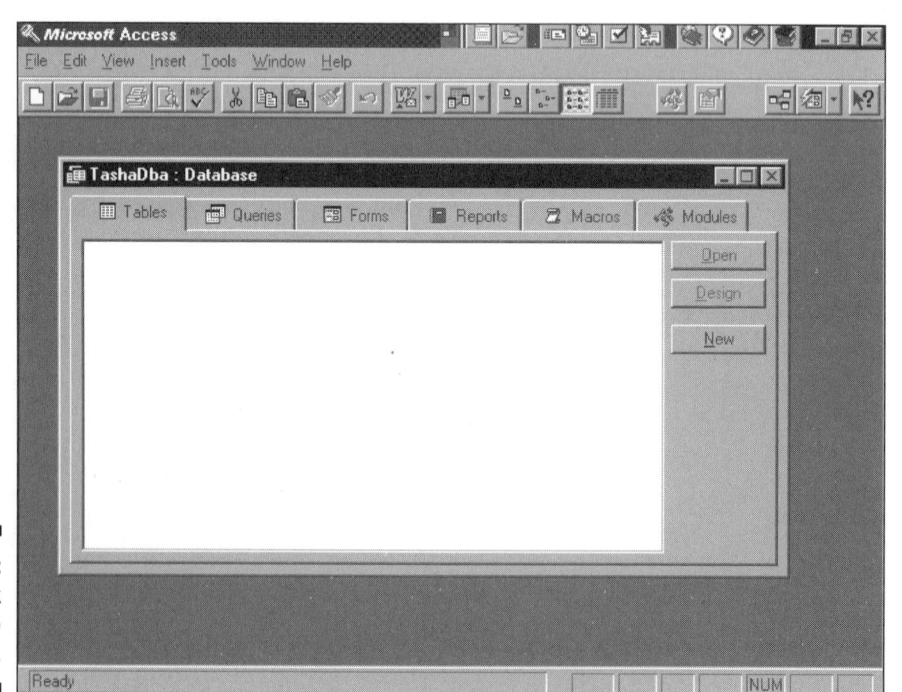

Figure 19-3: A blank database window.

Linking foreign files to Access

The capability to convert foreign database files into Access is great if you plan never to use a rival database again. If a stubborn co-worker insists on using dBASE while you're using Access, however, you can compromise and just link that file to Access without converting it. That way, you can share a dBASE file with others without having to endure the torture of learning to use the dBASE program.

The disadvantage of this approach, of course, is that, rather than have a single Access file to worry about, you have to worry about keeping track of separate dBASE (or Paradox or Lotus 1-2-3) files.

If you absolutely must keep data stored in its original file format yet still use it in Access, however, linking a foreign database file to Access is easier than switching to another database program.

To link a foreign database file to Access, follow these steps:

1. **Choose File⇨New Database.**

   The New dialog box appears (refer to Figure 19-1). (Skip to step 4 if you want to convert a foreign database file into an existing Access database.)

2. **Click the General tab, click the Blank Database icon, and click OK.**

   The New Database dialog box appears (refer to Figure 19-2).

3. **Type a name for your database in the File name box and then click Create.**

   Access displays a blank Database window (refer to Figure 19-3).

4. **Choose File⇨Get External Data⇨Link Tables.**

   The Link dialog box appears, as shown in Figure 19-4.

5. **Click the File of type list box and choose the file format you want to link.**

   If you have a Paradox file, for example, choose Paradox. A list of files that match your criteria appears in the Import dialog box.

6. **Click the file you want to convert and then click Link.**

   The Select Index Files dialog box appears.

7. **Click the index file that accompanies the file you chose in step 6 and then click Select.**

   Note: Not all database files have an accompanying index file.

8. **Click Close.**

   Access displays your newly linked database in the Database window, shown in Figure 19-5.

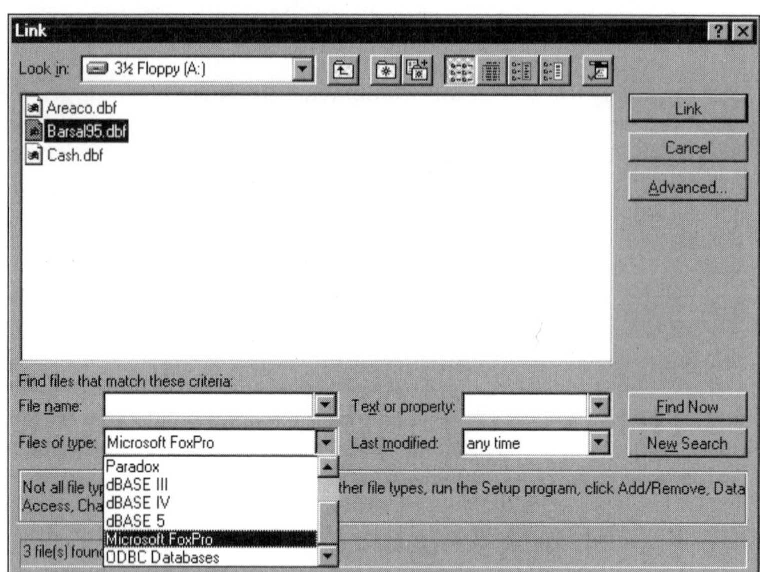

Figure 19-4: The Link dialog box.

Converting Access databases into another file format

Although you may use Access, your friends may be using a rival database program. If you've created a wonderful mailing list of people who are easy to con and you want to share this data with your friends, you may have to convert your Access files into another file format, such as dBASE or Paradox.

Converting an Access database to a different file format creates two copies of the same data stored in two separate files. If you update one file, Access has no way of updating the second file as well.

To convert your Access databases into a different file format, follow these steps:

1. **Open an Access database, click the Tables tab, and click the database table you want to convert.**
2. **Choose File⇨Save As/Export.**

   The Save As dialog box appears, as shown in Figure 19-6.
3. **Click the radio button labeled To an external File or Database and then click OK.**

   The Save Form In dialog box appears.
4. **Click the Save as type list box and choose a file format, such as Text Files or Microsoft Excel 7, in which to save the design of your form.**
5. **Click Export.**

Linked dBase file

Figure 19-5: The Database window shows a linked database.

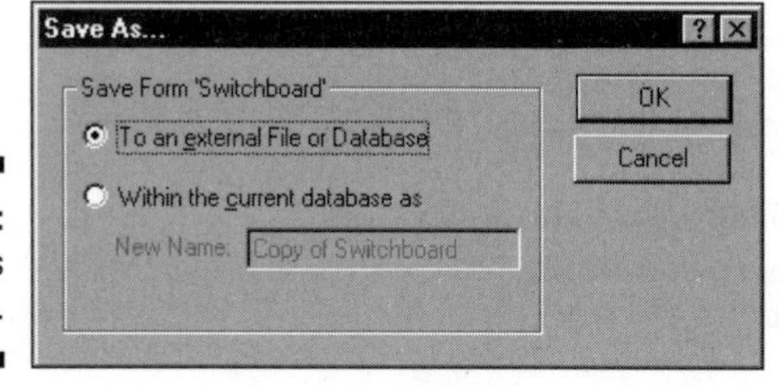

Figure 19-6: The Save As dialog box.

If the Save as type list box doesn't list the database format you want, follow these steps:

1. **Run the Microsoft Office Setup program again.**

   The Microsoft Office Setup screen appears.

2. **Click Add/Remove.**

   The Maintenance dialog box appears.

3. **Highlight Microsoft Access and then click Change Option.**

   The Microsoft Access dialog box appears.

4. **Highlight Data Access and then click Change Option.**

   The Data Access dialog box appears.

5. **Click the check box for the database drivers you want to use and then click OK.**

Creating a Startup Form

If you're the only person using a particular database, you can make it as sloppy and unorganized as you want, as long as you know where to find the data you need. If you want others to be able to use your database, however, creating a startup form is a good idea. (***Note:*** You can create only one startup form per database.)

The startup form acts like a program *splash screen,* which displays a window that can briefly explain how to use the database, describe what type of information is stored in it, or even relate tasteless jokes you want your co-workers to read for their amusement while they use your database.

Three steps are involved in creating a startup form:

- Design the appearance of your startup form
- Create a button to make the startup form go away
- Make the startup form the first form that appears

Designing your startup form

You can create a startup form that displays, at its simplest level, nothing but text. If you want to be more extravagant, you can modify the fonts and font size, draw lines and boxes on the form, or even add pictures. Because the appearance of your startup form is simply for the user's benefit, make it easy on the eyes.

To create a startup form, follow these steps:

1. **Open the database to which you want to add a startup form.**
2. **Click the Forms tab.**
3. **Click New.**

   The New Form dialog box appears.

4. **Highlight Design View and then click OK.**

   Access displays a blank form, shown in Figure 19-7.

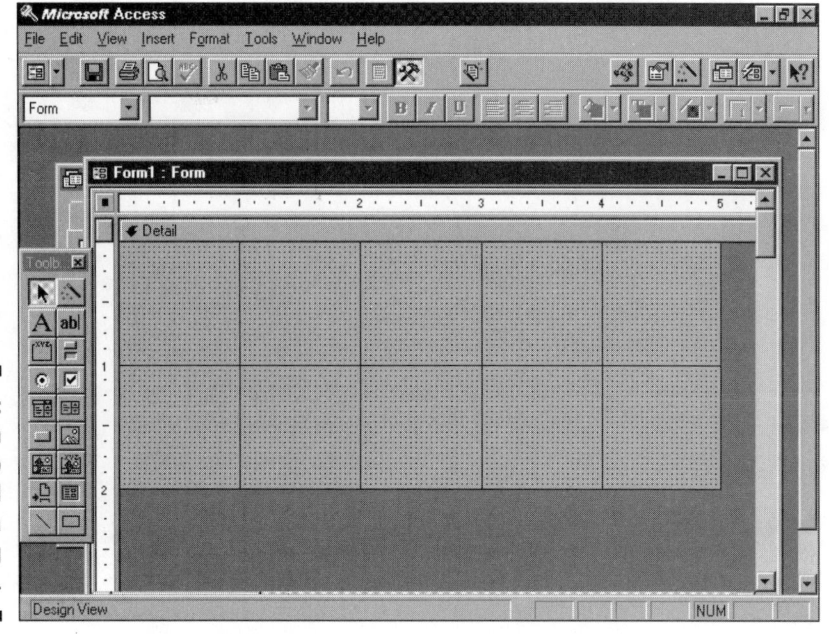

Figure 19-7: A blank form is ready to be turned into a dazzling startup form.

5. **Click the Label icon, draw a label on the form, and type any text you want to appear on the startup form.**
6. **Click the Image icon, draw an image box on the form, and choose an image you want to appear on the form.**
7. **Repeat steps 5 and 6 as many times as you want.**
8. **Click the Form Selector button and then click the right mouse button.**

   A pop-up menu appears, as shown in Figure 19-8.
9. **Click Properties.**

   The Form dialog box appears, as shown in Figure 19-9.
10. **Click the Format tab.**
11. **Click the Scroll Bars box and change the value to Neither.**
12. **Click the Record Selectors box and change the value to No.**
13. **Click the Navigation Buttons box and change the value to No.**
14. **Click the Auto Center box and change the value to Yes.**
15. **Click the close box in the Form dialog box.**
16. **Click the close box in the Form design window.**

    A dialog box appears and asks whether you want to save your changes.

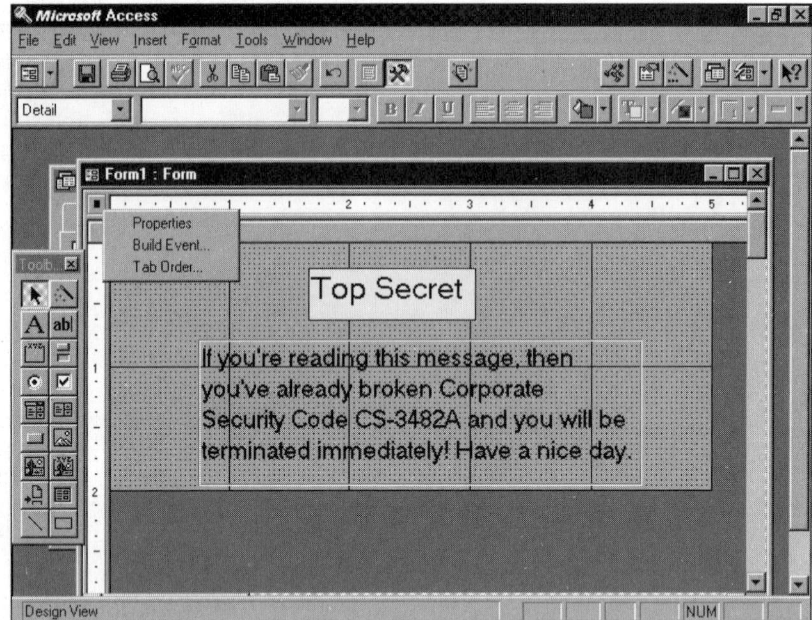

Figure 19-8: The right mouse button pop-up menu.

Form

Format | Data | Event | Other | All

Caption	
Default View	Single Form
Views Allowed	Both
Scroll Bars	Neither
Record Selectors	No
Navigation Buttons	No
Dividing Lines	Yes
Auto Resize	Yes
Auto Center	Yes
Border Style	Sizable
Control Box	Yes
Min Max Buttons	Both Enabled
Close Button	Yes

Figure 19-9: The Form dialog box.

17. **Click Yes.**

    The Save As dialog box appears.

18. **Type a name for your form (such as** Startup**) and click OK.**

Adding a button to close your startup form

By definition, a startup form appears immediately. After the startup form appears, however, you may want to display a button that makes it go away.

To create a button to close your startup form, follow these steps:

1. **Open the database that contains your startup form.**
2. **Click the Forms tab.**
3. **Click your startup form and then click Design.**

   Access displays your startup form, shown in Figure 19-10.

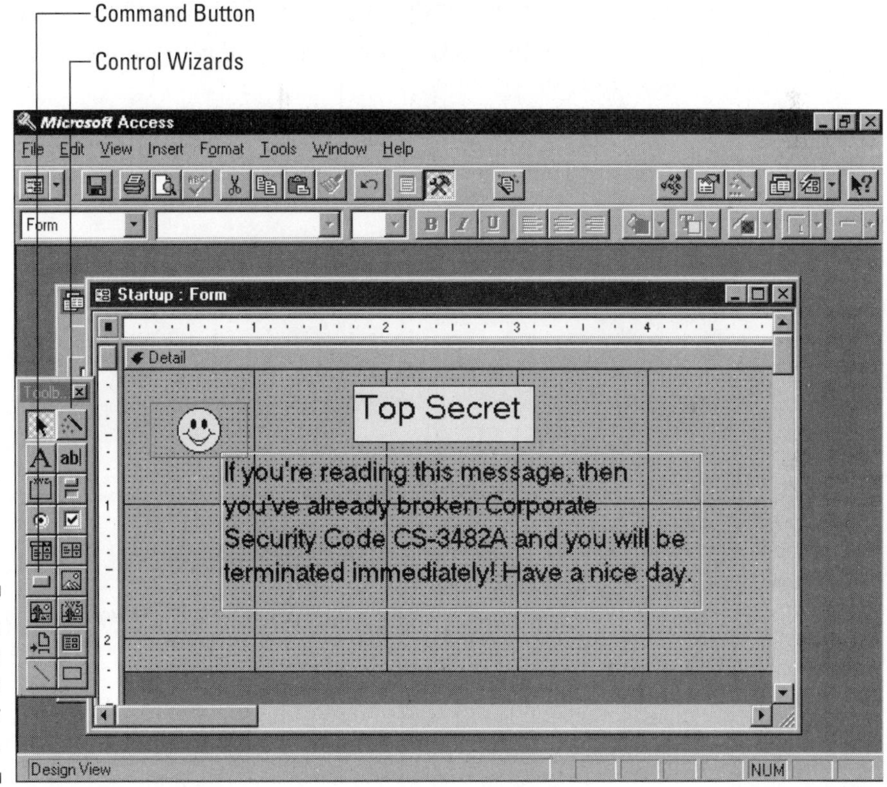

Figure 19-10: Your startup form is ready for modifying.

4. **Click the Control Wizards icon in the Toolbox so that it appears indented, or "pushed in."**

   If it already appears indented, skip this step.

5. **Click the Command Button icon and draw the command button on your form.**

   The Command Button Wizard dialog box appears.

6. **Highlight Form Operations in the Categories list.**
7. **Highlight Close Form in the Actions list.**
8. **Click Next>.**

   The Command Button Wizard asks whether you want to display text or a picture on your button.

9. **Click either the Text or Picture radio button and then click Next>.**

   The Command Button Wizard asks for a name for your button, shown in Figure 19-11.

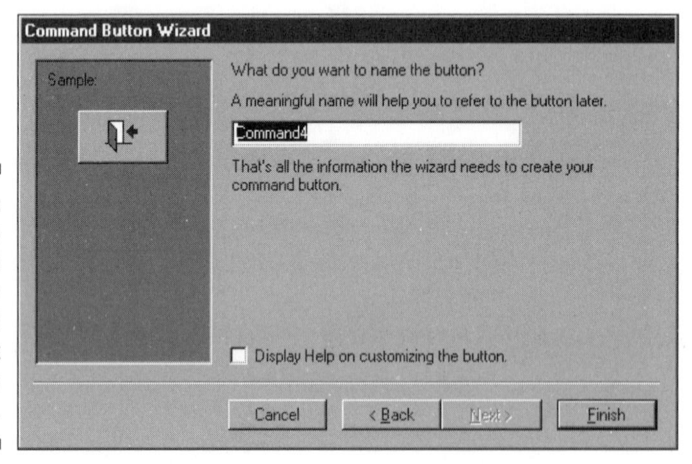

Figure 19-11: The Command Button Wizard dialog box asks for a name.

10. **Type a name for your button and click Finish.**

    Access displays your command button on the form.

11. **Click the close box for the Form design window.**

    A dialog box appears and asks whether you want to save your changes.

12. **Click Yes.**

Making your startup form appear

After designing your startup form and putting a button on it to make it go away, the final step is to make sure that your startup form appears as soon as you or someone else opens the database.

To make your startup form the first form to appear, follow these steps:

1. **Open the database that contains your startup form.**
2. **Choose Tools⇨Startup.**

   The Startup dialog box appears.
3. **Click the Display Form list box and choose the name of your startup form (such as Startup).**
4. **Click OK.**

   Now, whenever anyone opens your database, your startup form appears immediately, as shown in Figure 19-12.

Figure 19-12: The Startup dialog box.

Password-Protecting Your Valuable Work

What if you store valuable data that could get a president impeached if someone discovers it? In that case, you may want to take the additional precaution of password-protecting your database. If someone tries to view the information stored in your database, that person will need the correct password.

If you forget your password, you won't be able to use your database either, of course. Worse, if someone steals your password without your knowledge, your database may be wide open to prying eyes while you blissfully think that it's safe. Don't rely entirely on passwords.

Selling and distributing your Access databases

If you create databases for everyone else all the time, you'll notice one problem: For other people to be able to use your database, they also need a copy of Access on their computer.

If you would rather not install copies of Access on computers that belong to people who have no idea how to use Access, a better solution exists. Why not turn your Access databases into real programs?

With a copy of the Access Developer's Toolkit, you can turn your databases into programs you can distribute for free or for profit.

As another alternative, get a copy of the Visual Basic compiler (it's separate from the version of Visual Basic included in Access). This combination of Visual Basic and Access lets you create databases in Access and then use Visual Basic to design the look of your program.

With a little creativity and a lot of luck, you may be able to use Access to create — who knows? — the next best-selling program that will earn you millions, give you the chance to quit your job, and enable you to start your own software company that can compete with Microsoft.

Creating a password

Passwords can be as long as 14 characters and are case-sensitive, which means that NUGGET is a completely different password than Nugget. To make your password as confusing as possible, mix together numbers and uppercase and lowercase letters, such as NZ8sy4.

The more difficult it is to guess your password, the more difficult it is for you to remember, so be careful when you choose a password.

To password-protect a database, follow these steps:

1. **Choose File⇨Open.**

   The Open dialog box appears.

2. **Click the Exclusive check box so that a check mark appears in it.**
3. **Click the database you want to password-protect and then click Open.**
4. **Choose Tools⇨Security⇨Set Database Password.**

   The Set Database Password dialog box appears, as shown in Figure 19-13.

Figure 19-13: The Set Database Password dialog box.

5. **Type your password in the Password box.**

   Access displays your password as a series of asterisks, just in case a spy is snooping over your shoulder.

6. **Type your password again in the Verify box and click OK.**
7. **Choose File⇨Close.**

Opening a password-protected database

To open a password-protected database, follow these steps:

1. **Choose File⇨Open.**

   The Open dialog box appears.

2. **Click the database you want to open and then click Open.**

   The Password Required dialog box pops up, as shown in Figure 19-14.

Figure 19-14: The Password Required dialog box.

3. **Type the password in the Enter database password box and then click OK.**

   If the password is correct, Access grudgingly opens the database for you to edit, modify, or view to your heart's delight.

Removing a password

Passwords can be useful but also a nuisance. If you don't have anything worth stealing or if you just don't care about losing your data, you can remove a password so that Access doesn't continue asking you for one every time you try to open a password-protected database.

To remove a password from a database, follow these steps:

1. **Choose File⇨Open.**

   The Open dialog box appears.

2. **Click the Exclusive check box so that a check mark appears in it.**
3. **Click the database you want to open and then click Open.**

   The Password Required dialog box pops up (refer to Figure 19-14).
4. **Type your password in the Enter database password box and then click OK.**
5. **Choose Tools⇨Security⇨Unset Database Password.**

   The Unset Database Password dialog box appears.
6. **Type the database password in the Password box and then click OK.**

   Your database is now free of annoying passwords and is wide open to spying from people you probably don't like.

Part VI

Shortcuts and Tips Galore

"ALRIGHT, STEADY EVERYONE. MARGO, GO OVER TO TOM'S PC AND PRESS 'ESCAPE,'...VERY CAREFULLY."

In this part . . .

In this part, you discover how to use Microsoft Bookshelf to search for quotes from famous people who are probably dead by now. You also see where to search online for more information about using Microsoft Office, including the latest program updates and bug reports.

Chapter 20

Online Resources for Microsoft Office

In This Chapter

- The Microsoft Network
- CompuServe
- The Internet

In case you've already found the manuals that come with Microsoft Office virtually useless (you're not alone), let the fact that you can often get better help through your modem cheer you up. If you subscribe to the Microsoft Network or CompuServe, you can ask for help from complete strangers and pick up tips for using Office more productively.

If you have access to the Internet, go straight to Microsoft's computers and grab the latest files that provide bug fixes, program updates, and additional tools that can keep your version of Office up-to-date.

If you don't have access to the Internet or an online service like CompuServe or the Microsoft Network, you can still get latest Office news and files by dialing into the Microsoft Download Service Bulletin Board System at (206) 936-6735.

So don't despair. The next time you feel like tossing your computer (and your copy of Office) out the window, take a moment and look for help through your modem. Chances are good that you'll find a sympathetic ear from someone who has already suffered through the same problems you're going through right now.

Visiting the Microsoft Network

The Microsoft Network was Microsoft's ill-fated attempt to create an exclusive online service that would put America Online and CompuServe out of business. To achieve this goal, Microsoft threw in a free copy of the Microsoft Network communications program with every copy of Windows 95. Everyone in the world who has a copy of Windows 95 automatically has a copy of the Microsoft

Network communications program whether they like it or not. As fate would have it, the Microsoft Network wound up duplicating the Internet to such an extent that most people would rather access the vast resources on the Internet rather than the selection of resources available through the Microsoft Network.

In case you don't already know, the Microsoft Network is nothing more than a collection of computers located within the valuable property boundaries of Microsoft. By dialing into the Microsoft Network, you can read and write messages to others or chat in real-time with people from all over the world.

Naturally, using the Microsoft Network costs money. Besides paying for the cost of your phone call, you also must pay a monthly subscription fee, plus a per hour surcharge if you use the Microsoft Network extensively. Fortunately, the Microsoft Network isn't that interesting, so you probably won't use it too often. But if you do use it a lot, keep in mind that it can get pretty expensive in the long run. If you visit the Microsoft Network, you can find tips to make Microsoft Office easier, update files to fix bugs in Microsoft Office, or sample files that show you how someone created a fancy newsletter or brochure.

For more help on subscribing, using, and searching through the Microsoft Network, pick up a copy of *The Microsoft Network For Dummies* (IDG Books Worldwide, Inc.) by Doug Lowe. If you're not already a member of the Microsoft Network, this book shows you how to sign up.

To visit the Microsoft Network from within Office, follow these steps:

1. **Choose Help➪The Microsoft Network. (If you're within an Office binder, choose Help➪Binder Help➪The Microsoft Network.)**

   The Microsoft Network dialog box appears, as shown in Figure 20-1.

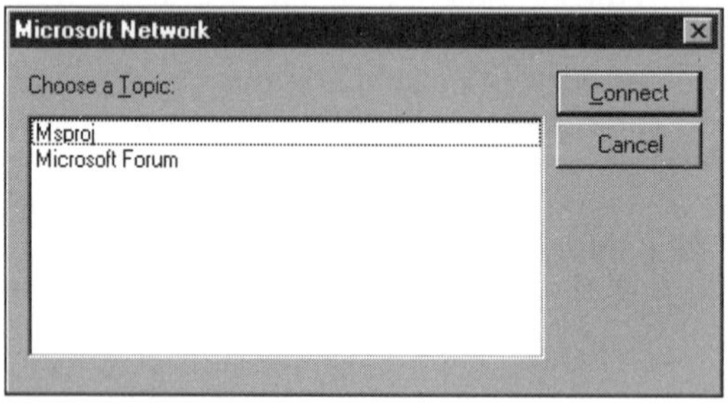

Figure 20-1: The Microsoft Network dialog box.

2. **Make sure that your modem is turned on and then highlight Microsoft Forum and click Connect.**

   The Microsoft Network Sign In dialog box appears, as shown in Figure 20-2.

Figure 20-2: The Microsoft Network Sign In dialog box.

3. **Type your member ID in the Member ID box, type your password in the Password box, and click Connect.**

   The Microsoft Forum window appears, as shown in Figure 20-3. (When you sign on with the Microsoft Network, Microsoft lets you choose your Member ID and Password.)

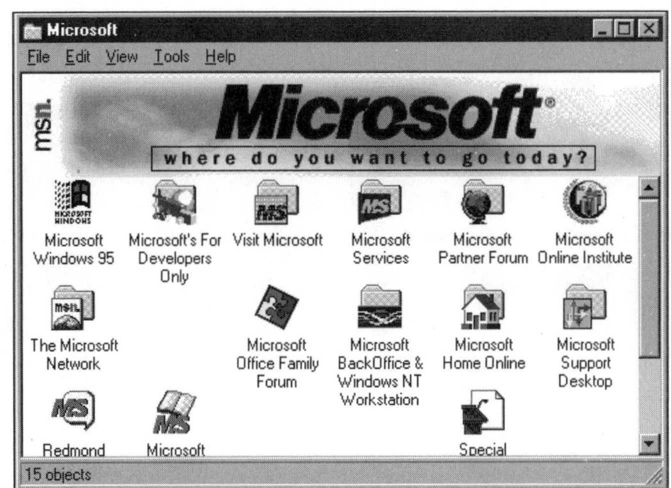

Figure 20-3: The Microsoft Forum window.

4. **Double-click the Microsoft Office Family Forum icon.**

   The Microsoft Office Family Forum window appears, as shown in Figure 20-4.

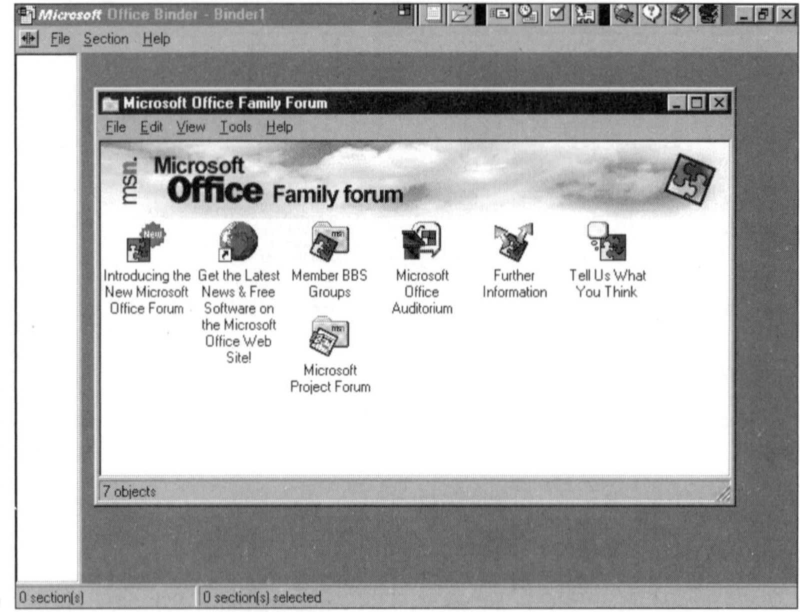

Figure 20-4: The Microsoft Office Family Forum window.

5. **Double-click the Member BBS Groups icon.**

   The Member BBS Groups window appears, as shown in Figure 20-5.

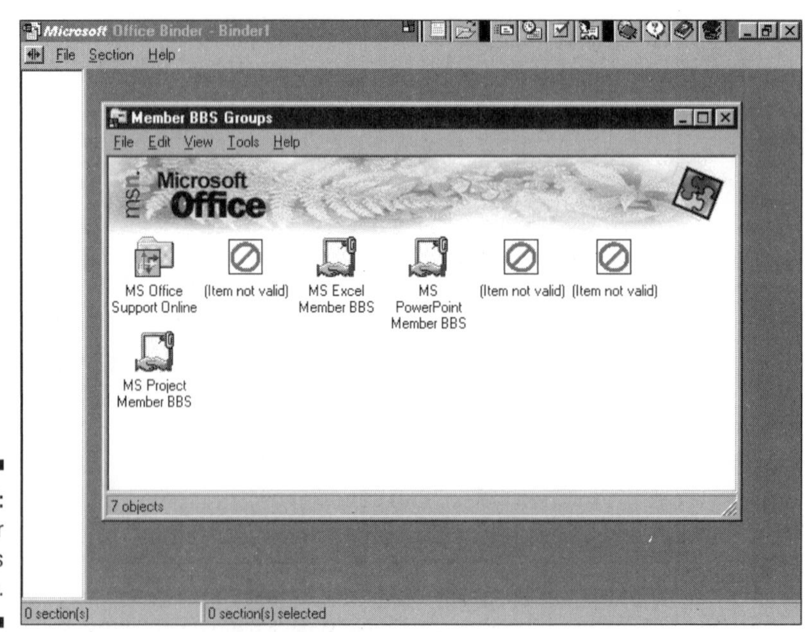

Figure 20-5: The Member BBS Groups window.

6. **Double-click a BBS icon to read or write messages about your favorite program such as Microsoft Schedule+.**

   Figure 20-6 shows a typical message BBS.

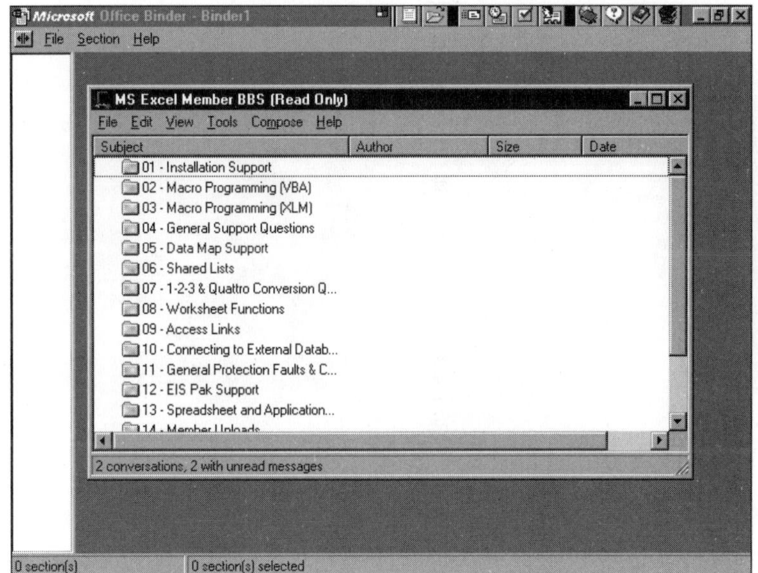

Figure 20-6: A typical message BBS.

7. **Choose File⇨Sign Out when you get tired of wasting time and money on the Microsoft Network.**

   A dialog box appears, asking if you really want to disconnect from the Microsoft Network.

8. **Click Yes.**

Getting Help from CompuServe

CompuServe is the oldest online service in the world and offers plenty of support for all of Microsoft's products. Of course, to use CompuServe, you have to sign up first. Like the Microsoft Network, CompuServe requires a monthly subscription fee plus an additional surcharge per hour.

Unlike the moribund services offered on the Microsoft Network, however, CompuServe provides many more files, messages, and information from people all over the world. You may run across macros to help you use Word, Visual Basic programs for customizing Access, or templates designed to help you create Excel worksheets for specialized uses such as for managing rental property.

Just keep in mind that the information you receive on CompuServe doesn't always come directly from Microsoft representatives, although that may not be a bad thing, because not even the people at Microsoft necessarily know what they're doing at any given time.

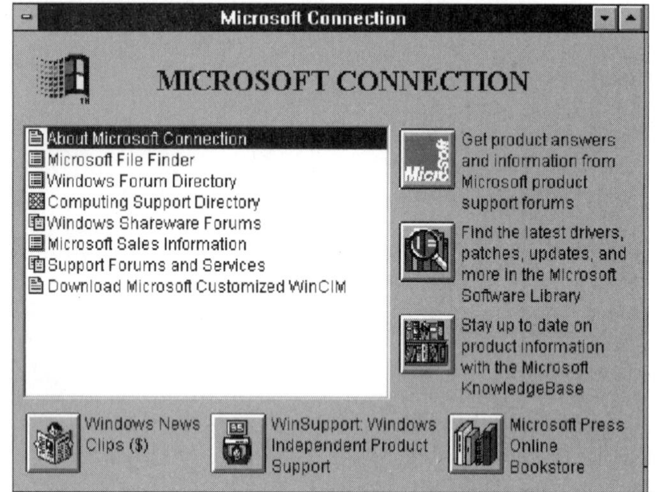

Figure 20-7: The Microsoft Connection on CompuServe.

To visit the Microsoft forums on CompuServe, just use the magic **GO MICROSOFT** command, which tosses you into the Microsoft Connection, shown in Figure 20-7.

For more help on subscribing, using, and searching through CompuServe, buy a copy of *CompuServe For Dummies* by Wallace Wang (IDG Books Worldwide, Inc.). If you're not already a member of CompuServe, this book shows you how to sign up as well as how to navigate around and find lots of useful files and news that can turn your computer into something more interesting than a boring word processor. In case you decide to cancel your CompuServe membership, call CompuServe at (614) 457-8650.

Microsoft Office on the Internet

Not surprisingly, most of the more current information about Office is available at Microsoft's Internet sites. If you just want to download files, visit their Internet (sometimes known as FTP or File Transfer Protocol) site at:

```
ftp.microsoft.com
```

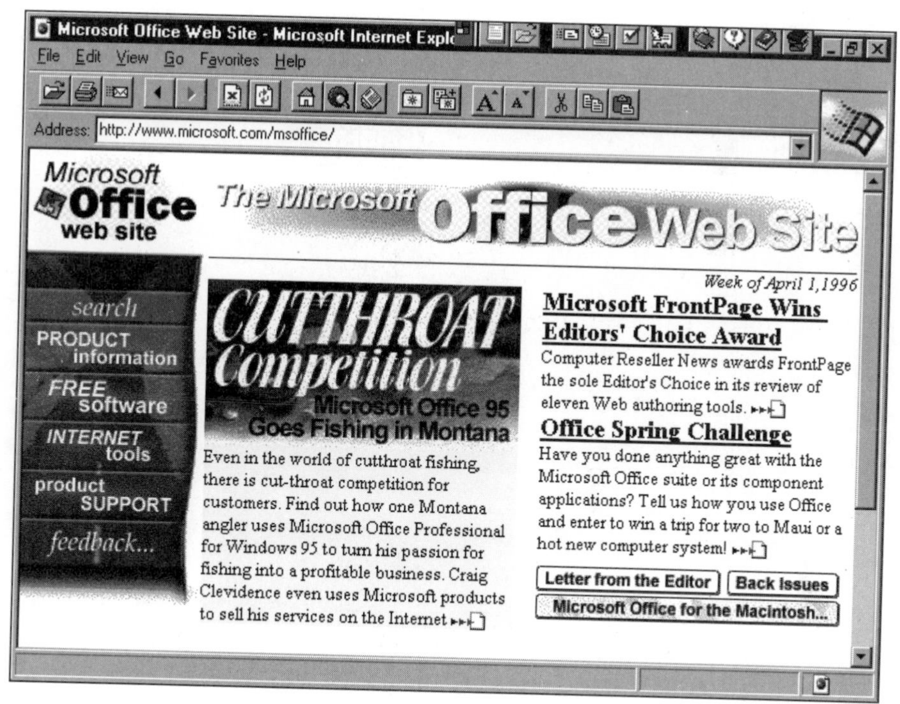

Figure 20-8: The Microsoft Office Web site.

If you prefer the flashy graphics of the World Wide Web, visit their Web site, shown in Figure 20-8, at the following address:

```
http://www.microsoft.com/msoffice
```

Some of the more useful files you can find at the Microsoft Web site are Internet Assistant programs for Word, Excel, and PowerPoint. These Internet Assistant programs let you convert ordinary Word, Excel, or PowerPoint documents into Web pages.

Other types of files you may find include free bug fixes (so that your programs actually work as advertised), updates (to add new features to your programs that you still probably won't ever use), or official information (propaganda) from Microsoft, explaining the wonderful ways you can use their products.

The Microsoft Web site mostly provides files directly from Microsoft. If you want a place to read and write messages, asking for help, you're better off calling the Microsoft Network or CompuServe.

Chapter 21

Making Microsoft Office Easier to Use

In This Chapter

- Starting up Microsoft Office quickly
- Looking up word definitions
- Finding fun stuff in an encyclopedia
- Using an online almanac

To give you as many options as possible (and to confuse you even further), Office provides multiple ways to do practically everything. Not only can you start up Office in several different ways, but you also have shortcuts for sharing data between Word, Excel, PowerPoint, and Access.

For those people who like knowing little secrets, dig through this chapter and find a shortcut that can make Office easier for you to use. Who knows? You just may be able to impress your boss enough with your Office skills that you can justify getting more money and then defecting to a rival company with your valuable knowledge.

Starting up Microsoft Office Quickly

Quick! Name all the different ways to start up Office. Now that you're done, check the following list to see how many ways you may have missed.

Click the Start button (and choose New/Open Office Document)

This method gives you a choice of opening an Office binder or loading an individual file created by Word or Access. To use this method, follow these steps:

1. **Click the Start button on the Windows 95 taskbar.**

   A pop-up menu appears, as shown in Figure 21-1.

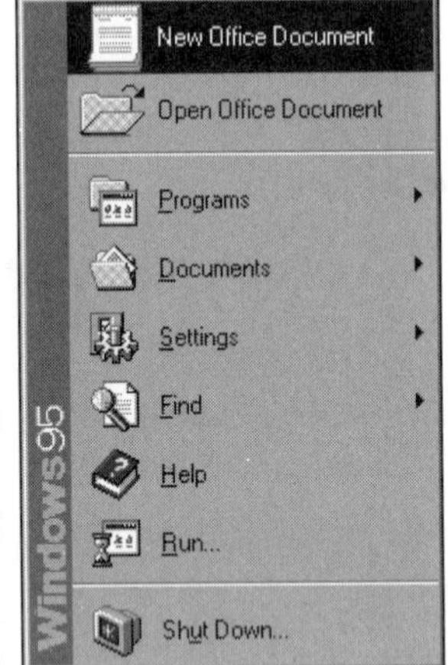

Figure 21-1: The Start button pop-up menu.

2. **Click one of the following:**

   - **New Office Document**
   - **Open Office Document**

   The New (or the Open) dialog box appears, as shown in Figure 21-2.

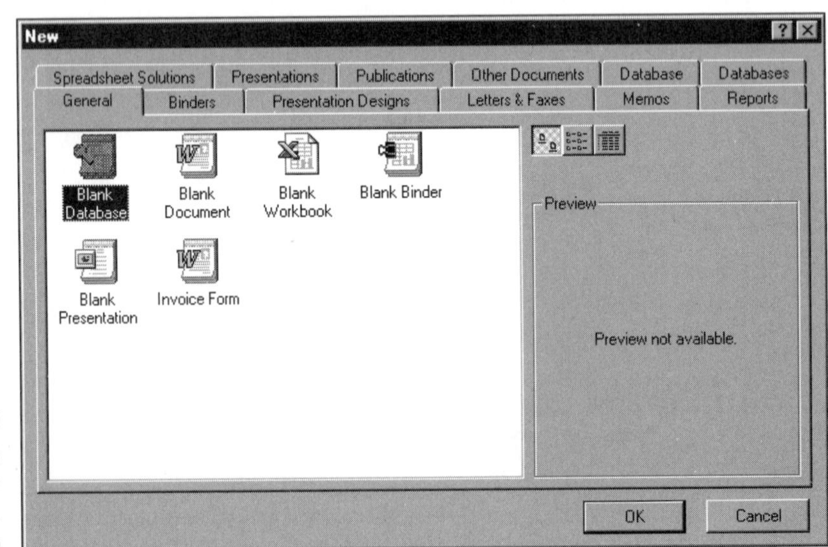

Figure 21-2: The New dialog box.

3. **Double-click the type of file you want to open or create.**

Click the Start button and use the Programs menu

This method is a bit clumsier than just clicking New Office Document or Open Office Document from the Start button. It still works, however, so you may as well know about it. To use this method, follow these steps:

1. **Click the Start button on the Windows 95 taskbar and highlight Programs.**

   A pop-up menu appears, as shown in Figure 21-3.

2. **Click one of the following:**

   - **Microsoft Binder**
   - **Microsoft Office File New**
   - **Microsoft Office File Open**

   The New (or the Open) dialog box appears (refer to Figure 21-2).

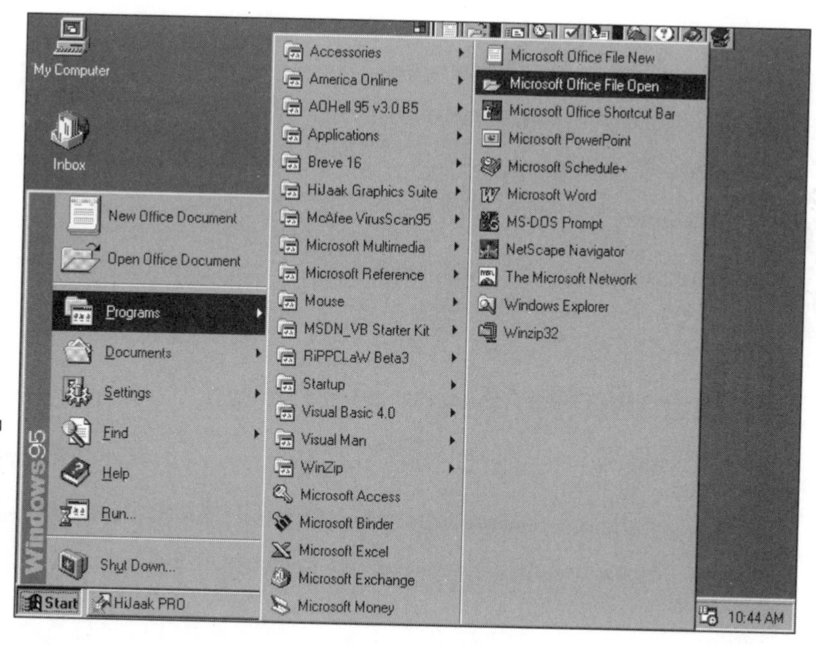

Figure 21-3: The Programs pop-up menu.

3. Double-click the type of file you want to open or create.

This method also lets you load individual programs, such as Word or Excel.

Click the Microsoft Office Shortcut Bar

If you have the Microsoft Office Shortcut Bar hovering on-screen, as shown in Figure 21-4, starting Office just by clicking one its buttons may be easier than clicking on the Start button.

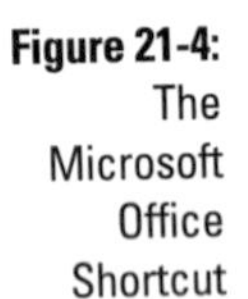

Figure 21-4: The Microsoft Office Shortcut Bar.

To use this method, follow these steps:

1. **Click one of the following:**
   - **Start a New Document**
   - **Open a Document**

   The New (or the Open) dialog box appears (refer to Figure 21-2).

2. **Double-click the type of file you want to open or create.**

If you click the Make an Appointment, Add a Task, or Add a Contact button, you can start Schedule+ right away.

Click the right mouse button

Here's a neat way to start up Office that most people never know about:

1. **Click the right mouse button anywhere on the Windows 95 desktop.**

   A pop-up menu appears, as shown in Figure 21-5.

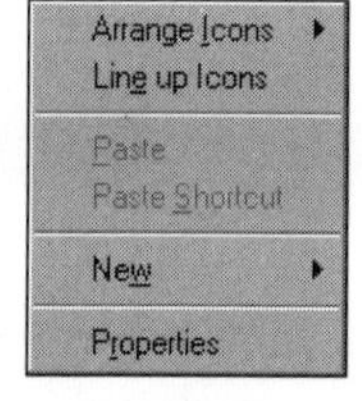

Figure 21-5: The right mouse button pop-up menu.

2. **Highlight New.**

   Another pop-up menu appears, as shown in Figure 21-6.

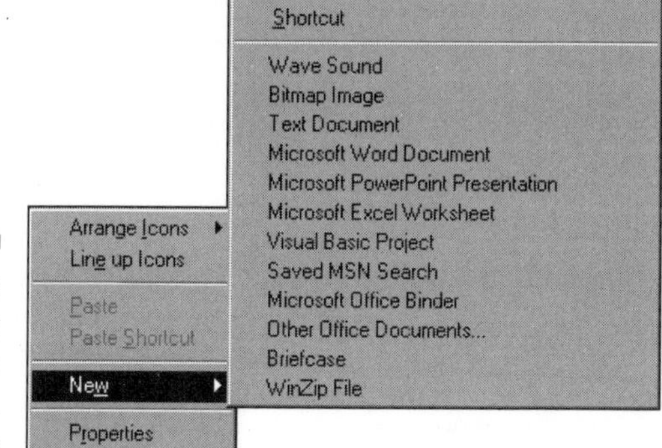

Figure 21-6: The New pop-up menu.

3. **Click Microsoft Office Binder.**

   Microsoft Office creates a New Microsoft Office Binder button on the Windows 95 desktop, as shown in figure 21-7.

Figure 21-7: The New Microsoft Office Binder button.

4. **Double-click the New Microsoft Office Binder button.**

You also can use this method to create a new Word, Excel, PowerPoint, or Access document, as well.

Use the Windows Explorer

If you want to open an existing file, use the Windows Explorer to do so by following these steps:

1. **Click the Start button on the Windows 95 taskbar and highlight Programs.**

   A pop-up menu appears (see Figure 21-3).

2. **Click Windows Explorer.**

   The Exploring window appears, as shown in Figure 21-8.

3. **Double-click the file you want to open.**

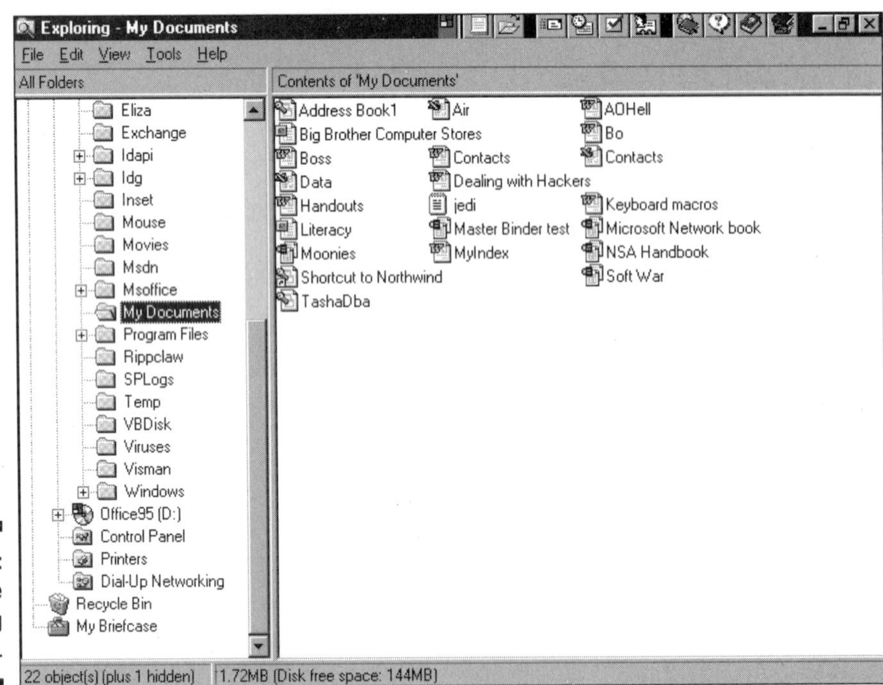

Figure 21-8: The Exploring window.

Click the Start button (and choose an individual program)

If you don't want to create or open an Office binder, you can open an individual program by following these steps:

1. **Click the Start button on the Windows 95 taskbar and highlight Programs.**

   A pop-up menu appears (refer to Figure 21-3).

2. **Click one of the following:**

   - **Microsoft Access**
   - **Microsoft Excel**
   - **Microsoft PowerPoint**
   - **Microsoft Schedule+**
   - **Microsoft Word**

Using Microsoft Bookshelf

If you bought the CD-ROM version of Microsoft Office Professional, not only did you get a copy of Access, but you got a copy of Bookshelf.

Bookshelf contains the complete text of the following books, stored for your convenience on a compact disc:

- A dictionary
- A thesaurus
- A book of quotations
- An encyclopedia
- An atlas
- A chronological timeline
- An almanac

You can load Bookshelf in two ways, shown in Figure 21-9:

- Click the Bookshelf button on the Office Shortcut Bar
- Choose Tools⇨Look Up Reference from within Word or Excel

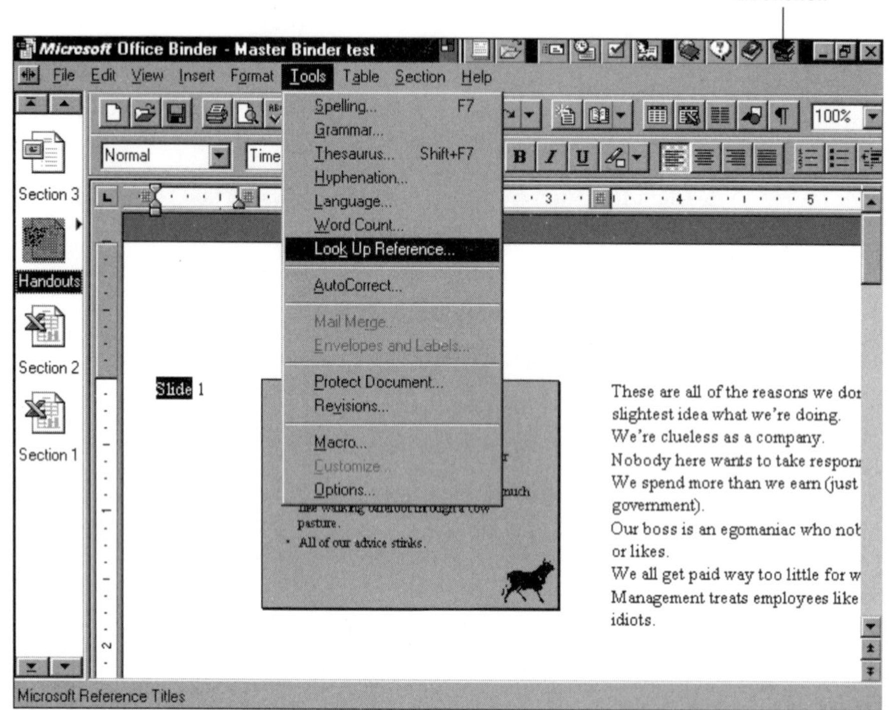

Figure 21-9: Two ways to load Bookshelf.

Clicking the Bookshelf button lets you run Bookshelf as a separate program. Choosing the Look Up Reference command lets you search for words stored in your current Word or Excel document.

Looking up definitions

You may be reviewing somebody else's Word or Excel document and have no idea what a particular word means. Rather than reach for your dictionary, let Bookshelf look up the word for you instead.

To look up a word within Word or Excel, follow these steps:

1. **Highlight a word within your Word or Excel document.**
2. **Choose Tools⇨Look Up Reference.**

   The Lookup Reference Title dialog box displays your highlighted word in the Text box, as shown in Figure 21-10.

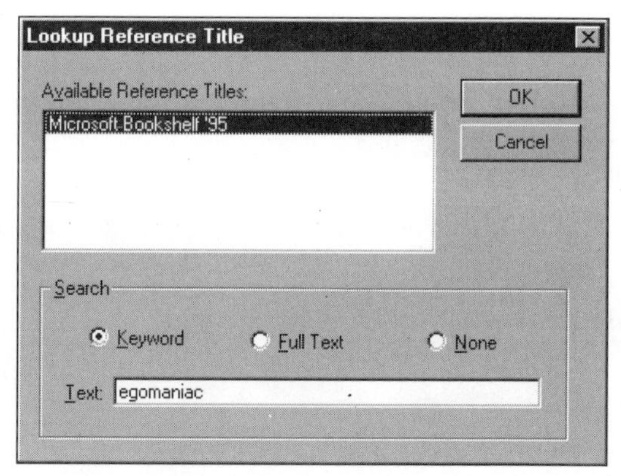

Figure 21-10: The Lookup Reference Title dialog box.

3. **Click OK.**

   The Bookshelf window appears.

4. **Click the Dictionary button.**

   The Bookshelf window displays a definition for your highlighted word, as shown in Figure 21-11.

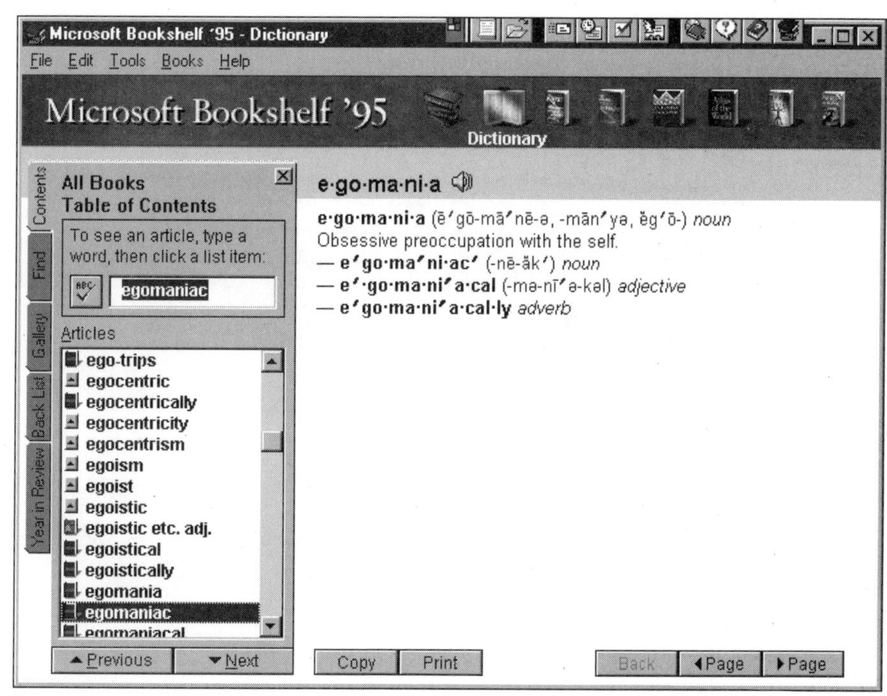

Figure 21-11: The Bookshelf window.

5. **Choose File⇨Exit.**

If you want to search for a word definition on your own, follow these steps:

1. **Click the Bookshelf button on the Office Shortcut Bar.**

   The Bookshelf Daily dialog box appears, as shown in Figure 21-12.

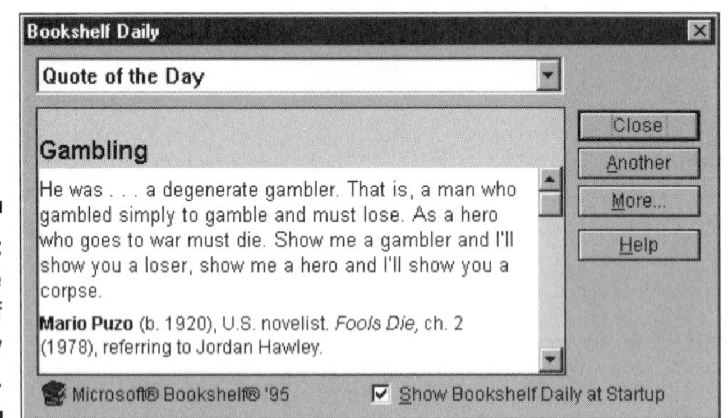

Figure 21-12: The Bookshelf Daily window.

2. **Click Close.**
3. **Click the Dictionary button.**

   The Dictionary window appears, as shown in Figure 21-13.

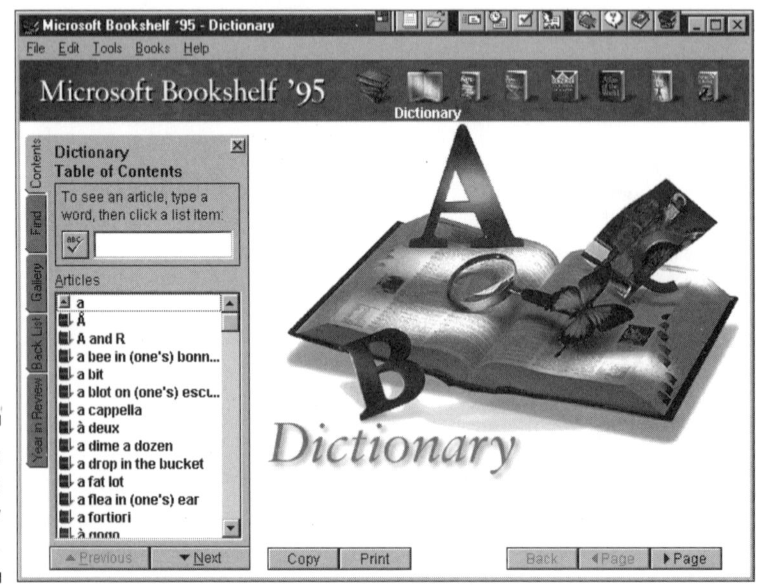

Figure 21-13: The Dictionary window.

4. **Type a word in the Dictionary Table of Contents box.**

   A list of words appears in the Articles list box.

5. **Double-click the word in the Articles list box that you want to view.**

   The Dictionary displays a definition, as shown in Figure 21-14.

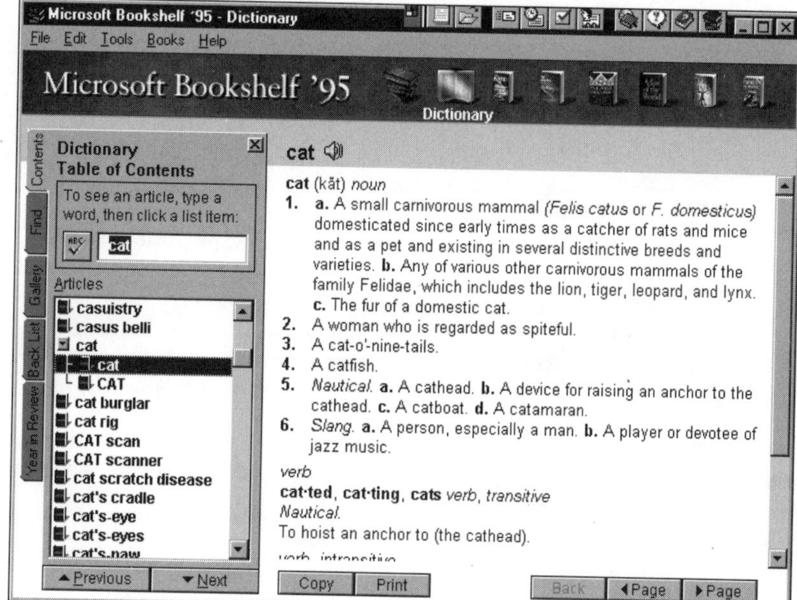

Figure 21-14: The Dictionary window.

6. **Choose File⇨Exit.**

Finding alternatives in the thesaurus

A thesaurus can be a wonderful tool to provide a more exact word or a clumsier euphemism that only clutters your message unnecessarily. To use the thesaurus from within Word or Excel, follow these steps:

1. **Choose Tools⇨Look Up Reference.**

   A Lookup Reference Title appears (see Figure 21-10).

2. **Click OK.**

   The Bookshelf window appears.

3. **Click the Thesaurus button.**

4. **Type a word in the Thesaurus Table of Contents box.**

   Bookshelf displays a list of words in the Articles list box.

5. **Click a word listed in the Articles list box.**

   Bookshelf displays multiple synonyms and acronyms, as shown in Figure 21-15.

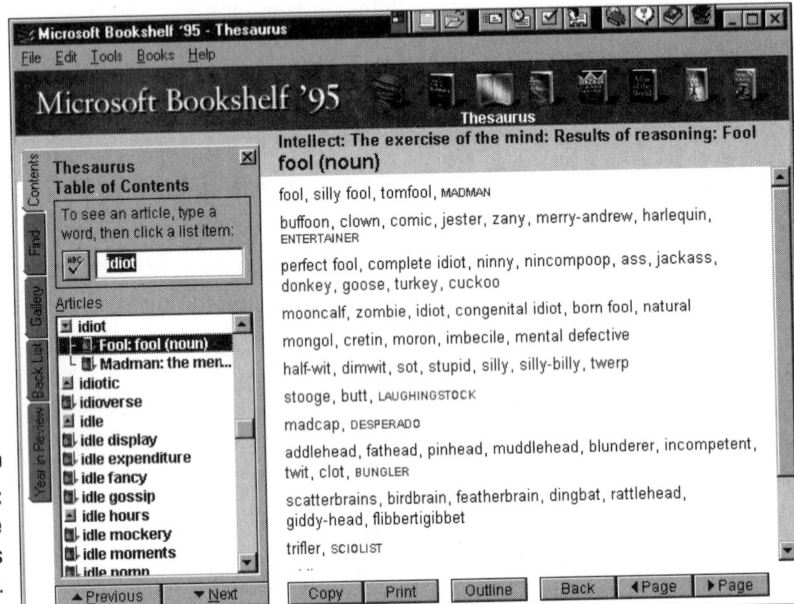

Figure 21-15: The Thesaurus window.

6. **Choose File⇨Exit.**

If you want to search the thesaurus on your own, follow these steps:

1. **Click the Bookshelf button on the Office Shortcut Bar.**

   The Bookshelf Daily dialog box appears (see Figure 21-12).

2. **Click Close.**

   The Bookshelf window appears.

3. **Click the Thesaurus button.**

4. **Type a word in the Thesaurus Table of Contents box.**

   Bookshelf displays a list of words in the Articles list box.

5. **Click a word listed in the Articles list box.**

   Bookshelf displays multiple synonyms and acronyms (see Figure 21-15).

Finding a neat quote

If you're writing a speech, report, or term paper and you want to add a touch of class to it, get a relevant quote from somebody famous. To find a quote from within Word or Excel, follow these steps:

1. **Choose Tools➪Look Up Reference.**

   The Lookup Reference Title dialog box appears (see Figure 21-10).

2. **Click OK.**

   The Bookshelf window appears.

3. **Click the Quotations button.**

4. **Type a name in the Quotations Table of Contents box.**

   Bookshelf displays a list of names and topics in the Articles list box.

5. **Click a word in the Articles list box.**

   Bookshelf displays a quote, as shown in Figure 21-16.

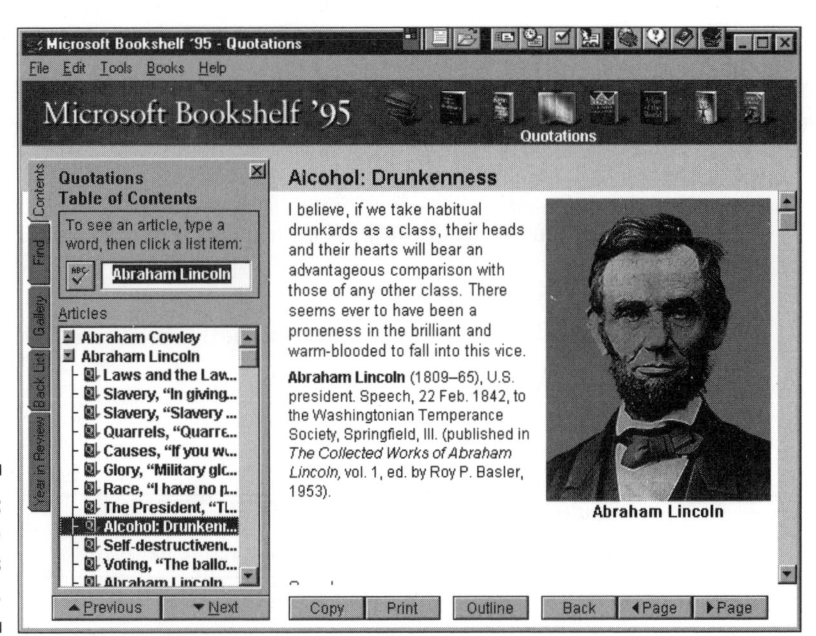

Figure 21-16: The Quotations window.

6. **Click Copy.**

   The Copy dialog box appears, as shown in Figure 21-17.

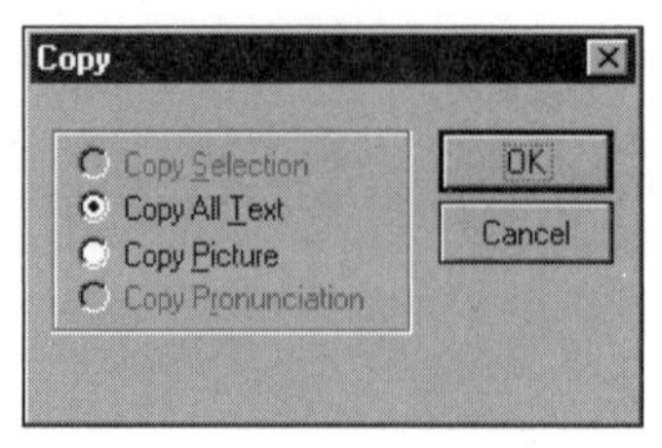

Figure 21-17: The Copy dialog box.

7. **Click a radio button and click OK.**
8. **Choose File⇨Exit.**
9. **Move the cursor in your Word or Excel document where you want the quote to appear.**
10. **Press Ctrl+V.**

    Your chosen quote appears.

Finding fun stuff in the encyclopedia

Encyclopedias are fun to look at because they contain all sorts of interesting information that won't help you get a job or find a spouse, but can liven up your day a bit when you learn that you can make laughing gas and oxygen by heating ammonium nitrate or that the Nobel Peace Prize was named after the inventor of dynamite.

To use the encyclopedia from within Word or Excel, follow these steps:

1. **Choose Tools⇨Look Up Reference.**

   The Lookup Reference Title dialog box appears (see Figure 21-10).
2. **Click OK.**

   The Bookshelf window appears.
3. **Click the Encyclopedia button.**
4. **Type a name in the Encyclopedia Table of Contents box.**

   Bookshelf displays a list of topics in the Articles list box.
5. **Double-click a word in the Articles list box.**

   Bookshelf displays additional text, as shown in Figure 21-18.
6. **Choose File⇨Exit.**

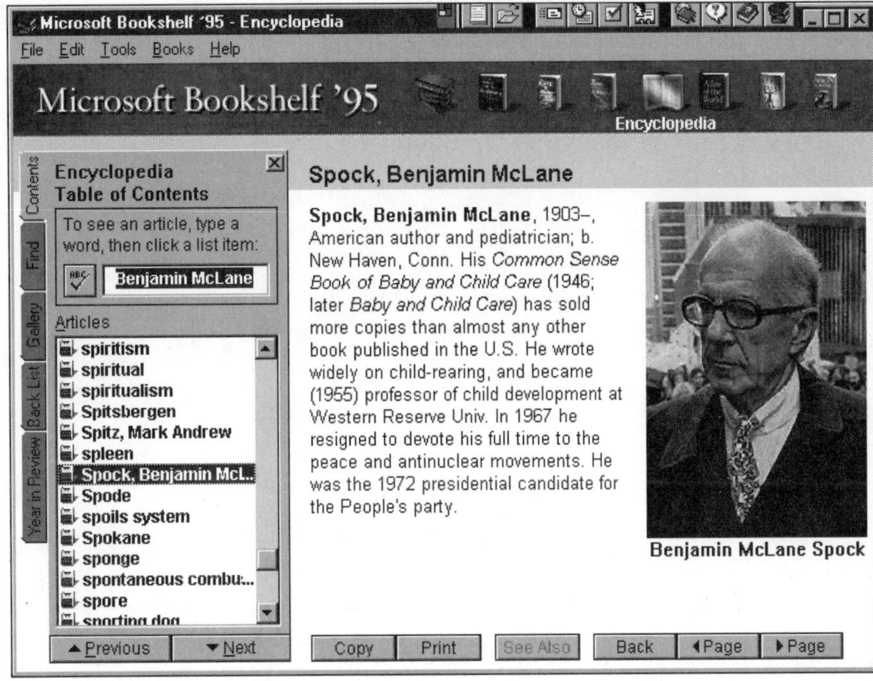

Figure 21-18: The Encyclopedia window.

Finding your country with an atlas

Most American high school students can't find the United States on a map, which makes the atlas in Bookshelf all the more valuable. To use the atlas from within Word or Excel, follow these steps:

1. **Choose Tools➪Look Up Reference.**

   The Lookup Reference Title dialog box appears (see Figure 21-10).

2. **Click OK.**

   The Bookshelf window appears.

3. **Click the Atlas button.**

4. **Type a name in the Atlas Table of Contents box.**

   Bookshelf displays a list of topics in the Articles list box.

5. **Double-click a word in the Articles list box.**

   Bookshelf displays additional text, as shown in Figure 21-19.

6. **Choose File➪Exit.**

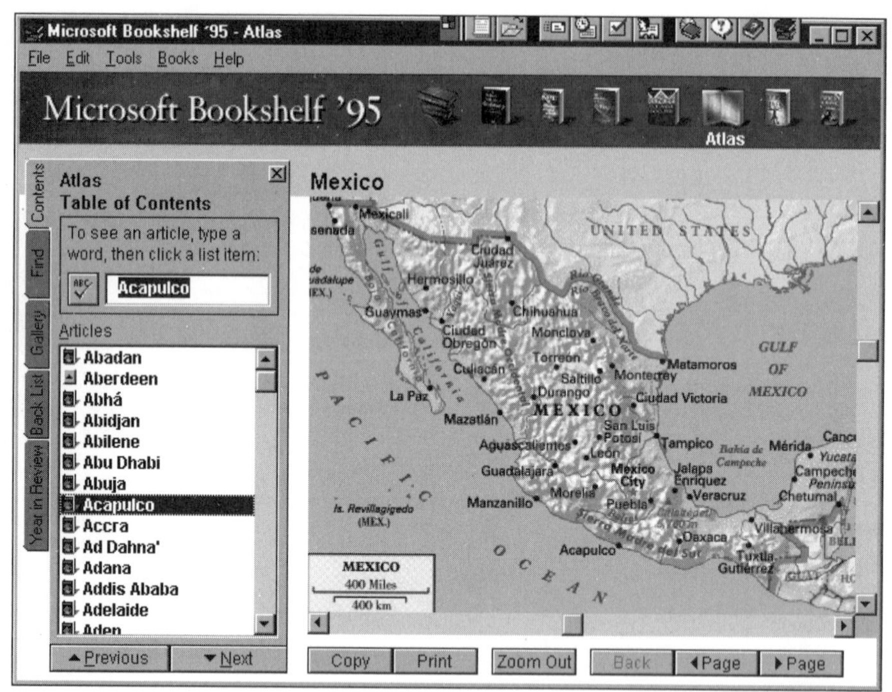

Figure 21-19: The Atlas window.

Somewhere in time

Want to know what happened in history? Since most people's sense of history extends as far back as last year's hit movie, take some time to browse through the Chronology book in Bookshelf and teach yourself interesting facts that could one day win you thousands of dollars on *Jeopardy*.

To use the Chronology book from within Word or Excel, follow these steps:

1. **Choose Tools⇨Look Up Reference.**

   The Lookup Reference Title dialog box appears (see Figure 21-10).

2. **Click OK.**

   The Bookshelf window appears.

3. **Click the Chronology button.**

4. **Type a name in the Chronology Table of Contents box.**

   Bookshelf displays a list of topics in the Articles list box.

5. **Double-click a word in the Articles list box.**

   Bookshelf displays additional text, as shown in Figure 21-20.

6. **Choose File⇨Exit.**

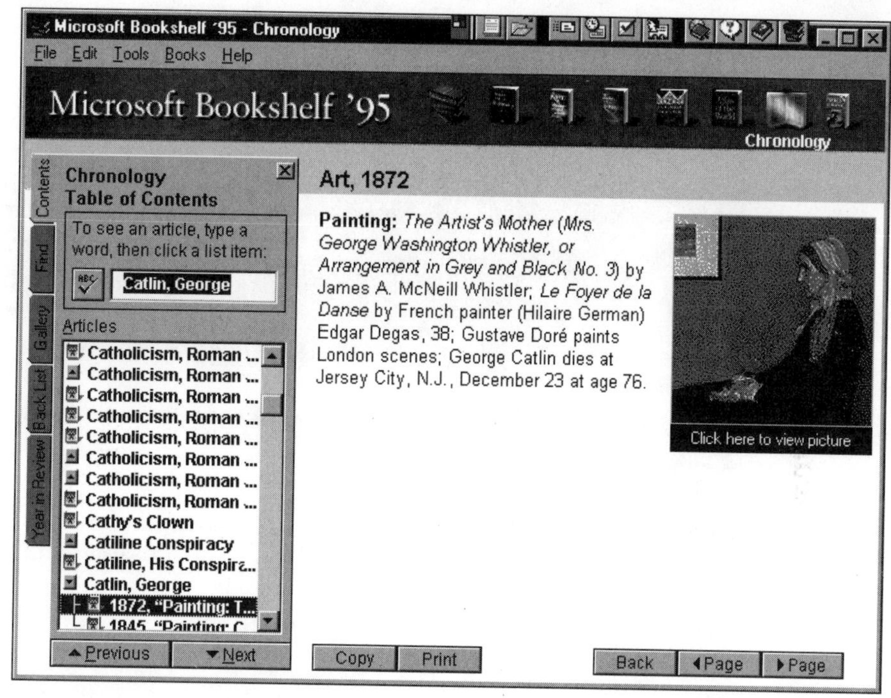

Figure 21-20: The Atlas window with text.

Using an almanac

Almanacs typically contain an oddball assortment of information that you may need occasionally but have no idea where to find otherwise. Some of the weird information you may find in the almanac includes the names of the Governor for each state, the nutritional value of Swiss cheese, the names of people who appear on the United States $500 bill, and the population of religious groups in Africa. If this type of information is vital to your work, then you'll be pleased that the almanac is just a click away from viewing.

To use the Almanac book from within Word or Excel, follow these steps:

1. **Choose Tools➪Look Up Reference.**

   The Lookup Reference Title dialog box appears (see Figure 21-10).

2. **Click OK.**

   The Bookshelf window appears.

3. **Click the Almanac button.**

4. **Type a name in the Almanac Table of Contents box.**

   Bookshelf displays a list of topics in the Articles list box.

5. Double-click a word in the Articles list box.

Bookshelf displays additional text, as shown in Figure 21-21.

6. Choose File➪Exit.

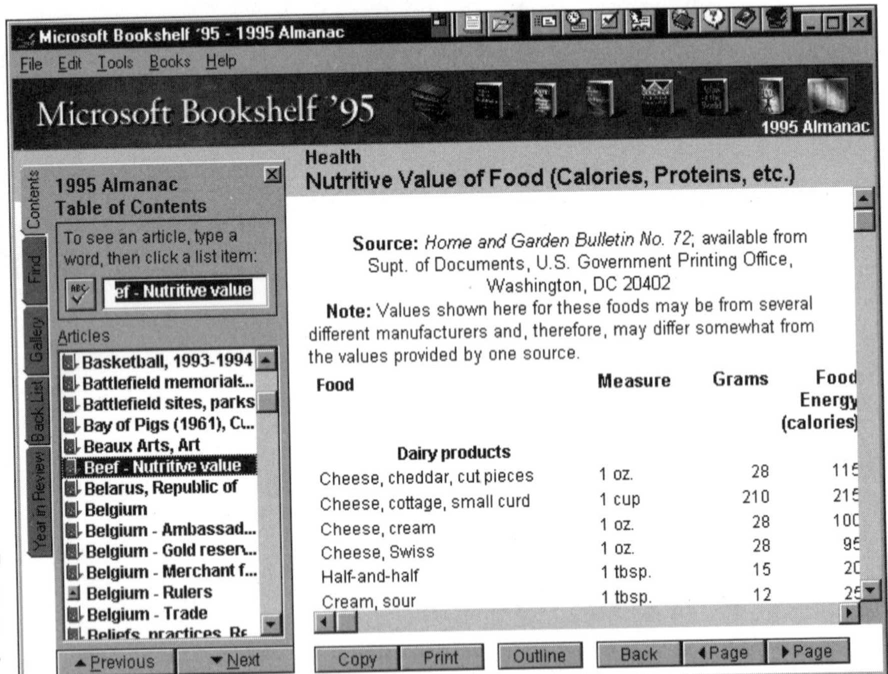

Figure 21-21: The Almanac window.

If you want to search for the almanac on your own, follow these steps:

1. Click the Bookshelf button on the Office Shortcut Bar.

The Bookshelf Daily dialog box appears (see Figure 21-12).

2. Click Close.

The Bookshelf window appears.

3. Click the Almanac button.

4. **Type a name in the Almanac Table of Contents box.**

   Bookshelf displays a list of topics in the Articles list box.

5. **Double-click a word in the Articles list box.**

   Bookshelf displays additional text (see Figure 21-21).

6. **Choose File⇨Exit.**

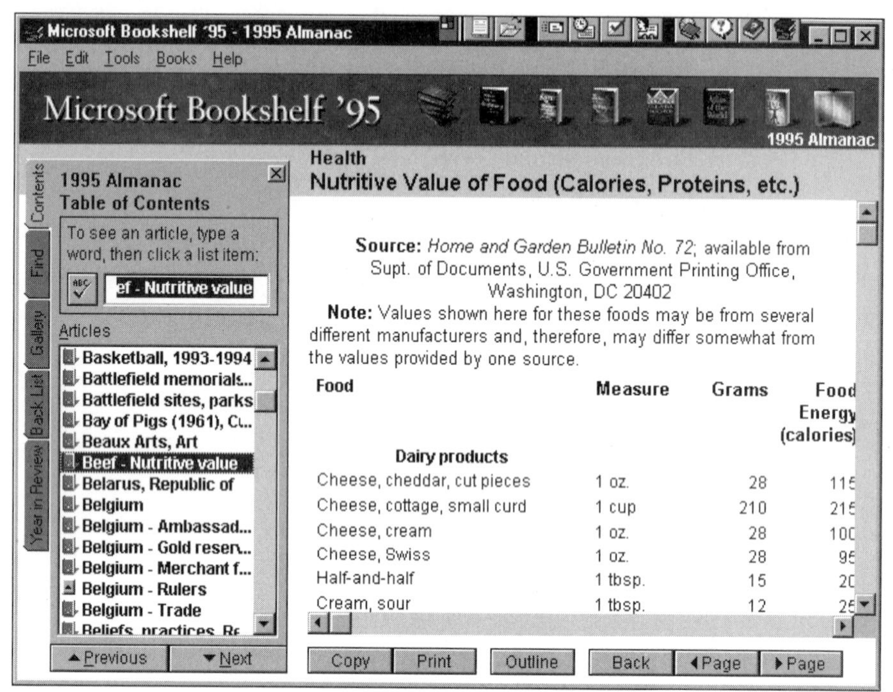

Figure 21-21: The Almanac window.

If you want to search for the almanac on your own, follow these steps:

1. **Click the Bookshelf button on the Office Shortcut Bar.**

   The Bookshelf Daily dialog box appears (see Figure 21-12).

2. **Click Close.**

   The Bookshelf window appears.

3. **Click the Almanac button.**

4. **Type a name in the Almanac Table of Contents box.**

   Bookshelf displays a list of topics in the Articles list box.

5. **Double-click a word in the Articles list box.**

   Bookshelf displays additional text (see Figure 21-21).

6. **Choose File⇨Exit.**

Index

Note: Page numbers in *italics* refer to charts and illustrations.

• G •

• H •

• I •

• K •

• L •

• M •

• S •

• T •

• V •

• W •

• Z •

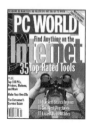

IDG BOOKS WORLDWIDE REGISTRATION CARD

Title of this book: MORE Microsoft® Office For Windows® 95 For Dummies®

My overall rating of this book: ☐ Very good [1] ☐ Good [2] ☐ Satisfactory [3] ☐ Fair [4] ☐ Poor [5]

How I first heard about this book:

☐ Found in bookstore; name: [6] ☐ Book review: [7]

☐ Advertisement: [8] ☐ Catalog: [9]

☐ Word of mouth; heard about book from friend, co-worker, etc.: [10] ☐ Other: [11]

What I liked most about this book:

What I would change, add, delete, etc., in future editions of this book:

Other comments:

Number of computer books I purchase in a year: ☐ 1 [12] ☐ 2-5 [13] ☐ 6-10 [14] ☐ More than 10 [15]

I would characterize my computer skills as: ☐ Beginner [16] ☐ Intermediate [17] ☐ Advanced [18] ☐ Professional [19]

I use ☐ DOS [20] ☐ Windows [21] ☐ OS/2 [22] ☐ Unix [23] ☐ Macintosh [24] ☐ Other: [25] ______ (please specify)

I would be interested in new books on the following subjects:
(please check all that apply, and use the spaces provided to identify specific software)

☐ Word processing: [26] ☐ Spreadsheets: [27]

☐ Data bases: [28] ☐ Desktop publishing: [29]

☐ File Utilities: [30] ☐ Money management: [31]

☐ Networking: [32] ☐ Programming languages: [33]

☐ Other: [34]

I use a PC at (please check all that apply): ☐ home [35] ☐ work [36] ☐ school [37] ☐ other: [38] ______

The disks I prefer to use are ☐ 5.25 [39] ☐ 3.5 [40] ☐ other: [41] ______

I have a CD ROM: ☐ yes [42] ☐ no [43]

I plan to buy or upgrade computer hardware this year: ☐ yes [44] ☐ no [45]

I plan to buy or upgrade computer software this year: ☐ yes [46] ☐ no [47]

Name: Business title: [48] Type of Business: [49]

Address (☐ home [50] ☐ work [51]/Company name:)

Street/Suite#

City [52]/State [53]/Zipcode [54]: Country [55]

☐ **I liked this book!** You may quote me by name in future IDG Books Worldwide promotional materials.

My daytime phone number is ______

IDG BOOKS®
THE WORLD OF COMPUTER KNOWLEDGE

YES!

Please keep me informed about IDG's World of Computer Knowledge. Send me the latest IDG Books catalog.

NO POSTAGE NECESSARY IF MAILED IN THE UNITED STATES

BUSINESS REPLY MAIL

FIRST CLASS MAIL PERMIT NO. 2605 FOSTER CITY, CALIFORNIA

IDG Books Worldwide
919 E Hillsdale Blvd, STE 400
Foster City, CA 94404-9691